W9-DHT-478

The Struggle for
Swazi Labour, 1890–1920

During the years between 1890 and 1920 the capitalist economy
of southern Africa rapidly expanded and white increasingly
dominated black. African societies, once self-sufficient, became
heavily dependent on migrant wage labour and purchased food.
Rural societies were transformed, and as a consequence many
Africans were impoverished.

The results of colonial expansion and capitalist penetration
have been examined in other localized studies. This work is the
first to look closely at Swaziland. It provides a carefully documented account of Swazi subordination to foreign political and
economic rule. The author shows the ways in which the Swazi experience differed from that of other peoples living on the rural
periphery of southern Africa's industrial revolution. He attributes
these differences to the pre-colonial political alignments of Swazi
society, the resistance of Swazi chiefs and commoners to colonial
policy, and the survival strategies of Swazi homesteads.

The Struggle for Swazi Labour examines the emergence of the
South African gold-mining industry as the dominant, though by
no means exclusive, employer of Swazi labour, and it looks at the
struggle within Swazi society for control over the migrant labour
flow. It shows how the local history of white settlement and land
expropriation influenced the pace and nature of Swazi incorporation into the new economy. The book will be helpful to anyone
wishing to understand the power base of the traditionalist Dlamini aristocracy in contemporary Swaziland, and to those looking
for an explanation for South African economic domination of
the surrounding countries.

Jonathan Crush is a Canada Research Fellow at Queen's
University.

The Struggle for Swazi Labour, 1890–1920

JONATHAN CRUSH

McGill-Queen's University Press
Kingston and Montreal

© McGill-Queen's University Press 1987
ISBN 0-7735-0569-5

Legal deposit 4th quarter 1987
Bibliothèque nationale du Québec

Printed in Canada

This book has been published with the help of a
grant from the Social Science Federation of
Canada, using funds provided by the Social
Sciences and Humanities Research Council of
Canada.

Canadian Cataloguing in Publication Data
Crush, Jonathan Scott, 1953-
    The struggle for Swazi labour, 1890-1920
    Bibliography: p.
    Includes index.
    ISBN 0-7735-0569-5
    1. Swaziland – Economic conditions. 2. Swaziland –
    Social conditions. 3. Social structure – Swaziland.
    4. Swaziland – Relations – South Africa. 5. South
    Africa – Relations – Swaziland. I. Title.
    HC925.C78 1987   330.9681'302   C87-093740-5

Cover Drawing of Swazi regiment tilling royal fields,
1890s. Royal village in the middle background.
Courtesy Swaziland Archives.

All photographs are from the Swaziland
Archives except for those from the institutions noted below:
BARLOW RAND: mine workers at Boksburg
JOHANNESBURG PUBLIC LIBRARY AFRICANA MUSEUM:
Swazi regiment on the march; tin miners;
ox-drawn wagon
KILLIE CAMPBELL AFRICANA LIBRARY: Swazi men
dressing hides
TRANSVAAL ARCHIVES DEPOT: Republican
administration, 1898; Swaziland Concessions
Commission

For Linda, Claire, and Genevieve

Contents

Figures

Tables

Preface

The present study provides an account of how one African society was incorporated into the regional capitalist economy of late nineteenth- and early twentieth-century southern Africa. It attempts to show how political subordination to Britain and growing economic domination by South Africa exerted a profoundly subversive effect on Swazi social organization. Yet it also demonstrates the important role Swazi chiefs and commoners played in setting the directions of change and the limits of transformation of their own society. In their drive to control the land and labour resources of Swaziland, agrarian and mining capitalists ran up against a society which still displayed much of its pre-capitalist vitality and integrity. The nature of the Swazi response, and its overall effectiveness, was strongly influenced by this and by the fact that Swazi society was not an undifferentiated whole. Pre-existing lines of division and contest within Swazi society helped shape the new colonial order in the country. The struggle over Swaziland's land and labour resources consequently emerges as a recurrent theme in this work. Consideration of the course and outcome of this struggle illustrates the deep historical roots of South African economic dominion over Swaziland and provides a better basis for understanding the persistence of traditionalist personnel and institutions in post-colonial Swaziland. In conception and execution this study has been heavily influenced by recent developments in the historical analysis of capitalist and colonial influence in southern Africa. As an exercise in historical geography it attempts to show the contribution which a geographical perspective might make to furthering an understanding of the origins of contemporary social and spatial domination in southern Africa. As well, the study seeks to demonstrate to historical geographers the value of moving beyond the description of untenanted landscapes to the experiences and struggles of those who actually hewed the landscape.

My own acquaintance with Swaziland extends back twenty years, ten as an academic researcher. The present work, however, is the product of intensive periods of fieldwork in 1977 and 1982, supplemented by shorter field trips in 1984 and early 1986. The state archives of Swaziland, South Africa, and Britain have been used in the past by political historians of colonial Swaziland. Yet they are also rich for the country's economic and social history. This study makes extensive use of these records and of archival deposits which will be new to Swaziland scholars. They include the Government Native Labour Bureau records in the Transvaal Archives, the High Commission papers at the Public Record Office, and the draft annual and monthly reports in the D and RCS series of the Swaziland Archives. Other relevant primary documentation included the Barlow Rand collection of H. Eckstein & Co., Native Recruiting Corporation records, missionary archives, and various collections of private papers in the Killie Campbell Africana Library, the University of Witwatersrand archives, the Transvaal Archives Depot, Rhodes House Library, and the British Library. I also obtained access to documents in private hands and am grateful to the holders for permission to make use of this material. During the course of my research, I became aware that there are other privately held collections of papers in South Africa and in Swaziland itself; perhaps in time the holders will open them to public scrutiny. There proved to be much published primary documentation of value, including commission reports, travelogues, and newspapers. The *Times of Swaziland* and the *Goldfields News* are particularly profitable sources of information. I was regrettably unable to pursue my plans to collect Swazi oral history relating to the period of study following an accident to a member of my family in Swaziland in 1984. In partial compensation, Philip Bonner gave me full access to the transcripts of his own interviews in Swaziland. I also discovered the detailed oral memoirs of a Swazi commoner who lived through the period discussed. These were recorded in the 1950s and are available at the Swaziland Archives. As well, there was much of relevance in the recently discovered and highly detailed British court records for the Hlatikulu district of Swaziland. These records, unsorted and uncatalogued, are now housed in the Swaziland Archives.

I am indebted to a number of people for their aid. The director of the Swaziland Archives, Mr Julius Dlamini, has always been unfailingly helpful. The archivists at the Public Record Office, Rhodes

House Library, Barlow Rand, the Transvaal Archives Depot, the Killie Campbell Africana Library, and the University of the Witwatersrand all provided valuable assistance. Messrs Jannie Ferreira of the Transvaal Archives Depot and C.D. Chalmers of the Search Department of the Public Record Office warrant special thanks for their help in tracking down obscure documentation. Mr Hylton Davis permitted access to the private records of the Native Recruiting Corporation. The staff of the Africa Evangelical Fellowship in London kindly lent me an original run of the magazine *South African Pioneer*. The directors of the Swaziland Archives, the Transvaal Archives Depot, the Killie Campbell Africana Library, the Barlow Rand archives, and the Africana Museum (Johannesburg) gladly consented to my use of photographs from their excellent collections.

Much of the groundwork for this study has already been laid by two scholars: Hilda Kuper and Philip Bonner. My intellectual debt to both will be apparent in what follows. Earlier versions of this work profited from readings by Phil Bonner, David Crush, Linda Crush, Leonard Guelke, Alan Jeeves, Paul Maylam, Randall Packard, and Barry Riddell. A number of scholars supplied perceptive comments on parts of the manuscript. They include Martin Fransman, Bill Freund, Noel Garson, Shula Marks, and Charles Van Onselen. I benefited considerably from related discussions with William Beinart, Alan Booth, Chris Rogerson, and Paul Wellings. Alan Jeeves and Ruth Edgecombe gave me access to some of their own research materials. Judy Weisinger translated documents from the Dutch. Ross Hough of Queen's University assisted with the initial preparation of cartographic material. The maps and diagrams were drawn by members of the cartographic laboratory in the Department of Geography, University of Alberta. My field research would not have been possible without the material support of my parents. Linda Crush assisted with archival research in 1982. I am also very grateful for her general help and encouragement.

Parts of this book have previously appeared in *Journal of Historical Geography* 12 (1986), *Journal of Southern African Studies* 11 (1985), and *Political Geography Quarterly* 4 (1985); I thank the editors for their permission to reproduce this material.

I have been fortunate to enjoy the financial support of a number of organizations. My original research trip to Swaziland in 1977 was made possible through assistance arranged by Dr Bruce Young of Wilfrid Laurier University. In 1982 my research was funded by a fellowship from the Ford Foundation/IDRC Social Science Research Program for Eastern and Southern Africa, and by grants from the

Social Science Faculty of the National University of Lesotho and the International Geographical Congress. In 1984–5 the Social Sciences and Humanities Research Council of Canada provided me with two generous research grants and a post-doctoral fellowship at Queen's University. These gave me the opportunity to build much new material into my original doctoral dissertation and to revise my interpretations on certain key issues. In 1985 I received supplemental funding from the Central Research Fund of the University of Alberta. Finally, a grant from the Social Science Federation of Canada made publication of this study a reality.

Abbreviations

AC	Assistant Commissioner
ACR	Annual Colonial Report
BA	British Agent Archive, TAD
BC	British Consul
BL	British Library
BRA	Barlow Rand Archives, Johannesburg
CA	Commission Archives
CAD	Central Archives Depot, Pretoria
CMAR	Chamber of Mines Annual Report
CO	Colonial Office Archive, PRO
CS	Colonial Secretary Archive, TAD
CT	Colonial Treasurer Archive, TAD
DNL	Director of Native Labour
ERPM	East Rand Proprietary Mines
GG	Governor General Archive, CAD
GNLB	Government Native Labour Bureau Archive, TAD
GOV	Governor of the Transvaal Archive, TAD
HC	High Commissioner Archive, TAD
HCR	Hlatikulu Court Records, SA
JP	Justice of the Peace
JPL	Johannesburg Public Library
JUS	Secretary for Justice Archive, CAD
KCL	Killie Campbell Africana Library, Durban
LTG	Lieutenant Governor Archive, TAD
MR	Monthly Report
NA	Natal Archives Depot, Pietermaritzburg
NAD	Native Affairs Department
NC	Native Constable

NGI	Native Grievances Inquiry
NRC	Native Recruiting Corporation
PM	Prime Minister Archive, TAD
PRO	Public Record Office
RC	Resident Commissioner
RHL	Rhodes House Library, Oxford
RM	Resident Magistrate
RNLA	Rand Native Labour Association
SA	Swaziland Archives
SAIRR	South African Institute of Race Relations Archive, UW
SANAC	South African Native Affairs Commission
SAR	South African Republic
SCC	Swaziland Concessions Commission
SNA	Secretary for Native Affairs Archive, TAD
TAD	Transvaal Archives Depot, Pretoria
TLC	Transvaal Labour Commission
TOS	*Times of Swaziland*
USPG	United Society for the Propagation of the Gospel Archive, London
UW	University of Witwatersrand
WNLA	Witwatersrand Native Labour Association

Glossary of Swazi Terms

emabutfo	age-regiment
emakhandzambile	pre-Dlamini clans
emasi	sour milk
etula	tribute to a superior in the form of a daughter for marriage
imbutfo	permanent regiment
Incwala	first fruits ceremony
Indlovukazi	queen mother
Ingwenyama	king
inkosi	monarch
khonta	give allegiance
kusisa	loan of stock
lichaba	platoon
lilima	communal labour
lobola	bridewealth
nduna	headman
neza ilikuba	form of agricultural ritual involving treatment of an implement such as a hoe
tindvuna	chiefs appointed by the king
ukwenizisa	arranged marriage
umbengo	pre-battle ritual involving slaughter of stock
umemo	obligatory tribute labour party
umnumzana	homestead head
umuti	homestead

Embekelweni royal village in the Ezulwini valley, circa 1890

A typical Swazi *umuti* in the 1890s. The portable beehive structure later gave way to a more permanent mud and thatch building in many parts of the country.

A Swazi *umuti* with maize crop picked for storage

Swazi women making beer from sorghum, 1895

Married Swazi men dressing hides, with women and children in background, 1896. The wooden headring was worn by all married men until the early years of British rule.

A Swazi regiment on the march

Members of a regiment, probably Mbandeni's Mgadhlela force

The Republican administration in Swaziland, 1898. J.C. Krogh is prominently seated in the centre of the picture.

Members of the Swaziland police, 1905

The Swaziland Concessions Commission. Johannes Smuts is seated fifth from the left; J.C. Krogh fourth from the right.

Members of the Swazi protest delegation to Lord Selborne, July 1905. Chief Silele Nsibande is second from the left.

Queen mother, Sobhuza, Queen Regent Labotsibeni, Resident Commissioner de Symons Honey, High Commissioner Lord Buxton, Mrs Honey, Lady Buxton, 1917 (from the left)

Horo gold mine in northern Swaziland, circa 1910

Gang of tin miners with white overseers

Ox-drawn wagon for transport of dressed tin to South Africa

Mine workers at East Rand Proprietary Mine, Boksburg

The Struggle for Swazi Labour, 1890–1920

Introduction

Swaziland is an unusual country.
                           Sir Alfred Pease, 1914

The discovery of gold in the central Transvaal in the late 1880s hastened the emergence of a regional political economy in southern Africa dominated by capitalist interests. Flows of labour, capital, and trade were redirected towards the new mining complex of the Witwatersrand which, a mere twenty-five years after the first discoveries, was the site of over fifty working mines and the home of over 200,000 people. The vast majority of these were migrant labourers drawn from throughout the sub-continent. Their experience on the Rand exercised, in turn, a profound influence on those districts from which they came, transforming peasant production, agrarian social structure, and forms of rural consciousness in a bewilderingly rapid fashion. Most Africans failed to benefit from this phase of unprecedented industrial growth. They suffered extensive expropriation of ancestral lands, were consigned to inhospitable and overcrowded reserves, and became dependent on a mix of wage labour and rural production for their means of survival. They were also subject to highly coercive forms of manipulation in the capitalist workplaces of the region and were now at the mercy of exploitative colonial overlords.

Yet, within particular societies and rural localities, not all Africans were equally affected or responded in identical ways. White settlement and land expropriation were extremely uneven geographically. The character, timing, and impact of various modes of colonial control varied considerably from place to place. In some areas, the tenuous control of African rulers over their subjects was actually strengthened; yet, in many more, strong rulers were brought to their knees. While labour migration was ubiquitous it was very uneven, reflecting great variation in the social and material conditions in the various supplier areas. Within each district only certain sections of the population migrated regularly for wage employment. Some of those who stayed at home had a brief period of relative prosperity as agricultural commodity producers; others tried to resist these new and threatening forces in various ways.

Given such diversity in the forms of capitalist penetration and African reaction, the general process of change must be examined in a way that is sensitive to local conditions. In the 1970s, revisionist analysis of the making of southern Africa's regional political economy emphasized the guiding hand of capital and colonial state.[1] More recently there has been an important attempt to re-examine the sub-continent's mining and industrial revolution and to reconstruct it from the outside in. This book joins a number of recent works which acknowledge the "power of the periphery" in affecting the form and content of capitalist penetration and colonial domination.[2] African chiefs and commoners, peasants and proletarians, acting singly and in concert, did mould the terms of their own incorporation into the new order and hence the very nature of that order itself. The undoing of the rural districts of the sub-continent might seem in retrospect to have been inevitable. At the time, however, nothing seemed inevitable to the various players in the drama. To assert that the countryside was not simply a receptacle of change does not, of course, tell us very much. It needs to be demonstrated historically that rural Africans were far from passive, that they responded quickly and creatively to the forces confronting them, and that their actions and struggles did have a material impact on the course of capitalist penetration.

By failing to venture very far into the countryside, the existing literature on Swaziland presents an impoverished view of the diversity and complexity of Swazi responses to the threats and opportunities of the new order. Swazi praise-poems, lauding the actions of the great men of the realm, find resonance within the country's historiography. Ordinary Swazi men and women consequently need to be removed as spectators from the touch-line of the past. Yet Swazis, like anyone else, made their history under conditions not of their own choosing. To evaluate the "power of the periphery" and the constraints on that power, a much clearer understanding is needed of the political and economic content of rural society. The history of Swaziland demonstrates the importance of such an understanding.

The social history and historical geography of many parts of southern Africa is still obscure. In sharp contrast to the attention lavished on the former British protectorates of Basutoland (Lesotho) and Bechuanaland (Botswana), all too little is said about the third member of the triumverate. Prior to the second colonial occupation of Africa in the years after World War II, Swaziland was often perceived in colonial circles as something of a colonial backwater. The tradition of neglect has been kept alive by the academic community. Although there have been a few perceptive studies, they do not amount to the kind of sustained discussion of the country's past that is urgently needed. There is still a profound ignorance about the crucial period of social and economic change between the death of the Swazi king Mbandeni in 1899 and the installation of his grandson Sobhuza II in 1921. Isolated political histories of the period pay scant regard to economic and geographical circumstance and transformation.

The reasons for neglect of Swaziland by scholars are open to conjecture. Alan Booth has noted that "it is small (out of the way perhaps), and less of a labour pool than most other countries in the catchment area. But limited size does not have to connote insignificance, and it can mean manageability. 'Insignificance' is a relative term; five percent or less of the labour flowing to the mines in any given year might not seem like much; but if that same migrant labour force constitutes thirty percent or more of the male working population, its impact on the contributing society becomes considerable."[3] Even if Swaziland is seen only as a "microcosm of issues covering a wider area" it cannot continue to be treated with such indifference. As an arena in which white settlement and extensive land alienation coincided with growing incorporation of Swazi men into the South African migrant labour system, the history of the country speaks to a number of controversial issues in the region at large.[4]

The period of Swazi history examined here appears to have seen the emergence of many of the classic symptoms of underdevelopment. A relatively self-sufficient African society was reduced to a state of heavy dependence on wage labour and imported foodstuffs. The migrant labour force leaving the country swelled from no more than a handful to over 10,000 per annum. Pre-capitalist political and social relations were dismembered and restructured by the colonial state. A large proportion of the land surface of the country was expropriated to make way for white settlement and Swazis were resettled in specially created reserves. Such broad continuities with the experience of other parts of the region should probably be noted at the outset. But the discontinuities and differences also command attention.

By the 1890s, many Africans in southern Africa were already firmly incorporated into the new capitalist labour markets of the region, but the vast majority of Swazi remained outside. African homesteads throughout the region insulated themselves against the demands of the labour market through agricultural commodity production, but the Swazi did not. The terms of participation in Swa-

ziland's extremely brief phase of peasant export production were
set by the pre-existing social relationships of Swazi society. In many
parts of southern Africa, increased participation in the Rand goldmines' migratory labour system led to agricultural decline in the
countryside. In Swaziland, such a limited view fails to explain the
massive shift in Swazi migration patterns towards the mines in a brief
period after 1908. African dependence on food purchase commonly
followed land expropriation; in Swaziland the order was reversed.
By the turn of the century relations between chiefs and commoners
had been severely eroded over a considerable part of southern Africa, including the eastern Transvaal where many Swazi were resident. The resilience of chief-commoner relations in Swaziland itself
is in marked contrast to this general trend. And the fierce local
struggles over land and labour witnessed in Swaziland set the country
apart from the "labour reserves" of the Bechuanaland Protectorate
and, particularly, Basutoland.

The course of capitalist penetration and colonial domination of
Swaziland was affected to a considerable degree by the internal relationships and productive activities of Swazi society. The roots of
the country's incorporation into South Africa's migrant labour system cannot simply be located in the external inducements of the
market and coercive labour practices adopted by capital and state.
Such a view has the potential to be fundamentally misleading since
the existence of internal forces precipitating and constraining participation in produce and labour markets are ingeniously denied or,
at best, relegated to a residual status. For Swaziland, a blind eye
would have to be turned to the different branches of the nineteenth-
century Swazi economy, homestead and chief-commoner relations,
the institutions of aristocratic dominance such as the country's *emabutfo* or regimental system, and internal political struggles between
Dlamini and non-Dlamini chiefdoms. As a result, no satisfactory
explanation could be advanced for the slow pace of capitalist penetration of Swazi society, the role and dilemmas of an often-divided
Swazi ruling class in mobilizing Swazi wage labour, and the uneven
character of early migrant movements. As I shall demonstrate, however, internal relations and institutions were also caught up in the
dynamic of transformation. They were refashioned by incorporation
into a broader political economy and this affected subsequent Swazi
participation.

The Republican and British colonial states played a major role in
releasing Swazi land and labour for South African and local capitalist
enterprise. Recent studies of the state in colonial Africa have high-
lighted the conflicting imperatives of accumulation and legitimacy

in much colonial policy. In Swaziland, such conflicts were particularly acute.[5] The policies of the British colonial administration built on those of its predecessor by providing land and, less successfully, labour for white farmers; they mobilized Swazi labour for the South African market; and they restricted Swazi freedom in that market. But several historical episodes cast doubt on any instrumentalist implications that might be drawn. The bluntness of early colonial tax policy, the gulf between settler demands and colonial practice over land policy, the geography of the partition, and the government of a competitive recruiting environment all suggest that the reasons for colonial actions need careful and sensitive scrutiny.

As areas like Swaziland were drawn into the developing capitalist economy of the sub-continent, the common project of white farmers and mining capitalists was to break African resistance to wage work through the use of political coercion. But farmers also tried to destroy or curtail severely African access to land and to immobilize labour on white farms and ranches. The infamous Swaziland land partition of 1907–8 sought to resolve these tensions by providing land for settler enterprise and subdividing the Swazi labour force in order to secure a cheap and stable supply of workers for settler-estate production. However, in the context of vigorous competition for labour which characterized this period, and the recourse of a rural subsistence base, wage workers could exercise some choice over locations and terms of employment. There was thus an inevitable hiatus between the mobilization of workers and their appearance at designated employment centres. The eventual rise of the Rand mines as the major employer of Swazi labour owed much to the response of Swazi homesteads and individual migrants to competitive recruiting conditions within the mining industry and to the intermediary role of white traders in the Swazi countryside.

The landscapes of historical geography are often bare of the people who made and experienced them. This book exemplifies an alternative perspective which explores historical geography "from below," but I also seek to emphasize the shifting and open-ended relationships within which ordinary Swazi, black and white overlords, and the agents of merchant, mining, and agrarian capital struggled with one another to define and realize their interests. The outcome of these struggles directed the overlapping geographies of frontier interaction and labour migration. If those geographies are to be understood, we must pay attention to the conflict between central and local chiefdoms over Dlamini control; between commoner homesteads and the Swazi ruling class over the fruits of rural and wage labour; within the homestead over *lobola* and the disposal of the

wage packet; among white landlord, Swazi chief, and labour recruiter over commoner labour; and by migrants and their homesteads against the forces restricting their control over the means of
production and the conditions of wage employment. The contest
for land and labour is a single unifying theme in my analysis. It was
this struggle, not the hand of capital, state, or ruling class, that
determined the course and pace of events in Swaziland.

Against this backdrop, the present study also has more parochial
concerns. The observer of present-day Swaziland is always struck by
two features: the strong economic hold of the neighbouring apartheid state over Swazi affairs and the remarkable, and not unrelated,
persistence of traditionalism in the political life of the country.[6] Both
are very old. In the period I examine, two interesting points emerge.
First, in the case of Swaziland at least, South African expansion was
hardly a "failure" as Hyam has suggested.[7] It is true that for many
of the reasons outlined by Hyam, Swaziland was never formally
incorporated into the Union. But in the economic sphere, largely
ignored in Hyam's analysis, South Africa rapidly achieved exactly
what it wanted: a client state acting as a labour reservoir for South
African industry. Second, it was the ability of the Swazi ruling class
(under the powerful leadership of the Queen Regent Labotsibeni)
to navigate the treacherous waters of capitalist demand and colonial
subversion that eventually gained their successors a pre-eminent
position in post-colonial Swaziland.

The effects of foreign domination and traditional resilience should
naturally be examined in the context of the colonial period as a
whole. By concentrating on the period from 1890 to 1920, I inevitably leave much unfinished. For the period prior to 1890, I assume
a familiarity with Philip Bonner's evocative re-creation of nineteenth-
century Swaziland and the extraordinary concessions era during the
later years of King Mbandeni.[8] To use Bonner thus has distinct
advantages: first, his work alerts us to the folly of seeing nineteenth-
century Swazi society as static, impregnable to outside influence, and
without internal dynamic. Second, it reminds us that the Swazi "nation" has historically been far from a seamless web which it was often
perceived as during the illustrious, but in many ways mystifying,
reign of the late Sobhuza II. I briefly revisit these earlier years in
order to draw more boldly the material base and productive mélange
of nineteenth-century Swaziland, and the main lines of cleavage and
centralization within Swazi society. Without such a backwards glance
it is difficult to interpret the significance of what follows. At the other
end of the period I conclude with Sobhuza's assumption of power

since, within Swazi society at least, this represented the beginning of an important new phase. Moreover by the early 1920s the major contours of colonial Swaziland's new political economy had been firmly drawn.

PART ONE

Swaziland in the Nineteenth Century

CHAPTER ONE

Homesteads, Chiefs, and Kings

With regard to labour I can but observe that the natives of this country are no exception to the rule which prevails wherever the Military System exists and the authority of the Chief is supreme. Some few Swazis do engage themselves to Europeans but the vast majority have yet to learn the dignity of labour.

Johannes Smuts, 1896

The nineteenth-century Swazi state has recently been called the principal collaborator of southern Africa.[1] There is justification for this claim. The regiments of Mswati I raided the Tsonga peoples to the north and east of Swaziland to supply slaves for Boer communities in need of labour; alliances were made (and broken) with particular factions in the Boer Republics to provide insurance against the powerful Zulu forces to the south; Swazi regiments were dispatched to assist both Boers and British in a series of operations against the fiercely independent African peoples of the northern Transvaal.[2] In 1879, some 8,000 Swazi soldiers fought alongside the British in their successful campaign against the Pedi under Sekhukhune. The Swazi themselves never took up arms against the regional white invasion and were consequently not subjected to the armed conquest which befell many other African societies in the area. The primary advantage of collaboration proved to be the retention of political independence until 1895 when the country finally came under the control of the Kruger Republic.[3] A hut and poll tax, accompanied by flogging and cattle confiscation, was not imposed until August 1898.

The relative lateness of colonial subjugation was partially responsible for the notable absence of Swazi on the capitalist labour markets of the sub-continent for much of the nineteenth century. There is no evidence of any large-scale movement of men out of the country in search of wage employment in the period of Swazi independence prior to 1895. Small numbers of Swazi did make their way to the distant Kimberley diamond fields in the 1870s and 1880s, but the movement was spasmodic and it is likely that these migrants were sent with a specific mission, probably to buy guns (table 1).[4] Certainly there was none of the massive migration from Basutoland and the northern Transvaal at the time.[5] Small groups worked from time to

TABLE 1
Swazi "New Hands" at the Kimberley Diamond Fields, 1873–84

Year	Kimberley Mine	Dutoitspan Mine
1872	6	
1873	20	
1874		
1875		
1876		
1877	6	
1878	90	20
1879	21	4
1880		
1881		
1882	32	109
1883	12	
1884	11	

Source: Sieborger, "Recruitment and Organisation of African Labour," 180–93.

time on the goldfields of the eastern Transvaal but the rapid development of the Witwatersrand gold fields after 1886 failed to tempt the Swazi for over a decade. In the absence of colonial coercion, the extensive labour resources of Swaziland remained outside the capitalist embrace until the late 1890s. The march of capital was stalled in Swaziland not only because it lacked coercive power, however. Immunity from the demands of the new regional economy is clear testimony to the internal resilience of Swazi society, given increasing evidence of significant pre-colonial labour migration from other parts of the sub-continent.[6] Such resilience was due to the productive independence of the average Swazi homestead and to the broader web of social relations in which each homestead was enmeshed.

Agricultural production in nineteenth-century Swaziland took place, as today, in an area of considerable environmental diversity. Early white travellers, missionaries and colonial officials often remarked on the varied environmental base of this "East African Tyrol."[7] The Swazi divide the country up into four distinct zones: the inkangalo (European highveld), live (middleveld), lihlanze (lowveld) and Lebombo (the eastern mountain range) (figure 1). These broad physical distinctions were later maintained by white settlers who saw in each different prospects for new forms of productive activity.[8] Modern scholars give each zone a set of distinguishing geomorphological,

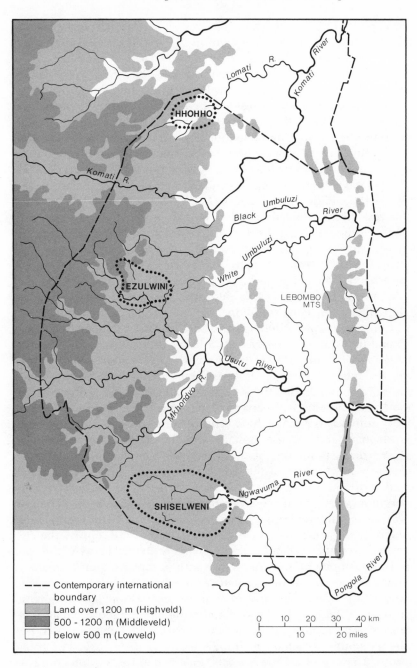

HHOHHO

Lomati   R.

Komati River

Komati R.

Umbuluzi   River

Black

White Umbuluzi

EZULWINI

LEBOMBO
MTS

Usutu   River

Mkhondvo R.

Ngwavuma   River

SHISELWENI

Pongola   River

--- Contemporary international
    boundary

Land over 1200 m (Highveld)

500 - 1200 m (Middleveld)

below 500 m (Lowveld)

0   10   20   30   40 km
0   10   20 miles

1 Swaziland: relief

ecological, and climatic characteristics.[9] They also stress the importance of this diverse environment in the rise of the Swazi state and the functioning of the nineteenth-century Swazi economy.[10]

In the late nineteenth century the bulk of a Swazi population, estimated at 50,000–80,000, was living in the middleveld zone. Almost as many Swazi were resident in the neighbouring highveld and lowveld reaches of the eastern Transvaal. The Swaziland highveld, with its steep, rocky, mountainous slopes and leached soils, was generally shunned by Swazi settlers, except along the river banks of the numerous gorges which slice through the region. The lowveld, while fertile, was ridden with malaria and tsetse fly and often had droughts. While the middleveld offered the best prospects for a reliable annual harvest, Swazi cultivators still faced the prospect of periodic crop failure especially towards the east. Widespread famine was rare yet most years there was still movement of population or homestead representatives from deficit to surplus areas to obtain food from kin or friends. The chiefs, as larger food producers, redistributed surplus produce to temporarily destitute homesteads, reinforcing the dependency of many commoners.

Constrained by technology and social relations from significantly expanding the area under cultivation, Swazi cultivators learned to cope with an uncertain environment. They sought out the most fertile land; cultivated fields were often widely scattered as a result.[11] Most homesteads practised shifting cultivation and many tried to obtain at least one river-bank garden for early planting and harvest.[12] Sorghum was the major food crop because of its greater resistance to drought and because its stalks were edible in times of famine.[13] The growing popularity of maize in the second half of the nineteenth century may have been related, at least in part, to its higher yields and shorter growing period. It was also less labour-intensive than sorghum, an important consideration for most homesteads. Yet maize was more vulnerable to drought, so both crops were usually cultivated by the same homestead.[14] By the turn of the century the cultivated area of Swaziland was about equally divided between the two.

Intercropping of the grain crops with pumpkins, gourds, melons, cowpeas, beans, and sweet potatoes was common. The Swazi also ate wild fruits, vegetables, and roots in normal seasons, even more so in times of famine. In the year following a crop failure the agricultural cycle was adjusted to include an earlier planting time – to put the seed out of reach of the hungry – and an early harvest of green crops. Underground storage pits, in which surplus grain could be kept for a number of years if necessary, were filled after a good harvest, to be used as a hedge against future crop failure.[15] The major insurance against drought and famine lay in the mixed character of the agricultural economy, however.

Small stock such as sheep, goats, and chickens were raised and eaten by most homesteads on a regular basis. Obtaining access to cattle, either through direct ownership or by *kusisa* (loan) from wealthier stockholders such as the chiefs, was a major goal of the Swazi homestead. Sour milk (*emasi*) was a major source of protein in the Swazi diet, and cattle could be slaughtered for meat at times of hardship.[16] Yet the social significance of cattle was such that only the chiefs regularly slaughtered for food. Pressure on livestock was mitigated by the proximity of the Swaziland lowveld, rich in large and small game. Swazi homesteads hunted more in the winters following poor harvests.[17] So, with these strategies, Swazi society was able to survive particularly serious droughts in 1876 and 1889 without recourse to wage employment.

The basic Swazi unit of domestic production for both the commoners and the ruling class was the homestead or *umuti*.[18] A normal polygynous *umuti* consisted of the homestead head (the *umnumzana*), his mother, his wives, their unmarried children and the households of his married sons with their dependents, as well as numbers of more distant relatives, such as widows and their children. The size of the *umuti* varied considerably, reflecting variations in status and wealth of the *umnumzana* and the stage reached in the developmental cycle of the homestead. As Alfred Gould observed in 1891, "some have 800 to 1000 huts in them, whilst others which you suddenly light upon in a day's journey are but miserable compilations of two or three huts and an apologetic cattle kraal; but one and all are constructed on one and the same lines, the smaller but minature representations of their greater contemporaries."[19] It was only the "great men of the realm" who could aspire to the upper echelons described by Gould, the bulk of the population living in "smaller native villages [which] only number eight to ten huts with from 20 to 60 inhabitants."[20]

At a particular juncture in the life cycle of the *umuti*, the households of married sons would break away from their father (all except the senior wife's first son who was invariably the heir) and form separate homesteads. Gould notes that this rarely happened before a man reached the age of forty, when he had probably acquired sufficient labour power, through wives and children, to reproduce the new *umuti*.[21] The death of the *umnumzana* was one certain cause of homestead fission. Most Swazi men aimed to ascend to the ranks of the *umnumzana* through marriage and the establishment of their own productive community. Whether marriage was actually feasible for the young man depended on the cattle resources of his father's homestead, fathers being responsible for paying the *lobola* or bridewealth of their sons. Here was the essence of a relationship of dependency which tied the sons to their fathers and which constituted a potential source of conflict between the two. Bonner comments, "for a son to establish his own homestead and hence to engage independently in subsistence production, he needed access to wives, but access to wives depended on access to cattle which the elders controlled [and hence] a dependent relationship was structured into homestead production."[22]

Bridewealth demands escalated sharply in the second half of the nineteenth century so that it would have been difficult for the young unmarried man to raise sufficient capital without an extended period of several years in wage employment. There is no indication that Swazi men were prepared to disregard their obligations within Swazi society and seek *lobola* elsewhere. Indeed as *lobola* demands increased the rate of new marriages probably declined. This may have led to the growing state of dissatisfaction among young males mentioned by elderly Swazi informants in the 1890s.[23] The daughters of the aristocracy and clan chiefs commanded much higher *lobola* than commoners. This guaranteed that cattle wealth tended to flow towards the wealthy. The tendency was reinforced by other political and juridical mechanisms and by the growth of strong ideological constraints on accumulation by commoners. The practice of *kusisa* developed, at least in part, as a defensive strategy by commoners to spread their cattle wealth and thereby reduce the possibility of forcible expropriation by local chiefs or the aristocracy. By the late 1880s most homesteads had at least a few cattle but the inequalities in cattle holding were marked. Royalty and the chiefs ran herds that numbered in the hundreds, and sometimes thousands, while most commoner homesteads probably had no more than five head.[24]

Cattle served as a means of subsistence, as the primary form in which wealth could be stored, and as the currency for the fundamental exchange transaction necessary for the reproduction of the lineage (the acquisition of wives through *lobola*).[25] Within the *umuti*, the rearing of stock (which commonly also included some goats and sheep) was the domain of men and particularly young boys. However, this sexual division of labour with regard to stock-tending was a fluid one. With massive appropriation of male homestead labour by the Swazi rulers in the nineteenth century, the range and scope of tasks demanded of women intensified. As well as being largely responsible for homestead agricultural production, women and girls became involved in the supposedly sacrosanct tasks of handling cattle. Kuper quotes two elderly informants who told her that women "often were left alone because the men, with the boys as carriers, went to the royal villages; sometimes the girls had to look after the cattle" and that "if the fathers were away and there were no sons at the homestead, who would do the milking? – the daughters of course."[26]

Within the homestead, the *umnumzana* orchestrated the agricultural activities, which ensured the reproduction of the various constituent households. Men did contribute in various ways to the reproduction of the homestead but the bulk of their labour time was absorbed in service outside the *umuti*. For much of the second half of the nineteenth century, the domestic subordination of women and children forced them to play the role of primary producers at the level of the homestead. Within the homestead, while men might help with clearing new land, the tasks of an onerous cycle of cultivation, which included breaking the ground (with digging sticks or hoes), planting, weeding, bird scaring, reaping, threshing, and food preparation were undertaken by wives and young girls. Each wife was allocated her own field or fields to cultivate (which was often performed collectively) and all women expended labour on the fields of the *umnumzana*. Female labour was drawn outside the homestead on a broadly reciprocal basis through voluntary participation in communal work parties for other commoner homesteads (*lilima*).[27] Women were also in charge of the homestead production of various kinds of handicrafts and other necessary items such as mats, clothing, and cooking utensils.[28] The systematic appropriation of male labour from the homestead forced women into an ever-wider and more exclusive role in domestic activity, which tended to immobilize them in the countryside. Male labour was much more mobile.

All chiefs systematically appropriated homestead labour from their followers through *umemo* (obligatory tribute labour). Failure to heed the chief's call for tribute could lead to heavy fines and eventual banishment. Chiefs made demands for *umemo* at all stages of the agricultural cycle and, in the winter months, for hunting. A chief's own fields were cultivated by those resident at his own homestead, supplemented by tribute labour. An additional field was worked solely by tribute and the surplus product was the chief's to dispose of. He might send a portion to the royal villages as tribute. Members of the chief's homestead and the tribute labour party itself, or destitute persons and visitors to the chiefdom, usually consumed the rest. A reputation for largesse on the part of a chief had the added advantage of drawing new followers into the chiefdom.[29] While all chiefs, great and small, demanded tribute labour on a periodic basis from their followers, many of the more important Dlamini and clan chiefs had contingents of young unmarried males drawn from the homesteads of their followers permanently in residence at their villages. Apart from the coercive power which this enabled the chief to command within the chiefdom, these contingents worked the fields of the chief and participated in hunting and raiding activities. The size of the local force varied over time and from chiefdom to chiefdom, but several powerful non-Dlamini chiefs in the south of Swaziland had well over a hundred men in residence in the late nineteenth century.

The ability of a chief to appropriate homestead labour through *umemo* and local labour contingents ultimately rested on the control which he exercised over land, the principal means of production. Descriptions which survive of the Swazi tenurial system as it developed in the nineteenth century stress the highly unequal rights of access of Swazi to the material base of the country.[30] The access of commoners was rooted in a dependent relationship of obeisance, allegiance, and tribute to local chiefs. Integral to the consolidation of the Swazi state in the nineteenth century was the assertion of nominal control over all land by the Swazi monarch. Mswati secured the right to any portion of land he chose for his own use (and indeed his fields were scattered throughout the country), to build royal villages at any location, to settle his personal followers anywhere in the country, and to create new chiefdoms with his own appointees as chiefs. The king acquired extensive grazing grounds (for royal cattle posts) in various choice areas of Swaziland and exerted absolute rights over natural resources, such as timber and reeds, which he often called upon local chiefdoms to supply. Local chiefs from whom the monarch took land for his own purposes were often compensated with land elsewhere in the country.[31]

For administrative convenience and to preserve local relations of domination, the allocation of land to commoners remained in the hands of the chiefs. The country was divided up into a large number of chiefdoms (more than one hundred by the 1890s) ruled by chiefs of the dominant lineage, hereditary clan chiefs, and *tindvuna* (appointees of the king).[32] The size of the chiefdoms varied considerably, as did the numbers of followers of a chief. In the early 1900s, for example, there were 41 chiefs in the southern Hlatikulu district alone with followings varying from as few as 15 to as many as 1,050 homesteads.[33] Local chiefs allocated land for building, cultivation, and communal grazing to commoners who offered allegiance and tribute in return. When the British later expropriated large tracts of Swaziland for white settlement in the first decade of the twentieth century, they were in fact launching an attack on the whole structure of pre-capitalist relations between chiefs and commoners (chapter 7). They were also threatening the position of dominance of the Dlamini clan and its ruling aristocratic lineage within Swazi society.

The historical roots of Dlamini domination are to be found in an ecologically diverse area in southern Swaziland known as Shiselweni (figure 1). Under their leader Ngwane, the Dlamini clan settled here in the late eighteenth century and began to assimilate the pre-existing population of the area by intermarriage and armed conquest.[34] Between 1815 and 1820 Ngwane's grandson Sobhuza 1 was driven northwards by stages to the Ezulwini Valley in central Swaziland, and then to the Dlomodlomo mountains north-west of present-day Swaziland, by repeated attacks from his southern neighbours, the Ndwandwe. In subsequent years Sobhuza reasserted his control over the north and centre of Swaziland. Hhohho and Ezulwini became the core areas of the expanding Swazi state, and it is noteworthy that along with Shiselweni, both contained superior soils, were well-watered and had a low incidence of drought.[35] An additional advantage was their proximity to the defensible highveld mountains. By the time of the first serious white settlement of Swaziland in the 1880s, the Ezulwini area was firmly established as the heartland of the Swazi state and the centre of Dlamini control.

The period after 1840, under Sobhuza's successor Mswati, was the great phase of Swazi state building. A far-reaching series of reforms were set in motion by Mswati and the Queen Regent Thandile which quickly transformed the institutional face of Swazi society.[36] Initially, Mswati intensified his efforts at territorial expansion and consolidation. Vigorous attacks on semi-independent clan chiefdoms, a policy of placing members of the aristocracy in charge of new chiefdoms, and the establishment of a comprehensive network of royal villages throughout the country all served this general purpose.[37] Mswati then forged a series of alliances with the more powerful clan groupings through extensive intermarriage and a tax on the country's chiefs to meet the *lobola* (bridewealth) for his senior wife. Regional chiefs anxious to consolidate their own position in the country assigned one or more of their daughters to the king. These *etula* women either became wives or concubines of Mswati or were married off to other chiefs for royal *lobola*. The same fate befell many women captured by Mswati's regiments in internal and external raiding.[38]

The cattle wealth of the aristocracy was augmented by continual tribute and raiding activities outside and within Swaziland, restrictive marriage practices, appropriation of the most favourable grazing grounds for the royal herds, and fines, confiscation, and seizure of cattle for various criminal and political offences.[39] Whenever a mar-

riage between two Swazi was concluded, the king demanded one or
two head of cattle as tribute. Mswati and his grandson Mbandeni
(1840–89) established royal cattle posts at various locations in the
middleveld and lowveld to house their abundant herds. One estimate
put Mbandeni's cattle wealth at close to 20,000 head by the late
1880s.[40]

In the 1840s and 1850s, Mswati curbed the ritual autonomy of
other clans and strengthened that of the aristocracy by instituting
various rituals of kingship. Foremost amongst these was the *Incwala*
ceremony, an annual event held over two weeks in December or
early January. Attendance by all men was compulsory. The centrality
of the *Incwala* as a ritual of kingly supremacy and supernatural
endorsement of Dlamini hegemony has been amply demonstrated.[41]
The ritual was also one element in the assertion of central control
over agricultural production in Swazi society. As a "first fruits" ceremony no Swazi could partake of the new harvest until after it was
celebrated. Earlier in the agricultural cycle, Mswati instituted a ceremony known as *neza ilikuba* where no homestead was allowed to
break the soil for planting until the king had publicly doctored an
agricultural implement.[42]

For our purposes, perhaps the most significant of Mswati's many
actions was his renovation of the Swazi regimental system which had
existed in embryo form under his predecessor Sobhuza. He established country-wide age-regiments (the *emabutfo*) into which all males
were automatically conscripted.[43] The *emabutfo* invested Mswati with
potential control over the rate of marriage and homestead formation
in Swazi society since a regimental group was given permission to
marry only when the oldest members reached their mid-thirties. At
this point a new regiment of adolescents was usually formed at the
behest of the king. The regimental cycle operated at five to ten year
intervals. At any one time there were four or five separate regiments
in existence, numbering anything up to 5,000 men each.[44] Within
the system as a whole there were different categories of soldier, a
distinction which tended to cut across regimental divisions.[45] A permanently mobilized force (the *imbutfo*) was stationed at various royal
villages in the country with the largest contingents in the Ezulwini
valley (figure 2).[46] *Imbutfo* members were drawn from all regiments,
young and old, but the backbone of the army were unmarried members of the king's own regiment; the Giba during Mswati's reign and
the Ndhlavela in that of Mbandeni (appendix A). At times in Mswati's
reign the *imbutfo* force may have numbered as many as 5,000 men.[47]
All other regimental members of whatever age or marital status lived
at their own homesteads or at those of local chiefs. They participated

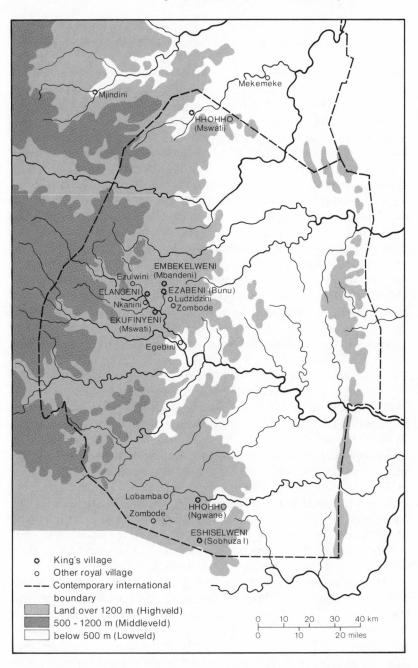

Mjindini

Mekemeke

HHOHHO
(Mswati)

EMBEKELWENI
Ezulwini (Mbandeni)
ELANGENI   EZABENI (Bunu)
Nkanini   Ludzidzini
             Zombode
EKUFINYENI
(Mswati)

Egebini

Lobamba
Zombode   HHOHHO
           (Ngwane)

ESHISELWENI
(Sobhuza I)

⊕ King's village
o Other royal village
— — Contemporary international
    boundary
▨ Land over 1200 m (Highveld)
▨ 500 - 1200 m (Middleveld)
☐ below 500 m (Lowveld)

0   10   20   30   40 km
0   10   20 miles

2 Royal villages

in the annual *Incwala* and were called periodically to the royal villages to perform specific military, agricultural, and other tasks.

The regimental system undoubtedly played a major role in the spread and consolidation of Dlamini dominance over much of Swaziland. It gave the aristocracy direct control over a vast reservoir of labour for military and agricultural purposes as well as providing them with a virtual internal monopoly of coercive power. The *imbutfo* soldiers performed a multitude of domestic tasks for the king and royal homesteads including building, gathering wood, cutting poles, and running messages. In the winter months they were deployed in the lowveld in large royal game hunts. These hunts were carefully organized and synchronized and could involve well over a thousand men at a time.[48] The *imbutfo* also worked in the royal fields at all stages of the agricultural cycle: breaking ground and planting (August to January), weeding (October to February), chasing off birds (January to April), and reaping and threshing (April to June). During periods of heavy labour demand (such as planting and threshing) the king issued a more widespread call for labour. He often used the opportunity provided by the presence of the *emabutfo* at the *Incwala* for some impromptu weeding of the royal fields.[49]

The surplus product of the royal fields appears to have been largely consumed within Swaziland, at least before the 1890s, in order to sustain the large royal villages and the *imbutfo* force. Royal villages often reached a considerable size (in the 1880s Embekelweni and Nkanini had populations of over 3,000 and 2,500 respectively to support).[50] Dudley Kidd reported seeing "huge stacks of grain for feeding the army" close to the royal villages around this time.[51] In the third quarter of the nineteenth century, cattle were regularly slaughtered at the royal villages to feed the population, which is an indication that grain production may not always have been sufficient to meet the total annual demand. In addition, many men in the *imbutfo* cultivated small plots near the royal villages to supplement their diet. The *Incwala* ceremony placed a large burden on royal resources since the numbers expecting to be fed would surge dramatically in the period when grain stocks were lowest.

Of fundamental importance in the nineteenth century was the role played by the regimental system in the establishment of the Swazi state. Major defensive efforts to resist Zulu encroachment, and various offensive campaigns in alliance with the British and Boers called for mobilization on a national scale. In periods of peace, regimental groups were regularly dispatched on raiding expeditions to the north and west of the country.[52] The booty, especially cattle, was primarily appropriated by the king but a proportion was redistributed in the barracks. The attraction of the permanent force for many commoners was that it provided an avenue of upward mobility, since those who performed well in the regiments could look forward to cattle or land as reward from the king.[53] Human captives from raiding were absorbed into Swazi society, boosting the labour resources of the royal homesteads, or sold off to Boers in the eastern Transvaal.[54]

In peace and war, the regimental system performed the vital role of socializing the young men of the non-Dlamini chiefdoms and refugee groups into the new state, cutting across regional and clan loyalties and forging a new national identity which demanded complete allegiance to the Dlamini aristocracy. Socialization into the ethos of the regiments began extremely early in a young Swazi's life since the junior regiment was composed of children aged 7 to 12.[55] From then on, through service in the regiments, a spirit of military discipline and fierce loyalty to the royal house saturated every facet of the Swazi male's existence. Even the most mundane of regimental tasks was performed with military precision and dedication, as one eye-witness account attests: "we came upon a regiment of 400 to 500 Swazi warriors in full uniform – shields, assegais, kerries etc; they were a splendid lot of men, all at work hoeing the King's land and all in perfect order; suddenly as we watched, the hoeing being finished, shields were seized, and still in the same order they fell in eight-deep and with a war-chant started on their march to the King's kraal."[56]

The strength of the permanent force and the intensity of central demands on the regiments varied. Periods of political insecurity or military aggression saw an increase in the number of *imbutfo* soldiers and more frequent mobilization of the *emabutfo*. During periods of peace it became more difficult to retain a large force. Whatever the political situation, the years of regency which commonly followed the death of a monarch tended to be times of greater regional autonomy, as many in the standing force were demobbed and the royal villages were consumed by intense, and often violent, factional struggles for the throne. Local chiefs seized the opportunity to reassert control over their young male followers. Between 1865 and 1874, for example, the Swazi state was kingless and the resulting decentralization of authority to the local level persisted well into the reign of the new king Mbandeni. The upshot of these periodic struggles over Mswati's refashioned regimental system was the retention of unarmed and subordinated local contingents of men at the homesteads of local chiefs.[57]

The Sekhukhune campaigns of the late 1870s appear to have

marked the onset of a new phase of centralization. In the 1880s the
Swazi king, Mbandeni, continued to consolidate his power through
the *imbutfo*. This process coincided with the expansion of new opportunities for wage labour in South Africa, after the discovery of
diamonds in Kimberley in the early 1870s. Service in the Swazi regiments and in local labour contingents bound many a young Swazi
man more firmly to the land at a time when other African societies
were beginning to send more migrant labourers onto the market.[58]
By the end of his reign, several thousand soldiers drawn mainly
from the Ndhlavela regiment were stationed at the royal villages at
Ezulwini and elsewhere. Contemporary observers such as Mathews
observed that Mbandeni had thousands of men at his "beck and call"
and Penfold describes how in the late 1880s Mbandeni called up
several thousand soldiers within the space of 48 hours to undertake
repairs at the royal villages.[59] Travel accounts from the period are
full of colourful descriptions of the magnitude and splendour of
Mbandeni's *Incwala* ceremonies. In the mid-1880s, some 3,000 to
4,000 men and women were present but by 1888 this number had
apparently swelled to as many as 9,000 men alone.[60] Shortly after
Mbandeni's death in 1889 several thousand soldiers built the village
of his successor Bunu, at that time still a minor.[61]

The experience of the thousands of Swazi in the eastern Transvaal
districts of Barberton, Carolina, Ermelo, and Piet Retief over which
Mswati had held sway had begun to follow a markedly different
trajectory by the 1870s.[62] Following extensive land expropriation, a
Transvaal-Swaziland border was demarcated in 1866 (and 1875) by
the Transvaal Republic. In 1880, a British Royal Commission under
James Alleyne gave more formal sanction to the earlier delimita-
tions.[63] For the Swazi on both sides the new boundary was extremely
porous and remained little more than a figment of the colonial car-
tographer's imagination. Yet the border did signify an increasingly
divergent set of material circumstances for the two Swazi peoples in
the second half of the nineteenth century. Wholesale land alienation,
Boer settlement, and the acquisition of 200 farms in the eastern
Transvaal by MacCorkindale for his New Scotland settlement reduced many Transvaal Swazi to the status of "squatters" on their
own land.[64] These new social relations between landlord and tenant
inevitably exercised a corrosive effect on relations with the more
distant Dlamini aristocracy inside Swaziland itself. In the lowveld
Barberton district less intensive white settlement, large blocks of
crown land, and the existence of royal villages established by Mswati
did mitigate these pressures somewhat.[65] It is certainly feasible, though
there is no direct evidence of this, that the gradual loss of control

over the manpower of the eastern Transvaal tended to intensify the royal claim on young men within Swaziland.

In the early 1890s the size of the *imbutfo* force inevitably declined somewhat as Mbandeni's Ndhlavela regiment was demobilized. In partial compensation, growing numbers of his heir Bunu's own regiment the Mgadhlela (aged 12 to 17 in 1890) were drawn to the royal villages to supplement the older standing contingent of Giba soldiers. Heavy demands were placed on the *imbutfo* in the spheres of agriculture, hunting, and internal cattle raiding. Without an external outlet for their energies, however, inter-regimental clashes around the royal villages became commonplace. Mass mobilization of the Swazi regiments in 1895 and again in late 1898 for abortive military actions provided clear evidence of the continuing vitality of the institution.

The close ties between soldier and king comprised a set of anterior obligations which capitalist employers had constant difficulty in breaking through until well into the 1890s. As Johannes Smuts observed: "it seems scarcely credible, but it is nonetheless true, that in this country containing thousands of able-bodied men, employers complain of the scarcity of labour. While I cannot say that the Paramount Chief forbids his people to work, I believe he encourages them to assemble at Zombode or to say they work for the King alone."[66] Obligations to the aristocracy were always felt most keenly and continuously by the regular *imbutfo* soldier. The bulk of the potential Swazi migrant labour force, adult males under the age of forty, consequently remained immobilized by its loyalty to and service in the regiments during the second half of the nineteenth century. Demobilized soldiers given permission to marry had little immediate interest in labour migration and could still expect periodic calls for service from the aristocracy. For these individuals, as well as for younger male adults in certain areas of the country, it was the character of local, rather than centre-periphery, relations which constituted the dominant inhibition to migrancy. The south of Swaziland, in particular, was never as firmly incorporated into the regimental system as the centre and north.

Generally speaking, the degree to which local relations between chiefs and commoners were over-ridden by the demands of the king depended on the extent to which the particular chiefdom was under Dlamini influence and control. Total subservience could mean a considerable and persistent loss of local male labour. In the centre and north of the country Dlamini overlordship was particularly strong in the second half of the nineteenth century, although several chiefdoms in the north-east managed to hold themselves at arm's length.

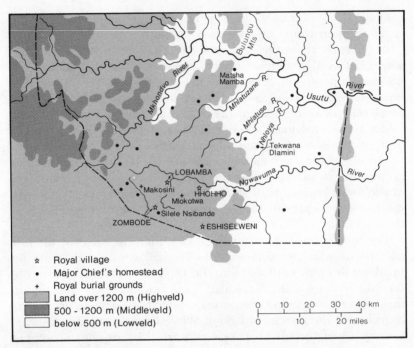

3   The "soft underbelly" of Swaziland

The pressures for regional autonomy were at their strongest in the
south of the country, however, where there were many chiefdoms
actively opposed to central control. The labour of the young men
of a number of these chiefdoms was only sporadically available to
the aristocracy, if at all.

While the consolidation of Dlamini dominance was largely achieved
through the regimental system, the maintenance of supremacy required continual vigilance throughout the country. The heteroge-
neous nature of the clan groupings under Dlamini sway, the uneasy
mix of coercion and co-optation in Swazi politics, and the existence
of chiefdoms whose loyalty to the crown was little more than nominal
inevitably meant that the effectiveness of central control ebbed and
flowed. Struggles for the throne led to the coalescence of regional
interests around rival claimants, exacerbating many of the tensions
latent in Swazi society.[67] The traditional "soft underbelly" of the
Swazi state was the area between the Usutu and Mkhondvo rivers,
and the southern boundary of Swaziland (figure 3).[68] While the region was of immense religious and symbolic importance to the aristocracy, they never succeeded in subordinating it as firmly as they
did other parts of the country. In the 1820s, for example, the Mamba

chiefdom of the south-east was granted *de facto* independence for assisting the Dlamini to regain control of Shiselweni. The Mamba chief of the day, Maloyi, was permitted to retain his ritual autonomy (the Mamba having their own version of the *Incwala*), to raise his own regiments, and to give sanctuary to refugees from the king. The Mamba hence became a veritable state within a state. The male labour of the chiefdom was rarely available to the aristocracy and, in later years, the question of Mamba autonomy became an object of re- peated conflict between the Dlamini and the Mamba. At such times, whenever retreat became expedient, the Mamba withdrew into the natural cave fortress of the Bulungu mountains nearby.[69]

In the last quarter of the nineteenth century Dlamini-Mamba re- lations deteriorated markedly. Bonner reports that Mbandeni's in- itial appointment as king was resisted by the south, and it is possible that the Mamba chief, Matsha, was in the vanguard of this move- ment.[70] Certainly Mbandeni and Matsha were on very poor terms towards the end of the latter's reign. James Stuart mentions a major disagreement between the two but does not note its origin, beyond "an insulting remark made of the former indirectly by the latter."[71] It may well have been related to a permanent grant of land in the south of Swaziland by Mbandeni to a white settler in 1887. This land, which was subsequently purchased by the South African Republic for over £40,000, covered a massive 100,000 acres and incorporated much of the Mamba chiefdom.[72] Not only would such a grant have been an assertion of Dlamini rights over the area, but it may have been Mbandeni's hope that Boer settlement of the concession would break Matsha's independence.

The south of Swaziland contained a number of important non- Dlamini clan chiefs in addition to the Mamba. Some, such as the Nsibande and Mdhluli, had been co-opted by the aristocracy as care- takers of royal graves and as clans from which the chief wives of the monarch could be drawn. The Nsibande also played the role of regional commander at the old royal village of Zombode.[73] In the 1880s, however, there was a falling-out with Mbandeni. In 1888 the Nsibande chief, Silele, was forced to flee from Swaziland, as a result of his complicity in a coup against the throne.[74] Although he was subsequently allowed to return by Mbandeni, a portion of his chief- dom was expropriated to make way for a new Dlamini chief, an action which alienated his affections still further.[75] Although there were a number of Dlamini chiefdoms in the south, many were on poor terms with the central authorities. In the 1890s, for example, Sicunusa and Makaheleka Dlamini were in charge of chiefdoms which had earlier been severely punished by Mswati's army.[76] Tekwana

Dlamini, a son of Sobhuza I, ruled a populous southern chiefdom
where Zulu culture was much in evidence. Tekwana spent an extended period in exile in Zululand during Mswati's reign and eventually returned to Swaziland where his loyalty to the king remained
much in doubt.[77]

The final component in the heterogenous mix of southern inhabitants was the large Zulu population of the area. The largest Zulu
chiefdom in southern Swaziland was that of the Simelane, who had
come as refugees to the country earlier in the century. While ad-
mitting Dlamini overlordship, the Simelane chief retained a semi-
independent status which included ritual autonomy and a greater
degree of control over the labour of his male subjects.[78] Many royal
wives were drawn from the Simelane over the years, an indication
of the Dlamini need to cultivate relations with a populous and cul-
turally distinct clan. After about 1860 the Zulu population of southern Swaziland was augmented by a wave of Zulu colonization across
the Pongola river. By 1875 there were over 30,000 Zulu resident on
the north bank in a belt of settlement which extended well into south-
west Swaziland. When the southern boundaries of the country were
drawn, numerous Zulu were incorporated. One Zulu chief Sitambe
Ntshongise who lived in the Piet Retief district of the Transvaal had
several hundred followers in Swaziland in the 1890s. These people
were settled in the south west of the country under an *nduna* (or
headman) of Sitambe's and refused to acknowledge the overlordship
of the Swazi king.[79]

The south of Swaziland was consequently a populous and relatively
cosmopolitan area. In the early 1890s it was described by James
Stuart as "for the most part very densely packed with kraals."[80] The
area was dominated by important clan chiefs with large followings
whose relationship with the Dlamini rulers was often of a nominal
character and who were always willing to seize the opportunity to
loosen central control. One of the major implications of this, and
the consequent regional differentiation in Dlamini control in the
country as a whole, was that the chiefs of southern Swaziland acquired and retained a greater degree of control over the labour of
their own followers. In the case of the Mamba, with male labour
resources of over 2,000 men by the 1890s, this control was virtually
absolute. But in general, the south was under-represented in the
force of *imbutfo* soldiers at the royal villages. Successive Swazi kings
and regents were acutely aware of the importance of the south and
repeatedly tried to bring it under closer central supervision.

In the 1880s, the Swazi king Mbandeni launched a serious campaign to curtail southern autonomy. He pursued a systematic policy

of inter-marriage, avidly seeking a stronger political alliance and broadening the range of "acceptable" clans. In order to curb the territorial control of the powerful southern chiefs, a number of loyal Dlamini chiefs were placed in the area on land expropriated for the purpose.[81] Mbandeni, and later Bunu, mounted a series of attacks on the cattle wealth of the weaker chiefs. Perhaps the most dramatic incident of the 1890s occurred in late 1895 when Bunu ordered a massive call-up of the Swazi regiments to prepare for a full-scale military campaign. The *umbengo* ceremony, which had not been conducted in Swaziland since 1879 and the dispatch of the Swazi regiments to battle the Pedi, was performed in a dramatic preparation for war.[82]

According to a number of contemporary accounts, Bunu's objective was to launch an assault on the south and bring the independent Mamba chiefdom to heel. Certainly there was considerable consternation in the Mamba camp itself; urgent messages pledging loyalty and asking for protection were dispatched to the Republican Special Commissioner at Bremersdorp, homesteads were abandoned, and many residents of the chiefdom fled to safer ground in nearby hills or crossed the border into Natal.[83] The threatened attack failed to materialize and the regiments were disbanded without seeing action. For missionary observers, it was a clear case of divine intervention. For others, such as the inexperienced British Commissioner, Johannes Smuts, an attack on the Mamba was never really intended.[84] All accounts attest that the *umbengo* ceremony itself went badly wrong and that Bunu himself was furious with its outcome. It is certainly possible that this evil omen, taken with the simultaneous death of the former Queen Regent Thabiti, convinced him that the time to subdue the Mamba forcibly had not yet arrived. Bunu's good humour soon returned. In a meeting with the Public Prosecutor from Bremersdorp, he proposed a wager that he had had no hostile intentions towards the Mamba: "I shall take a bet with you for everything that I own and for everything you own that no such thing will take place because I would very much like to have your goods."[85] The offer was declined. Whatever Bunu really intended for the Mamba, the call-up did serve to show "that he [Bunu] is head of the Nation and still retains the power to call his men together," a vital consideration at the outset of his reign.[86] On the eve of the imposition of Republican colonial rule in Swaziland, the mobilization certainly issued a timely warning to Kruger that he proceed cautiously.

Swaziland thus entered the colonial period with its regimental system essentially intact, with Mamba autonomy conserved and with clear regional differences in the degree of control exercised by the aristocracy over the male labour resources of the various chiefdoms. The struggle between centre and periphery over the loyalty and labour of the young men of the kingdom intensified dramatically thereafter. Attempts to reintegrate the south, and its male personnel, into the centralizing institutions of the Swazi state continued after the imposition of colonial control. But new and powerful forces, including widespread land alienation, colonial emasculation of the powers of the chieftainship, and growing participation in wage labour, now threatened to undermine the institutions themselves.

CHAPTER TWO

Cattle, Capital, and Commodity Production

As a miner, or labourer of any kind, the Swazie is useless ... He thinks it a disgrace to work for the white man under any conditions.

Goldfields News, 7 July 1896

Swazi participation in the developing regional economy was desultory for much of the nineteenth century. Before mid-century there was a limited trade in iron goods and calico cloth with the Portuguese at Delagoa Bay. Thereafter, white hunters and traders from the Transvaal, bartering cattle, ivory, and skins for horses and guns, periodically traversed Swaziland. Although these visits occurred with increasing regularity in the 1860s and 1870s, European commodities did not become integral to homestead reproduction or the reinforcement of chiefly or aristocratic dominance in the country.[1] Merchant capital did not, in fact, establish a significant presence in Swaziland prior to the penetration of mining and venture capital in the 1880s.

In the 1870s and early 1880s, Swaziland was inundated by Boer cattle graziers seeking the rich winter pastures of the highveld zone. With the Swazi themselves making only limited use of the highveld, the king and local chiefs were quite willing to lease land in exchange for what they regarded as tribute in cash and particularly kind.[2] As the 1880s progressed, the winter trekkers increased in numbers, pushed further eastwards into the middleveld and lowveld, and sought more formal sanction from the Swazi rulers through written leases. One visitor to Swaziland observed that "it seems to be absurd to speak of Swazieland as belonging to the Swazies, when the country right up to the Bombo Mts. is marked out in what are termed grazing concessions, and during the winter months Swazieland to all intents and purposes changes hands, the natives as possessors of the land are effaced, and the Boers take charge."[3] The majority of the leases were acquired directly from the Swazi king, Mbandeni, an implicit acknowledgment of his pre-emptory control over the country's resources. However, many graziers and white settlers made further payments directly to local chiefs, since their sanction was usually required as well. In one case on record a Boer grazier, Mulder, paid £50 to a chief and a rental of £3 per annum to the king for a grazing concession.[4] This connivance by local chiefs in granting concessions has traditionally been ignored by historians who have concentrated all their attention on the machinations at the royal villages in the Ezulwini valley.

In the mid 1880s, the news of another Eldorado spurred a wave of British and South African mining speculators and prospectors into Swaziland. They initially sought Mbandeni's permission for their operations and by 1889 the entire country had been parcelled out into over 50 mineral concessions. Many of the mining syndicates, together with traders and farmers, obtained land concessions which invariably conflicted with the grazing leases held by Boers.[5] The country was eventually covered by a morass of overlapping mineral, grazing and land leases, and land grants in perpetuity. About half of the 400 concessions granted conferred some form of agricultural right.[6] The various leasehold rights were given legal sanction in 1890 by a judicial body appointed jointly by Britain and the South African Republic. White settlement and farming activity was limited in the 1890s but when the British colonial state defined concession boundaries and transformed leasehold rights into inalienable property rights in 1907, the stage was set for white settlement and farming on a larger scale.

With concession incomes flowing to the Swazi rulers in the late 1880s, a flock of traders were drawn to the country. They too acknowledged the authority of the monarch and the country was quickly divided into a series of monopolistic trading concessions, which in two cases at least conferred the right to import goods duty-free. The traders brought the European commodities, particularly liquor, which allowed ostentatious displays of consumerism at the various royal villages and chiefly homesteads of the country. The closing years of Mbandeni's reign witnessed what Bonner forcefully describes as a "descent into anarchy."[7] The concessions spree got completely out of hand with the assistance of a number of duplicitous white advisers, through whom the Rand mining houses and agents of the government of the South African Republic acquired a series of speculative industrial and administrative monopolies. Factionalism in the Swazi royal house intensified and opposition to the concessions policy generated a spate of political killings. Bitter disputes over resources amongst the concession holders and with local chiefs and commoners ensued. The white advance could no longer be contained by the Swazi rulers and imperial intervention soon followed. The designs of the Kruger state on Swaziland as a potential "road to the sea" and as an arena for Boer settlement, and the tortuous negotiations with Britain from 1889 to 1895 which followed, have been documented in detail elsewhere.[8] In 1895, in the face of sustained protest by the Swazi chiefs, Swaziland became a protectorate of the South African Republic and the first formal colonial administration was installed in the country. This doomed Swazi independence.

Against the backdrop of political uncertainty and intrigue, the 1880s and 1890s were unprofitable years for the gold, tin, and coal miners of Swaziland. Between 1882 and 1899, eight gold concessions were worked at various times. The fledgling industry spent half a million pounds in prospecting and the erection of stamp batteries. But heavy operating costs, inadequate transport facilities, and perennial labour problems forced the companies to stumble along from year to year. Only the gold mine at Forbes Reef northwest of Mbabane consistently made a profit and by 1897 the entire industry had ground to a halt.[9] Tin and coal were mined on a small scale after 1895 without much success. In contrast, the 1890s were prosperous for traders in Swaziland, who clustered around the royal villages, the homesteads of important regional chiefs, and the small mining camps in the centre and north of the country, selling luxury goods and trading in grain and cattle.

Before 1893 most traders operated their own stores and canteens, dispatching Swazi hawkers into the surrounding districts in order to expand their market threshold.[10] In that year a trading concession owned by Albert Bremer and his partner Wallenstein was floated as a limited liability company in London. The Mercantile Association of Swaziland, in which trading houses at Durban and Delagoa Bay were major shareholders, became the premier trading organization. Duty-free goods were imported by ox-wagon to the company headquarters in Bremersdorp and distributed to stores at Mbabane, Mahamba, Bulungu, and the royal village of Nkanini. Forced by its shareholders to buy goods through Delagoa Bay, the Association never made large profits, although it was able to save £11,000 in duty between 1894 and 1899. A major competitor was the German Gustav Schwab, another duty-free concession holder, who established three stores in different parts of the country in 1893.[11] Between 1895 and 1899 Schwab's trading activities garnered an annual profit of £4,000–5,000. A further fifteen to twenty individually owned stores and canteens were scattered about the country. The most successful of these was J.C. Henwood who held a monopoly trading concession over a massive area of 573,000 acres in southwest Swaziland. Henwood worked the concession from a single store with the aid of a large staff and as many as 18 ox-wagons. Starting with capital of £500 in 1889, he was worth over £23,000 at the outbreak of the Anglo-Boer War ten years later.[12]

Apart from a wide variety of trading goods imported for Swazi use, a substantial liquor trade grew up in the Ezulwini valley and around the homesteads of several regional chiefs. After the imposition of Boer colonial rule, sporadic efforts were made to control the illicit sale of liquor to Swazis. In one roundup in 1896, Albert Bremer and a number of other traders were prosecuted by the Kruger administration. But the trade was a lucrative one and with the connivance of local officials, it continued largely unabated. The Swaziland Concessions Commission later estimated that between 1894 and 1899, the Mercantile Association and Gustav Schwab alone imported over 33,000 gallons of illicit wine and spirits into the country.[13]

For many traders a less risky and equally lucrative activity was participation in a burgeoning cattle trade. Swaziland acquired a reputation as the "stockyard" of southern Africa in the 1890s as Swazis disposed of large numbers of cattle to white and black buyers. A *Times of Swaziland* editorial commented on the trade:

Several thousands must be expended annually by Tonga and Portuguese natives, who, returning from the goldfields, elect to invest their money in Swazie stock and pay good prices too, for their acquisitiveness. Hundreds of head find their way to the Delagoa Bay market through enterprising white traders and generally the cattle trade is a source of great profit and revenue to the territory.[14]

The investment of mine wages in Swazi cattle by miners was probably one way to circumvent restrictive conditions governing marriage transactions in southern Mozambique. The export of cattle to the Transvaal was somewhat inhibited by a duty of 10 shillings per head plus 7 per cent of market value. Yet Swazi stock still found its way onto the meat markets of Natal, Johannesburg, Pretoria, and Barberton, as traders smuggled cattle into the Transvaal behind the backs of South African border officials.[15] Traders in Swaziland were the major buyers but several Transvaal firms employed white and black travelling agents to procure cattle in the country. Between 1896 and 1899 officials of the Kruger state found ample time to augment their salaries through cattle trading.[16]

For Swazi homesteads participation in the trade was conditioned by access to livestock. In this respect the aristocracy and the chiefs were particularly well placed. With their large herds accumulated in the second half of the nineteenth century, they were able to dominate, if not to completely monopolize, the trade. Most homesteads of commoners entered the trade at a price and would therefore have parted with their cattle only after careful consideration of the alternatives and implications. Where there is evidence of commoners disposing of cattle it was usually as barter for grain or agricultural implements such as hoes, picks, and ploughs, rather than luxury goods. The commodification of livestock did, however, lead to an erosion of some of the mores governing livestock transactions in Swazi society.

Cattle-raiding by agents of the Swazi chiefs and aristocracy was a constant feature in nineteenth-century Swaziland, but never before had this been motivated by the prospect of acquiring trade goods through barter and sale. Since it was certainly more advantageous to sell someone else's stock than to part with one's own, there was a dramatic upsurge in stock theft. The young Swazi king Bunu, with considerable coercive power at his command, was in the vanguard of this development. The herds of wealthier commoners and powerless minor chiefs were constantly raided by *imbutfo* soldiers on a whole variety of pretexts. But it was difficult for the king's own herders to adequately police the large royal herds which were depleted by stock thieves who sold the proceeds to cattle traders in Swaziland and the Transvaal.[17] Boer graziers from the Transvaal wintering in Swaziland also lost heavily. The devastating rinderpest epidemic of 1897–8 eventually spelled the end of these activities and the lucrative cattle trade as a whole, but not before many thousands of Swazi cattle had entered the meat markets of the region and the African societies of southern Mozambique.

In order to gain access to trade goods two further possibilities confronted the Swazi chiefs and *umnumzana*: to rearrange the productive activities and consumption patterns of the homestead to generate a marketable surplus or to promote labour migration for wage employment. Given that the male and female labour force of the country was already embroiled in military and agricultural pursuits, it is unsurprising that few chose the latter option. Writing some fifty years later, Allister Miller, a journalist who first came to Swaziland in 1888, witnessed how traders began to export grain from the country to the Lourenço Marques area and the mining communities of the eastern Transvaal.[18] Swaziland's "peasant boom," such as it was, was of very short duration and ended as abruptly as it had begun. The terms on which it was achieved were set, as with cattle trading, by the pre-existing social structure of Swazi society and particularly the preferential access to land, labour, and oxen enjoyed by the Swazi chiefs.

During the 1880s, mining companies and white settlers in Swaziland were often unable to obtain grain within the country and sent out for their supplies. Missionaries at the southern settlement of Mahamba noted that money was "very unusual" in the area and that Swazi homesteads only occasionally bartered small stock and grain with itinerant traders and hawkers.[19] In the early 1890s, however, when Elias King established a trading store at Mahamba, he was soon able to export wagon loads of maize to the eastern Transvaal.[20] Traders in other parts of the country also started to buy grain from Swazi homesteads around this time. The bulk of the purchased maize seems to have come from the middleveld and, within that zone, from the centre and south of the country. One of the major southern entrepôts was a store at Bulungu in the Mamba chiefdom where the illegal sale of liquor was rife and the export of maize amounted to some 600 to 700 bags a year.[21] Unfortunately no record of general grain exports was kept, although when Godfrey Lagden toured the country in 1892 he discovered that most traders were buying from 500 to 1500 bags of maize a year.[22] This would suggest a total export figure somewhere in the range of 5,000 to 10,000 bags.

After a particularly severe drought in 1889, the next five years brought good rains and excellent harvests. Many middleveld homesteads consequently had quantities of surplus grain which, rather than storing as in past years, they decided to barter with the traders.[23] Yet it would be incorrect to imply that there were no changes taking place in the organization of Swazi agriculture. Although there are no figures available, a number of contemporary accounts document an expansion in the area of grain under cultivation between 1890 and 1897. This was initially orchestrated by the chiefs who were the first to incorporate the mould-board plough into the rural agricultural cycle "in lieu of the primitive method of breaking up the soil with picks."[24] The chiefs' unfettered access to land and their control over the labour resources of the homesteads of commoners through umemo and local labour contingents allowed them to intensify their demands for labour from their subjects. In this way they were able to increase production and dispose of the surplus grain to traders. Although there is no direct evidence of royal participation in grain trading, it is known that imbutfo soldiers were kept busy in the royal fields during the 1890s and it is possible that some of the traditional surplus of grain was sold to traders. However, most of the grain probably still went on the upkeep of the royal villages.

The main reason for selling cultivated grain was not, as in other parts of the sub-continent, to obviate the pressures of colonial taxation but to secure additional access to trade goods. Following the lead of the chiefs, some larger and more established homesteads of commoners began to barter cattle for ploughs in the early 1890s and, where local chiefs were willing to grant additional land, to expand the area under homestead cultivation. There was quite probably a degree of communal ploughing and, in one case at least, a Swazi farmer from the eastern Transvaal came over the border to plough for his relatives in Swaziland.[25] The integration of the plough into the agricultural cycle of a number of Swazi homesteads was generally a mixed blessing for the women of those homesteads. The plough was almost always worked by men, so that women were released from the difficult task of breaking new ground with digging sticks and picks. Conversely, as the cultivated area expanded, the demands on their labour power at all other phases of the long agricultural cycle probably intensified.

Several commentators later noted that the introduction of the plough immediately brought a more diffident attitude to agricultural labour on the part of Swazi women. This is belied by contemporary evidence from the 1890s.[26] What is perhaps more likely is that female labour was now stretched over an expanding cultivated area, so that the attention given to any one field inevitably declined. Even so, the acquisition of the plough through cattle trading and its adoption by chiefs and a number of commoners was an important aspect of Swaziland's ephemeral phase of agricultural commodity production. Swazi agriculture in the mid-1890s seemed set for a major period of expansion which, so long as market accessibility held out, might have brought more widespread prosperity to the country and certainly increased rural stratification. As it was, the process was rudely shattered in 1896 by a series of ecological calamities.[27] When Swazi homesteads again began to sell grain after the Anglo-Boer War it was under a very different set of economic conditions, and with very different results (see chapter 3).

In the 1880s and 1890s the only employers of note within Swaziland itself were local mines and the larger trading concerns. The majority of workers in a small mine labour force of less than 2,000 were immigrant Zulus and Mozambicans. The footpaths of Swaziland were worn smooth by these migrants who transformed the mines of Swaziland into "a halting if not a kindergarten for boys travelling Randwards" by stopping no longer than a month or two in the country.[28] On their return journey many more mineworkers passed through Swaziland to acquire stock from Swazi sellers.

Employers on the neighbouring goldfields of the eastern Transvaal complained continually about the difficulty of getting Swazi men to work on the mines.[29] The handful that did appear for work refused to sign contracts, would only work for short periods, and were extremely difficult to control:

There is only one opinion amongst employers of Swazi labour and that is that it is about the poorest labour that can be got in or on a mine. The Swazi workman stays only a short time at work, probably two months at the outside, and then clears off with his £3 or £4 back to his kraal. He refuses to go down a mine at all.[30]

In July 1896 when twenty Swazi workers deserted from Moodies Mine near Barberton after being issued identification badges and passes under a new Republican law, they left the offensive articles neatly stacked outside the Mine Manager's door before they left.[31]

A few Swazis worked on the mines within Swaziland but here too their lackadaisical attitude, and unwillingness to work for more than a few weeks, infuriated mine managers.[32] Some Swazi men provided periodic and irregular domestic, agricultural, or transport-riding service to concession holders, but Boer graziers were generally unable to obtain shepherds during their winter sojourn in the country.[33] Those Swazi who did seek work were probably drawn from the ranks of the poorest stratum of Swazi society. It is possible that many of them also came from the south of the country where the demands on their labour-time by the central authorities were considerably muted. Certainly this was true for the one case for which there is detailed evidence.[34]

John Gamede was born in 1874 in the southern Mamba chiefdom and his father died when he was still an infant. His mother went to live with an uncle of his, according to the Swazi levirate custom. When Gamede was ten this uncle died as well, and his mother and a sister moved again to live with another member of his father's family. At the age of about fourteen, Gamede was befriended by a trader who was selling cloth in the district. The trader asked Gamede to return to Bremersdorp to work for him. His widowed mother agreed since she was finding it increasingly difficult to provide for her family. Gamede spent the next two years in Bremersdorp looking after the trader's stock. Then, after an argument with the trader, he deserted and returned home, where he remained until his mother sent him out to work again. He returned to Bremersdorp where he worked for a time as a cook and groom to a local settler. Some months later Gamede was arrested on suspicion of assaulting a white woman and was held for a week before being released uncharged. Soon after this incident he met and travelled with a group of Zulu migrants who were passing through Swaziland en route to Barberton.[35] He went with them to Barberton where he found employment with a local farmer and border policeman named Strijdom. Gamede worked for Strijdom ("this man treated me like one of his own children") until 1896 as a cattleherd and then a border guard. When Strijdom left the area for Pretoria, Gamede went to Barberton considering mine employment. Instead he found work in a sawmill for a month before deserting on pay-day "because it was too dangerous."

The subsequent phase of John Gamede's migration sheds considerable light on the first major surge of Swazi labour out of the country. After 1894 Swaziland was hit by a series of unprecedented environmental disasters. For four successive years rainfall was well below normal, rivers dried up, and crop yields plummeted.[36] Moreover, the surviving crops were ravaged by swarms of locusts. The harvest of 1896 was almost entirely destroyed by the pest. In subsequent years, only certain regions were affected, but crop loss was still considerable.[37] The traditional mechanisms for coping with famine were in constant use and locusts were eaten in large numbers. Meat was consumed in quantity and cattle trading for imported grain experienced a sudden upsurge.[38] Homesteads who had earlier avoided the cattle trade were now forced to dip into their limited holdings as their ability to feed themselves was put under considerable strain. Some men sought work from local missionaries and settlers in exchange for maize and in late 1896 there was a sudden, but brief, movement of Swazi migrants out of the country to seek work in the eastern Transvaal.[39] The harvest of 1897 was a better one but the locusts returned in 1898 and 1899. Towards the end of 1897, the country was finally devastated by the rinderpest epidemic which had been sweeping the sub-continent.

Rinderpest came late to Swaziland but it came with a vengeance. Within weeks the country was convulsed by the epidemic first introduced by Boer transport riders. The effect on the rich cattle stocks of the Swazi was little short of catastrophic. According to the rough estimates of colonial officials, within a month 7,000 cattle were dead; by the end of 1897, 30,000; by March 1898, over 50,000. The final toll was estimated at around 100,000 or approximately 80 to 90 per cent of the country's stock.[40] While the southern reaches of Swaziland were not seriously infected until mid-1898 no area remained immune. Matsha Mamba, the important southern chief, eventually lost well over 5,000 head. The royal cattle posts were denuded.[41] The impact on commoner homesteads was disastrous. The whole countryside was thrown into a state of turmoil as destitute families sought out friends and relatives who could provide them with sustenance. In many cases, wives and children migrated back to their original homesteads because their husbands could no longer supply food.[42] This sudden increase in impoverishment and destitution threatened to tear apart the whole fabric of Swazi society and quickly succeeded where years of capitalist exhortation and fulmination had failed; the sons of the Swazi homestead were dispatched to the labour markets of the region on a life-saving mission.

John Gamede left for Johannesburg, along with scores of other young Swazi men, "so that I could feed my mother during the great famine." His experience on the Rand provides insights into the trauma experienced by this first wave of Swazi migrants. As he later recalled:

I went to Nigel and up in Nigel I worked in the canteen where meat was sold to mine workers. Every day I worked I wrote down my money in a little booklet one, one, one and every strike I made in my book it meant 1/– because I worked for a shilling at a time. The man for whom I was working was a drunkard. He wasn't the actual owner, but he was the manager of this place. One day the owner came in and found him drunk and he kicked him and told him to go out because he didn't want him anymore and he came and said "John, I can't pay you. Your money was 160/– but this drunkard has taken it."

Gamede left the mine penniless after working there for six months. He bumped into a friend who suggested he go and work on an unpopular mine who were always looking for workers. In desperation, he heeded the advice but it was not long before he was in trouble again: "I worked for 10 days in the Mine. Then I got ill. It seemed to be an outbreak of dysentry right throughout South Africa. After a month I recovered and went back to the mine to work again. The boss boy was a drunkard and he would give his men beer to drink, but I would not drink so he chased me away." Gamede approached an American compound manager who paid him £3 for the days he had worked. He returned to Swaziland, eventually became an evangelist with the Scandinavian Alliance Mission, and never went back to the mines.[43] Not all Swazi migrants were so lucky. Many received no pay or were cheated out of their wages by unscrupulous labour touts and white mine employees. Others never returned to Swaziland at all. With the abysmal working and compound conditions of the era, mortality rates were extremely high. In one much-publicized case, all three sons of a Swazi chief died on the Rand.[44] Nevertheless, the distress in Swaziland itself was such that the risk had to be taken.

The statistics are not available to chart this migrant movement with any great accuracy. We do know that the number of Swazis engaged for minework on the Rand jumped from 188 in 1897, to 1,127 in 1898 and to 1,177 in 1899; in September 1899, at the outbreak of the Anglo-Boer War, 1,898 Swazi were working on the mines.[45] The closer gold and coal mines of the eastern Transvaal were besieged by men looking for work. Some migrants even sought employment on Boer farms in the eastern Transvaal, which certainly indicates their desperation.[46] The total number of migrants leaving the country was probably well in excess of 5,000 in 1898 and 1899. In the months of October and November 1898, and March 1899 alone, over 1,000 work passes were issued to Swazi work seekers.[47] Later, especially between 1899 and 1902, Swazis tended to look more towards Natal and especially Durban for employment.[48]

The local representatives of the Kruger state observed the movement of Swazi migrants out of the country with approval. With a mandate from the Volksraad to generate labour migration from Swaziland, the local administration headed by J.C. Krogh was hamstrung by its inability to impose taxation.[49] Now, not only could corrupt local officials make a small fortune trading grain (to add to their booty from the illicit liquor trade), but the recalcitrant Swazi were being driven to work in increasing numbers.[50] Krogh was well aware that the migrant movement was probably only a temporary phenomenon and that there were still strong internal constraints on the unconditional release of Swazi labour. In early 1898, for example, between 2,000 and 3,000 Swazi migrants waited to leave for work until after they had taken part in the *Incwala* ceremony. Later that year, when Bunu mobilized the Swazi regiments to counter a possible coup engineered by the Kruger state, he forbade Swazis from leaving the country to work and recalled those who had already left. The response was immediate. South African employers reported that Swazis at work in all parts of the Transvaal were dropping their tools and returning to Swaziland to aid their king.[51] These incidents provided an ominous indication of the continued hold of the Swazi monarch over much Swazi labour, even at a time of great physical hardship.

Three complementary strategies were devised by Krogh to try to mobilize the maximum number of Swazis for regular participation in wage work. The first of these was to break the power of the Swazi monarchy. Bunu's brief but eventful reign (1895–9) is notorious in Swazi lore as a period of despotic and quixotic rule. There can be little doubt that Bunu had a penchant for personal cruelty although the legends which grew up around his actions were often highly exaggerated.[52] Many of his actions are perfectly explicable given internal political struggles to strengthen Dlamini hegemony, the desire to secure central control over cattle trading, and growing frustration at the arbitrary, coercive, and confining character of Boer rule. Bunu's activities were seen as a "continual menace" by an administration that was attempting to subordinate the Swazi ruling class to its own whim.[53]

On the night of 9 April 1898, Bunu inadvertently provided Krogh with grounds for attack when an important Swazi chief, Mbhabha Nsibande, and two others were murdered at the Zombode royal village.[54] Kruger immediately tried to turn the situation to his own advantage by prosecuting Bunu and laying the groundwork for the abolition of the office of the Swazi monarchy. Krogh proposed to replace the king with four minor sub-chiefs who would control the districts. Failing that, he planned simply to depose Bunu and substitute a more suitable and manipulable candidate, "a tool trained by themselves."[55] The person Krogh had in mind was Masumpa, like Bunu a son of Mbandeni, who was being harboured in the Piet Retief district of the Transvaal by Memezi Dlamini, his exiled uncle. In some Swazi circles, Masumpa was regarded as the rightful heir to the throne and Bunu and his mother, Labotsibeni, shared an unbridled hostility towards Masumpa and Memezi.[56] The Boer plan to overthrow Bunu was eventually dropped under relentless pressure from Milner and Chamberlain who repeatedly called on Kruger to reject any precipitate action, despite a private conviction that they were supporting "a worthless creature in Bunu."[57] Bunu was eventually fined after a show trial in Bremersdorp and further restrictions were placed on his powers of internal jurisdiction over Swazi affairs.[58]

The second strategy adopted by Krogh in pursuit of Swazi labour was the imposition of taxation. The Charlestown Convention of 1894 gave Kruger leave to impose taxes in Swaziland from January 1898, but realizing that there might be resistance to collection Krogh decided to delay until August that year. The tax was exceedingly onerous and was rendered still more pressing by the impoverished state of many Swazi homesteads. To a tax of 10 shillings per hut and a road tax of 2s 6d per head, the Volksraad added a poll tax of forty shillings per male adult. Unlike the Transvaal, no remission of the poll tax was allowed for evidence of six months labour service.[59] Fraser, the British Agent at Pretoria, commented: "the great object of the Government was not so much to bring in revenue ... but to show the Swazis that the necessary payment of these taxes would oblige them to gain sufficient money by labour ... and so to induce the Swazis to take to agricultural or mine labour."[60] The Swazi chiefs were bluntly informed that "the labour markets at Johannesburg and elsewhere are open to the Swazi people" when they protested the harshness of the tax.[61] The local British representative, Johannes Smuts, signalled approval for the Kruger strategy agreeing that "the natives need some incentive to labour and material benefit will ensue if the numbers of men who at present idle about the kraals ... leave the country for a time to labour in the mines."[62] British concern that the tax may have been unnecessarily heavy was studiously ignored by Republican officials, and a request from Bunu that he be allowed to supervise the collection of tax was turned down, despite the favourable write-up given to the system by Smuts.[63] In August 1898 tax collection began for the first time. Cattle traders accompanied the tax collectors and used the opportunity to buy confiscated stock. Although tax evasion was common Krogh managed, through a combination of force and threat, to collect about £15,000 within six months.[64]

Krogh's third strategy was the reverse of the first, since it carried an implicit acknowledgment of the control of the Swazi king over the labour power of many of his subjects. Krogh first approached Bunu in early 1897 and urged him to order his followers to go and look for work. He offered to appoint a white labour agent with whom Bunu could deal and suggested that the king might draw a percentage of the workers' wages as recompense. While Bunu's initial reaction was favourable, he later declined to have anything to do with the proposal, possibly fearing the risks of overt collaboration with a colonial state that was universally disliked by the Swazi people. However, the environmental disasters of late 1897 and 1898 put a very different complexion on the matter.

The Swazi royal villages were under increasing pressure at this time as their cash requirements became acute. Money was needed to purchase grain, to meet tax needs, and to rebuild cattle stocks. Krogh's refusal to allow Bunu to collect tax foreclosed one option, while the Kruger state's monthly payment of concession revenues to the king proved insufficient.[65] A strategy therefore had to be devised by Bunu in order to appropriate a proportion of the earnings of Swazi men who were being forced by circumstance to migrate for employment in increasing numbers. His idea was that all migrants should leave the country under his direction and submit a portion of their wages to him on their return. But he was also concerned about the wider ramifications of an uncontrolled migrant movement, as James Stuart pointed out:

[Bunu] represents that the procuring of labourers in Swaziland by labour agents without his knowledge or consent is a hardship and tends to undermine such authority as he at present possesses among his people. It is abundantly clear that if labour agents, European and natives, may act independently of the Paramount Chief, it will cause natives to pay him less respect ... [and he] desires that all labourers recruited in Swaziland should, before proceeding to Johannesburg or elsewhere, come to his kraal Zombode and there obtain his permission to leave the country.[66]

The Dlamini rulers were thus not opposed in principle to the migration of Swazis out of the country for employment, but they were equally aware of the threat that uncontrolled migration might pose to their position of supremacy within Swazi society. Here was a dilemma which was to haunt the aristocracy well beyond the 1890s.

For its part, the Kruger state saw Bunu's stance as the means to mobilize additional Swazi labour. Officials realized that Bunu was the key and hoped that more labour might be released at his discretion or on his order. Out of this community of interest between the state and the Swazi king arose another offer from Krogh to provide a single labour agent who would work with the king to channel all Swazi labour to the mines. The news of the potential monopoly was greeted with relish in certain circles. The Chamber of Mines' recruiting arm, the Rand Native Labour Association (RNLA), was having its own problems in forcing rival recruiters out of the market.[67] In Swaziland at least, the prospects now appeared somewhat brighter. By securing an agreement with Bunu as the exclusive purveyor of Swazi labour the stage could conceivably have been set for similar deals elsewhere in the region. In November 1898, S.T. Erskine of the RNLA wrote to James Stuart, the Acting British Consul in Swaziland, offering his services to conduct all Swazis to the mines, to place them, and to ensure that their wages were paid. He also offered to pay the way of Swazi headmen who, as he put it, "can see that the kafirs are well treated."[68] Erskine clearly imagined that the best strategy was to obtain the support of the British representative in Swaziland. Stuart saw distinct advantages in centralized recruiting arguing, probably on the basis of his experience in Natal, that it might help to hinder "the loose morality learnt at the mines [being] put into practice in a more or less innocent community."[69] It is unclear, however, whether Stuart declined to press the RNLA's case or whether he did so and was unsuccessful. Either way, the result was the same. The RNLA application was rejected and the contract was offered to a local Boer recruiter from Ermelo, Thuys Grobler, with connections in high places.[70]

In mid-1899 an extraordinary document agreeable to all parties was drawn up vesting Grobler with a monopoly over the mine labour supply from Swaziland (appendix B). Johannes Smuts was sceptical of the ability of either Bunu or the Kruger state to enforce the monopoly on the grounds that he failed to see how "Bunu or anyone else can prevent Swazis from engaging themselves to any employers they may select."[71] Its mettle was never tested. The contract sat on Kruger's desk awaiting the final approval which never came because the region was engulfed by the Anglo-Boer War in late 1899. It is probable that Smuts' prognosis was correct given subsequent events. Attempts to enforce the contract could well have been resisted by many regional chiefs and by the migrants themselves who, by 1899, had acquired a healthy disrespect for recruiters of any genre.

In the chaotic regional labour market of the late 1890s Swaziland, like many other areas of potential labour supply, was besieged by black and white labour touts. Some opted to work through the local chiefs and Bunu and were accorded a favourable reception.[72] Others went directly to the Swazi homestead. While several large batches of approximately 50 to 70 workers went to the mines under the aegis of labour agents in the early part of 1898, the majority opted to leave the country independently since "a rumour is current that the white men sell them to the mines and the independent spirit of the Swazie rebels against anything in which others may make capital of which he is not a sharer."[73] The rumour was well grounded in fact. Many an early migrant had "gone out to work as a poor man and returned in much the same plight."[74] The practice in the mines of deducting exorbitant capitation fees paid to labour touts from the workers' wages ensured that. Many Swazi migrants made only one visit to the mines, preferring to look elsewhere on subsequent trips.[75] The rural information network diffused a deep suspicion of the labour agent: "When this man gets back to his own people, he starts a preaching tour and his text is 'Beware of the whiteman – he will cheat you.' This native makes more converts in a week than John Wesley made in a lifetime. When the honest agent comes along for boys he finds that his task is an all but impossible one – not because he is a labour agent but because he is a white man."[76] Swazi hostility towards the labour recruiter was to extend well into the twentieth century.

At the outbreak of the Anglo-Boer War there were some 2,000 Swazi working on the Witwatersrand. Most of these joined J.S. Marwick's famous overland trek of Zulu workers to Natal, parting with the main company at Volksrust.[77] Many, but by no means all, young Swazi migrants settled back into a rural existence. Those from homesteads still in need of cash supplements turned their attention to the labour markets of Natal and moved southwards in search of employment. The War also threw up its own opportunities, particularly in the British forces, who paid Swazi workers as much as £6 per month for their services.[78] With the War came the lifting of colonial control and temporary environmental respite. Individual Swazi homesteads were periodically looted for food but little serious damage was wrought in the country by either British or Boer, the Swazi rulers carefully maintaining "cordial relations with both sides and preserving Swaziland's neutrality and nominal independence for the duration."[79] Some homesteads were able to recoup some of their cattle losses from rinderpest through theft from Boer herds in the eastern Transvaal. The War also provided the Dlamini aristocracy with a fleeting chance to regroup and reassert some of its lost powers. This task was made difficult by the early death of Bunu soon after the commencement of hostilities and by the designation of an infant as his successor. The Swazi Queen Regent, Labotsibeni, did embark on a limited campaign of cattle raiding to rebuild the royal herds and Boer cattle seized by several southern chiefs were confiscated on her order. Several contemporary accounts attest that the Regent also took the chance to settle some old political scores, actions which involved some loss of life.[80]

In the 1890s Bunu's agreement with Grobler aimed to mobilize labour for the South African mines under the control of the Dlamini aristocracy. In the first decade of British rule these two imperatives, at first complementary, proved to be contradictory. The strong, though often ineffective, complicity of the Kruger state with mining capital has been demonstrated elsewhere.[81] As a colonial state, its policy in Swaziland was unambivalent as it sought to mobilize Swazi labour for the mines and farms of the Transvaal. How successful this strategy might eventually have been is open to speculation. After the Anglo-Boer War, the British colonial state was faced with a similar challenge and the same problems in meeting it. The British role was complicated, however, by the competing demands of a local mining and nascent settler-estate sector. Their attempts to resolve these various pressures by freeing land and generating labour for capitalist enterprise, while simultaneously attempting to maintain social order, reveal important continuities with Kruger policy and give some indication of the fate which might have befallen the earlier project.

PART TWO

Mines and Migrants

CHAPTER THREE

Coercion, Co-optation, and Taxation

There are a number of young men in the country who are roaming about doing nothing but eating up the food supply of the elders. Let these young men go out to labour for money.

Lord Milner, 1904

At a point known as Makosini, nine miles south-east of Mahamba on the southern border of Swaziland, lie the remains of the two great Swazi kings of the nineteenth century, Sobhuza I and Mswati. The official caretaker of these graves during the early years of British rule was chief Nzama Mdhluli. Nzama was also the acting head of a branch of the Mdhluli clan during the minority of the heir to Nlulini the previous chief. He was one of the more important chiefs in the area with a following of over 300 homesteads. Only six other chiefs in the heavily populated Hlatikulu district had more. From the colonial viewpoint Nzama was a bland ruler. He was seen simply as "reticent" and "weak" and appears to have discharged his duties to the Swazi rulers and the colonial state without demur.[1] On 7 March 1911, however, Nzama was sentenced by the Assistant Commissioner's court at Hlatikulu to one month's imprisonment with hard labour. The sentence arose from an incident at Makosini several days before.

In early 1911 it became obvious that the year's harvest was in danger as the country was in the grip of an unexpected drought. To salvage the crop all available labour had to be carefully marshalled. It was therefore not surprising to find that Nzama had ordered a large tribute-labour party or *umemo* to weed his fields. According to Mtsheleni Ntshangase, a Native Police Constable, he and two other policemen approached the party in search of tax defaulters. They discovered that ten men had not got tax receipts and, moreover, three of the party were visitors from the Transvaal without travelling passes. The altercation between the police and the work party was interrupted by the arrival of Nzama and a group of armed men. Nzama demanded to know why the police were patrolling his district without first informing him and told them that if they were going to arrest men for not carrying their tax receipts then they must arrest the whole party. The custodians of colonial law declined his invitation and attempted to arrest the thirteen offenders. A group of women from the *umemo* blocked their path and shouted insults at the police. Nzama's men, acting under his orders, then surrounded them. Nzama pointed to the police and asked his followers: "why do you look on while these people come here and kill us. They are so proud of their little white people." At that the police were attacked and driven out of the area.[2]

The colonial administration decided not to overlook the incident as it constituted a spontaneous local challenge to the state's coercive apparatus in the country. Nzama and his men were punished accordingly. The tax collection machinery of the state depended for its effectiveness and legitimacy on coercion, co-optation of the country's chiefs, and the establishment of a force of black constables to search the countryside for tax evaders. By 1911 this machinery was working relatively efficiently; its annual demands ensured a recurrent assault on the independence and integrity of the Swazi homestead. While it bred nothing but bitterness and resentment towards the state and its agents, only occasionally did the subterranean tensions boil up into open conflict and confrontation. As this chapter shows, the erection of the tax machinery in the first decade of British rule was far from being a harmonious and consensual process.

When the British assumed control of Swaziland in 1902 the imposition of taxation was a formality. In Milner's blueprint, the country was to be administered as far as possible as a district of the Transvaal and heavy Transvaal taxation rates were immediately applied to the Swazi population. Over the first twenty years of British rule 55 to 75 per cent of an ordinary colonial revenue of £40,000 to £52,000 was generated through poll, hut, and dog tax. A further £1,000 to £3,000 was raised each year by means of court fines and the issue of travel and work passes.[3] A large proportion of this revenue was swallowed up by administration (18 to 25 per cent per annum) and the costs of coercion (as much as 42 per cent in 1907–8). Establishing the conditions for settler-estate production in Swaziland placed an additional heavy burden on the colonial budget. Between 1904 and 1911, £190,000 was disbursed on various aspects of the land partition. Just over half of this amount came from loans (including £70,000 from the much healthier Basutoland treasury) and the remainder from ordinary revenue.[4] As a result, the colonial state in Swaziland was continually strapped for funds and spent little on services except those benefiting white landowners and mining companies. The subsequent temptation to turn to the Swazi for additional revenue proved irresistible.[5]

There is abundant evidence that British colonial officials, like their earlier Republican counterparts, viewed taxation as a device to "spur the natives to labour" and they were keen to impress this view on the Swazi.[6] As early as 1901, Johannes Smuts claimed that on the basis of his knowledge of Swaziland in the 1890s, "some incentive to labour is necessary" and that "every facility should be given and every provision made for natives going out to work in the mines of the Transvaal."[7] This view was echoed by colonial officials on all rungs of the colonial ladder. In public pronouncements they sought to assure their doubting listeners of the disinterested benevolence of the state. As the Transvaal Governor Milner pointed out: "the able-bodied men could earn enough in a month [to pay tax]. Nowhere was it so easy to pay the tax as in South Africa, where there was always plenty of good work and good wages for natives. The country was starving for want of labour and the British law ensured that a man would be paid the wages he was promised."[8] In private they were much less sanguine. District officials in Swaziland were instructed to "persuade the young men of the Clan to go out to earn wages instead of spending their lives in idleness and debauchery."[9]

The first colonial report on Swaziland was extremely pessimistic about the contribution the country might make to the labour force of the Transvaal. It noted that there were probably no more than 7,000 to 8,000 Swazi available for work and that of these it was unlikely that more than 3,000 to 4,000 could be induced to leave Swaziland in any one year, even under the most favourable recruiting conditions, and assuming that taxation was imposed on Transvaal lines. By way of explanation the report observed that "this tribe of all those in South Africa, habitually yields the fewest numbers of men to the labour markets, probably owing to the survival of their military organization, their innate laziness and scorn of labour."[10] This gloomy prognosis was later confirmed by witnesses to the Transvaal Labour Commission who were questioned at length on the attitudes of the Swazi towards wage employment in South Africa.[11] Even in a moment of great optimism, Godfrey Lagden, the Secretary of Native Affairs in the Transvaal, only conceded that he could see Swaziland as an eventual source of labour for the eastern Transvaal but not to any great degree for the Witwatersrand.[12] Colonial taxation clearly had a vital role to play in helping overcome Swazi reticence to employment in South Africa.

The initial rate of taxation in Swaziland included a poll tax of £2

per annum on each male adult over the age of 18 and a hut tax of
£2 per annum for each wife (in effect a tax on the productive capacity
of the homestead).[13] In early 1903, there was considerable appre-
hension in the Transvaal Native Affairs Department about how the
Swazi might react towards taxation. The Swaziland administration
was instructed to use no pressure or harassment in collecting tax but
to use its influence "only to guide the inclination of the Swazis."[14]
The news of taxation was greeted in Swaziland with a mixture of
alarm and resignation. As Lagden noted at the time: "the people
seem to regard the tax as quite beyond their ability to meet, and
with their fatalistic tendencies, do not appear to be prepared to make
any extra effort to do so, but to await eventualities. I fear that it
would be nearly impossible to collect the tax from them, and that
only with a stern distraint of their livestock, which I cannot advise,
for it would sooner than anything else cause serious disorder among
the natives."[15] The many-wived Swazi chiefs were particularly concerned by the unlimited hut tax and warned that it would lead to
abandonment of married women and a rapid growth in prostitution.
Conscious of the social disruption this might cause, local officials
immediately recommended an annual tax ceiling of £6 per adult
male. The proposal was accepted by Milner and incorporated into
the colonial tax structure.[16]

The tax collected from the Swazi in 1903 took officials rather by
surprise, although there was widespread evasion in outlying areas.[17]
In the central Mbabane district an estimated 87 per cent of the
anticipated tax was forthcoming (table 2). The reserves of cash circulating in Swaziland permitted the generous response. Money acquired in the late 1890s through cattle trading and migrancy was
supplemented during the Anglo-Boer War by earnings from employment in Natal and with the British forces. Money was also raised
by selling small stock and by borrowing from relatives in the Transvaal. The wealthier stratum of Swazi society in particular had little
difficulty in paying the tax. It was claimed that one southern chief,
Makaheleka Dlamini, would have no trouble in paying a tax as high
as £100 per annum although this would have been a "drain on his
capital."[18]

If the tax was paid relatively freely in 1903, the situation only a
year later could not have been more different. The first collection
and an extremely poor harvest bit into homestead reserves and extensive food purchases were necessary in early 1904.[19] In addition,
an epidemic of East Coast Fever further denuded Swazi herds. In
1904 there were only an estimated 10,000 cattle left in the whole
country (less than 10 per cent of the pre-rinderpest figure).[20] The

TABLE 2

Tax Collection in Mbabane District, 1903–7

Paid in Year	In Respect of Year					Total(£)
	1903	1904	1905	1906	1907	
1903	12,410					12,410
1904	830	7,338				8,168
1905	748	3,138	8,272			12,158
1906	184	664	2,208	4,575		7,631
1907	122	274	585	871	4,902	6,754
Unadjusted Total	14,294	11,414	11,065	5,446	4,902	47,121
Arrears	0	1,424	2,130	1,339	2,172	7,065
Total	14,294	12,838	13,195	6,785	7,074	54,186

Source: SA, D19/07/1141, AC Mbabane, MR, September 1907.

memory of rinderpest itself was still fresh in Swazi minds and the advent of another major setback in the painstaking process of rebuilding cattle stocks filled the country with "much alarm." The prospect of raising funds through cattle trading had also evaporated. In 1904, the chiefs and wealthy commoners again paid their taxes without demur, but many homesteads were in dire straits. There were many responses to the heavy taxes.

Homesteads attempted to raise the necessary funds without migrating either out of choice or because they did not have the labour resources. Few homesteads were in any position to generate or sell surplus agricultural produce in order to pay taxes (chapter 4). Rather, the demands of the taxes induced some homesteads to sell some of their own food. In 1902 and 1903, traders were unable to buy grain in the country. But from mid-1904, an increasing number of homesteads sold grain to traders immediately after the harvest in order to raise cash for taxes. This practice invariably produced food shortages later in the year, a situation of which traders quickly took advantage. Maize bought from Swazi homesteads for as little as 5 shillings per bag in May when taxes were being collected was often resold at 30 shillings per bag in September. Oblivious to their own role in forcing this change, colonial officials blamed the Swazi farmer for selling cheap and buying dear: "the natives in this part of the district are by no means wealthy; in fact the reverse is the case. They seem to lack foresight and do not appear to save for a 'rainy day' ... Instead of filling their pits in case this year's crops were a failure, as they have proved to be, they sold their grain almost before it was dry, and consequently have nothing to fall back on. I think not more than 50 natives in the whole district filled their mealie pits last year."[21] This strategy was at best a palliative to cope with the immediacy of the taxes since the alternative was prosecution and a heavy fine or an extended prison sentence with hard labour. Migration for wage labour during the summer months was often the only means of acquiring the money to buy foodstuffs at inflated prices before the new harvest was brought in.[22]

Some Swazi homesteads acquired tax money from other sources, including livestock sale or various "informal sector" activities such as collecting and selling wood to Europeans for building and fuel, the sale of chickens and eggs, and beer brewing.[23] In the latter case, the transformation of a traditional product into a marketable commodity was partially responsible for an increase of beer production and consumption in Swaziland during the first decade of this century.[24] Sorghum beer was sold by Swazi brewers to workers on local gold and tin mines within the country, and to migrants passing through the country from Mozambique to South Africa and back. The existence of migrant labourers in some homesteads thus allowed others, through the redistribution of migrant earnings, partially to insulate themselves from taxes. The costs of participation included continual harrassment by the state and the conversion of a food crop into a market commodity which often led to food shortages later in the year.

Another means of raising money to pay taxes was through the "sale" of children. This had first taken place on a small scale in the late 1890s in response to the combined pressures of Republican taxation and ecological collapse. At that time, a number of workers at the coal mine in the Swaziland lowveld took advances on their wages in order to purchase young Swazi girls from impoverished homesteads "under cover of eventual marriage."[25] In the early years of British rule Swazi homesteads started to sell children to each other. How widespread this became is difficult to determine but it did cause an official Swazi complaint that they were forced "to sell our children in order to pay tax which is heavy."[26] A protest to the Colonial Office by the Aborigines Protection Society produced a flurry of correspondence within the colonial state. The explanation offered by Swaziland officials was that although the "so-called sale of girls to obtain money" might be repugnant to "civilized ears," Swazi fathers "frequently betroth their infant daughters in order to benefit by the *lobola* cattle in advance of marriage."[27] The appeal to their vanity seems to have satisfied the Society. In a sense colonial officials were perfectly correct. *Ukwenizisa* (or arranged marriage) was not uncommon in Swazi society, particularly between wealthier Swazi homesteads anxious to establish alliances with other clans or lineages. What the British official did not care to mention was that colonial taxation was forcing a new form of *ukwenizisa*; the betrothing of daughters by poor homesteads to men of substance in order to meet their economic obligations to the state.[28]

The opposition of homestead heads to the enforced and premature "marriage" of their daughters can be traced to three factors. First, it represented an early loss of productive labour to the homestead since the girl would leave before she reached a marriageable age. Second, the *umnumzana* may have been forced into accepting a low payment for their daughters when they might reasonably have expected to reap a higher bridewealth payment in cattle at a later date. And third, unlike bridewealth paid in cattle, the homestead would have nothing to show for enforced participation in *ukwenizisa*, since the payments went immediately into the coffers of the state. In many ways the practice could only have led to greater impoverishment and discontent among poorer homesteads. And indeed the same must be said for all of these methods of coping with colonial demands.

After their surprising success in collecting tax in 1903, colonial officials were eager to press home their advantage. In 1904, the Transvaal Native Tax Ordinance of 1902 was therefore extended to Swaziland.[29] Legal machinery was now in place for the prosecution of tax evaders. House-to-house police searches and the vigorous prosecution of offenders began almost immediately. In addition to demands for back tax, offenders were fined £2 for each month they were in arrears.[30] An essentially voluntary tax was transformed at an administrative stroke into a forced tax in a situation where the capacity of the Swazi homestead to make payments had been sharply eroded. The first sign that something was seriously amiss in the Swazi countryside came in mid-1904 with persistent rumours from outlying districts that a rising was imminent. These reports detailed massive discontent with the tax burden and suggested that the people were "anxious to rise against and throw off European control."[31] The dissatisfaction of the commoners was not only directed against the colonial state. The taxation structure, an early instance of regressive legislation, discriminated in favour of the wealthier elements of Swazi society. The fact that a man with three wives was subject to the same tax as a chief with ten times that number was undoubtedly extremely irksome.[32] Many homesteads heads had also contracted a larger number of wives through the Swazi levirate custom. To have to pay taxes on women acquired by this custom produced further discontent.[33]

The tensions within Swazi society caused by taxation penetrated to the most basic level. The *umnumzana* were generally unwilling or unable to migrate for wage employment and relied either on the various cash sources detailed above or on the wages of other homestead members in order to meet their taxation obligations and to purchase grain for the reproduction of the homestead.[34] This reliance inevitably bred tension between fathers and sons over control of the wage packet. The constant temptation for sons who did seek employment was to work only for as long as it took to raise sufficient funds to meet their own needs. While there was a certain degree of wage remittance, it is doubtful that this was adequate to meet the total taxation obligation of the homestead, given the limited time period that most Swazi were prepared to spend at work. In addition, young unmarried Swazi males who had migrated primarily with the object of obtaining money for bridewealth resented and probably resisted the products of their labour being appropriated by homestead heads or local chiefs to meet their own needs and obligations (chapter 4).[35]

The Swazi chiefs had their own specific objections to taxation. Wives acquired after 1903 were subject to tax irrespective of the number of wives a chief already possessed, and additions to the productive capacity of the homestead meant extra recurrent costs for the chief. The chieftainship also had a vested interest in securing lower taxes for their followers since their own ability to appropriate a portion of the wage was being inhibited. These grievances, taken with the growing stress within Swazi society, ensured that the commoners spoke to the colonial state through the medium of the chiefs. An initial appeal for relief directed to Milner elicited an unconvincing reply: "there was a complaint about the tax, that people were poor, had lost their cattle, and could not pay. No-one was sorrier for this than himself. But the loss of cattle was common to all South Africa, to white men as well as natives, and to the Government itself. It was impossible to allow that the people as a whole were too poor to pay tax."[36] Milner's twisted logic cut little ice with the Swazi chiefs, whose appeals against the tax became more strident and impassioned.[37] Pleas for the reduction of the tax burden met with intractable responses: "there are numbers of idle men in the country who could with ease earn sufficient money."[38]

The failure of the Swazi chiefs to bend the will of the state called for more drastic measures on the part of their followers. The obvious alternative to raising funds for tax was to avoid payment altogether. Tax evasion (or "defaulting" in the colonial lexicon) reached epidemic proportions in Swaziland between 1904 and 1907. By September 1906, an estimated amount of over £21,000 was in arrears.[39] A finer indication of the extent of tax evasion can be garnered from the Mbabane district tax records (table 2). In 1903, 87 per cent of expected tax was forthcoming while in 1904 the proportion plummeted to 57 per cent. In 1905 and 1906 it was still way below expectations, despite far more rigorous tax collection methods. If tax evasion was widespread in the accessible Mbabane district, where policing was considerably more organized, it was endemic in the peripheral districts of Hlatikulu, Ubombo, and the Peak. Various strategies were adopted by Swazi men in their attempts to avoid payment. Not all were as drastic as those of an elderly lowveld man who reportedly committed suicide rather than go to jail for tax evasion.[40] In 1904, tax defaulters simply stayed away from tax-collection camps, but in 1905 and 1906, with the institution of homestead inspections by police, more active measures were called for. Homesteads invariably heard about police raids well in advance and the all-female homestead was a frustratingly common sight for the tax collectors.[41] Where the homesteads were near the Swaziland border, many men slipped into the Transvaal or Natal for a brief period. Alternatively, they would hide in the vicinity until the frustrated police had left the area. It is possible that there was a degree of collusion, that the Swazi police themselves gave notice of their intentions. Certainly the colonial state found imported Zulu policemen to be far more effective in matters such as tax collection and consequently tried to employ a large proportion of Zulu in the 170 members of the black police force.[42]

Some homesteads managed to circumvent the tax collector by circulating old tax receipts. The palming off of receipts was not always an unqualified success, particularly if the guilty party was known to the police.[43] With cases of evasion and refusal to make payment mushrooming alarmingly, the colonial administration acted in late 1905 to try and remedy the situation by summoning all current and back taxes. The chief business of colonial courts became "the work of instilling into the minds of the native population the necessity for contributing their mites towards the upkeep of the country." The local settler newspaper commented sarcastically that the range of excuses proffered by tax defaulters was as "ingenious and varied as the personal adornments of the defendants." However, with local jails "about as full of the defaulters as it is advisable to fill them" the pressure on tax evaders slackened at the end of 1905.[44]

In sum, the assault on the defaulter was unsuccessful. The police were spread too thin on the ground, defaulters invariably elected to serve prison sentences rather than pay fines so that additional revenue was not collected, rudimentary prison facilities could not cope with the level of demand, the new element of naked force led to still greater dissatisfaction in the country, and the assault largely failed in its most basic aim of precipitating a mass movement of labour migrants out of the country.[45] Those who left Swaziland for short-term employment did so not to acquire tax money in the first instance but to secure cash for *lobola* or food purchase. Rather than acting as a "spur to labour," the heavy rate of taxation may even have reduced the labour supply for some South African and local employers. In 1904, the numbers of Swazi working in the labour districts of the Transvaal remained virtually constant. Certainly there was a steady increase in 1905 but there was an equally steady decrease in 1906, so that by the end of 1906 there were only 132 more Swazis employed than there had been two years earlier. The number of Swazi employed on the Transvaal mines increased from 441 in January 1904 to 851 in December 1906 (with a peak of 1,089 in February 1906) but these figures remained well below those of the late 1890s and did not satisfy colonial officials who were keen to move large numbers of Swazis onto the South African labour market. Even local employers within Swaziland failed to benefit from heavy taxation and the complaints about labour shortages were echoed by white settlers and local mine managers. Local employers were the first to complain that the taxation system was having a negative effect, for it encouraged a defeatist attitude and opposition to, rather than participation in, labour migration.[46]

After closely monitoring events in Swaziland for several months, the High Commissioner was forced to act. Aware of mounting opposition of the chiefs to his land policy and the bitter complaints in the country regarding taxation, Selborne decided to trade one off against the other. By affording relief from the heavy taxes, he hoped that there might be a more favourable disposition towards his land policy. First he delayed collection of the 1906 tax and, after visiting Swaziland and hearing representations from the chiefs, he slashed the tax in half.[47] His compromise failed. Opposition to colonial land policy was maintained at fever pitch throughout 1907 and there was no immediate reduction in tax defaulting. In September 1907, a year after the new tax structure was put in place, over 50 per cent of taxpayers in the heavily policed Mbabane district were still in arrears.[48]

A more systematic assault on the Swazi homestead was needed. The authoritarian Robert Coryndon, appointed Resident Commissioner in mid-1907, provided just the right stimulus for such a policy. Coryndon immediately reviewed and began to reconstruct the local administrative apparatus, adopting a set of "stringent measures in the very numerous cases of wilful default to pay."[49] To ensure a greater concentration of colonial personnel and more intensive policing, the number of districts in the country was increased from four to five (figure 4). Within each district the state erected machinery for the enforcement of taxation and the hunting down of tax evaders under the rigorous provisions of the Transvaal Native Tax Ordinance. A comprehensive tax register was compiled and a definite collection season established (from May to September). Coryndon was also convinced from his experience in Central Africa that an efficient tax collection system could not be established without the full co-operation of the Swazi chiefs. He therefore made immediate attempts to draw the chiefs into the coercive apparatus of the state. Given the poor relations with the Swazi chiefs which then prevailed, he quickly realized that any voluntary co-optation was unworkable, and decided instead to force their assistance.

The chiefs were made responsible for bringing their followers to tax collection camps. When Mgudhula Mtetwa arrived in Mbabane to pay tax with only 20 of his 1,100 followers in July 1907, the Assistant Commissioner refused to accept payment until Mtetwa brought "a proper number of his men."[50] Chiefs were ordered to arrest and forward tax defaulters for prosecution. Any balking was rigorously punished. In August 1907, for example, three major southern chiefs, Mzila Nhlabati, Bokweni Mamba, and Silele Nsibande, were all fined for failing to toe the new line.[51] In the same month a Ubombo district chief, Mpundhle Maziya, was prosecuted when he appeared at a tax camp with less than 50 of his 247 followers. This action reportedly had "a most salutary effect on other chiefs who when called upon to attend did so accompanied by every ablebodied follower, whether in possession of tax money or not."[52] The high point in the colonial campaign came in October 1907 with the arrest of chief Giba Dlamini on a charge of obstructing the police in the course of a round-up of tax defaulters. Giba's resistance to the new colonial code got him 6 month's imprisonment with hard labour.[53] The forced incorporation of the chiefs into the state apparatus proved to be necessary for effective tax collection. The prosecution of a number of chiefs in 1907 hastened this process, yet it might still be questioned why the bulk of the chiefs appear to have given in so easily, given their opposition to colonial land policy and the pervasive dissatisfaction of commoners with the taxation system. The answer is to be found in a particular conjunction of events in

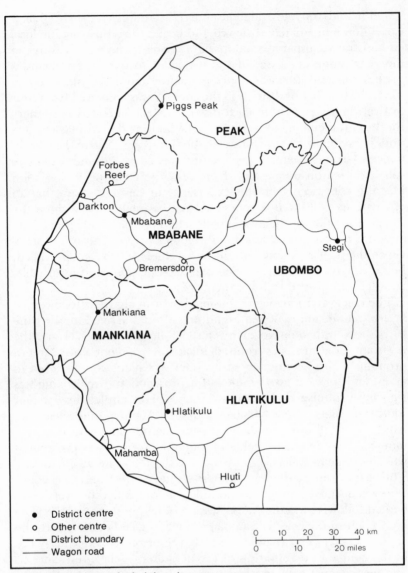

- ● District centre
- ○ Other centre
- – – District boundary
- —— Wagon road

0   10   20   30   40 km
0   10   20 miles

4 Colonial districts and administrative centres, 1907

1907–8 which led them to try to turn colonial taxation to their own advantage.

When the chiefs were informed by colonial officials of the "absolute need for them to use every endeavour to impress upon their followers the urgent need and duty of every able-bodied man to proceed to work," the appeal was largely redundant.[54] Faced with colonial opposition to their attempts to secure funds to pay lawyers' and advisers' fees and to finance a delegation to Britain to protest land policy at a higher level of the colonial apparatus, the Swazi chiefs had resorted to various forms of compulsory levy from 1905 onwards. Initial collections from homesteads in late 1905 and early 1906 were rather fitful and disguised as calls for rain tribute.[55] These exactions paled next to the heavy demands of 1907–8. In mid-1907, Queen Regent Labotsibeni imposed a minimum national levy of £5 per chief and £1 per male adult and ordered the confiscation of cattle when payment was not forthcoming.[56] Local chiefs all over the country cajoled their followers to seek work to meet the levy. Considerable numbers of men, who might otherwise have remained on the land, left in search of wage employment.[57] Whether the chiefs would have been quite so successful in mobilizing their followers without the aid of colonial taxation is difficult to say. What is certain is that while colonial officials viewed the motivations of the chiefs with considerable disquiet, they were more than pleased with the eventual outcome. The question then became one of besting the chiefs in the struggle to appropriate the earnings of labour migrants. The contradictory effects of colonial land and labour policy consequently forced the chiefs and aristocracy to work in tandem with the colonial state to facilitate Swazi participation in wage labour when, in a different set of circumstances, they might equally well have tried to inhibit it and extend the lifespan of the tax evasion epidemic of 1904–7.

Colonial officials were still aware that the chiefs could not be relied upon as components of the tax machinery, particularly in apprehending tax defaulters, since such participation would have been seen as an open acknowledgment of their collaboration with the state.[58] They therefore mounted a sustained and systematic attack on those tax defaulters among the commoners. Small police patrols were dispatched into the countryside at random, to surprise "natives wilfully evading hut tax regulations." Since many defaulters still managed to evade these patrols, large numbers of police were concentrated in a limited area for saturation sweeps through the countryside.[59] No part of the country was immune. Even the Queen Regent's Zombode village was ransacked for defaulters, much to her displeasure. Those who obstructed the course of colonial justice by interfering with the inspection of tax receipts were ruthlessly prosecuted.[60] The whole draconian operation was construed by infantile colonial officials as a sort of game hunt:

Another most successful capture was brought about through the arrest of an old man of some 60 years for eluding the pass regulations. On being cautioned and advised that he should take out a 1/– pass, he informed my *nduna* that he had not that amount, but would show him 4 tax defaulters if he could procure his freedom. A police patrol acting on this information succeeded in capturing the 4 men who had not paid since 1903.[61]

No one was safe from the rigorous activities of the police and stiff fines and jail sentences were handed out for defaulting and obstruction of justice. In 1909, the administration cast its net still wider as colonial officials began to make annual trips to collect taxes on the Witwatersrand from workers who were away from Swaziland during the regular collection season.[62]

From late 1907, Assistant Commissioners began to report the "desirable effects" of their campaign. The number of Native Travelling Passes (NTP's) issued by the local administration jumped from 4,268 in 1906–7 to 11,857 in 1907–8. The issue of work passes increased by over 3,000 within the space of a year and some districts were reported to be "empty of natives," who were away working.[63] Although the number of Swazi migrants on the goldmines increased by several hundred, the majority of workseekers still tended to avoid the Rand. The colonial onslaught and the demands of the Swazi chieftainship ensured that mass participation in migrancy became entrenched from 1907–8 but neither had direct control over where the migrants would actually seek work (chapter 4). Within Swaziland, the collection of back taxes began to swell the impoverished colonial treasury and the roads of Swaziland were in a better state of repair than at any time past. Convict labour was employed almost continuously on the building and upkeep of roads. In later years, the quality of the roads was a ready visual index of the degree of tax defaulting among the people.

There was an immediate decline in tax defaulting after the colonial onslaught began in 1907–8 (table 3). Tax evasion was never completely eliminated, however, and tended to surge in years of poor harvest, economic depression, or immediately after an increase in tax demands such as in 1916. Some men also managed to evade tax payment for many years. It was not until April 1911 that the state caught up with N. Nsibandi who was £33 in arrears for the period 1903–10. Zihlele Gwebu was even more elusive, and it was 1919 before his claim that he had never been able to earn money for tax fell on, deaf colonial ears.[64]

Colonial taxation is generally viewed as the major coercive lever used by colonial governments to force Africans off the land and into capitalist labour markets. There is little doubt that in many cases it

TABLE 3
Tax Defaulters Prosecuted by District, 1907–15

Year	Hlatikulu	Mbabane	Mankiana	Ubombo	Peak	Total
1907/8	1,691	683	224	318	150	3,066
1908/9	1,217	394	429	223	66	2,329
1909/10	399	171	185	228	42	1,025
1910/11	130	191	239	200	43	803
1911/12	143	338	58	81	10	630
1912/13	131	118	87	295	14	645
1913/14	266	195	63	111	83	718
1914/15	137	186	126	138	57	644
1915/16	272	241	242	198	49	1,002

Source: ACR, 1907/8–1915/16; SA, Draft ACR, 1907/8–1915/16.

was a very effective lever, particularly where local ruling classes were incorporated into the tax collection apparatus. In Swaziland taxation initially proved to be a "blunt instrument" in mobilizing Swazi labour and in directing it towards particular markets.[65] Before 1907 Swazi homesteads created sufficient space for themselves in order to respond to colonial tax demands without recourse to sustained labour migration. The responses of Swazi commoners were thus far from consistent with colonial designs. The reformulation of colonial labour policy which followed was rendered inevitable by a taxation system which served only to fuel social discontent and threatened to produce the kind of armed revolt being witnessed in neighbouring Zululand.[66] The co-operation of the Swazi chiefs was not won without a struggle and the relationship with the state was always fragile and unstable. The colonial state was unable, through financial constraint, to offer the material rewards which often accompanied collaboration in other parts of British Africa. The massive grievances which the Swazi aristocracy and chiefs entertained against the state throughout this period, particularly over colonial land policy, inhibited full collaboration except insofar as they could turn such collaboration to their own advantage. When, as at Nzama's, the zealous guardians of colonial domination violated what were highly contentious rules governing tax collection in the countryside, the response could be dramatic.

CHAPTER FOUR

Rulers, Regiments, and Recruiters

We would sooner go poor men in our own country than die at the Rand with money in our hands.

Swazi saying, 1904

As the Anglo-Boer War drew to a close, South African employers in urgent need of black labour moved quickly to exploit any areas of potential supply, Swaziland included. In late 1901, John Major applied for a licence to introduce 300 labourers from Swaziland for twelve months' service at St George's Colliery, Dundee, in Natal. In early 1902, recruiters sought official permission to recruit 500 Swazi for work at Durban docks for periods of three to six months.[1] In late 1902, Thuys Grobler and Helgard de Jager attempted to resuscitate Grobler's 1899 monopoly recruiting agreement with Bunu, but were blocked by the Transvaal Native Affairs Department.[2] Both the Barberton goldfields and the Rand mines, through the agency of the Witwatersrand Native Labour Association (WNLA), set up recruiting facilities in Swaziland and black labour touts entered the country in some numbers.[3] The potential Swazi workforce was estimated at 10,000 by Enraght Moony in June 1903, and 15,000 by David Forbes in 1904.[4] Forbes calculated that 3,000 Swazi had worked outside the country at some stage between 1901 and 1904, while Moony's more generous estimate was that in the fifteen months between September 1902 and December 1903, 5,000 men left Swaziland for work in South Africa for short periods.[5] These early migrants and their sending agencies, such as chiefs and homestead heads, made decisions about migration destinations according to limits set by the South African reconstruction economy.

In the early years of the century there were a number of alternatives to employment in the Rand gold-mining industry. These included the coal mines and sugar plantations of northern Natal, the farms and coal mines of the eastern Transvaal, sundry informal sector activities such as domestic service, washing, transport riding (and crime), and extensive public works programs on roads, docks,

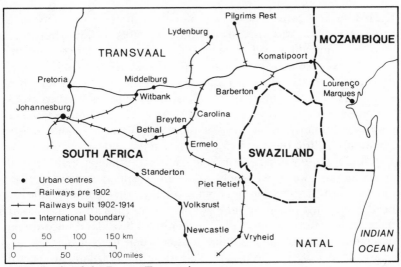

5 Swaziland and the Eastern Transvaal

and railway works throughout the region.[6] Swaziland was centrally situated in relation to many of these places of employment and there were many options available to the Swazi migrant. The Rand was certainly one of the highest wage centres but the more favourable conditions and terms of service elsewhere proved a considerable counter-attraction. Swazi migrants took full advantage of the various alternatives to mine work, as is seen by early spatial patterns of migration.

Non-mining employment towards which the migrants tended to gravitate included urban domestic service in the towns of the eastern Transvaal, road and railway works in the Transvaal (particularly the Springs-Breyten and Ermelo line), and various urban areas in northern Natal (figure 5).[7] In 1904, for example, there were 200 Swazi working on roadworks in the eastern Transvaal town of Ermelo, 285 in the coal mining district of Newcastle in Natal and a further 155 as far afield as Durban.[8] Swazi migrants seem to have been aware of employment opportunities outside the country, probably from their relatives in the eastern Transvaal and from the resulting free flow of visitors and information across the border. The major advantages of many of these forms of employment were their relative accessibility and the absence of written contracts which tied migrants down to specific periods of service.

Several hundred Swazi migrants, mainly from the centre and north of the country, sought work on the gold mines of the eastern Transvaal around Barberton and Pilgrim's Rest. These mines were less

hazardous and considerably healthier than those of the Witwatersrand. Barberton was also attractive to migrants seeking short-term
work and travelling on foot, who did not have the desire or means
to pay their own transport costs to Johannesburg. As Godfrey Lagden noted "the Swazis don't care about going too far in search of
employment."[9] Shortages of labour at Barberton allowed migrants
to extract more favourable terms of service. Mine managers quickly
discovered that there was little point trying to recruit labour in Swaziland itself "for they will not go to a mine unless on their own
account."[10] Swazi workers refused to contract for longer than a month
at a time and were extremely reluctant to spend more than four
months away from home. This meant that they could juggle the
need for a wage with the other demands on their time and labour
from within Swazi society. The proximity of Swaziland encouraged
desertion when conditions failed to meet their demands.[11]

The farms of the Transvaal, like those in Swaziland, were studiously avoided by migrants. Gold mining employment on the Rand
was also widely shunned and when Swazi migrants did appear they
generally refused to work underground.[12] The proportion of Swazi
in minework in the labour districts of the Transvaal was less than
30 per cent in early 1904, and it was not until late 1907 that the
mines finally outstripped other forms of employment in these areas
(table 4). The average number employed in the mines was only 710
in 1905 and 688 in 1906. In 1907–8, when the number of Swazi
migrants dramatically increased under intense pressure from the
colonial state and the Swazi chiefs, the majority still tended to avoid
the Witwatersrand. Between April 1907 and March 1908, almost
12,000 travel passes and 8,000 work passes were issued in Swaziland,
while there were fewer than 2,000 Swazi on average in the gold
mines in 1907 and 1908.

The unpopularity of the Rand among Swazi migrants had much
to do with the longer contracts demanded of recruits and the atrocious working and living conditions of minework. These had showed
little improvement over the late 1890s. Compounds were grossly
over-crowded, squalid, disease-ridden, and poorly heated and ven-
tilated. A vigorous work regimen was imposed on a labour force
whose inadequate diet left them wholly unfit for minework. Underground, the work was physically taxing, there were few controls over
brutal white gang bosses, and miners were constantly in danger from
malfunctioning machinery and rock bursts. Back on the surface,
workers emerging from the hot and stifling conditions underground
into the bitterly cold Johannesburg were prime candidates for pneumonia. Indeed "the combination of exhaustion, hunger and chill

TABLE 4

Swazi Employment in Labour Districts of the Transvaal, 1904–18

Month	1904 M/W	Other	Total	1905 M/W	Other	Total	1906 M/W	Other	Total	1911 M/W	Other	Total	1918 M/W	Other	Total
Jan	441	1,153	1,594	830	1,050	1,880	1,051	1,644	2,695	2,848	1,330	4,178	4,458	428	4,886
Feb				983	1,047	2,030	1,089	1,652	2,741	2,820	1,185	4,005	4,669	442	5,111
Mar	461	864	1,325	1,032	1,061	2,093	1,034	1,600	2,634	2,891	1,048	3,939	4,812	447	5,259
Apr	488	732	1,220	1,022	1,025	2,047	952	1,646	2,598	2,838	1,114	3,952	4,792	437	5,229
May	439	748	1,187	954	1,078	2,032	872	1,511	2,383	2,848	1,119	3,967	4,822	438	5,260
Jun	438	719	1,157	978	1,115	2,093	784	1,401	2,185	2,898	1,081	3,979	4,837	436	5,273
Jul	482	754	1,236	1,031	1,133	2,164	733	1,344	2,077	3,023	1,081	4,104	4,832	433	5,265
Aug	445	761	1,201	916	1,148	2,064	702	1,293	1,995	3,359	1,148	4,507	4,918	452	5,370
Sep	454	767	1,221	918	1,229	2,147	661	1,202	1,863	3,515	1,167	4,682	5,121	455	5,576
Oct	499	851	1,350	1,053	1,376	2,429	567	1,207	1,774	3,822	1,228	5,050	4,973	436	5,409
Nov	454	767	1,221	1,083	1,464	2,547	608	1,273	1,881	4,095	1,201	5,296	4,728	451	5,179
Dec	629	899	1,528	1,041	1,482	2,523	851	875	1,726				4,681	470	5,151

M/W = Mines & Works

Source: TAD, GOV 147–1084; CAD, GG 1420–33.

could not help but contribute to the ill-health of all but the most robust worker."[13] Mortality rates were extremely high as pneumonia, pulmonary tuberculosis, and other diseases took their toll. Swazi aversion to these conditions easily outweighed the fact that Rand wages, although pitifully small by any standard, were higher than those elsewhere.[14] Swazi reactions were not simply based on hearsay. The brief flirtation with the gold mines in the late 1890s had left the workers exceedingly bitter. In 1903, David Forbes interviewed a number of migrants about their attitude towards the mines. He discovered that the mines were universally associated with bad working conditions, poor health, and high death rates.[15] Chiefs and *umnumzana*, many of whom had lost sons before the Anglo-Boer War, also regarded the Rand with great distaste. The epigraph of this chapter typified the general attitude. Forbes' attempts to reassure Swazi migrants were unsuccessful.

Yet for some, the potential benefits of gold mining employment outweighed the hazards since, as noted above, there were always several hundred Swazi on the mines before 1910. It is significant that many of these migrants made their own way to Johannesburg without the assistance of recruiters. In 1907, for example, 70 per cent of Swazi mine workers fell into this category of non-recruited labour – called "voluntaries" or "independents."[16] This allowed them some latitude in avoiding the worst of the mines and signing on for surface rather than hazardous underground work. The separation of recruits and independents is somewhat artificial in this context, however. The recruiters who were successful in Swaziland recruited for the handful of mines that the Swazi were prepared to work at anyway. Recruits and independents consequently mingled in the compounds of the "two or three mines in Johannesburg which are in great favour with the Swazis."[17] Contract breaking was particularly common among Swazi workers whose desertion rates were well above the industry average. By proceeding independently to the Rand, the migrants were able to maintain some control over the terms and conditions of their own employment, as the external demands on Swazi labour power intensified. The crux of the problem facing capital and the colonial state was that although Swazis could eventually be induced to work, they could not be forced to labour at designated places for specified lengths of time. These variables were to a considerable degree determined by the migrants themselves. Even the eventual capitulation to the mine recruiter occurred at the instigation of Swazi workers and homestead heads who saw here the means to further their own interests (see chapter 5).

The years before 1907 were characterized by sporadic and casual participation in wage employment by a fairly narrow band of Swazi men. While the imposition of taxation may have been responsible for some of this movement, most migrants had their own reasons for going to South Africa to seek work. The majority seem to have been young unmarried males aged from 15 to 35, cohorts of the deceased Swazi king Bunu, who rarely left the country for more than a few months at a time. In a sense they resembled the classic "target worker" migrants who worked only for as long as was required to raise their target income before returning home. However, they were neither the "radio and bicycle" workers of colonial mythology and industry propaganda nor the "forced target" workers of more recent radical historiography.[18] Their target was basically twofold: money for grain purchase and *lobola* payments. When the heavy demands of the state and the Swazi ruling class began to bite after 1907, the Swazi migrant force expanded to embrace many married men and younger *umnumzana* as well.

In the first two decades of colonial rule the *umnumzana* were largely unable to meet the demands of their unmarried sons for bridewealth payments. In some cases the *lobola* obligation was dispensed with altogether, but in general the cash payment became the dominant form of bridewealth amongst commoners. In order to secure the means for marriage, sons were forced to migrate for wage employment rather than depend on their fathers as in previous times. Many homestead heads were so desperate for funds that the practice of marriage on credit became widespread with demands for a downpayment of no more than a single beast or £2 to £3.[19] As East Coast Fever was brought under control after 1910 with the aid of a colonial dipping program financed by a 2 shillings tax on each adult male, Swazi cattle holdings were rapidly rebuilt. Cattle were gradually reinstated as the major form of *lobola* and the temporary expedient of cash bridewealth, introduced to meet the exigencies of the post-rinderpest years, slowly fell away. Even so labour migration continued to be a major way for young Swazi men to acquire access to marriage.[20]

This new accessibility of marriage to young Swazi men was to have profound social repercussions. The major implication of cash *lobola* was that unmarried sons had greater independence in the marriage market. The overall result was an accelerated rate of marriage in the late 1890s and early 1900s. In 1905, David Forbes noted that in the 1880s it had been rare to see a man under the age of 25 who was married but that after only a decade's participation in wage labour, many Swazi "marry when quite boys."[21] Through participation in wage labour there was no longer any pressing need for newly married sons to wait for the internal development of a viable productive community before hiving off from the family homestead.[22] Here were the roots of a practice that had become commonplace by the 1930s: "Whereas before economic security depended on the land that men obtained from their fathers, and the cattle they received as part of their heritage, modern youths become independent of both land and cattle by living in town or on European-owned land, and supporting themselves on money wages that they invest as they please. As long as they remain in the homestead the patriarch exercises control, so many a son, unwilling to be completely bound ... moves a short distance from the ancestral centre and establishes his own homestead."[23] Married sons of longer standing also took the opportunity provided by new material resources to separate from their fathers' homesteads. The rate of new homestead formation consequently increased quite dramatically in the early years of colonial rule, and with it came a noticeable decline in homestead size.

In the first two decades of British rule, food purchase continued to ensure the reproduction of the majority of homesteads. For some years after the Anglo-Boer War, agricultural production was seriously inhibited by inclement environmental conditions. Droughts in 1903, 1905, 1908, 1911, and 1916 and the ravages of locusts, aphids, and caterpillars hobbled Swazi productivity, making homesteads increasingly dependent on imported grain. In 1903 the colonial state distributed £2,000 worth of maize to destitute homesteads, but in subsequent drought years the Swazi were left to fend for themselves.[24] Homesteads with some food were forced to husband their resources more carefully and there was consequently much less internal redistribution of food.

Access to the game resources of the Swaziland lowveld, a traditional hedge against hunger, was restricted by colonial legislation and the advent of white hunters from the Transvaal. The colonial state limited Swazi hunting to a few months every year and prohibited it in the period when game was needed most as a food source, before the new harvest was brought in. Severe penalties for poaching completed the criminalization of this traditional means of acquiring food. In contrast, white hunters from the Transvaal were allowed free reign during the limited hunting season. With firepower now denied by legislation to Swazi hunters, the whites rapidly decimated the wildebeest and impala herds of the lowveld, shipping wagonloads of biltong out of Swaziland to the urban centres of the Transvaal.[25] The pool of game on which Swazi homesteads could draw was rapidly diminished. In 1907, in response to protests by local white settlers, the activities of the hunters were circumscribed by the declaration of two game reserves.[26] One of these reserves covered the entire lowveld in the Hlatikulu district, effectively barring Swazi residents access to game in this populous part of the country.

With Swazi cattle stocks at an all time low other traditional responses to famine – *kusisa*, stock slaughter, or exchange of stock for grain – were denied many homesteads. *Emasi* (sour milk), an important source of protein in the pre-colonial diet, became a luxury item.[27] Without draft oxen those homesteads which had invested in ploughs in the 1890s were unable to break up as much land and the area under cultivation declined appreciably.[28] In a survey of 288 homesteads conducted by the Swaziland Concessions Commission in 1905, 172 (60 per cent) had no cattle and a further 71 (25 per cent) had less than five head. Over 80 per cent of surveyed homesteads reported owning cattle before the rinderpest epidemic of 1897–8. Only 5 per cent of the homesteads had access to *kusisa* cattle, most from the holdings of local chiefs or the royal herds.[29] Between 1911 and 1921, however, the number of cattle owned by Swazi increased from under 40,000 to over 200,000. From about 1912 reports became common of Swazi homesteads with cattle yet lacking cash income, reluctantly bartering cattle for grain in the hungry season following a poor harvest.[30] Yet a census of homesteads conducted in 1914 reveals that the rebuilding of herds, and the possibility of acquiring grain through barter, was highly selective. Well over 50 per cent of surveyed homesteads in most areas, and as many as 70 per cent in the highveld Mankiana district, held no cattle at all (table 5). Between 60 and 80 per cent of homesteads had less than five head.

Given this set of constraints on the vitality of homestead reproduction, the *umnumzana* repeatedly directed homestead members to migrate for short periods to obtain cash for food and, where they were unable to do so, looked for work themselves. The length of time spent by Swazi in wage employment was thus to some degree related to the quality of the annual Swazi harvest and the fluctuating price of imported maize, at the same time mediated by the complicating factors of colonial taxation and the episodic demands of the chieftainship. In rare years of particularly good weather and harvest, the number of Swazi on the labour market could drop appreciably. Yet poor harvests were more the norm and Swaziland became a consistent importer of grain from the Transvaal after the turn of the century (16,700 bags in 1908–9, the last year in which exports were officially recorded).[31]

The deepening reliance of the homestead on grain purchased from local traders or hawkers from the Transvaal was gradually

TABLE 5
Cattle Holdings of Swazi Homesteads, 1914

Number of Cattle	Percentage of Households		
	Mankiana	Mbabane	Peak
0	70.4	68.9	50.8
1–5	9.0	2.9	11.8
6–10	8.6	9.3	12.2
11–15	5.2	9.3	6.1
16–20	2.6	3.9	7.4
21–30	3.3	3.9	6.5
31–40	0.7	0.8	2.6
41–50	0.1	0.5	0.4
>50	0.1	0.5	2.2

Source: SA, RCS 405/14.

reinforced by a change in the division of labour in the homestead. The labour force at the command of the *umnumzana* declined, but not it seems through the loss of male labour. The integration of migrant wages and purchased grain into the reproductive cycle of the homestead seems to have underwritten a widespread, though unorchestrated, withdrawal of labour from homestead fields by Swazi women.[32] Much less effort was expended in agricultural pursuits than in the nineteenth century and more time was devoted to other productive and non-productive activities. While this trend was actively contested by the *umnumzana* they were unable to subordinate and control women's labour as completely and effectively as they had previously. In the second decade of the century, as participation in wage labour became more widespread and the *umnumzana* managed, primarily through the advance system (see chapter 5), to acquire a greater degree of control over the wage packet, income was also invested in agricultural innovation. By 1921, 20 per cent of homesteads owned mould-board ploughs. While the total area under cultivation may well have increased there is no evidence of a corresponding increase in agricultural productivity or indication of a drop in food imports.

It is therefore quite possible that the adoption of the plough was hastened, not by any attempt to raise production levels to generate market surplus as in other areas, but by the refusal of women to revert to more intensive methods of breaking up the soil for planting. In addition, even with an expanded area under cultivation "owing to the indifferent cultivation, a large number of natives prefer to get money to buy food from a labour agent, than by endeavouring to grow their own."[33] As an alternative to working continuously in the fields some women were prepared "to walk 20–30 miles if they know of a store where they can buy mealies a little cheaper than they can get them locally."[34] Women with access to migrant earnings were also known to purchase additional sorghum from traders for conversion into beer. The proceeds of beer sales were sometimes used for homestead needs but also to acquire some imported luxury goods for their own consumption.

Male labour, which in the nineteenth century had been almost exclusively utilized outside the *umuti*, was increasingly embroiled in homestead production for ploughing between July and September. In smaller homesteads, the *umnumzana* or young boys became directly responsible for this task, and in the larger ones single male sons wielded the plough.[35] Males were also more active in homestead agricultural activity at the harvest in April and May. The full dimensions and possible regional variations in the emergence of the new homestead division of labour are difficult to determine, but one effect was the development of a marked seasonal pattern to labour migrancy. Significant numbers of migrants adjusted to a regular oscillatory pattern, leaving Swaziland for work for six months after ploughing operations were complete and returning in time for the harvest in April-May (figure 6).[36] This was not the case with all migrants. Older men who worked for shorter periods either in Swaziland or in the eastern Transvaal and single mineworkers from larger homesteads whose incorporation into homestead reproduction was not so advanced were not bound by quite the same constraints.

Many regional chiefs and the Swazi central authorities at Zombode encouraged participation in wage labour by young Swazi men. In July 1904 the Queen Regent informed Milner that "we do not allow our boys to stay at home and do no work."[37] A proportion of the initial migrant movement occurred at the direct behest of the Swazi ruling class who sent their followers out to acquire cash for the purchase of commodities and grain and for taxes. The release of labour by the chiefs was far from unconditional, however, since Swazi men were also required to till their fields during all phases of the agricultural cycle. Chiefs encouraged their followers to seek work in the off-peak periods of agricultural demand. As a result, many early Swazi migrants tended to work only for short periods outside the country in the winter months when the internal demands on their labour were at a minimum, and only for as long as it took to acquire the funds necessary for grain purchase on behalf of the homestead

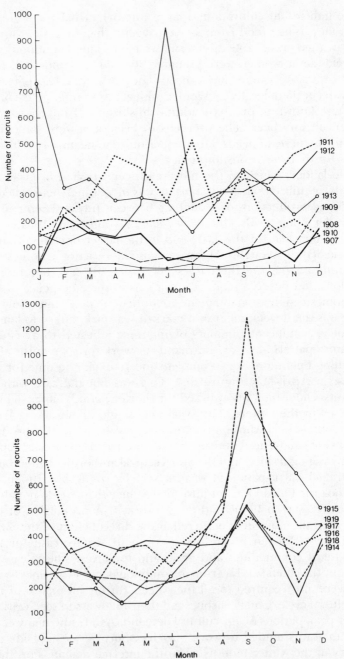

6 Monthly distribution of recruits received by WNLA/NRC members from Swaziland, 1907–20

or chief. In 1907–8 the numbers of migrants in the labour market sent by the Swazi rulers did, of course, increase dramatically. Thereafter, as mass participation in wage labour became entrenched the Swazi ruling class were increasingly concerned with controlling rather than simply mobilizing Swazi labour.

The longer-term problem which faced most chiefs was how to secure a degree of leverage over the growing number of migrants who went to work of their own accord or at the behest of the *umnumzana*. Chapter 1 illustrated how, in the nineteenth century, labour was extracted from the homestead either through obligatory *umemo* or through the semi-permanent mobilization of young males at the chief's own village. In both forms of tribute chiefs saw the means of acquiring money for their own purposes. Rather than trying to force their followers to surrender a portion of the wage under duress, many chiefs levied a cash payment in lieu of tribute-labour.[38] This tactic of substitution, although widely practised was particularly feasible for two types of chief; those with large followings and those whose followers were not incorporated into the Swazi regimental system and who therefore exercised a greater degree of control over the male labour of their own chiefdoms. It is significant that there was a concentration of both types of chiefdom in the southern districts of the country where Dlamini influence was at its weakest. The most important of these remained the Mamba chiefdom under Matsha's heir, Bokweni.

In general, migrants from the southern reaches of Swaziland did not have quite the same constraints on their time as the followers of smaller chiefs, whose labour was required for agricultural purposes, or of chiefdoms more firmly under central control. The result was that an absence during periods of peak agricultural demand could be "paid for" by directing a proportion of the wage earnings to the chief. Migration for longer periods to centres such as the Rand, the selective acceptance of mine contracts, and the lack of any marked seasonal pattern to migration were all natural extensions of the relative freedom of southern migrants. In the south, the closer ties between local chiefs and commoners also meant that the latter were more easily mobilized for work when the occasion demanded. In 1907–8, the southern chiefs proved particularly effective in sending out their followers. Between June and August 1907, for example, almost 2,000 migrants left the Hlatikulu district, and almost 70 per cent of work passes issued in 1907 and 1908 were for Hlatikulu migrants.[39]

In many southern chiefdoms, the primary contest over control of migrancy and the migrant wage occurred at the local level, between chief, the *umnumzana*, and the migrant himself. In most parts of the country, however, and the south was no exception to this, these struggles were complicated by the demands of the Dlamini aristocracy at the royal villages. After the death of Bunu in 1899, and the failure of the ruling council to elect an adult king in his place, most Swazi resigned themselves to a long period of regency. The size of the force of *imbutfo* soldiers started to decline as men returned to their home districts. This process of demobilization was hastened both by the calls of the *umnumzana* and by local chiefs who seized the opportunity to try and reassert control over their male followers. The dilution of Dlamini powers during periods of regency was not a new phenomenon; the prospective length of that period (approximately 20 years) certainly was. Unprecedented participation of Swazi men in wage labour and the needs of both local chiefs and the royal villages for cash resources gave added impetus to the conflict. Occasional national levies, such as that imposed in 1907, were successful because they had the support of local chiefs who had a common interest in contesting colonial land policy through orthodox channels, but these could not in any way be seen as a permanent solution.

When the Swazi Queen Regent, Labotsibeni, began to devise a strategy to exert central control over migrancy it was to the south that she gave closest attention. The distinctive demography of the area ensured that. At the time of the 1911 census, almost 40 per cent of the adult male population of the country lived in the Hlatikulu district and between 1907 and 1916 approximately 50 per cent of the "legal" migrant labour force came from this one district (table 6). After 1910 over 60 per cent of Hlatikulu migrants went to the Rand gold mines (compared with 10–30 per cent in the Mbabane and Mankiana districts) and between 1912 and 1915, 58 per cent of the Swazi mine workforce were Hlatikulu men (table 7).[40] Control of the south was the key. And the Swazi regimental system was the means by which the aristocracy attempted to secure central control. But before they could do so it was necessary to forge an alliance with local white labour recruiters in order to secure a conduit to the mines. This particular alliance was not long in the making since both parties stood to gain. Its likely success, however, was conditional on the attitude of Swazi migrants themselves. Here there was much less ground for optimism.

Between 1902 and 1910, labour recruiters had a lean time in the Swazi countryside. This was largely a function of Swazi aversion to mine work, but for those prepared to go to the mines, the legacy of the 1890s was still strong. Recruiters were consequently treated with suspicion and even outright hostility. Itinerant recruiters were par-

TABLE 6

Territorial Distribution of Work Passes Issued, 1907–8 to 1916–17

Year	Hlatikulu		Mbabane		Mankiana		Peak		Ubombo		Total
	Number	%	Number	%	Number	%	Number	%	Number	%	
1907–8¹	4,973	62.9	1,677	21.2			591	7.5	665	8.4	7,906
1908–9	2,966	49.1	1,376	22.8	887*	14.7	453	7.5	362	6.0	6,044
1909–10	2,265	41.1	1,519*	27.5	1,013	18.4	518	9.4	202	3.7	5,517
1912–13	4,204	50.5	1,951	23.4	1,091	13.1	643	7.7	431	5.2	8,320
1913–14	2,698	46.5	1,290	22.2	1,166	20.1	306	5.3	345	5.9	5,805
1914–15	4,210	55.6	1,167	15.4	1,586	20.9	280	3.7	335	4.4	7,578
1915–16	4,631	51.0	1,861	20.5	1,400	15.4	676	7.4	520	5.7	9,088
1916–17	3,302	48.4	1,523	22.3	1,150	16.9	448	6.6	400*	5.9	6,823

¹ In 1907–8, Mankiana district was divided between Hlatikulu and Mbabane districts. All figures are for year ended 31 March.

*Extrapolated figures.

Sources: ACRs, 1907–8 to 1916–17; SA, Draft ACRs and MRs.

TABLE 7
Territorial Distribution of Swazi Mine Recruits, 1912–16

Year	Hlatikulu			Mbabane			Mankiana			Peak			Ubombo		
	1	2	3	1	2	3	1	2	3	1	2	3	1	2	3
1912–13	2,778	66.1	56.2	1,435	73.6	29.0	444	40.7	9.0	34	5.3	0.7	256	59.4	5.2
1913–14	1,688	62.6	57.8	516	40.0	17.7	522	44.8	17.9	0	0.0	0.0	195	56.5	6.7
1914–15	2,797	66.4	60.1	847	72.6	18.2	872	55.0	18.7	0	0.0	0.0	135	40.3	2.9
1916–17	3,150	68.0	55.4	1,344	72.2	23.6	1,037	74.1	18.3	0	0.0	0.0	150	28.8	2.6

1 Number of Mine Recruits.
2 Recruits as a percentage of Work Passes Issued in District.
3 Recruits as a percentage of Total Recruits.

Sources: ACRs, 1912–13 to 1916–17; SA, Draft ACRs and MRs, 1912–13 to 1916–17.

ticularly unsuccessful. Apart from the opposition by chiefs to their unannounced presence, the fact that they were not residents of the country and were therefore unknown to their potential clients intensified the level of distrust. The handful of trader-recruiters doing business in the southern districts of the country were slightly more successful since they were generally recognized figures in the rural areas and could advance small quantities of goods, such as maize, on credit. They were also in a favourable position to take advantage of the surge of migrant labour in 1907–8. Attree and Howe, the only permanent recruiters in the Hlatikulu district, secured 423 recruits between October 1907 and March 1908; 60 per cent of the total number of Swazi recruits during this period.[41]

The major casualty of Swazi distaste for mine work and mine recruiters was the Witwatersrand Native Labour Association (WNLA). The undistinguished career of WNLA and its subsequent collapse after 1906 was, of course, common to all of British southern Africa.[42] The problems it faced and the reasons for its demise were mirrored in Swaziland with one obvious exception. In other areas the constant problem was the infidelity of Chamber of Mines' members to their own recruiting organization. In Swaziland workers tended to avoid recruiters of any genre, particularly before 1907. Until April 1903 an agreement with the Barberton Chamber of Commerce excluded WNLA from recruiting in Swaziland. As pressure mounted on WNLA to extend its operations and the Barberton mines failed to obtain any recruits there, the agreement was rescinded and WNLA began work in the country on condition that they did not recruit in the Barberton area itself or intercept Swazis proceeding independently to Barberton.[43] Initially WNLA activities in Swaziland were small-scale and experimental. Long-time white residents took charge of recruiting on a part-salary, part-capitation fee basis.[44]

At the end of the year the operation was reviewed. Less than 300 recruits had been forwarded from Swaziland in a nine-month period, at an exorbitant cost of £9 per recruit, and the majority of these were for surface, not underground, work.[45] In early 1904, after Swaziland had been given its "fair trial," the local manager concluded that "no adequate results would be obtained by maintaining the organization." The WNLA operation was therefore reconstructed. All salaried employees were dismissed and the number of capitation fee recruiters was increased to five. Recruits were supposed to be delivered at Barberton or Volksrust for a fee of 20 shillings per head.[46] This method proved even less successful. In 1904, only 35 recruits were forwarded, in 1905 there were 39, and in 1906, none at all (table 8). Even a reduction of the contract period to four months in

TABLE 8

Swazi Migrant Labour to the Rand, 1903–10

	1903			1904			1905			1906			1907			1908			1909			1910		
Month	WNLA	OR	LO	WNLA	OR	LO	WNLA	OR	LO	WNLA	OR	LO	WNLA	OR	LO	WNLA	OR	LO	WNLA	OR	LO	WNLA	OR	LO
Jan				32					66			71		13	177		29	147		36	45		156	45
Feb									165			98		13	118		211	112		223	56		224	52
Mar									124			153		30	136	2	147	150		40	72		282	100
Apr	60						12		34			107	5	28	97		127	56		75	65		448	86
May	18						3		48			107		9	76	5	146	68		37	44		402	46
Jun							24		59			66		7	68		41	97		44	36		274	44
Jul	69								54			103	11	22	140	8	58	77		28	32		505	54
Aug	5								52			91	16	5	270		53	75		112	45		193	42
Sep	28								47			76	17	26	229		81	81		51	38		375	41
Oct	19								72			133	31	43	286		101	92		177	61		145	33
Nov	25			2					84			61		85	225		24	58		88	35		187	45
Dec	49			1					37		13	179		132	225		162	91		220	93		130	39
Total	273			35			39		842		13	1,245	80	413	1,047	15	1,180	1,104		1,131	622		3,321	627

WNLA = Witwatersrand Native Labour Association Recruits.
OR = Other Recruits.
LO = Locals. These include voluntaries, transfers from other mines, and transfers from other forms of employment on Rand.

Sources: CMAR, WNLA Annual Reports.

1904 (following several other areas where the same experiment was tried) failed to overcome Swazi inertia.[47] Eventually, in November 1906, Swaziland, like the Transvaal, was officially opened to private recruiting by the Rand mining houses and their agents.

Perhaps the most interesting aspect of the ephemeral WNLA operation was an attempt by the local manager to incorporate the Swazi ruling class into the recruiting apparatus. Local chiefs were asked to bring their influence to bear on their followers while the Swazi Queen Regent was provided with more tangible incentives. As David Forbes later explained: "[I told] the Queen that it was necessary to teach the Swazis that it was in their interest to come up here to work for the white men, and the more they turned out, the more it would be of interest to the country and themselves, and I asked the Queen to teach these people this, and I said that the Labour Association would allow her £30 a month for teaching her people this. I did not put it to her that she was actually a recruiter, but pointed out that she had to teach her people to come up here and that it would be to her interest to do so."[48] Transvaal legislation, which barred recruiters and African chiefs from concluding formal contracts, prevented WNLA from coming to a definite agreement with the Regent. WNLA officials were nonetheless convinced that any approach by recruiters other than through Labotsibeni would not have any effect in "bringing the Swazi out." Underlying WNLA's strategy to employ the Queen Regent as a recruiting agent was a belief that the Swazi regimental system could be used to generate labour for the mines. Although the Queen Regent proved to be a willing ally, this method of recruiting failed to deliver more than a handful of labourers.[49]

The spirits of labour recruiters were not dampened by the failure of WNLA. In early 1907, a plan was devised by Prince Malunge and two agents of the Queen Regent – Albert Bremer and Josiah Vilikazi – to recruit Swazis for minework in Johannesburg. Since Vilikazi thought there would be some difficulty in persuading the Swazi migrants themselves, the three schemers decided to appeal to them on the grounds that *izinkomo zakwe Ngwane ziyemula* (the King's cattle were being looted) and that it was their duty to replenish the royal herds. Vilikazi returned to Swaziland to put the plan to the Queen Regent while Bremer, who was *persona non grata* with the administration in Swaziland, was to be found in the bars of Johannesburg boasting that he could supply 5,000 men to the mines. J.S. Langerman of the renegade Robinson Mining Group took the bait and offered Bremer a capitation fee of £2 per head for his "boys."[50] When colonial officials heard about the scheme they quickly intervened.

Selborne informed the Colonial Office in March 1907 that while

there was "no objection, quite the contrary" to the recruiting of
Swazis for minework, the involvement of Bremer required further
investigation. Moony, the Swaziland Resident Commissioner, was
resolutely opposed to the plan. He recalled that Bremer had been
acting as a "quasi-adviser" to the Queen Regent on colonial land
policy and noted that "his political intriguing has been conducive to
a great deal of discontent and obstruction towards the Administration and I could only view his presence in Swaziland as trying to
keep this spirit alive." Bremer's participation in the recruiting scheme
could only have one interpretation: "I have reason to believe that
the project of recruiting labour is to be undertaken with the purpose
of raising funds by way of capitation monies for the purpose of
prosecuting whatever action against the Administration the Chief
Regent and her advisers may decide to take."[51] Moony recommended
that the deal be aboıted and Selborne agreed.[52] He informed J.B.
Robinson that while he had no objection to the appointment of "an
agent of good character," Albert Bremer fell outside this category.[53]
Nevertheless, a more modest and secretive agreement was concluded
with the Robinson Group in July 1907 to supply 500 mineworkers
to the Robinson mines (appendix c).[54] There is no indication that
the colonial state had knowledge of this agreement, nor is there
evidence that it was ever fulfilled. Indeed, it is unlikely that Bremer
was any more successful than WNLA before him in tapping *emabutfo*
labour.

Some months earlier, in late 1906, a local mining concern, Swaziland Tin Ltd, had also sought to resolve its labour shortages by
concluding a contract with Zombode. Sidney Ryan, who was in charge
of recruiting for the tin mines, went directly to the Swazi capital
where he was permitted to address a general meeting of the Swazi
council of chiefs on the labour needs of the company. Later he met
privately with the Queen Regent and Malunge and "interested them,
by means of presents and promises of a capitation fee, in getting
the young men of the Nation to work at the mines."[55] Ryan was
confident that the labour problems of the company were at an end
when he concluded an agreement with Prince Malunge in September
1906 for the supply of 500 labourers (appendix d). Malunge's con-
fidence that he could get the labour was short-lived. In the following
months he supplied a mere 30 workers (most probably from his own
personal following) for which he received a modest payment of £20.[56]

The next attempt by recruiters to mobilize labour through the
emabutfo occurred at a time when migration for wage employment
by Swazi men was entering a new phase of expansion and the quest
for centralized control was magnified accordingly. In 1908, a re-

cruiter for the York Mine in Krugersdorp, Bonnar Armstrong, devised a plan to "open the floodgates of an imprisoned reservoir and
deluge the Rand with enthusiastic Swazis seeking employment."[57]
The York Mine, a "West Rand storm centre," was experiencing constant problems with its labour force and was anxious to secure a
compliant and homogenous supply of labour, possibly to counteract
the pernicious influence of the lumpenproletarian "Regiment of the
Hills" who were well ensconced in the mine compounds.[58] After first
securing the approval of H.M. Taberer of the Government Native
Labour Bureau in Johannesburg, Armstrong went to Swaziland where
he held lengthy meetings with the Swazi Queen Regent, Labotsibeni.
He eventually persuaded Labotsibeni to call together and commission a Swazi *lichaba* (platoon) to work at the York Mine on conditions
to be determined by mine management. Her only reservation was
that the platoon would work for no longer than six months. The
platoon was instructed to "spy out the Rand as a workshop for the
Nation" and report back favourably on conditions at the York Mine.
This was supposed to allay Swazi apprehensions about the Rand and
prefigure a massive mobilization of regimental labour for work on
gold mines.
    In early September 1908, the first platoon was called together at
Zombode and left for the Rand. It consisted of representatives of
four Swazi *emabutfo* (the Ngulube, Halaza, Lisaka, and Mgadhlela),
two members of the immediate family of the Queen Regent, and,
as a tacit recognition of the health problems likely to be encountered
on the Rand, a herbalist. The platoon of fifty men was accompanied
to Johannesburg by the Swazi Prince Regent, Malunge. Before leaving they signed an unusual contract which was enthusiastically endorsed by colonial officials in Swaziland (appendix E). A.G. Marwick,
the Assistant Commissioner of the Mbabane district, noted that "although this is not the accepted form of contract between a recruiter
and a native engaged by him, in deference to the wishes of the natives
I allow it to stand, for the reason that it shows the individual and
collective spirit in which these natives are proceeding to work on the
Rand."[59] Colonial officials, not normally noted for their deference
to Swazi wishes, were as aware as anyone of the implications of the
scheme in mobilizing Swazi labour for the mines. A month later, in
October 1908, a second platoon was commissioned at Zombode and
sent to the York Mine. The York management reported that the
first batch of workers though "raw and green" were acquitting themselves well underground and were proving to be superior to the
"weedy gangs from Portugese territory." Armstrong was lauded by
the local press as a "miracle worker" and an "enterprising Peter the

Hermit." Only six weeks after leaving Swaziland, however, the first group of workers deserted from the York Mine and returned to the country "fat, box-laden, blanket-bedecked, but grumbly."[60] The men complained bitterly about the conditions at the York Mine and claimed they had been cheated out of their wages. The Queen Regent immediately recalled the second group of workers from Krugersdorp before any further damage could be done.

In early 1909 Armstrong and the Queen Regent tried to repeat the experiment by dispatching a third platoon to the Rand. On their arrival in Johannesburg all of the workers deserted Armstrong's charge and went to work on mines of their own choice. Labotsibeni's attempt to raise yet another contingent in mid-1909 was thwarted by the complaints of rival recruiters and the intervention of the colonial state. After several years absence, Thuys Grobler returned to Swaziland and joined forces with Bonnar Armstrong as a labour recruiter. Warned off by colonial officials, Grobler sent a small batch of recruits who had been supplied directly by Prince Malunge back to their homes. A stiffly worded directive from the administration to the Queen Regent informed her that "people who were forced to go and work would make trouble" and advised her to stop ordering migrants to join her mine platoons.[61] As the *Times of Swaziland* commented, not without a hint of irony, "the peaceful conquest of the Transvaal by Swazi impis is indefinitely delayed."[62]

With the number of Swazis at work on the mines escalating rapidly, the advantages of pre-empting other recruiters and securing a monopoly on mine labour supply were increasingly apparent. Yet another recruiting organization, the South African Merchants Corporation Ltd, therefore attempted to resuscitate the Grobler-Bunu agreement of 1899 in a letter to Resident Commissioner Coryndon: "I claim that no one but this Corporation can recruit labour in Swaziland for work in as much as we claim that all other recruiting is illegal. It is our intention to put the necessary legal machinery into motion to stop that recruiting. Wherefore I shall be much obliged if you will kindly furnish me with a list of all the Labour Agents who are operating in Swaziland so that I may take steps accordingly."[63] The Corporation's threat raised the alarm among colonial officials who finally decided to put an end to recruiting deals with Zombode after a decade of indecision.

The colonial state had taken an ambiguous attitude towards the various schemes outlined above. While any semblance of "forced labour" would be conducive to social unrest, this had to be set against the need to use all justifiable means to prise Swazi men into the

capitalist labour market. The Transvaal regulations prohibiting recruiters from making contracts with chiefs were thus selectively applied in Swaziland, depending on the particular circumstances of
each case. Those schemes which promised purely and simply to
mobilize more labour for the South African mines were thoroughly
approved of. Those which threatened to inhibit the labour flow or
which had ulterior political motives subversive of the authority of
the state were quickly scotched. Hence, Grobler's attempt to secure
a monopoly in 1902, the Bremer-Vilikazi-Robinson deal and the
Merchants Corporation bid in 1910 were frowned upon, while the
plans of WNLA, Swaziland Tin Ltd, and Armstrong (at least initially)
received explicit or implicit colonial endorsement.

In response to the appeals of rival recruiters Marwick & Morris
and Howe & Murray, whose own operations were threatened by the
prospect of monopoly agreements, the administration began to consider amending the existing legislation.[64] An exchange of correspondence between Coryndon and Selborne ensued. Legal opinions
were sought (and challenged by the Merchants Corporation) and
legislation was drafted to counter the "extremely objectionable" Bunu-
Grobler contract.[65] In late 1910, the Transvaal Labour Agents regulations (in force in Swaziland) were modified to control competitive
recruiting and a clause was added which prescribed a heavy fine or
jail sentence to any chief or headman who compelled any Swazi to
sign a mine contract.[66] This legislation reflected colonial fears that
the Queen Regent retained the power to control the Swazi migrant
movement and interfere with the "free flow" of Swazi labour.

Officials also realized that forcing Swazi migrants to work in the
Queen Regent's platoons at unpopular mines was causing great discontent in the countryside, as the testimony of one migrant worker
made clear:

When I left the Chief's kraal about two weeks ago a messenger from the
Queen Regent was there, having come to call out a gang of forced labour
by the Queen's order. A large number of natives were assembled, and the
messenger said:– "The Queen requires all members of the 'Halaza', 'Gavu',
'Ngulube' and 'Mgadhlela' regiments to go to her kraal to be sent ... for
mining work, as the others who were sent are about to finish their Time."
The messenger questioned the Chief as to the reason why he had not sent
natives when previously ordered by the Queen, and the Chief replied he
had no men to send. The old men spoke, stating that if the Queen was
going to imprison them and their chief, the young men had better go to
work ... the young men then said to the chief – "As you are arrested on our

account we will go in compliance with the Queen's order" ... the natives belonging to my tribe are most unwilling to go ... and will only comply out of fear that their Chief will be punished or killed by the Queen.[67]

That Labotsibeni's strategy began to flounder, even before colonial intervention, was hardly surprising given (a) the resistance of local chiefs and *umnumzana* to her attempts to call together platoons for minework and (b) the resistance of Swazi migrant workers towards attempts to impinge upon their freedom of choice in the labour market. Colonial legislation constituted the final blow, not only to the Merchants Corporation bid for a monopoly, but also to the Regent's policy of control. It is somewhat ironic that a monopoly agreement which in 1899 was enthusiastically endorsed by the Kruger state as a means of generating labour was seen, only ten years later, as a means of stemming the flow of labour. While much is made of the monopsonistic drive of the South African mining industry, it is important to note the Swaziland colonial state's encouragement of competitive recruiting conditions.

The various schemes were intended to be forerunners to a mass mobilization of Swazi labour for mine work under centralized Dlamini control. When the Queen Regent told Armstrong that "if my people are pleased with the treatment, you will have done a lot of good for my people and me too" she was speaking from the heart.[68] All the schemes are consistent with what was known at the time as the "one gate" policy of the Queen Regent. The concept of monopoly control over migrancy had strongly appealed to Bunu in 1898–9. After the Anglo-Boer War its appeal was maintained. The "one gate" policy was first enunciated in 1904 when Moony was asked to refuse work passes to any Swazi who did not first come to Zombode. It was later repeated to Milner when the Queen Regent insisted that "we want them all to go in a lump to work in a certain place, not to be taken by any chance white man."[69] The request was refused. The colonial state already had sufficient problems in mobilizing Swazi labour without this additional complication.

After 1907, when Swazi labour migration was undergoing a period of rapid growth, the "one gate" policy became even more critical if the aristocracy was to exercise a sufficient degree of control over migrant labour to further Dlamini interests. For one thing, they could not appropriate any of the fruits of labour migration that took place outside their control. For another, any uncontrolled migrant movement threatened the primary functions of the *emabutfo* within Swazi society; namely its role in allowing the Dlamini to appropriate labour from homesteads and its centralizing role in forging a national identity which cut across regional and clan loyalties. The Queen Regent could clearly not afford to dispense altogether with more traditional forms of labour appropriation and her plan was to dispatch the *emabutfo* for mine labour during periods when the agricultural demands were slackest. Hence she insisted in the agreement with Armstrong that no regimental labour could be spared for any longer than six months at the outside; a condition which the York Mine found unsatisfactory.[70]

The Queen Regent feared as well that extended periods spent on the Rand by Swazi migrants would not only deprive the aristocracy of labour in the sphere of agricultural production, but would generate new forms of consciousness hostile to traditional authority. As she pointed out to Armstrong, she had no desire to present Sobhuza with a "weak nation" as the legacy of her period at the helm.[71] Labotsibeni was as keen as the York Mine to have a mine stocked entirely with Swazis where traditional attitudes, loyalties, and solidarities would be less threatened by exposure to other Africans, and to pernicious urban-industrial influences destructive of rural authority. The fact that Swazi workers did tend to congregate at certain Rand mines was for rather different reasons, and it is significant that the York Mine was not among them.

CHAPTER FIVE

Traders, Runners,
and Recruits

It is certainly not a pleasing spectacle to see half a dozen white men running after the same native.

F.O. Buckle, 1914

After 1908 the number of male Swazi leaving Swaziland for work in South Africa each year varied between 7,000 and 10,000.[1] This is clear evidence that the South African economy was consolidating its hold over Swazi society. There was still one major change in spatial patterns of Swazi migrancy before the 1920s, however.[2] Prior to 1910 there were always fewer than 2,000 Swazi working on the Witwatersrand goldmines. Within three years this figure doubled and from then until the late 1920s fluctuated around 4,000 to 5,000, rising to over 6,000 some years and falling in years of particularly good harvest (such as 1920) or industrial unrest on the Rand (such as 1913–14) (figure 7).[3]

Contemporary observers with a vested interest in the flow of migrant labour reacted warmly to this "relatively considerable increase" in the mine labour supply from Swaziland.[4] By 1912, 48 per cent of the work passes issued in Swaziland were for minework and by 1915 this figure had reached over 80 per cent. Within the labour districts of the Transvaal there was a marked switch to the mines. As table 9 indicates, by 1914 over 90 per cent of Swazis employed in the labour districts were in the mines. To some extent this reflected changing employment opportunities within the Transvaal itself brought on by general economic depression in the years leading up to the Great War. But it was also a function of a growing preference for minework amongst Swazi migrants.[5]

From early 1910, the number of Swazi actually recruited for minework increased dramatically (table 10). Between 1910 and 1912, for example, 10,339 Swazi migrants were recruited by the mines compared with only 2,819 in the preceding three-year period. The relative importance of recruited and non-recruited mine labour also underwent significant change (table 11). By 1912, the vast majority

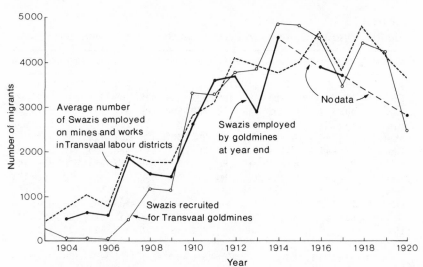

7 Swazi migration to the Witwatersrand, 1903–20

TABLE 9
Swazis Working in Transvaal Labour Districts at Year End, 1905–20

| | Mines & Works | | Other Employment | | |
Year	Number	%	Number	%	Total
1904	629	41.2	899	58.8	1,528
1905	1,083	42.5	1,464	57.5	2,547
1906	718	34.0	1,395	66.0	2,113
1907	2,221	59.3	1,522	40.7	3,743
1908	2,310	63.8	1,311	36.2	3,621
1909	1,897	64.9	1,028	35.1	2,925
1910	2,989	69.6	1,302	30.4	4,291
1911	4,095	77.3	1,201	22.7	5,296
1913	3,149	87.9	434	12.1	3,583
1914	4,749	94.2	293	5.8	5,042
1915	5,231	93.6	358	6.4	5,589
1916	4,235	92.3	353	7.7	4,588
1917	4,196	91.2	406	8.8	4,602
1918	4,681	90.9	470	9.1	5,151
1919	4,728	89.2	571	10.8	5,299
1920	2,967	83.6	581	16.4	3,548

Sources: Chamber of Mines Annual Reports; TAD, GOV 897.

TABLE 10

Monthly Distribution of Swazi Recruits for Rand Mines, 1907–20

Month	1907	1908	1909	1910	1911	1912	1913	1914	1915	1916	1917	1918	1919	1920
Jan	13	29	36	156	141	147	742	193	290	496	247	466	419	288
Feb	13	211	223	224	169	109	322	354	188	406	264	333	262	223
Mar	30	147	40	282	188	154	365	202	196	344	234	382	232	210
Apr	33	127	75	448	204	135	272	342	132	280	137	351	233	139
May	9	146	37	402	189	252	282	362	133	234	122	380	184	150
Jun	7	41	44	274	197	942	267	280	245	338	220	379	219	116
Jul	33	66	28	505	245	260	132	387	356	414	213	372	258	145
Aug	21	53	112	193	286	300	249	483	530	382	331	362	333	134
Sep	43	81	51	375	354	303	391	1235	930	475	508	508	574	269
Oct	74	101	177	145	332	360	307	490	736	403	369	354	590	224
Nov	85	24	88	187	443	356	201	204	624	347	417	156	427	213
Dec	132	162	220	130	489	463	281	357	476	392	429	390	483	358
Total	493	1195	1131	3321	3237	3781	3811	4889	4836	4511	3491	4433	4214	2469

Sources: Chamber of Mines Annual Reports; NRC Annual Reports.

TABLE 11

Swazi Recruits, Independents, and Locals Engaged on Rand Mines, 1907–20

	New Hands				Locals	
	Recruits		Independents		Mine	Other
Year	Number	%	Number	%	Number	Number
1907	493	25.5	1,440	74.5	62	545
1908	1,195	64.9	647	35.1	65	392
1909	1,131	79.6	291	20.4	108	223
1910	3,321	92.1	285	7.9	120	222
1911	3,237	87.7	455	12.3	100	208
1912	3,781	85.7	632	14.3	190	263
1913	3,811	91.9	337	8.1	222	162
1914	4,889	90.6	509	9.4	203	183
1916	4,511	82.8	934	16.2	248	88
1917	3,491	76.2	1,092	21.7	365	82
1920	2,469	76.0	780	24.0	207	72

Sources: Chamber of Mines Annual Reports; WNLA Annual Reports.

of the Swazi mine workforce was forwarded by recruiters. The non-recruited Swazi contingent in the mines began to rise again thereafter to about one in four new hands by 1920. Nonetheless, strong forces were clearly at work to overcome Swazi aversion to the goldmines in general and the recruiter in particular. The reasons for these changes must be sought in reduced alternative employment opportunities and in altered recruiting conditions in the rural districts of Swaziland itself.

The years between 1906 and 1912 have been characterized as a period of "anarchy" in the mine labour market, as the Rand mining houses, sometimes corporately, more often individually, struggled ferociously against one another to secure an ample supply of black labour for their operations. As Alan Jeeves and David Yudelman have recently noted:

Temporarily shelving their bid for a labour monopsony, the large mining groups now began to compete aggressively with each other for labour. Recruiting costs increased dramatically; hundreds of whites and thousands of blacks were drawn into the industry as recruiters and runners; the government service was plundered for the talent needed to head up the recruiting services which the individual mining groups were now forced to establish. They made allies of the country traders and local headmen ... and devised powerful incentives to tempt blacks into mine employment and the country traders into service as recruiters. In the years after about 1906–7, the mining industry supplied huge sums in the form of cattle and cash advances on wages.[6]

This period of intensely competitive, but wasteful and expensive, labour recruiting injected large sums of money into the rural economy through the advance system. African workers in many parts of southern Africa responded quickly to this new situation. The amount of black labour arriving on the mines from throughout the region increased rapidly after 1906. This period of competitive "anarchy" was eventually brought under control by state intervention in the form of the Native Labour Regulation Act of 1911, and by the formation of the monopsonistic Native Recruiting Corporation (NRC) by the Chamber of Mines in late 1912. However, it was not until 1920, with the demise of the last of the independent labour contractors, that the NRC exerted full control.

The central importance of competitive recruiting conditions in the mobilization of black mine labour is well established.[7] Swaziland was no exception since it did not take long for these conditions to spill over the Transvaal border into the country, when the first wave of independent labour contractors and recruiters arrived in 1907. These recruiters were not initially particularly successful in their endeavours, however. As Swaziland acquired a reputation as a poor hunting ground among recruiters, less effort was made to establish viable recruiting operations in the country. It was not until 1910, with the reorganization of recruiting methods by labour contractors and the influx of a second wave of independent labour agents, that recruiters experienced sustained success in the country.

A fundamental aspect of this reorganization was the "capture" of local traders within Swaziland by the various competing recruiting companies. The speed with which this occurred is explicable once the plight of the trader in the first decade of this century is understood. If the 1890s had proved to be a profitable period for traders, the years from 1901 to 1910 provided an acid test of their capacity for survival. In the earlier period traders made a lucrative business out of cattle trading and the provision of imported commodities to Swazi homesteads. After the Anglo-Boer War, by contrast, they struggled to find a niche. When the traders returned to the country in 1902–3 they found that the Swazi and the Anglo-Boer War protagonists had not dealt kindly with them in their absence, and that the prospects for trade were far from favourable:

A great number of them have suffered severely by the ravages of war, in most cases having their stock of merchandise looted and buildings gutted and ruined. These men will have a terribly uphill work in re-establishing their businesses for, in addition to the loss and damage sustained, they have had to face an exceptionally hard year owing to the failure of crops, cattle disease and difficulty in transporting their merchandise.[8]

Not only did many traders have to begin again from scratch, but they discovered that one of their major sources of profit in the 1890s, cattle trading, had evaporated. Swazi cattle stocks had been reduced to a bare minimum and those homesteads who did retain cattle held on to them very tenaciously, only offering them for sale at inflated prices or when their need for grain became acute.[9] Traders able to convince the stockholder to part with his cattle were faced with quarantine restrictions which thwarted any attempt to tap the South African market.

Liquor trading, another earlier profit source, offered better prospects, at least in theory. In practice, the traders found that the Swazi chiefs and people had turned their backs on imported liquor almost completely.[10] Their cash resources were now needed for more pressing concerns: food purchase, colonial taxation, and fighting colonial land policy. In his evidence to the Transvaal Labour Commission in

1904, Godfrey Lagden noted that the Swazi "have not got to jam yet."[11] His quaint message was one which the Swaziland trader was not at all anxious to hear. The primary customer for merchant capital in the 1890s had been the chiefly stratum within Swazi society, but as wage labour became more pervasive there was every prospect that mass consumption of "kaffir truck" and other commodities might ensue, as it had in other parts of the sub-continent. The consumption of imported commodities by Swazi homesteads was very limited, however, and by some accounts even declined after the Anglo-Boer War.[12] Country traders bemoaned the fact that "the Swazis do not utilise imported articles to the same extent as do most other tribes" and that "very little is spent by the natives beyond the bare necessities."[13] The hard-nosed colonial ideologue had his own interpretation for this state of affairs: "The Swazis as a tribe are certainly far behind other native tribes of South Africa if use of imported articles may serve as an index of civilization. That it does so serve is of course indisputable."[14] The explanation of the trader was at once more pragmatic and more convincing: "Trade has never been worse in Swaziland ... owing to the fact that the natives have very little money, and traders attribute their impoverished condition to the following: tax, loss of cattle, shortage of food and continual calls on them by the Paramount Chief for money to assist her in paying for the deputation and subscribing to her agents."[15] With the income of Swazi homesteads immediately assailed from all sides, it was not surprising to find that the reserves available for purchase of imported commodities, other than maize, were minimal.

The one area still open to the traders was the local maize trade due to persistent shortfalls in Swazi food production. In 1903, Swazis were seen streaming into Barberton and northern Natal to buy grain, but in subsequent years the activities of traders in Swaziland itself made this unnecessary.[16] Imports of maize and maize products from the Transvaal and Natal rose rapidly. The trade was extremely competitive and traders eventually had to resort to price-fixing to maintain their profit margins.[17] Other competition, less easy to control, came from local white farmers and itinerant maize hawkers from the Transvaal. One potential market which was lost to the traders was the local mines, who preferred to deal directly with grain merchants in the Transvaal in order to minimize production costs.[18]

Traders were able to make some money through buying cheap maize from Swazi homesteads and later reselling at inflated prices (see chapter 3). It was primarily through this practice and the sale of imported maize that most traders kept going from year to year. In 1909, in the Hlatikulu district, virtually all of the 38 general dealers licences and eight hawkers licences were issued "solely for

selling mealies to natives."[19] Maize trading continued to provide a
staple means of support for traders in Swaziland after 1910, but
many diversified their activities to include labour recruiting which
as well as being a source of income, improved their competitive
position in the maize trade.

Prior to 1910, some traders did try labour recruiting as a sideline,
following the lead of trader-recruiters elsewhere in southern Africa,
but the attitude of Swazi workers to the Rand and to recruiters
mitigated against any sustained success. At the end of 1909, there
were a mere eight labour recruiters in the country, five of whom
were recruiting for the labour contractors, Marwick & Morris. By
contrast, during the course of 1910, over 60 licences were issued.
In 1911, 80 were issued and in 1912, the number jumped to over
100. When the NRC was formed in October 1912, there were 70 white
recruiters with innumerable black "runners" actively at work in the
Swazi countryside. These recruiting agents operated on behalf of 18
South African and five local recruiting agencies in 1912 (table 12).

Two different types of recruiter could be observed. First, there
were itinerant labour agents who recruited for the various mining
houses, their labour recruiting departments, or independent labour
contractors such as A.M. Mostert. These recruiters came to Swaziland in the periods of peak labour emigration (particularly the last
third of the calendar after the ploughing season) and stayed no
longer than a few months in the country. While there was a general
upward trend in the overall number of recruiters in the country
they peaked each year in October, with the arrival of the itinerants (figure 8). Second, there were the resident trader-recruiters.
Although a number of new trader-recruiters established stores
between 1910 and 1912, many of these individuals were traders already in the country who began recruiting as a sideline. They were
used by all of the more successful cullers of Swazi labour, including
Marwick & Morris, Howe & Murray (a local syndicate recruiting
for General Mining's Van Ryn GM Cò) and Taberer's Labour Organization. The labour contractor, A.M. Mostert, first used itinerants and
then switched to trader-recruiters by poaching from other organizations. Marwick & Morris took the lead in forging a connection
between the Rand mines and the Swazi homestead via the trader-
recruiter.

The largest East Rand employer of black labour in this period was
the reconstructed East Rand Proprietary Mine (ERPM) of the Farrar/
Anglo French Corporation. After the repatriation of Chinese labour
in 1908, ERPM turned to "model contractors" such as Barecke &
Kleudgen and Marwick & Morris in order to maintain their labour

TABLE 12
Recruiting Organizations in Swaziland, 1910–13

Recruiting Organization	Number of Recruiters			
	1910	1911	1912	1913*
Rand Mines				
Native Recruiting Corporation			17	36
Marwick & Norris	19	21	29	21
A.M. Mostert	16	11	11	2
J.E. Palmer & Co	4	3	2	
Taberer's Labour Organization	3	11	10	
Howe & Murray	6	5	7	
H. Nicholson	1	1	1	
B. Bantjes	2			
Goerz Group	1			
Neumann Group	2		5	
Consolidated Goldfields		8	4	
Consolidated Mines Selection		1	3	
Jupiter GM Co	1	1	1	
Worcester GM Co	1	1	1	
Luipaardsvlei GM Co			1	1
Sub-Nigel GM Co	1	1		
Premier Diamond		1	7	
East Transvaal Mines				
French Bobs GM Co	1			
Sheba GM Co		1		
Breyten Collieries		1		
Other South African				
L.C. Gillespie			1	
Transvaal Landowners Assoc.			1	
R. Acutt			1	
S.A. Wattles	1	1	1	
Local				
Swaziland Recruiting Agency	2	3	1	
Swaziland Tin Ltd		1	1	
Piggs Peak Development Co	1	4	1	
Kobolondo Mines	1	1	1	
Swaziland Corporation		1		
McCreedy Tins		1	1	
Polongeni Tin		1		
Total	63	81	108	

*January to June 1913   Source: High Commissioner's Gazettes, 1910–13.

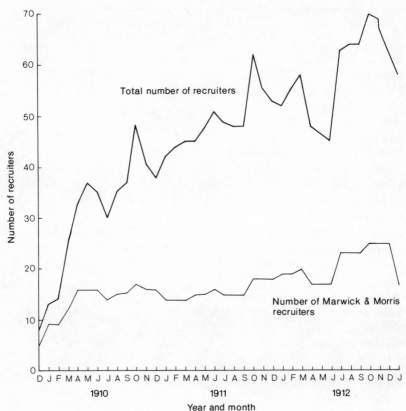

8 Number of recruiters in Swaziland, 1910–12

strength.[20] Marwick & Morris (known as *Kwa Muhle* by their African clients) was formed in 1907 by Transvaal Native Affairs Department officials, J.S. Marwick and Colonel George Morris.[21] Pooling their knowledge and experience of Swaziland and Zululand, and encouraged by the relatively significant complement of Swazi and Zulu "independents" at ERPM, the two men attempted to break into under-exploited recruiting territory. In 1909, they obtained a ten-year contract from ERPM to supply 5,000 workers per annum for underground work at a rate of 8 pence per shift worked.[22]

J.S. Marwick's first sortie into Swaziland was not a great success. He went to Mbabane with a view to obtaining labour but discovered, like many before him, that "the natives continue to shirk going out under engagements and prefer to seek work for themselves."[23] A later venture into the south of Swaziland was no more successful. R.P. Jones, a Marwick & Morris representative, spent two weeks in the Hlatikulu district in January 1909 but had his visit cut short when he injured himself by falling off a mule while investigating potential sources of recruits.[24] In November 1909, J.S. Marwick and George Morris made a third attempt to secure Swazis for mine work, coming to Swaziland and "making arrangements for the more effective organization of their labour supply."[25]

Their first task was to draw the Swaziland trading community into the operation. Traders were employed as recruiters and money was lent to them with which to make cash and maize advances to prospective recruits. To expand the range of advances on offer, Marwick & Morris started the nucleus of a cattle herd which could be drawn upon by company recruiters to make stock advances to migrants who preferred cattle to cash.[26] All traders were asked to establish a network of black runners to advertise company services and to canvass for labour in the countryside. Both recruiters and runners were paid on a salary, rather than capitation fee basis and as a result Marwick & Morris "obtained the services of the best agents and the most influential natives as runners."[27] Recruits were offered a contract which, in length at least, was deemed to be more attractive to the Swazi. The standard contract length was set at six months for underground work and a limited number of three month surface work contracts were put on offer as well (appendix F). While this contract was tailored to the existing pattern of oscillatory migration, the shorter contract "captured" some of the short-term migrants common in the central districts of the country.[28] Marwick & Morris concentrated most of their effort in the Hlatikulu district from which the greater proportion of the existing Swazi mine force was coming but recruiting operations were established in all the other districts as well. In the Ubombo district, a retired colonial official, M. Whitridge, took charge of recruiting.[29] The close personal ties of the company with members of the Swaziland administration facilitated matters; Marwick's brother, A.G. Marwick, was the Assistant Commmissioner in the Mbabane district. At the ERPM mine itself, a separate compound was established for *Kwa Muhle* workers and the Swazi chiefs were encouraged to appoint mine police there.[30]

Marwick & Morris then took steps to control the marked propensity for desertion displayed by Swazi workers. Desertion from the Rand was a rather selective phenomenon. In 1909, for example, the desertion rate was 17.6 per cent for minework, and only 3.6 per cent for other forms of employment (table 13). J.S. Marwick's unwieldly solution was to circulate lists of previous deserters to pass issuers in Swaziland so that when they took another contract their passes would be endorsed accordingly. The Government Native La-

TABLE 13
Desertions by Swazi Workers from Gold Mines and Transvaal Labour
Districts, 1908–20

(a) Transvaal Labour Districts

	Average Number Employed in Labour Districts		Desertions		Desertion Rate (%)		Recovery Rate (%)	
Years	Mines	Other	Mine	Other	Mine	Other	Mine	Other
1906	985	1,441	112	79	13.1	5.5	18.6	27.8
1909	1,786	1,634	315	58	17.6	3.6	55.6	41.4
1913	3,969	804	170	15	4.3	1.9	84.1	53.3

(b) Gold Mines (NRC members excluding contractors' recruits)

Years	1	2	3	4
1908	1,730	221	12.77	9.73
1910	2,386	182	7.62	2.36
1912	3,376	37	1.09	1.45
1914	3,497	24	0.68	1.31
1916	4,335	7	0.16	0.83
1918	4,223	14	0.33	0.80
1920	3,501	15	0.42	0.61

1 Average Number of Swazis Employed
2 Total Number of Desertions
3 Desertion Rate (%)
4 Overall Mines Desertion Rate (%)

Sources: (a) TAD, GNLB Annual Reports; (b) Chamber of Mines Annual Reports.

bour Bureau reacted favourably to the idea and passed Marwick's
first list of 70 deserters to the Native Affairs Department in the
Transvaal. However, the plan was dropped when the Department
protested that to be effective the scheme would have to be universal
and that this, in turn, would precipitate "a most embarrassing deluge
of paper, such as would paralyze any effort to trace individuals."[31]

As a partial solution, Marwick & Morris recruiters in Swaziland were warned to avoid recruiting known deserters for a second time. With tighter policing by the South African state the recovery rate of Swazi deserters rose dramatically from 18.6 per cent in 1906 to 84.1 per cent by 1913. Swazi desertion rates, in common with those of other groups of African workers, had fallen precipitously by 1920.

Other recruiting organizations interested in exploiting the Swazi labour supply followed the lead of Marwick & Morris, and intense competition developed to secure the services of Swazi runners and local traders.[32] Taberer's Labour Organization placed a number of trader-recruiters on the payroll and used the services of the local manager of Swaziland Tin Ltd to head up its operation in the country.[33] The Neumann Group, J.E. Palmer & Co. (recruiting for Johannesburg Consolidated Investment), and General Mining all used trader-recruiters. The latter had a syndicate of seven southern Swaziland traders, Howe & Murray, recruiting for their Van Ryn Mine. Despite the new-found success of these labour recruiters in Swaziland after 1909, Swazi migrants continued to regard them with distaste:

The native is despising the European engaged in getting labour for the mines. This is unfortunate; for there are really good and honourable men employed in this work, but it is a fault of human nature that the few unworthy ones should discredit the rest ... Our Bantu have come across a few Europeans who have gulled them, or kowtowed to them, and so they are disposed to despise the white man as a whole.[34]

Success itself was rooted in the material incentive of the cash advance for minework.[35] For the first time, the Swazi migrant could acquire cash for tax, food purchase, or *lobola* prior to embarking upon a mine contract. This was a highly significant development for it spelled the decline (though never the demise) of a number of well-established responses to taxation demands such as selling cheap maize to Swazi traders, or tax defaulting followed by prosecution, fine, or imprisonment (see chapter 3). Among poorer homesteads and those without access to mine advances these practices continued.[36]

Prior to 1910, chiefs and *umnumzana* had had to rely on remittances or representation at the mine compound to acquire a portion of the mine wage.[37] W.A. Challis identified the basic problem which this presented when he noted the breakdown of the "old Bantu traditions of the children helping their fathers" and the emergence of a social environment in which "the young men help themselves, keep or spend their wages, neglect their homes, disappear from their kraals without warning, and are sucked down in the whirlpool of Johannesburg."[38] The cash advance now allowed the Swazi *umnumzana* and local chiefs a potentially greater degree of control over the mine wage of sons and followers. The advantages of cash in Swaziland before work on the Rand were only too apparent to chiefs and homesteads heads, who heartily endorsed the switch to recruiters. For the migrant himself, be he the head of a young family or a single man, the temptation of cash virtually on demand to meet taxation and other expenses was considerable. If the migrant's family approached the local trader-recruiter for cash while the migrant was away, the money would also be advanced and deducted in Johannesburg from the worker's wage packet.[39] The size of the advance was boosted by the competitive nature of the recruiting environment. By mid-1912, potential recruits could obtain advances of as high as £20 to £30.[40] This meant that the recruit could be sure of obtaining the wage for a whole mine contract before leaving the country. The trader-recruiters had little compunction about offering the money of their principals to recruits in the hope of securing the all-important capitation fee for themselves.

The lack of restraint on advances proved to be shortlived, however. In 1910, the standard advance in South Africa was limited to £5 by the Union Government. In January 1912, through the South African Native Labour Regulation Act of 1911, the advance was further reduced to £2. Subsequently, in late 1912, it was again raised to £5. In November 1911, WNLA approached the South African Department of Native Affairs about the possibility of limiting advances in Basutoland, Bechuanaland, and Swaziland to £2 "in order to ensure uniformity of treatment." The request was passed on to the High Commissioner who promulgated legislation limiting advances in the three territories to £2.[41] Initiatives to control the size of cash advances consequently came from outside the country and were only reluctantly acceded to by local officials. Indeed, no sooner was Gladstone's legislation on the books than the Swaziland Resident Commissioner, Coryndon, appealed to him to raise the advance on the grounds that "many of the natives will refuse to go to work unless they can make adequate provision for their families pending such time as they can remit money from the mines."[42] The £5 advance was reinstated in early 1912.

Despite regulation of the size of advances, recruiters were able to use other methods to push the amount above the legal limit. Thus, for example, they advanced money to potential recruits to pay current and back tax, and court fines, over and above the basic cash advance. As the tax collection season got under way, recruiters were besieged by men wanting money to pay tax and avoid prosecution as defaulters. The cash was usually advanced without question and was often sufficient to cover the tax of the non-working relatives of the recruit.⁴³ The money advanced for tax purposes could reach considerable sums, and recruiters made little effort to ascertain whether a request was genuine or not. Recruiters were always ready to advance funds to pay fines for the numerous possible violations of the oppressive colonial legal code. Workers penalized under the country's taxation and recruiting legislation could obtain money from recruiters to pay fines. Recruiters would also ensure that deserters from their own employ were prosecuted. They would then bail out the deserter by paying his court fine, increasing his debt still further.⁴⁴

Some trader-recruiters made a practice of advancing maize, and occasionally stock, to Swazi families on credit as a book entry which did not even appear on the mine contract as an advance. Indebtedness was exacerbated by the high prices charged for maize at the season of peak demand.⁴⁵ The exploitative practices to which this gave rise caused the colonial state some concern and in 1913, as part of exhaustive regulations governing recruiting in the country, the state ordered that no labour recruiter could "lend or supply money, stock or any other articles to any native labourer with whom he is executing a contract for labour ... over and above the advance authorised."⁴⁶ How effective this prohibition was is difficult to say, but there are few comments in the historical record after 1913 which suggest the widespread indebtedness to traders elsewhere in the region. In addition, there is no evidence of traders being prosecuted under this clause. It may well be that the Swazi themselves shunned the possibility of falling heavily into debt, except where this was absolutely unavoidable.⁴⁷

Although itinerant recruiters and local trader-recruiters offered advances to potential recruits, the latter group had a definite competitive edge. Since they lived in the country the trader-recruiters were more familiar with the rural districts, and could afford to make larger advances since the chances of recovering the money in the event of desertion were much greater. Many Swazi homesteads were used to dealing with traders in their capacity as merchants of maize, and while their business practices can hardly have endeared them to their customers, most had lived in the country for long periods, many could speak SiSwati and, unlike the itinerants, they were well known to their clients.⁴⁸ One of the major uses to which advances were put was the purchase of grain. The trader-recruiter consequently performed a dual function on the same premises. Nevertheless, in a cut-throat recruiting environment, no recruiter could afford to sit back and wait for recruits to arrive at his trading store.

A more aggressive strategy was therefore adopted by the successful trader-recruiters.

Recruiters did not abandon local chiefs despite new opportunities for forging direct links with the homesteads of commoners through the medium of the advance. Although chiefs were prohibited by law from forcing their followers to accept mine contracts, a good working relationship with the local chief remained important. Bribery of chiefs was not unknown in Swaziland. One source notes that chiefs were paid a sum of ten shillings per head by recruiters, certainly a worthwhile investment for the recruiter given that capitation fees were often five times that sum.[49] The legal prohibition was easily circumvented, provided the chief could secure the consent of his followers. In July 1909, for example, a southern labour agent recruited some 40 followers of the Hlatikulu chief, Ntshingila. As the Assistant Commissioner at Hlatikulu noted, "Each individual was asked if he was going voluntarily, and all stated they were going of their own free will."[50] How effective and how enduring such practices were depended very much on the individual chief and his own following. No evidence is available of large batches of mineworkers being sent to the mines after 1910; the majority of workers on record proceeded to work centres in small groups, often with only one or two relatives or friends.[51]

Recruiters found it important to cultivate good relations with local chiefs for other reasons as well. Peripatetic maize trading and the mine contracts that went with it were sometimes organized from the homesteads of chiefs. There is also evidence to suggest that chiefs were involved in the provision of advances to recruits. Before 1913, when black runners were prohibited from carrying advance money, the runners often left large sums with the local chief for safekeeping. In their struggle to secure a competitive advantage some recruiters spread information deleterious to the interests of other recruiters and poached their recruits. In theory, a recruiter should always have been aware if a potential recruit had already accepted an advance since his tax receipt would have been stamped to that effect. Many recruiters either did not bother to inquire after a tax receipt or deliberately ignored the evidence. Even if there was no guarantee of the recruit accepting the contract, the tactic was worthwhile. His services were then secured for a subsequent tour either voluntarily or through the prodding of a colonial court of law. If the recruit was arrested at any stage for accepting two advances (perhaps at the instigation of an irate competitor), the recruiter was perfectly safe from prosecution since ignorance was an acceptable plea in court.

In order to expand the pool of recruitable labour, recruiters began to sign on underage (less than 18 years) Swazi males for minework. Given the difficulty of establishing the precise age of recruits, they were able to get away with this practice until the abuse became too blatant. In 1912, for example, Marwick & Morris were instructed by the Government Native Labour Bureau (GNLB) that the "large number" of underage recruits who were working in their compounds on three-month surface work contracts would be returned to Swaziland at their expense. Marwick & Morris immediately warned their recruiters in the field not to forward any other underage recruits until further notice. The Director of the GNLB attempted to control the practice at the administrative level by appealing to the South African Secretary for Native Affairs that "in view of the restrictions against recruitment within the Union of natives under the age of 18, I shall be grateful if representations can be made with the view to prohibiting their recruitment in Swaziland."[52] Legislation was enacted in Swaziland soon thereafter, but in the face of persistent evasion by recruiters and the problems in determining a man's real age, the recruiting of minors continued.[53] Stolen or borrowed tax receipts were often used by underage men to acquire passes from suspicious, but helpless, colonial officials.[54]

Recruiters in Swaziland made a practice of advancing money to migrants from Mozambique and Natal, and some even sent their runners into surrounding territories to recruit labour.[55] There was certainly a greater degree of risk in this since the advance was more difficult to recover in the event of desertion. In 1912–13, as many as 400 "illicit migrants" from southern Mozambique who had come to Swaziland to sign on with local recruiters were arrested for contravening colonial pass regulations.[56] Since it is unlikely that all of those who came were detected, the actual numbers were undoubtedly even higher. In the first half of 1912, when advances in Swaziland were higher than those in Natal and the Transvaal, an indeterminate number of Africans came to Swaziland to engage for minework in Johannesburg. Another upsurge in 1916 precipitated an official crackdown since "unless such practices are suppressed in their infancy there will be an exodus of Union natives into Swaziland to take advantage of the higher advances permitted there."[57]

If it was the advance which lubricated the recruiting apparatus of the traders, an essential cog in the machine was the African runner. Without the development of a mutually beneficial, if unequal relationship, between the recruiter and his runners, it is doubtful that the former would have had the same impact in the Swazi countryside. Runners were usually ex-mineworkers and running was, in general, a highly desirable profession. *Kwa Muhle* paid its runners a generous salary; other runners received a capitation fee of 5 to 10 shillings per recruit. Both groups of runners stood to make much larger sums of money than on a mine contract. Trader-recruiters tried to take advantage of this situation by holding down runner fees and using unlicensed runners. The unlicensed runner could be paid a lower fee and the recruiter was spared the expense of a licence. In one case, an unlicensed runner, Kukumba Shongwe, was prosecuted for canvassing labour for a recruiter named Maritz at 2 shillings per head. When Maritz refused to stand up for him in court, Shongwe commented ruefully that "Maritz has not played the game."[58]

It is impossible to determine how many runners were scouring the Swazi countryside for recruits. The problem of the illicit runner was serious enough, however, to prompt the colonial state to include a clause in its Regulations governing recruiting in Swaziland which prescribed that "every runner shall wear in a conspicuous position upon his outer garments a badge, clearly indicating that he is a runner and the name of his employer."[59] In 1913, as part of a joint agreement governing the terms of recruiting in Swaziland, the NRC and Marwick & Morris arranged to limit their recruiters to three runners apiece (appendix G). Seeing no advantage in such a restriction, recruiters on both sides of the fence refused to implement it.[60]

The tasks of the runner were many and opportunities abounded for manipulation of the system, sometimes in cahoots with the recruiter, sometimes acting independently. His basic role was to canvass the rural areas for recruits: "every country storekeeper is an agent and aristocratic Native Touts are employed. These are to be found in every nook and cranny where natives congregate, and entrusted by their employers with large sums of money frequently used as bait in making advances, sometimes for many months in advance."[61] The "nooks and crannies" inhabited by runners included tribute labour parties and weddings. Runners also loitered around colonial tax camps and courtrooms with money at the ready. No part of the countryside was untouched by the runner and, after 1914, white farmers in Swaziland were continually incensed by the ease with which runners could entice farm labour away. Runners, often relatives of the aristocracy or chiefs, had a high profile in the rural community and were well known as a source of ready cash. They sought out families or individuals they knew to be in debt to traders, the colonial state, or other Swazis. Up until mid-1913, runners were free to traverse the countryside with "a lot of money to advance as opportunity offered."[62] In May of that year, recruiters were barred from giving money to runners, but many continued to do so. Other clandestine methods adopted by runners to make on-the-spot advances to migrants included private arrangements (with a witness present) which could later be publicly denied if necessary, and "personal loans" by runners to recruits. Alternatively runners took the tax receipt of the potential recruit to the recruiter for stamping and then ferried the advance back again; a practice not technically against the law. Runners also acted independently to maximize their own benefits. Some obtained licences to work for one agent but touted for a number of others as well. This meant that the runner could offer the potential recruit a broader range of choices. He could thus obtain his fee even if the potential recruit was not favourably disposed towards the recruiter who was officially represented. Runners also arranged for friends or relatives to use their licences in order to increase the time actually spent in the field.

A good proportion of the runner's time was spent in "non-productive" activity. Runners were responsible for calling up workers given a "leave period" by the recruiter and for tracking down potential recruits who had absconded with their advance. Since these deserters often proved to be extremely elusive, this could be very time-consuming. Methods therefore were adopted to speed up the process. One of the more ingenious of these was the habit of dressing in police uniforms and imitating local African police, to the extent of "arresting" deserters and ferrying them, not to colonial jails, but to the trader's store. For obvious reasons, this practice met with severe colonial disapproval in the 1913 legislation which proscribed a heavy fine for "any runner who shall clothe himself in a manner that is an imitation of the uniform of the Swaziland Police or any other police or military force, or who shall clothe himself in such a manner as would reasonably cause any person to mistake such runner for a member of any such force."[63]

It was not unusual to find runners defrauding both employers and potential recruits, although the longer-term benefits of such actions were probably questionable. The terms of employment were misrepresented to entice the potential recruit, particularly if he was proceeding to work for the first time and was unfamiliar with conditions on the Rand. Some runners also cheated recruits out of their advances, causing some concern to the recruiting companies. As J.S. Marwick noted in 1913: "the number of disputes arising out of such transactions is largely on the increase and we are constantly having to deal with cases in which runners have converted monies to their own use and are without means of making good the deficit."[64] In court, it was the word of the recruit against that of the runner and since the latter usually had the backing of his employer, he was virtually immune from prosecution.

Swazi mineworkers were never passive victims of recruiters and runners, however, since there was ample opportunity to "play" the system themselves. It appears that the bulk of Swazi recruits proceeded "legitimately" to the mines, via a runner and recruiter. Yet for many the inducement of a standard advance was insufficient. While it is important to resist the temptation to generalize certain types of behaviour, as the students of "worker consciousness" are prone to do, it is of interest to lay out the variety and ingenuity of Swazi migrant workers' strategies against which the colonial state felt compelled to legislate. The most common methods used by Swazi migrants to defraud recruiters were desertion after acquiring one or more advances, and taking two or more advances prior to leaving for work on one of the contracts.[65] Desertion was both active and passive. In the latter case the recruit made little effort to avoid the recruiter or his runners but persistently refused to embark on a mine contract. In court, two types of explanation were usually offered. The first stressed unforeseen rural obligations to chief or homestead and the second emphasized personal health reasons. Neither was acceptable to the judges.

The question of when a recruit could be called a "deserter" was a constant source of dispute between recruiters and recruits. Recruiters would not receive their capitation fee until the recruit arrived at the mine. Yet to secure a potential recruit's services advances often had to be made on demand. Recruiters thus had to accept reluctantly that there would be a delay or "leave period" between the signing of a contract and the recruit actually leaving Swaziland. While the recruiters worked tirelessly to shorten this period, delays of up to a year were known. As long as there were numerous recruiting organizations in the country, the leave period was an important selling point for the recruiter and bargaining chip for the recruit. In 1913, Marwick & Morris and the NRC agreed to hold all new recruits to a three-month leave to check "the habit which is growing amongst the natives of borrowing money and remaining at their kraals in idleness for long periods."[66] In late 1914, the two companies tried unsuccessfully to restrict the leave period even further to two weeks. It was not until 1916 when the Native Recruiting Corporation acquired exclusive mine recruiting rights in the country, that the recruiters combined to shorten the leave to a standard period of two weeks to a month. What had been an issue of contention in a competitive recruiting environment, became an instrument of control in a monopsonistic one, and there was a dramatic increase in deserters after 1916, as the NRC tightened its control.

Recruits who actively deserted would leave the district where the advance was taken for another part of the country or for South Africa. Zululand and the eastern Transvaal were popular desertion spots and some migrants who were going to work in these districts would avail themselves of a mine advance before leaving. Mbilini Lunga, for example, took an advance of £5:8s in October 1912 from John Murray who was recruiting for the Van Ryn Mine in Johannesburg. He left Swaziland a week later to work in a small Transvaal town and was not discovered and brought to trial until March 1915.[67] Other deserters simply remained in their home district and attempted to avoid the runners and police by sleeping in the veld when either was in the vicinity. They sometimes did this very successfully. Nine months passed before Mgudwa Gamede was finally arrested at a beer drink and it took over two years for the colonial police to track down Mbambeni Magagule.[68] Conviction was no guarantee that the worker would not desert again. Basi Mnisi deserted four times from the service of Marwick & Morris between 1909 and 1914.[69]

To defraud recruiters, Swazi migrants also took two or more advances. Recruiters did connive in this practice but there are many cases of recruiters being "duped" by potential recruits. If a worker intended to acquire more than one advance he generally went to recruiters in different towns or went to another district altogether to obtain the second advance. He also studiously avoided taking advances from recruiters working for the same organization, which suggests he was aware of the possibilities offered by a competitive recruiting environment. After acquiring two advances, many workers would proceed to Johannesburg on one of the contracts. In October 1912, for example, Mayiyane Twala took an advance of £7 at Hlatikulu from Rowland Winn of Marwick & Morris. When called up by Winn's runners to go to East Rand Proprietary Mines he could not be found. He had gone to Bremersdorp where, on 28 January 1913, he took a £5 advance from Vallance Stewart of A.M. Mostert and went to work in Johannesburg on that contract.[70]

Some migrants took a second advance using a pseudonym. The easiest way to do this was to use the tax receipt of someone else, an elderly relative or a friend or relative who was not going to work that year. There is also evidence to suggest that stolen tax receipts were circulated in the Swazi countryside. It is possible that forged tax receipts were in circulation as well. In more than one case colonial officials found it impossible to locate the supposed taxpayer in the colonial register. The number of offenders brought before colonial courts for accepting more than one advance declined over time, and it is unlikely that this was a result of the slackening of the colonial or recruiter vigil, or the development of more sophisticated techniques of evasion, although these cannot be entirely discounted. Rather, it seems to have resulted from the tightening of control by the NRC and better liaison between recruiters.

In October 1912 the Chamber of Mines established its monopsonistic Native Recruiting Corporation. The period of hectic competition which followed the collapse of WNLA in 1906 and which had led to a massive regional conversion to mine labour, slowly came under control. The competitive environment, while unavoidable for a season, was counter-productive and costly in other ways. After a long struggle within the ranks of mining capital, monopsony was once again within reach, although the continued activities of the independent labour contractors ensured that it was never the mechanically precise system that some scholars have glibly constructed. Within Swaziland, over half of the trader-recruiters were immediately drawn under the NRC umbrella. By June 1913, 36 of the country's 60 recruiters were working for the NRC. The contractor A.M. Mostert reduced his presence in Swaziland to nominal levels in early 1913, leaving Marwick & Morris as the only other Rand recruiter in the country between October 1912 and 1916. In other areas, the NRC recruited for ERPM, but there was a tacit agreement that recruiting in Swaziland for this mine would remain in the hands of Marwick & Morris. From the inception of the NRC until June 1914, 6,801 contracts were signed by Swazi workers for the mines of NRC members, as opposed to 3,000 for Marwick & Morris. In the first month of recruiting, 45 per cent of recruits signed with the NRC and over the next two years this proportion fluctuated between 35 per cent and 55 per cent. But Marwick & Morris continued to be a major force in the country until 1916 and this ensured that strongly competitive recruiting persisted for a season (figure 9).

In mid-1913 the NRC abandoned its policy of "undermining the influence" of Marwick & Morris by poaching their recruiters and runners and sought a cooperative agreement.[71] This gave Marwick & Morris the exclusive right to recruit for ERPM in Zululand and Swaziland in exchange for concessions on recruiting methods (appendix G). The agreement itself was regularly abused by recruiters of both companies who often saw little personal gain in following central directives. Even after 1916, individual trader-recruiters continued to compete with one another under the NRC umbrella, although the opportunities for manipulation by migrants were much reduced.

With a greater degree of communication and less competition between recruiters, the regulation of advances at a lower level, and the curtailment of the leave period, independent travel to the mines

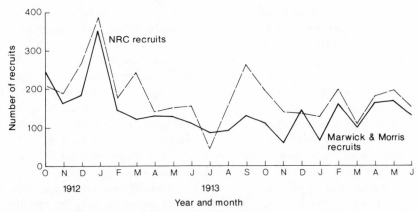

9 Number of Swazis recruited by NRC and Marwick & Morris, 1912–14

again became an increasingly attractive proposition.[72] A surge in non-recruited labour also reflected a growing partition of the Swazi workforce. First-time migrants sought the relative security of a contract, whereas the growing number of married migrants with homestead responsibilities wanted the flexibility of going independently to the Rand.

In 1917, the Natal coal-mining companies, which had just secured a large contract with the Railway Administration, Admiralty, and several shipping companies, made a big push to secure labour. This included an attempt to overcome traditional Swazi resistance to coal-mining employment with a vigorous recruiting drive in southern Swaziland. Recruiters from the coalfields began recruiting with a fleet of runners offering large advances in excess of £20.[73] The competitive recruiting environment of earlier years was briefly revived and there was a sudden surge in offenders taking more than one advance and in the number of Swazi working on the coalfields. On the Hlobane Mine near Vryheid the Swazi workforce jumped from 57 to 254 between July and October 1917. By December 1917, there were 320 Swazis at the mine.[74]

NRC recruiters responded by quickly drawing the attention of the authorities to recruiting malpractice. Their objections proved to be redundant. The Swazi workers rapidly discovered for themselves that their longstanding avoidance of the coalfields was amply justified. The long history of abysmal working and compound conditions on the Natal coalfields, and at the Hlobane mine especially, were revealed in independent inquiries by the Secretary of Native Affairs in 1910 and the GNLB in 1917.[75] The GNLB investigation revealed that conditions at Hlobane had deteriorated markedly since 1913 when a massive outbreak of scurvy had occurred at the mine.[76] Typhus and dysentery were rampant and medical facilties virtually non-existent. An Indian orderly, Frank, was the only "medical" attendant for 1,600 black workers. Impromptu medical inspections of ill workers, some of whom were housed outdoors, were made by the compound manager who claimed to have "no medical training but a long experience with sick natives."[77] In mid-1917, the death rate on the mine which had jumped sharply was blamed by mine management on "the weak debilitated class of native attracted, his want of acclimatisation [and] insufficient clothing."[78] Over-crowded tin shanties for barracks, poor sanitation, and hopelessly inadequate rations were compounded by continual on-the-job abuse. Workers' tickets were often not marked at the end of shifts and white gangers repeatedly abused and physically assaulted workers underground. The sordid catalogue of brutality by white worker against black is amply documented in the statements of 59 Swazi workers recorded in January 1918.[79] Complaints to compound managers were greeted with verbal insults and threats of further violence. Other workers did not bother to air their grievances through this channel. As Kufa Nsibande pointed out, "I made no complaint. I didn't go because I thought it was useless on account of what others told me."[80]

Labour unrest was not uncommon at Hlobane but the state came down heavily on the side of mine management. In February 1917, for example, 75 striking Xhosa workers at the mine were imprisoned as far away as Pietermaritzburg and Ladysmith for two months' hard labour.[81] Promises by mine management to exasperated recruiters that conditions would be improved went unfulfilled and Swazi workers, along with those from other areas, began to desert in droves. The effects were compounded when workers on the way to the mines received reports from the deserters and turned back to Swaziland before reaching Hlobane. As Mjanje Ngwenya recalled:

I met natives coming from the Hlobane mine and they told me it was a very bad place and I turned back with them. I will not go and work there as all the natives are deserting from there and are returning to Hlatikulu to get money to pay [the recruiters] back. One could fill this room with people who have run away from there.[82]

The trickle of deserters in mid-1917 had swelled to a flood by the end of the year. The colonial state was forced to act and in early 1918, over 50 Swazi deserters were arrested and tried at Hlatikulu.[83] The case proved to be something of a landmark, since it was the first significant victory by a group of Swazi workers in a colonial

court of law. With labour recruiters and mine representatives com-
mitting blatant perjury and the workers resolutely and vividly re-
constructing the conditions at the mine, the colonial state had little
option but to free the workers and absolve them of all responsibility.[84]
Sharp rebukes were also issued to the Hlobane representatives, and
the Hlobane mine continued to experience chronic labour shortages.[85]

There is no evidence that the Swazi workers ever returned to
Hlobane to see if the mine had kept its promise to "improve matters"
on the coalfields. The brief Swazi flirtation with the Natal coalmines
reveals, however, that as in 1910-13, large cash advances had the
potential to divert the flow of migrants into new channels. If, as in
the Hlobane case, these channels had very rough edges, it was merely
a temporary diversion. As long as there were employment alternatives Swazi workers continued to be extremely sensitive to working
conditions that affected their health and physical welfare.

The victory of the Swazi workers in the Hlatikulu courtroom takes
on added significance when set against the colonial state's handling
of recruiting activity in Swaziland in the first two decades of British
rule. In an environment of stiff competition, the trader-recruiters
required and received considerable state support. Pre-existent but
perennial colonial taxation demands proved a considerable boon to
the recruiter, and colonial officials had little objection to the presence
of recruiters and their runners at colonial tax camps. In the years
when advance money was flowing freely, the recruiters required
direct intervention from the colonial state to curb Swazi manipulation of the system, and to guarantee that recruited labour would
proceed to the Rand. Stiff penalties were imposed on recruits who
deserted or accepted more than one advance. When prosecuted,
workers were always ordered to proceed to the Rand after com-
pleting their sentence, on pain of violating colonial contempt of court
regulations. Two cases clearly illustrate the draconian nature of colonial labour legislation and taxation policy. In 1911, Madhlohlo
Magagule was fined a massive £40 or four months' imprisonment
with hard labour for defaulting on his tax of £9, and for deserting
after accepting a £5 advance.[86] Other workers were subject to double
prosecution if they accepted two advances and went to work on one
of the contracts. Mangebeza Ngobe was tried in 1913 for accepting
two advances and for deserting from the employment of the other
recruiter. His punishment was a fine of £20 or four months'
imprisonment.[87]

If the prosecuted worker opted to pay the fine he was further
indebted to the recruiter, and if he chose to serve in prison, then
he was unable to work for as much as half the year. Workers who

claimed sickness as an excuse for desertion were rarely given a medical examination. Often the amateur opinion of the trader-recruiter was enough to secure a conviction. When Ndhladle Bhembe claimed he had not gone to Langlaagte Block в to work his contract because "I am a very sickly person and my chest is bad," the opinion of labour recruiter Homa that "he does not look ill to me" was sufficient to earn Bhembe one month's imprisonment.[88] Even the impromptu diagnosis of a runner was sometimes sufficient. When Zondiwe Hlope set out for work but came back with chest and back pains, a runner's opinion that he did not seem sick landed Hlope a three-week prison sentence.[89]

The recruiters also required state support in bringing recruits to trial. While their runners could track down deserters, they had no powers of arrest. Swazi police were at the disposal of the recruiters for finding and arresting offenders, not only within Swaziland, but as far afield as the Rand itself. The case of Mashingiliza Nhlengetwa shows the extent to which some Swazi workers were in thrall to the colonial state and how little clemency they could expect from its black agents. Owing £26 in back tax for himself and his three wives, Mashingiliza took an advance of £5 on 6 March 1913 from Howe & Murray to work at Van Ryn for seven months. He then deserted to Zululand where he was finally tracked down and arrested by a Swazi constable, Dhlodhlo Dlamini. Dlamini described the arrest:

He said "I will not go, you can kill me. Who gave you the right to arrest me. Shoot me with your gun." I tried to force him to go and he resisted and struggled with me. My bandolier was broken. He also tore my putees. I struggled with him for a long time. Nohlokuku assisted me and we could not make him go with us. The next morning NC's Myanga and Kohliwe came to my assistance. The accused got several wounds in the struggle. I could not help hurting him. It was his own fault.[90]

Despite a medical report that attested that he had been "roughly treated," Mashingiliza was fined a further £12 and ordered to proceed to Van Ryn.

Any abuse of the recruiting system was thus a calculated risk. Colonial states throughout the region regularly intervened to manage the dirty struggle for recruits. When they failed to, social discontent in the rural areas grew. Thus, legislation was enacted, and to some degree enforced, to regulate the demand side of the equation. All of the pre-Union colonies in South Africa had their own legislation which, while congruent in broad contours, was adapted to the local situations.[91] After Union in 1910, a search was instituted in South Africa to secure "simplicity and uniformity in methods of recruitment," which culminated in the Native Labour Regulation Act of 1911.[92] Inside Swaziland, the Transvaal Labour Agents and Compound Overseers Proclamation of 1901, proved entirely adequate for the colonial state to monitor a situation where minimal recruiting activity was taking place. However, "greatly increased energy on the part of recruiters of labour" in 1910 forced colonial officials into an immediate search for a set of measures to contain the avaricious recruiters, whose activities were not particularly conducive to good government. In September 1910, the colonial state passed legislation to control the recruiters and their runners, establishing an elaborate licensing procedure and outlawing the poaching of recruits and misrepresentation of contract terms. The legislation was virtually a carbon copy of that passed in the Transvaal in 1907.[93] The only substantial difference lay in its provisions for dealing with the relationship between chiefs and recruiters (see chapter 4).

While state regulation was probably resented by many trader-recruiters insofar as their opportunities for abusing recruits were restricted, they were themselves dependent on outside help to dissuade the Swazi migrant from playing the system to his own advantage. It is therefore not surprising to find embellishment of the Swaziland legislation in 1911, and again in 1912, to control mounting abuse by Swazi migrants.[94] The Swaziland legislation was retained until 1913 notwithstanding the passage of the 1911 Act in South Africa. Under pressure both from the Union Government and local officials in Swaziland, who found the existing legislation "very defective and obscure," the High Commissioner finally assented to bringing Swaziland into line with South Africa, and the Native Labour Regulation (Swaziland) Proclamation of 1913 was passed in September 1913.[95] The local colonial state was no slavish imitator of its South African counterpart, however. Although the two sets of legislation were in many respects identical, the Swaziland version contained several clauses dealing with local conditions, particularly concerning the activities of runners and the control of labour on the local mines.

CHAPTER SIX

Brewers, Workers, and the Local Mines

There will be no hardship in making the Mine labourer a Servant. The necessity of doing so arises because of the custom which the local tin miners have adopted of leaving their work at any time and for as long as they wish and returning when they feel inclined to.
                              Robert Coryndon, 1910

The mines of Swaziland were an integral component of the labour market confronting Swazi migrants during the first two decades of the twentieth century.[1] The local mining industry had recurring problems with labour mobilization and worker control, even with a large potential labour supply. The mining companies' attempts to get enough labourers and to discipline and control them, were constantly undone by the nature of the labour process on the mines, the growing domination of the Witwatersrand in the regional labour market, and the demands of the Swazi ruling class on local mineworkers.

All the small-scale mining syndicates of the 1890s (see chapter 2) collapsed during the Anglo-Boer War and the mining concessions which showed some promise were absorbed by Rand mining houses or British-based companies.[2] In the years immediately following the war very little mining was carried on. In 1906–7, world tin prices soared above the £200 a ton mark, and Swaziland tin again became a viable proposition. With a renewed influx of foreign capital both gold and tin mining operations expanded fairly rapidly. By 1911 there were five tin properties and eleven gold mines in production (figure 10). The peak years for the gold mines were between 1910 and 1915 and for tin during the First World War when tin prices went above £300 per ton on the world market.[3] In the 1920s, both industries went into rapid decline. Between 1905 and 1920 gold and cassiterite tin constituted over 70 per cent of Swaziland's exports by value. The success of the industry was consequently important to the fledgling British administration in the country.

The major gold-producing mines in the country were controlled by British capital. The Piggs Peak Development Company Limited (with 80 per cent of the country's gold output in 1911–12) also had

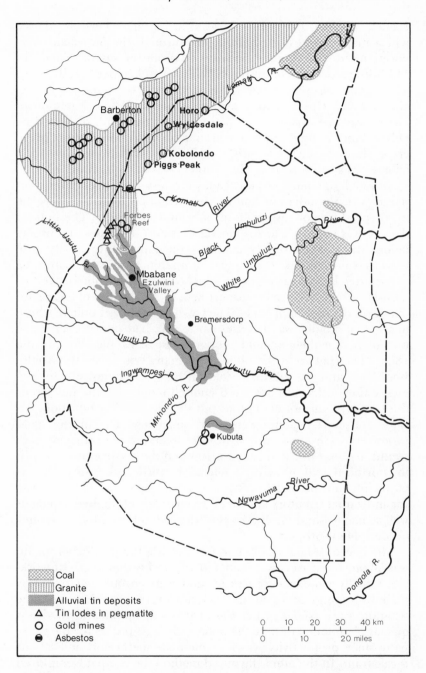

10 Minerals and mines in Swaziland

French backing. The South African industrialists Lewis & Marks, had a major interest in the industry through the Swaziland Corporation Ltd. The country's primary tin producer was Swaziland Tin Ltd (with 75 per cent of output in 1911–12 and 90 per cent by 1919) which went into production in 1905 after the Rand mining house, H. Eckstein & Co., had taken over the company. The Eckstein property covered an area of 100 square miles to the south of Mbabane. Other Rand mining houses acquired interests in tin but these properties showed much less promise and were mainly worked on a tribute basis by individual white miners or small syndicates.[4]

Although the mines of Swaziland were very small operations compared with the adjacent South African mines, Swaziland was the major producer of cassiterite tin in southern Africa.[5] The bulk of the ore was exported to Britain via Lourenço Marques. Transportation difficulties constantly hampered the mining industry. Because there was no rail link to the port, all machinery and ore had to be transported by ox-drawn wagon. This boosted production costs enormously.[6] The lack of rail transport kept the coal mines of Swaziland out of production completely. The Swazi Coal Mines Limited, whose major shareholder was H. Eckstein & Co., had mined over 2,000 tons of coal at their lowveld property east of Bremersdorp in the 1890s. The coal sat at the pithead for many years after the Anglo-Boer War, and was gradually sold off to Swazi homesteads for domestic use.[7] Eckstein's advanced enough money for the upkeep of the property but not enough to put the mine into production, because transport facilities were so rudimentary. The tin and gold producers were more successful in overcoming the transport constraint, because of the high tin prices and the relative proximity of the northern gold mines to a railhead. Nevertheless, transport costs bit deeply into potential profits and kept wages low. This was true for individual tributors and small syndicates with limited capital as well as major Rand mining houses who did not want to lose money on peripheral properties.

The cost of wages was important, because the production of tin was labour-intensive. Swaziland Tin adopted two methods of working. Initially white tributors (21 in 1906) were encouraged to employ their own gangs of 10 to 20 black labourers on each creek. The tributors were paid £33 per ton of dressed tin. This method was quickly abandoned despite the potentially high profits for the Company since productivity was low, methods inefficient, and labour recalcitrant. In the other, favoured method the company employed gangs of 20 to 40 labourers to remove overburden and to sluice the rich gravels at the bottom of creeks. Each gang had its own black

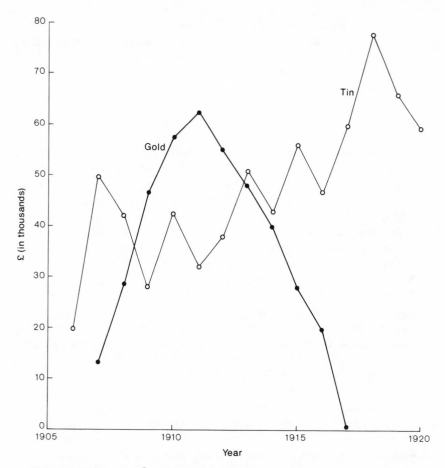

11   Tin and gold exports from Swaziland, 1905–20

nduna and a white overseer was put in charge of several gangs.[8] The alluvial nature of the tin deposits and the sluicing method of recovering tin ore demanded a lot of labour. A network of drainage furrows, some up to 20 km in length, had to be dug in order to tap and channel the headwaters of the area's drainage systems. Then the overburden had to be broken up (which varied in thickness from 2 to 20 metres), the gravel shovelled into sluice boxes, and the cassiterite removed after sluicing. In 1911, the companies made an important technological innovation when hydraulic monitors were introduced to break up the overburden. Labour demand slackened, productivity and output increased dramatically, and the cost of recovering cassiterite dropped from £41 to £25 per ton (figure 11).[9]

Feeding the workforce was another costly enterprise. Miners' rations were usually small helpings of maize meal once or twice a day. The mines were unable to obtain enough local maize from either white settlers or peasant producers, and were forced to import from trading firms in the eastern Transvaal, who were never averse to a little price gouging.[10] To compensate for the high costs, and to re-capture a portion of the mine wage, the companies established small stores on the mine properties where miners could supplement their meagre diet with meat, sugar, and vegetables.[11]

In addition, the companies had real difficulties obtaining sufficient labour. Before 1907, local mines resorted to intercepting Mozam-bican labour en route to the Rand. Although it is not clear exactly how many Mozambicans passed through Swaziland, several hundred Tsonga migrants (663 in 1908–9 and 462 in 1909–10) took out travelling passes every year. It is likely that this was to legitimize a rather longer stay than the two or three days it took to cross the country on foot.[12] For those Swazi homesteads who did release labour for capitalist enterprise, the low mine wages were unattractive. Even when the wage rate was raised by one of the mines, the impact seems to have been minimal; in 1906 the Forbes Reef Gold Mining Com-pany was unable to raise its labour complement from 250 to 550 by temporarily doubling wages.[13] Local mine managers and members of the Swaziland Chamber spoke repeatedly of the difficulties and gloomy prospects for the industry:

We have had frequent experience of the scarcity of unskilled labour available even for the modest requirements of the present ... It seems very curious but it's a fact and if tommorrow we required 1000 or even 500 unskilled labourers we would be at a loss to find them – locally at any rate ... The authorities are entirely sympathetic but unfortunately under present con-ditions they, like the employers, are helpless for the remedy lies with the Swazi himself.[14]

Although mine managers appealed to the local administration for assistance in meeting their labour needs, the state had limited powers in directing labour their way.

In late 1906, the mine managers presented a strong case to the High Commissioner that without firmer state assistance the industry would collapse. Selborne immediately declared open support for the local mines although he did not abandon the state's overarching commitment to the South African labour market. In an address to the Swazi people in Mbabane he urged that:

All those men who can work ought to go and work for it is necessary for their prosperity and that of the country that they should do so. Particularly do I wish the Paramount Chief and the chiefs to see that of those young men who seek work, a sufficient number should seek work in the mines and industries of Swaziland. It is well for Swaziland that many Swazis should go and seek work in the Transvaal, but it is bad for Swaziland that so few should seek work in Swaziland itself.[15]

Selborne wanted the local mines to prosper, because the colonial state gained revenue through taxation on mining profits, and he wanted local labour in the mines, because capital was being drained from the country through Mozambican migrants' wages. Given the inability of the state to move Swazi labour to the Rand it seemed logical that they should work locally and buttress the revenue-starved administration. Despite Selborne's appeal that Mozambican workers should be replaced by Swazis, it was a year before the labour needs of the local mines were fully met.

Given the prevailing Swazi attitude towards minework, the mine companies were aware that despite the advantages of location, they would have to battle to secure a share of the small migrant labour force. This was a major contradiction for the Rand mining houses which considered investment in peripheral properties. By obtaining migrants for their major mines, there was always the chance that the labour supply of their peripheral operations would suffer. Local mine managers were often left with the uphill task of securing and stabilizing their own labour supply. With the Swazi who would not work and with those who left the country independently of recruiters very little could be done. But when the labour supply was challenged directly by recruiters, the response was swift and forthright. In mid-1906 a band of labour touts entered Swaziland in search of labour for construction of the Carolina-Ermelo railway extension and attempted to recruit on the Swaziland Tin property. The offer of £3 per month had the predictable effect of "unsettling the Company's boys" when compared with their own wages of less than 30 shillings per month. The company responded by temporarily raising the wages of their longer serving-employees and "arranging much information to be circulated to the detriment of the Railway works."[16]

In pursuit of Swazi labour, the mines hired recruiters, who then had the same difficulty finding recruits as other recruiters (see chapter 4). Swaziland Tin appointed four white recruiters and a number of black runners under one Albert Mabaso in 1906. The white recruiters managed to obtain only 29 recruits in the eighteen-month period from July 1906 to December 1907. The most successful black runner, Kaptain, recruited 51 labourers in the same period but the other runners – Miner, Longone, Solomon, Skakaza, Majack, Sixpence and Carriage – only managed 51 between them.[17] The lack of success of the recruiters and runners led the mine manager, Sydney Ryan, to try to work through the Swazi rulers, in the mistaken belief that this was the only sure way to obtain the necessary labour (see chapter 4).

The coercive methods adopted by the colonial state in mid-1907 to smash general Swazi aversion to wage employment, and the mobilization of labour by the Swazi chiefs later the same year, heralded a change in fortune for the local mines. In the President's address to the Swaziland Chamber in August 1907, a new note of optimism was sounded: "The main handicap during the year was lack of native labour but the past 3 months have shown a marked improvement in this respect and the forces which have operated to bring about a change not the least of which is the sympathetic attitude of the Administration and the amenability of the native to tactful control. One mining company that could barely keep 400 natives as the standard of its labour role has now 1000 native employees on its books."[18] Numerous Swazi men in the centre and north of the country began to turn up for work on the local tin and gold mines. The "sympathetic attitude" of the administration, to which the President made reference, included a decision not to prosecute tax defaulters at work on the mines. Mine managers later began to advance tax money to defaulters as a means of procuring their services.[19]

The improvement in the labour situation at the local mines is graphically illustrated by the case of Swaziland Tin which was able to dispense with its recruiting operations altogether (table 14). The monthly average of black workers on the mines jumped from under 600 in 1906 to 1,087 in 1907–8, and continued to rise steadily to 1,563 in 1908–9, 2,017 in 1909–10, and 2,897 in 1911–12.[20] The greatest proportion was employed on the tin mines. In 1908–9, for example, the monthly employment rolls averaged 1,106 for tin and 457 for gold (2,337 and 561 in 1911–12). After 1912 the gold mining industry went into a tailspin. In 1917, when the Piggs Peak Development Company closed the final gold mine in the country, and turned the property over to trek-sheep farmers from Ermelo, only 250 workers had to be laid off.[21]

Other problems facing the industry were less easily resolved. Competition with South African employers over Swazi labour intensified again after 1910. In 1911, in an uncanny echo of the period before 1907, the mining industry reported that its most serious handicap was the shortage of labour. The causes were now somewhat different. Earlier, Swazi aversion to local mine conditions had led to labour

TABLE 14
Workers Engaged by Swaziland Tin Ltd, 1906–8

Month	1906 Number Engaged	Recruits	1907 Number Engaged	Recruits	1908 Number Engaged	Recruits
January			71	5	128	
February			57		166	
March			101	10	245	
April			150	14	224	
May			162			
June			182	8		
July	53	1	210	12		
August	32		166	6		
September	48	1	195	9		
October	124	14	206	11		
November	116	26	237	3		
December	123	34	187	5		

Sources: SA, RCS 100/15

shortages; in 1911, however, a "battalion of labour recruiters invaded and disorganized the local supply" (see chapter 5).[22] Appeals for colonial assistance were again sympathetically received. The colonial state was committed to the view that "it is only just that persons exploiting minerals in the country should have first-claim on the adjacent labour available," and legislation was passed to bar recruiters and their Swazi runners from the mining properties.[23] Nevertheless, the local mines were forced to resurrect their recruiting operations.

Another major problem facing the local mines was an extremely high labour turnover. Some indication of this can be gleaned from figures for the years 1911–12. In the gold mines the average monthly labour force was 561, but a total of 6,728 workers were actually hired during the same period.[24] In the tin mines the figures were 2,337 and 9,350 respectively (table 15). For the mining industry to secure a monthly workforce of 2,900 employees, almost six times as many workers had to be engaged during the course of a year.[25] One reason for the high labour turnover was the presence of the Mozambican miner. These migrants rarely stayed for longer than a month or two in Swaziland on their way to the Rand. Swazi workers who were

TABLE 15
Local Mines Annual Return, 1911–12

(a) Gold

Mine	Output (oz.)	Value (£)	White	Black
			Labour Engaged	
Alluvial Mines	35.25	150	9	83
Avalanche Mine			22	144
Black Diamond	123.35	523	44	247
Daisy Mine	1,147.27	4,873	68	676
Forbes Main Reef			95	614
Ivanhoe			1	1
Kobolondo Mine	1,483.16	6,300	69	777
Lomati Mine	281.63	1,196	21	390
Piggs Peak Dev Co	11,706.99	49,728	388	3,769
Primrose Mine			3	20
Waverley Mine	2.98	12	4	7
Total	14,780.63	62,782	724	6,728

Average Number at Work: White 60.3; Black 560.75

(b) Tin

Mine	Output (tons)	Value (£)	White	Black
			Labour Engaged	
Forbes Reef Tins			24	92
McCreedy Tins	64.43	6,101	23	935
Polongeni Tins	15.08	2,019	24	1,087
Swaziland Tin Ltd	233.34	24,277	202	7,236
Total	312.85	32,397	273	9,350

Average Number at Work: White 68.25; Black 2,337.5

Source: SA, RCS 44/12, Draft ACR, 1911–12.

forced into the workplace simply to acquire money for food purchase
or to make tax payment were also disinclined to spend extended
periods in wage employment. Swazi chiefs' attitudes and actions towards their followers in the mines were just as significant.

Most Swazi workers came from the central and northern districts
of the country which were near the mines. Hence there was no
marked spatial separation of home and workplace. They lived on
the tin and gold properties while at work, but home was close enough
to permit regular (usually weekly) visits and irregular sojourns to
assist with various agricultural activities. This sort of pattern was not
unusual in peripheral mining operations. What made the Swazi case
somewhat unusual was the resiliency of chief-commoner relations in
the countryside. The mines were close to the royal villages and the
homesteads of several important chiefs. That miners remained tied
by a web of obligations to local figures of authority impinged directly
upon the degree and timing of their participation in wage labour.
There was little problem where an agreement existed between the
chief and commoners that the commoners would migrate for employment, but when the chiefs demanded tribute labour, the working
period was constrained or interrupted. The chiefs' demands for
labour invariably meant that the mines had the most difficulty maintaining a full complement of labour during peak agricultural activity.
Regular employees on the tin mines would work for only two or
three days in the month leaving mine production "at the mercy of
their labourers."[26]

Swazi workers on three- or four-month oral contracts usually spread
the contract over a longer period, working sporadically and "returning when they feel inclined to."[27] In early 1910 the mine managers attempted to tackle the problem by bringing the Masters and
Servants Law to bear on a Swazi worker in a test case. Despite Resident Commissioner Coryndon's firm support for the move, it was
rejected in court. Swazi workers quickly heard of the decision and
there was an immediate upsurge in desertions. The companies appealed to the colonial state for less ambiguous legislation. While
colonial officials were very sympathetic, and even drafted anti-desertion
legislation, they realized that the signing and registration of contracts
was a necessary prerequisite for the enforcement of any law.[28] Local
mine managers were aware that an attempt to enforce written contracts on Swazi workers would be totally counterproductive and took
the line of least resistance, preferring a labour force prone to "continual desertion" over none at all.[29]

The strong feelings of Swazi workers, together with ever-present
cost constraints, prevented the mines from instituting more rigid

institutions of worker control such as the compound. Workers were
simply housed in camps of ramshackle, corrugated-iron shacks with
minimal service and sanitation, thrown hastily together on mine
properties. In other areas mine managers did what they could to
raise worker productivity. In 1908, the new manager of Swaziland
Tin, W. Knight, was commended by his superiors as someone who
could "teach a good deal to our Managers on the Rand as to the
organization of coloured labour."[30] Knight segregated the workforce
on ethnic lines and appointed *ndunas* who were of the same ethnic
background as their gangs. Wherever possible *ndunas* were also the
sons of chiefs. Knight later went to Potgietersrus to advise on the
labour problems of their tin mines.[31]

The various alluvial creeks of the tin properties were spread over
a large area which made continuous supervision of workers difficult.
The companies consequently depended heavily on their *ndunas* to
enforce work discipline. The lack of compound facilities inhibited
the mechanisms of social control needed to manipulate an essentially
undisciplined work force. The use of alcohol as a means of worker
control in southern Africa has been well documented.[32] Initially, in
Swaziland, mine workers tended to purchase beer from Swazi brewers since "all the large Kraals around cater for [the miners] on Sunday, making huge pots of beer and having dances."[33] The Transvaal
Liquor Licensing Ordinance, in force in Swaziland, prohibited the
manufacture of sorghum beer for sale and its implementation tended
to push Swazi brewers farther away from the mines where arrest
and prosecution were less likely. Yet these actions had a negative
effect on work discipline since "bodies of natives working on Mines
go great distances to obtain kaffir beer and they are, at the beginning
of the week, through excessive drinking and fatigue, unable to work
in a proper manner."[34] Finally, in 1913, after repeated appeals from
the mining companies the colonial state gave them permission to
brew beer and distribute it to employees at the end of a shift.[35]

The question of "illicit" brewing brought out one of the contradictions at the heart of colonial tax policy. Many of the brewers were
from homesteads who were trying to meet the colonial tax burden
through the sale of beer (see chapter 3). In mobilizing labour for
capitalist labour markets in South Africa, colonial taxation thus tended
to generate a set of conditions which constantly undermined the
productivity of local mine workers. It is possible, though there is no
direct evidence, that the state assault on brewing was also an attempt
to eliminate it as an alternative to labour migration by cutting off
another source of homestead income.

The administration was largely unsuccessful in its campaign to outlaw the sale of beer. As early as September 1906, Selborne warned that he was displeased to hear that because of excessive drinking at the homesteads of the chiefs, miners were sometimes unable to work for several days in the week and that if they failed to "cure the evil for themselves" he would legislate against the drinkers.[36] Here was another peculiar problem arising from the position of a capitalist enterprise in an agrarian setting. The chiefs' demands for labour did not automatically dissipate when their followers began work at adjacent mines. Apart from the temptation to return home at regular intervals, there is much evidence to suggest that the chiefs of the area took advantage of the proximity of their followers and called them to *umemo* or to organized hunts, particularly on weekends. At the conclusion of these activities there was usually a beer party, so that the workers returned to the mines in a rather different state than that demanded by capitalist enterprise.[37]

Tension between the local mines and the chiefs was exacerbated by the proximity of the royal villages. The Queen Regent even advised workers on labour relations. In July 1908, in order to facilitate collections for the campaign against colonial land policy, she ordered mine workers to strike for higher wages.[38] More typically, Swazi miners were called upon to perform agricultural and other tasks by the Queen Regent. In 1907, for example, workers on the tin mines in the Ezulwini valley and at the gold mines at Forbes Reef were ordered to Zombode to assist in building cattle byres on Sundays for the Queen Regent.[39] The mine managers responded to these weekend calls by introducing a system of Sunday labour to raise ailing productivity and to thwart the demands of the chiefs and aristocracy. In 1912, the administration declared that Sunday minework would not be permitted, but proceeded to turn a blind eye to a practice which continued unabated.[40] In 1916, disgruntled mineworkers informed proselytizing missionaries to "go and preach to the whitemen and tell them not to make us work on a Sunday."[41]

In response to the other problems of labour control, the state was quick to introduce some vigorous legislation. Clause 22 of the Native Labour Regulation (Swaziland) Proclamation of 1913 noted that "any native labourer in Swaziland who (a) neglects to perform any work which it is his duty to perform; (b) unfits himself for the proper performance of his work by having become or being intoxicated during working hours; (c) refuses to obey any lawful command of his employer or any person lawfully placed in authority over him; (d) uses any insulting or abusive language to his employer or any person lawfully placed in authority over him; or (e) commits any breach of any rules prescribed for good order and discipline or health on any mine or works" would be liable on conviction for a fine of not more than 40 shillings (at least two months' wages).[42] The workers, with the weapon of desertion at their disposal, paid limited heed and the legislation became almost impossible to enforce.

The difficulties of labour control in a small-scale, undercapitalized, and labour-intensive industry were compounded by the agrarian setting. Where the mines were unable to enforce the kind of work-discipline required for profitable production, the colonial state was willing to lend its weight. In practice, such legislation was of minimal assistance. The stance of the colonial state was necessarily more am-biguous on the question of labour mobilization for the local mines. While colonial officials were anxious to bolster the position of the local mines' labour supply they could do little more than offer gen-eral indications of support and exhortations to the Swazi themselves. The local mines were able to reap some spin-off benefits between 1907 and 1910 when the state moved to crush Swazi resistance to wage labour in general. But thereafter, when Swazi labour migration patterns underwent a significant reorientation in the direction of the Rand, a move which the administration supported, the local mining companies were given little help. In this they were not alone. Other employers within Swaziland, such as white farmers and ranch-ers, experienced similar difficulties and dilemmas.

PART THREE

Land and Labour

CHAPTER SEVEN

Land, Labour, and the Settler-Estate

We can now work to transform the country into the home of a well-ordered, prosperous and contented British community.

Robert Coryndon, 1908

On 12 July 1905, a young Swazi man was arrested by a Swazi police sergeant, brought to the Mbabane Magistrate's court, and charged with arson. The charge related to an incident the week before at the Swaziland Corporation's experimental cotton plantation at Loch Moy on Mawalawela Island on the Usutu River. R.M. Cauvin, the plantation manager, was away in Mbabane on business and his wife, four children, and a missionary guest were left behind. Two men appeared on the island at night and, after failing to gain entrance to the Cauvin residence, razed the building in which they were sleeping and severely beat an Indian servant who attempted to intervene. Cauvin's family escaped unhurt although their belongings were destroyed. In addition to the house the entire year's experimental cotton crop, which had been picked and was ready for export, was destroyed by fire. One of the arsonists who had exacted such "inhuman vengeance" was a former employee of the Corporation who had been dismissed.[1]

The Swaziland Corporation was one of a number of major concession holders in the country, whose intentions to sell land to incoming white settlers complemented the British colonial design for Swaziland. The Corporation's experimental agricultural activities on Mawalawela Island were designed to show prospective settlers that the country was suitable for estate production. The land companies, and settlers already holding concession rights in the country, depended on colonial intervention for establishment of the pre-conditions for agrarian capital accumulation. These included titular security, unfettered land control, and a property market. In 1907, through legislative edict, over 60 per cent of the land area of Swaziland passed out of Swazi hands. The land partition, as it is euphemistically known, left several hundred resident and absentee white landowners with title to an enormous 40 per cent of the land. By the late 1920s this grew to 58 per cent through crown land purchase.[2] Another precondition was an abundant supply of cheap, reliable labour.[3]

The unnamed assailant's attack on the Mawalawela plantation arose directly from his feelings of injustice about the treatment he had received at the hands of the Swaziland Corporation. The majority of Swazis seeking wage labour avoided agricultural employment. Farms in the Transvaal and Swaziland were shunned by Swazi workers, except under conditions of dire need. The treatment of Swazi who worked on the farms discouraged many others. It is probable that the arsonist's extreme reactions commanded sympathy in the local community. The general unwillingness of Swazi migrants to accept farm employment pushed white settlers towards more radical solutions which tied colonial land and labour policy very closely together.

The resettlement of Swaziland by whites after the Anglo-Boer War proceeded hesitantly. Between 1904 and 1911, the period during which the future of white settlement in Swaziland was under review, the white population increased by a mere 22 per cent (from 890 to 1083).[4] The first white settlers to enter Swaziland in any numbers were welcomed neither by the Swazi nor by the new British administration. They were generally indigent Boer "bywoners" – poor whites – who had been squatting in southern Swaziland in the 1890s and returned to the district after the war. British colonial officials tried to regulate this influx without much success. They regarded the bywoner presence as highly undesirable and as conducive to social unrest. As early as 1904, disputes between Boer and Swazi over land had become commonplace. Such incidents were usually provoked by the bywoners who colonial officials found to be "very intolerant and regardless of native rights."[5]

The bywoner households scraped a living out of the soil by planting a few acres of maize and vegetables each season for their own consumption. Extremely low productivity reflected their primitive techniques of cultivation. Most households lacked the labour resources and draft animals to break up new soil. In 1909, when the colonial state loaned animals to several families, they were only able to double their cultivated area. Very little surplus was produced for market and in famine years the bywoners suffered particular deprivation and hardship. They were locked into a cycle of low productivity by shortages of capital and the marked aversion of Swazis to accept employment with them.[6] A number of British settlers who managed to produce small surpluses of maize for local sale were interspersed with the bywoners. Some also cultivated a few fields of tobacco and cotton. In addition to the permanent settlers, Boer graziers from the eastern Transvaal resumed their annual trek to the Swaziland highveld for winter grazing of sheep. They numbered close to 500 and brought in as many as 100,000 to 200,000 sheep each year. Some trek farmers brought their sheep over 200 km to the superior Swaziland grazing grounds. The benefits of trekking outweighed the problem of ubiquitous stock theft which the trekkers encountered in Swaziland.[7]

The white community was sharply differentiated by nationality and mobility and was also highly fragmented geographically. The diverse and conflicting nature of its interests in Swaziland was also divisive. Only in the mining industry had there been any centralization of control over concessions acquired in the 1880s. A mere 14 land concessions (6.3 per cent) were owned by companies and there were 56 British and 152 Boer owners. The Boers had achieved some small measure of unity since 68 concessions were controlled by grazing syndicates.[8] Nevertheless, internal differences among the white concession holders in the pre-War period, were quickly subsumed in a common quest to consolidate control over Swazi labour and land. The basis for co-operation was clearly laid out by Godfrey Lagden: "If the European concessionaires were content to let all the natives on their concession remain in undisputed possession of their holdings and to allow them to plough new ground at will and utilize water and wood, there would be no difficulty. But they are not content to do so, desiring to appropriate the best ground for themselves, to stop indiscriminate cultivation and to displace any natives not required for their own purposes."[9]

A united front proved to be necessary for collective bargaining with the colonial state. In order to have an effective lobby, the various concession holders in the country resuscitated the Swaziland Mining, Commercial and Industrial Chamber (first formed in 1898). The Chamber saw itself involved in the "persistent fight to rescue Swaziland from native absorption and to maintain through years of inoperation, cost and loss, those properties which by purchase and judicial confirmation were European property."[10] In October 1905, the Chamber was assured of the support of the eastern Transvaal concession holders (a rather fickle loyalty as it transpired) and the white farmers of Swaziland who had banded together into a number of Farmers' Associations.[11] The unified white voice was orchestrated by the local representatives of several South African and British land companies. The companies with the most active capital involvement and extensive potential landed interests were also the most vocal; they included the Swaziland Corporation and the Henderson Consolidated Corporation.[12] The controlling interest in the Swaziland Corporation was held by South African industrialists Lewis & Marks. The Corporation had extensive interests in mining, land, and industrial monopolies and was the most important of the land companies. The magnitude of these interests forced the colonial state to make special arrangements with the Corporation outside the normal channels of colonial land policy.[13] The Henderson Consolidated Corporation was a subsidiary of the South African land company Henderson Transvaal Estates which owned over one million acres of land in the Transvaal.

Stanley Trapido has recently argued that the land settlement schemes of the British reconstruction administration in the Transvaal, while primarily of ideological and political intent, suited the needs of the land companies who looked forward to unloading large tracts of land onto the market.[14] Swaziland was no exception to this. Milner's settlement policy for the country sprang both from the pressure brought to bear by the local land companies and from his "grand design" for South Africa as a whole.[15] As Mashasha has pointed out, the policy adopted in Swaziland dovetailed neatly into Milner's reconstruction plans. Milner assumed that Swaziland would be incorporated into the Transvaal, and it had a part to play in the large scale settlement of British "yeoman" farmers in the Transvaal and Orange River Colony.[16] Unlike South Africa, where inadequate funding for land purchase and the lack of sufficient powers of expropriation provided considerable obstacles to his plans, Milner foresaw more suitable conditions in Swaziland once the "concessions' net" was unravelled. The Swaziland land companies and Milner were united in wanting to sell large tracts of land to British settlers. For example, in a draft agreement drawn up by Milner and the Swaziland Corporation's local manager, Allister Miller, the Corporation agreed to set aside a minimum of 50,000 acres for immediate purchase by British settlers on easy terms.[17] This particular agreement got no further than the planning stage, because Milner's successor, Selborne, was determined to reduce the Corporation's potential land control.[18]

The concession-holders' vision of Swaziland as a settler-state was fired by the speculative value of their concessions.[19] Allister Miller and the Swaziland Corporation were prime movers in these plans. They were pressing the Corporation's claim to almost one third of the land in the country. The banner was quickly taken up by the Swaziland Chamber.[20] The potential of Swaziland for settler-estate production and the role of the Swazi in these developments were feted: "If European energy and capital are devoted to the agricultural development of these productive areas the prosperity of the native will follow. He will soon learn to imitate what the higher race initiates and a close industrial inter-mixture of the two peoples will assist towards the regeneration of the native race."[21] This faith was based largely on the results of experimental agricultural work on a variety of cash crops, ranching, and timber by both the Swaziland Corporation and the Henderson Consolidated Corporation.[22]

The directors of the Swaziland Corporation believed that settlers would come to them for land but they also actively solicited settlers by devising a "broad and liberal scheme" of settlement.[23] It became clear how broad and liberal this scheme was to be when a pamphlet was issued by the Swaziland Chamber in 1907. The Chamber proposed that landowners in the country sell 2,000 acre blocks of high-veld land at 10 shillings per acre, and 300 to 500 acre middleveld blocks and 1,000 acre lowveld blocks at 20 shillings per acre.[24] The degree of speculation implicit in these selling prices is worthy of note. In 1907, the Swaziland Concessions Commission valued high-veld and middleveld land at 1s 9d per acre and lowveld at 9d per acre. It was hardly surprising, then, that settlers did not flock to take advantage of these "liberal" conditions, particularly when crown land was much cheaper.

Johannes Smuts, erstwhile British Consul in Swaziland, first recognized Swaziland's potential role in whitewashing the Transvaal countryside. He laid out what was to become the keynote to colonial policy on white settlement in the early years of British rule:

As to its agricultural and pastoral possibilities I have no doubt whatever. Swaziland in general will be well worth the attention of the farmer ... We may look forward to the country being occupied by white men in considerable numbers. That being so, it is essential that the land question be placed on a firm basis.[25]

The policy was perpetuated under Milner's successors. On a visit to Swaziland in September 1909, Selborne compared the situation in Swaziland with that in Basutoland in the following terms:

I have never considered that the future of Swaziland can or ought to be the same as that of Basutoland. There is the greatest difference between the two ... To show you what was in my mind as regards the position of whites in Swaziland in the future, when I issued my partition proclamation, I took power to insist that the whites who own the land should occupy it; which shows you what my conception was, not of men in Swaziland owning farms and farming Swazis but of white men living in Swaziland and farming themselves ... Looking forward as I do to a time when that part of the country which belongs to whites will be really peopled by them, when the white man's farms will be covered with homesteads.[26]

Selborne's experience in South Africa, however, had taught him that plans often went awry. He was justifiably concerned that if large areas of productive land were locked up by absentee landlords the rich agricultural potential of Swaziland would not be realized. As he did not want this to occur in Swaziland, he restricted the claims of the land companies. He noted at the time that "I want to prevent the land accumulating in the hands of large companies who simply farm kaffirs. I hold that it is in the public interest that large tracts of land should not be held in Swaziland, either by individuals or companies, without any beneficial occupation by white men and simply for the purpose of farming kaffirs. That this evil is not an imaginary one, experience in Natal and the Transvaal only too clearly proves."[27]

Selborne was well aware that his plan meant that "the Government will take upon itself the risk of the development of a large part of the country," a chance he was prepared to take.[28] The continuing commitment of the British colonial state to white settlement worked itself out in several ways; ensuring that large areas of the country were freed for settler-estate production, providing support services for settler enterprise, commissioning investigative reports of Swaziland's agricultural potential to attract "men from over the sea of the right stamp," and in colonial policy on the handling of crown lands in the country.[29]

The fate of the country's crown lands provides a clear example of the colonial vision for a white Swaziland. While the colonial state could do no more than encourage the land companies to sell their holdings to settlers, it controlled the fate of 22 per cent of the country designated as crown land after the land partition of 1907 (figure 12). Both the Colonial Office and local colonial officials in Swaziland understood that, in order to pacify the Swazi chiefs, this land would be incorporated into newly demarcated Swazi reserves.[30] Selborne reserved the right to put the land to other uses, declaring "I do not consider myself prohibited from putting a white man on any crown land which may now or hereafter become available" and rebuking any local official who thought otherwise.[31] He studiously ignored Swazi opposition to his plans for crown lands and courted the assistance of the Swaziland Chamber on the disposal of the land.[32]

Sale of crown land would also generate income for a beleaguered administration which was heavily in debt after settling the issue of

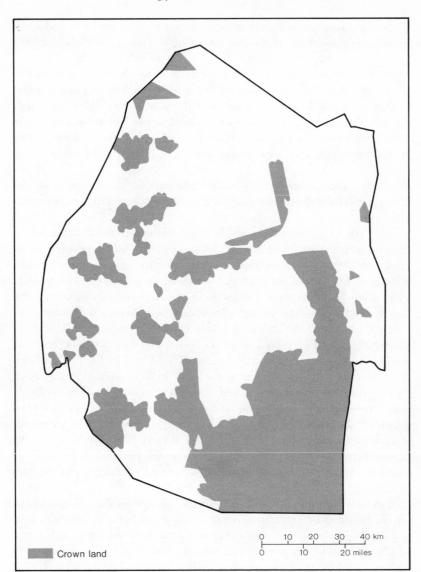

Crown land

0   10   20   30   40 km

0   10   20 miles

12 Crown lands in Swaziland, 1909

the concessions. In a letter to the new High Commissioner Gladstone in May 1910, Selborne urged that crown land be sold to selected farmers in order to liquidate the administration's debt of £80,000. Since Swaziland was eventually to be transferred to South African control, Selborne also deemed it imperative that the country be stocked with British settlers:

I would lay great stress on our doing all we can to dispose of this land while Swaziland is under the High Commissioner, because if the High Commissioner does it, then he can assure himself that a really good class of farmer is set down there, whether from other parts of South Africa or from England. If – and it is most important that a really good white population be settled there and not a rotten one – if the land is not sold by the High Commissioner, when Swaziland is transfered to the Union Government it will be used as a dumping ground for poor whites ... [who] will simply live on the surrounding natives and sink more and more to their level.[33]

Although this policy was roundly criticized by the Union government, crown-land sales began to accelerate under Gladstone's watchful eye.[34]

The sale of crown land to individual settlers and corporate interests generated an income of £135,000 for the state between 1910 and 1925.[35] Indigent bywoners received initial allocations of small blocks of 60 to 600 acres in the south of the country. Thereafter, crown land was dispensed to incoming settlers directly or under the aegis of the Mushroom Land Settlement Scheme, a privately financed plan "to acquire land suitable for the settlement of Britishers in Swaziland." The purchase of 60,000 acres of crown land in 1910 by "anonymous public spirited men assisted by Lord Lovat and the Earl of Selborne" was similar to a scheme in the eastern Orange Free State which had been established after the Anglo-Boer War to obtain land for soldiers from Lovat's Scouts and the Fife and Forfar yeomanry.[36] Two other large blocks were sold before 1920 to ranching companies, and throughout the First World War, blocks of 50 to 1,500 acres at prices of 3 shillings to 3s 6d per acre were sold to settlers. After the war, 1,000 acre lots were distributed to over 100 returning white soldiers on easy terms (3s 6d per acre when land prices were running around 10 shillings per acre on the open market). In addition, over 250,000 acres of encumbered crown land was sold to the holders of the encumberances (usually for grazing) for 1 shilling to 2s 6d per acre.[37] The sale of crown land ensured a steady influx of white immigrants after 1910.

The colonial vision of Swaziland as a haven for white settlers fitted in with the reality of white concession holding and settlement, and the place of Swaziland in the broader design for South Africa. Despite changing circumstances, the vision never faded. In 1907, Robert Coryndon's arrival from Northern Rhodesia as Resident Commissioner brought a new local impetus to the drive for white settlement in Swaziland. However, the British failure to attract large numbers of settlers to the Transvaal, and local conditions in Swaziland, ensured that Coryndon's self-appointed task of transforming the country into "the home of a well-ordered, prosperous and contented British community" never really came to fruition.

Upon taking power in Swaziland in 1903, the British colonial state was presented with a tangled morass of conflicting land, grazing, and mining concessions. Selborne called it "the most amazing chaos that the white man ever inflicted on a native tribe."[38] The colonial state attempted to resolve two basic issues: first, whether there should be a general expropriation of land and grazing concessions from the holders, and second, when this was rejected, whether land should be partitioned between the indigenous and European claimants or whether both should occupy and utilize the land concurrently. This latter question taxed the administrations of both Milner and Selborne.

On the basis of investigative reports by J. Rubie and Johannes Smuts in 1901 and 1902 respectively, Milner advocated a land partition which would give the Swazi and the concession holders different sections of the country.[39] Both reports pointed out Swaziland's suitability for white settlement, provided that white concession holders were given freehold title to land. Milner's policy was re-examined by Selborne in 1905 and 1906. Prior to September 1906, Selborne still countenanced a "policy of drift" but saw it as posing insurmountable difficulties for white farmers.[40] Despite mounting opposition from the united Swazi chiefs to any colonial attempt to "cut up the land," Selborne quickly decided on a policy of partition. As he later commented: "At the request of the concessionaires, at their request, not at the request of the Swazis, I am dividing the country between the concessionaires and the Swazi. In my opinion, the concessionaires were quite right to clamour for partition, because the concessions over the land are worthless so long as the natives had unrestricted right to prior use."[41] The Swazi rulers came close to changing his mind in late 1906, however. In meetings in Mbabane in September, from which white settlers were rigorously excluded, Selborne was taken aback at the ferocity of the Swazi case. Over 2,000 traditionally armed Swazi, including local mine workers, had come to the meetings. Attacks by Malunge, the Swazi Prince Regent, and Labotsibeni, the Queen Regent, on the illogicality of British land policy earned the arrogant Selborne's grudging respect.[42]

The High Commissioner concluded that unless he was very careful a land partition would lead to unrest and open revolt. The incident was described by Allister Miller as "the greatest blow to the long years of struggle to fertilize the spread of European influence in Swaziland."[43] Fearing that the causes of the Bambatha Rebellion in neighbouring Zululand were being replicated in Swaziland, Selborne decided to follow what he called a policy of "expediency dictated by nervousness." He responded positively to the white concession holders and several colonial officials about a partition, while simultaneously exercised a high degree of dexterity in fielding Swazi protest.[44]

Soon after the Anglo-Boer War it also became obvious to agricultural employers in Swaziland that it would be difficult to get an adequate farm-labour force. The aversion of Swazi males to any form of farm labour was quickly recognized and lamented by settlers.[45] Some Swazi chiefs had discouraged their followers from accepting farm labour as a form of passive protest against colonial land policy. But the conditions of farm work did not provide migrants with much incentive either. Farmers in southern Swaziland complained that "most of the inhabitants of this district are unable to offer sufficient wages to induce them to work on the farms and at present they are unable to obtain any labour."[46] Capital shortages were largely responsible for the fall in farm wages from a high of 25 shillings per month in 1904 to 10 shillings per month by 1909.[47] Farm wages were well below those at the local mines and various employment centres in South Africa, including the farms of the eastern Transvaal where farm wages could be as high as 60 shillings per month.[48]

The problem of providing competitive wages even beset those who could offer better rates for farm work such as the land companies and some maize farmers. The maize farmers faced a market that fluctuated sharply from year to year, depending on the adequacy of the Swazi harvest and the price of imported maize, and high labour costs bit deeply into meagre earnings.[49] A good Swazi harvest tended to depress the cost of maize (to below 15 shillings per bag) so that the farmers could afford fewer labourers the following season. A poor harvest would send the price of maize sky-rocketing (to over 40 shillings per bag), but white farmers would be unable to take advantage of higher maize prices because their harvest would be poor too. A further impediment for maize farmers was the seasonal nature of their labour requirements. The periods of peak demand for ploughing and harvesting coincided with those of Swazi agriculture so labour was invariably tied up. It was small wonder that from 1907 on, the local settler newspaper began to exhort farmers to move away from maize cultivation.[50]

The land companies in Swaziland engaged in experimental cash-cropping were no more successful in obtaining farm labour. This did not bode well for the future of settler-estate production in the country. As Allister Miller noted in 1904, "the shortage is not inconveniently perceptible at present, but very little development would make the shortage acute."[51] On the Henderson Consolidated Corporation's lowveld property the Manager was completely unable to obtain labour to assist with fencing operations in 1906.[52] Later, Dove, in his report to the Corporation, said that the one serious drawback to their property was that the male labour supply was "solely spasmodic and cannot be relied upon."[53] The Swaziland Corporation had similar difficulties and both it and the Henderson company resorted to female and child labour from the surrounding area. Apart from the reduction in wages, the seasonal problem was less acute, at least for cotton picking since the harvest came later in the year. Landowners soon saw female and child labour might form the backbone of any future cotton industry in the country.[54]

The difficulties of labour shortage were compounded by problems with labour productivity. At the Swaziland Corporation plantation, the manager complained that "although the native women and children take kindly to the work [we] have not succeeded in training them in the use of both hands."[55] At fixed wages of less than 5 shillings per month for children, and only double that for women, their recalcitrance was hardly surprising. Miller's experience with the Swazi worker in two different settings led him to the conclusion that low farm productivity was a selective phenomenon: "today, on the farm, he is practically a loafer. If we could only get natives on the farm to work like they do up at our properties at Forbes Reef in shafts and tunnels ... really it would be absolutely a pleasure to farm in the country but we cannot. They do not take an interest in their work."[56] The diffident attitude of farm labourers was a direct result of the onerous conditions of farm work and the inability of farmers to exercise direct and continuous supervision of the labour process.[57]

In July 1905, the President of the Swaziland Chamber harangued the members on the farm labour issue. In his speech he described many elements of the landowners' thinking about how to develop a farm-labour force:

We all know, some of us to our cost, that the detribalization of the native and the development of the agricultural industry are contingent upon one another. We have only to look at the local condition of affairs to see that ... for every 4 natives who work, 14 are idling at their kraals. It is quite impossible for any country to develop under these circumstances, and it will simply drive the agriculturalists to press for legislation or cheap imported labour. We know that the country can produce and whilst the agriculturalist is quite willing to pay a fair wage, he must have continuous labour, which he is quite unable to obtain under existing circumstances.[58]

From the start, white landowners attempted to solve the problem of obtaining a "class of labour that will give the country districts the benefits of cheap native labour."[59] Two solutions were commonly proposed before 1910: one involved importing foreign labour, and the other, tampering with the social structure of Swazi society.

Although no systematic plan for importing foreign labour was ever developed there are numerous references to the idea. However, it was hardly likely that employers unable to pay wages commensurate with those of local or South African mines would have had sufficient capital to meet the costs of importing labour on a large scale. Rather, these suggestions show the frustration of Swaziland employers with the reluctance of young male Swazis to accept farm employment. When Selborne was in Swaziland in September 1906, for example, he was approached by W. Pott, Swaziland Manager of the Henderson Consolidated Corporation, who had the idea of importing Egyptian or Indian labour to their lowveld concession. The response of the colonial state was an immediate and unequivocal refusal to countenance this "sanguine plan."[60]

Somewhat more realistic was the proposal of the Swaziland Chamber that the cotton industry use imported female labour from Mozambique.[61] Landowners also suggested the controlled importation of farm labour from the Transvaal.[62] They were naturally opposed to the free flow of ci-devant Swazi migrants from the Transvaal to Swaziland since they saw this as a "plank in the policy of the Swazi rulers."[63] Imported labourers would be strictly prohibited from offering allegiance (khonta-ing) to any Swazi chief. The eastern Transvaal was having its own labour difficulties at the time and farmers from that area who owned property in Swaziland were just as interested in generating a reverse flow of labour from Swaziland to their Transvaal estates.[64]

Internal solutions to the farm-labour problem presupposed a far greater degree of state intervention and yet were pursued with much greater vigour by landowners. When giving evidence to the South African Native Affairs Commission (SANAC) in 1904, Swaziland settlers David Forbes and Allister Miller, returned repeatedly to the Swaziland farm-labour issue, drawing on their experiences in the eastern Transvaal.[65] David Forbes saw heavy colonial taxation as a major obstacle to securing a stable and compliant farm labour force. As an employee of WNLA, Forbes argued that "everything should be done to secure labour for the Mines that is in reason but do not let it be done by a total disregard of farming interests." The high taxes demanded by mining capital as a lever against stubborn African populations were clearly counter-productive to white farmers, contended Forbes, since they pushed up farm wages. He suggested that Swaziland deploy a differential tax on farm labour which would encourage Swazis "to place themselves and their labour under the control of the European." He noted that Swazis would see the advantages if farm labour was taxed at £2 per head and 10 shillings per hut while all other homesteads were taxed at £2 per head and £2 per hut. Forbes anticipated that this would also weaken the chiefs' authority in Swaziland because "any native who would elect to remain permanently under the chief's control will have to pay for the privilege."[66]

Miller had one of the most revolutionary and improbable plans. Drawing on nineteenth-century social Darwinism and examples from as far afield as the American South and West Africa, Miller argued for the summary abolition of communal responsibility, the land-tenure system, and chiefly privilege in Swaziland. Miller's plan was a recipe for full rural proletarianization, except that he allowed for a small Swazi land-owning class which would have fixed 10-acre allotments in 500-acre blocks scattered throughout the country.[67] The eldest son would be the sole heir and the other offspring would be ejected onto the labour market:

We cannot say to the native "You must go and work" because it is against our principles to force labour and it would be misinterpreted in other countries. But we have now come to the time when somebody has to say that; somebody has to be hard to the native if he is not to grow up a miserable, flabby, good-for-nothing man. In a country like Swaziland somebody has to say that he must go to work, and that somebody is his parents who will have to say "I am not going to support you boys; you must do something for yourselves."[68]

Such a scheme was not, of course, a logical answer to the question of how to provide for a rural proletariat, since divorcing Africans from their means of production was no guarantee that they would accept farm work. As Miller noted, "unfortunately, the native is too anxious to go off the farms to the towns [although he] is far better off on the farm than he is in the town; he is better behaved and everything else."[69] The possible incentive of higher rural wages was rationalized away by appeal to the target-worker phenomenon.[70] For Miller, the long term solution was "industrial education," educating Swazi men "first of all as ploughmen, agriculturalists and growers generally." Miller suggested establishing two state-run schools in Swaziland at which Swazi youths could be trained for a period of five to six years before working on the farms.

The concept of the "unbounded estate," the view that the Swazi had control over too much land and that this was at least partially responsible for their resistance to wage labour, was a recurrent theme in settler thinking before 1907. Miller also argued that land tenure should be individualized; this reflected his antipathy towards "communalism," leaning on one's neighbour in times of hardship or distress instead of adopting the "civilized" solution – migration for wage labour. Communalism had to be replaced by an ideology of "individualism" and land reform was the fastest means to this end.

Less sophisticated expressions of the "unbounded estate" concept were more common. As early as 1902, the Swaziland Chamber asserted that "large native reserves tend to destroy any possibility of assimilation, inasmuch as the native is removed from intimate contact with Europeans, his wants are simple and every facility is here afforded for supplying these wants with minimal effort."[71] David Forbes, in his SANAC evidence, said that "at the present time [the Swazi] have more ground in Swaziland than they have necessity for, and that does not encourage them to work."[72] The settler mouthpiece, the *Times of Swaziland*, argued that "it is quite an error to imagine that taxes, Plakkers Wets and other subsidiary laws will make the native a worker so long as he finds squatting place where he can grow his food and live his life of practical idleness."[73] Sentiments such as these, along with the desire to obtain the most land for white settlement, blossomed into a series of proposals by concession holders. They called on the colonial state to restrict severely Swazis' access to land in the partition. If these proposals had been implemented, the Swazi would have had between 100,000 and 300,000 acres of land or less than 10 per cent of the land of Swaziland.[74]

A basic premise of these proposals was that no provision need be made for increasing population:

The coming generation is the present generation. A man with one wife has three children; one is a girl, and the other two are boys. One of the boys is going to inherit that ground, and the other is going out to work, and the only consideration one has for the future generation is for the heir of the house and he will possess the ground which his father possessed.[75]

Concession holders who were not primarily interested in the farm-labour supply tended to be more generous, at least before the emergence of a unified landowner front in late 1905. Boer concession holders who wished to obtain freehold highveld grazing grounds for winter trekking from the Transvaal and displace resident Swazis from their properties, and some settlers in southern Swaziland, initially were willing to part with up to two-thirds of the area of their concessions.[76]

Other contrasting proposals were put forward by various colonial officials. While they also wished to restrict the "unbounded estate," they had other pressures such as the Swazi chiefs' tenacious defence of their landed interests. In 1901, Johannes Smuts, who later sat on Milner's Swaziland Concessions Commission, developed a set of proposals for dealing with the Swaziland concessions' issue in which Swazis would have been almost totally dispossessed of land. In his recommendations to Milner in 1902, J. Rubie, another Commission member, was similarly uncharitable, although he wished to set aside one or two reserves for Swazi use.[77] By 1904, however, the atmosphere had become distinctly chilly towards similar settler proposals.

Officials became reluctant to commit themselves, in public or private, to *a priori* statements about the "native requirement." This was in marked contrast to the definitive statements of the concession holders. When pressed to provide figures, they were consistently more prodigal in their estimates. Lord Milner, whose land policy led to the establishment of the Swaziland Concessions Commission, refused to be pinned down to actual figures in private meetings with Allister Miller in 1904.[78] The British Special Commissioner in Swaziland, Enraght Moony, who emerged from several battles with settlers bloodied but unbowed, was resolutely opposed to setting an arbitrary minimum standard required to support a Swazi family. When asked to comment on whether 15 per cent of the land surface of Swaziland would be sufficient for Swazi needs, Moony replied:

Fifteen percent is too small. The natives are joint owners and entitled to more. There is also the political reason that if we tried to deprive them of too much there may be trouble. I think we should reserve practically half. They would not be satisfied, but they would become reconciled. Their idea of protection is that we should sit around and prevent them from being disturbed.[79]

Godfrey Lagden was also very reluctant to commit himself to a definite figure when pressed by the Swaziland Concessions Commission.[80] Those officials who did give figures were far more generous than the concession holders. Even H.M. Taberer of the Transvaal Native Affairs Department, whose firm conviction it was that "it is against the interests of the country and the natives themselves to provide for more than the present generation" and who was as keen as any Swaziland settler to see "surplus population" channelled to labour centres, concluded that at least half a million acres was necessary, a figure considerably in excess of even the most magnanimous landowner estimate.[81]

Milner pondered throughout the early part of 1904 how best to resolve the concessions' quagmire in Swaziland. He finally issued his infamous Proclamation in October and made provision for establishing reserves in Swaziland for Swazi occupation.[82] The Swazi rulers immediately petitioned against this Proclamation and stated their abhorrence of any colonial attempt to alienate land, "to place us in the position of kaffirs to the whites."[83] While Milner attributed the contents of the petition to the Queen Regent's white legal advisers, he was aware that his Proclamation "was certain to produce a not unnatural excitement in the Swazi mind."[84] When details of the Swazi protest reached the Colonial Office, Milner was cautioned that the Swazi should have "no just cause to complain of their treatment," a directive which he passed on to his Commission just prior to leaving office in mid-1905.[85]

When the Commission went to Swaziland under Selborne's watchful eye in October 1905 to begin the partition of land, they were armed with the conviction that while it was vital to free the larger part of Swaziland for white settlement, it was also necessary to treat Swazi land claims with liberality. The Swazi were to be allowed 40 to 60 acres of land per homestead. Nevertheless their generosity had definite bounds for they anxiously stressed that they did not want to create "native enclaves within which a native could pass a life of idleness."[86]

Milner had recommended that in creating reserves the Commission should disturb the Swazi population as little as possible and that no large homesteads, or chiefs' homesteads, should be moved to reserves under any circumstances. This recommendation was a result of Resident Commissioner Moony's reading of the situation in Swaziland:

A possible source of danger exists in the question of the removal of old established chiefs' kraals during the course of the demarcation. The people attach a very strong sentimental value to these old villages so that should any attempt be made to carry out any general movement of the people it might consolidate the various parties which now exist and lead to active opposition.[87]

The Commission viewed a mass resettlement of Swazis as highly impolitic and argued that landowners would have to be content with the areas of the country unoccupied by Swazi homesteads. They recognized that confinement of any sort was an anathema to the Swazi, but were convinced that partition could occur "without the nation as a whole, or any large section, simultaneously feeling it," a crucial consideration in state policy at this time.[88]

It is remarkable that Commission members with as much Swaziland experience as Johannes Smuts and J.C. Krogh could not have foreseen what would happen. It rapidly became obvious that the land being used by the Swazi varied considerably from homestead to homestead, but in all cases was greater than the "liberal" 60-acre estimate. The settlers' bluff was called. Not only were they suddenly in danger of losing well over half of the land to the Swazi but their plans to resolve the farm-labour issue through severe constriction of the "unbounded estate" were thwarted. An unprecedented display of anti-colonial acrimony and settler unity quickly followed.[89]

Amidst the furor of settler commination, Swazi hostility, and impassioned appeals to the Colonial Office by the Aborigines Protection Society, the Swaziland Concessions Commission was hastily recalled.[90] Selborne immediately began to rethink the whole partition issue. Simultaneously, the concession holders were developing a new scheme which was somewhat of a capitulation to the Swazi protests. An early version of this plan was mooted in the *Times of Swaziland* in October 1905. The complete plan was given to the Swaziland Concessions Commissions in December 1905 and to Selborne in March 1906. It proposed that (a) 20 farms aggregating 120,000 acres be laid aside for the Swazi chiefs and their immediate followers – two to the Royal household and the other 18 to the more important regional chiefs, (b) commoner homesteads be allotted 60 acres of land each, a total of 880,000 acres. In order to accomplish this, each concession holder would surrender an area proportional to the size of his concession (about one third), and (c) the Swazi would be moved to reserves gradually.[91] These were highly significant concessions by the white settlers. Not only were they prepared to give over one million acres for Swazi reserves and to consider a different solution to the farm-labour problem, they were now calling for a hierarchical land partition which favoured the Swazi ruling class. Each of these concessions deserves closer consideration.

The new proposals about the size of reserves represented a response to Swazi demands and colonial "nervousness."[92] The concession holders had accepted Selborne's conviction that the colonial state needed to be able to accommodate the entire black population of Swaziland as well as population increase in the near future. Colonial officials assumed that longer-term population growth would be supported by improved agricultural productivity with more intensive methods of cultivation. Selborne was convinced from early on that one-third of the land was sufficient for this and was not prepared to go much higher although there were considerable pressures on him:

In one respect ... opinion varies as to the results which might be expected if HMG authorised me compulsorily to partition the land. All are agreed that if the Swazis receive an ample proportion of the soil, judged both by quality and quantity, that there would be no serious trouble, although the Regent and her councillors would maintain a sulky and protesting attitude. Some of them, however, think that there would be no trouble, even if the amount of land which the Swazis received was not more than one third of the whole, provided that the land was of good quality and favourably situated. Others among them, however, express a distinct opinion that when the Swazis found that the concessionaires had obtained two-thirds of the whole country, there would be serious trouble.[93]

As Godfrey Lagden noted, it was a time to go gently. Selborne agreed although he found it "very trying to decide between being too cautious and taking risks."[94]

Throughout 1907, Selborne carefully avoided any public reference to the amount of land the Swazi might end up with, while remaining convinced that one third was ample. In the final delimitation of reserve boundaries in 1908–9 by the Partition Commissioner, George Grey, the Swazi were allocated 37 per cent of the area of the country, and what Grey believed to be at least 50 per cent of the quality soil. Through calculation of homestead production and grazing needs, Grey argued that there was sufficient land to accommodate the entire Swazi population and a 52 per cent increase.[95] He realized that the Swazi would "ultimately fill any portion of country now set aside" but he failed to anticipate the possibility of a rapid rebuilding of Swazi cattle stocks once East Coast Fever was under control after 1910, and the resilience of pre-capitalist forms of landholding in the reserves. Both these unforeseen developments hastened the degradation of the reserves at a rate far faster than Grey expected at the time.

The settlers' second major concession in 1906 was their support for a hierarchical land partition favouring the Swazi chieftainship. To appreciate the significance of this, it is necessary to return briefly to the 1880s. In the early days of white settlement, the settlers were anxious to conserve the authority of the Swazi monarch, Mbandeni, "because they knew his authority was of a friendly character to Europeans."[96] Just over a decade later, at the outset of British rule in Swaziland, they had performed an abrupt *volte-face*. Initially, collaboration with the Swazi chiefs had facilitated the acquisition of lease-hold rights over resources in Swaziland; now those same chiefs were a barrier to freehold title and Swazi labour power. The settlers wanted cheap labour and resented the Swazi chiefs' control over the home-steads of commoners, and the relationships which constituted the basis of that control.[97] They devised three complementary strategies to remake the situation to their advantage.

First, they argued that the chiefs should be divested of their powers of land allocation and their control over commoner labour. Although curtailing the amount of land the chiefs controlled would have helped to achieve their end, they believed that this was insufficient. This led to Miller's SANAC recommendations for individual tenure. The chiefs' powers of land allocation would be exorcised completely and replaced by a state-controlled market in freehold plots. When the settlers realized that the colonial state was not prepared to do this, they added a subsidiary condition that Swazi reserves should be fairly well distributed throughout the country so that all chiefs would lose some land.[98]

Second, the settlers called for the abolition of anachronistic "tribal laws and customs." The demise of customary mechanisms of chiefly accumulation – such as *lobola* – was viewed as a natural concomitant of "the assimilation of the principles and practices of civilization." However, they thought that the process could be hastened by heavy hut tax and legislative edict which set a ceiling on *lobola* payments.[99]

Finally, the settlers argued for dismantling the political power of the Dlamini aristocracy and the institutions, such as the *emabutfo* system, by which that power was sustained. In November 1902, just prior to the assumption of British control, the settler project was laid out with characteristic Miller gusto: "After over 14 years intimate intercourse with natives my opinion of the best way to deal with them is to govern them by dividing them, to destroy completely the central oligarchy, to transfer all the power to the Government proper, to prepare them for de-tribalization by establishing only minor chiefs – responsible only to white Government officials who may be ex-pected to emulate one another in their proofs of loyalty to the power that creates them."[100] David Forbes, who was familiar with the locus of power within Swazi society, proposed the names of 18 such co-lonial lackeys in various parts of the country who might act as in-termediaries in the colonial structures of control.

The turnabout in settler thinking in late 1905 and early 1906 requires explanation in the light of these "exceedingly robust views on the subject of breaking up the power of the chiefs."[101] Official statements about how best to deal with the Swazi ruling class also underwent the same metamorphosis, albeit at a much faster rate. In 1901, Johannes Smuts had laid out a series of far-reaching proposals on this question under which:

The position of the Paramount Chief would, to all intents and purposes, cease to be recognised – they would strike at the root of the whole social system of the country and would mean the practical break-up of the Swazis as a nation ... with the abolition of the office of Paramount Chief, the regulation of land occupation would also be vested in the British Government and the military system would fall to the ground. A very drastic change would therefore be effected which must come sooner or later, for, unlike Zululand and Basutoland, we have the European element owning rights in the country and we cannot perpetuate indefinitely the present system.[102]

In a fine example of colonial double-think, Smuts maintained that his proposals would "undoubtedly better ensure liberty and justice to the general run of natives." Enraght Moony, who became aware of the considerable difficulties in attempting to dismantle the Swazi chieftainship, at first argued that "we must assume power in an active manner, eventually displacing chieftainship as a governing factor."[103]

The Swazi had emerged from the Anglo-Boer War with more *de facto* autonomy and more intact than any other African society of the region. For the colonial state, good government and labour mobilization required the chiefs' collaboration. Colonial officials soon realized that the Swazi ruling class would accept only a limited restructuring; and even this was fiercely contested.[104] The only feasible strategy was rule through the existing structures and any move towards a more suitable form of indirect rule would be very slow. As Lagden commented: "great care is necessary not to depose any authority which by tradition exists, until there is something ready as a substitute, or an overwhelming public opinion has to be created, and it cannot grow until all fear of individual expression has disappeared ... and expectation of early results may be discounted."[105] This view was soon accepted by all officials, much to the irritation of Swaziland's concession holders.[106]

Settlers' proposals for hierarchical land partition thus reflected a fundamental reorientation in thinking brought about by the colonial state's wish to accommodate, rather than shatter, the Swazi monarchy and chiefs. There is little evidence to suggest that this proposal was taken seriously by the colonial state, however. It would have been very costly to obtain suitable farms for the Swazi chiefs in an already intolerably expensive situation. Instead, two alternative strategies were pursued by the state. First, legislation was passed prohibiting

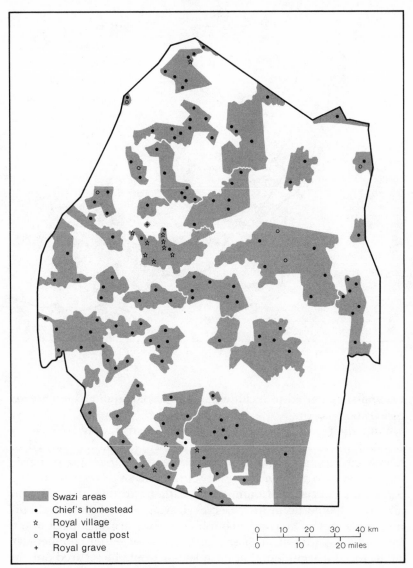

13 Spatial distribution of chiefly elements and Swazi reserves, 1909

private property and individual tenure in the reserves. Second, following Milner's suggestion, the chieftainship and the material indices of its internal dominance (cattle posts, royal graves, chief's homesteads and fields) were disturbed as little as possible by including these elements within the reserve boundaries (figures 13, 14, and 15).[107] In addition, in order to avoid mass relocation, the Partition

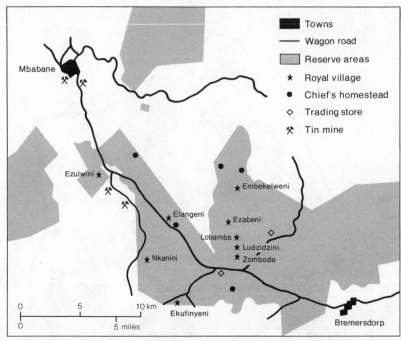

14 Map of Ezulwini Valley showing location of royal/chiefs' villages and reserve boundaries

Commissioner tried to include many Swazi commoner homesteads inside the reserves.

With their plans to generate a farm-labour supply stymied by colonial sensitivity and Swazi intransigence, the settlers turned to labour tenancy, a form of farm labour control with a long pedigree in southern Africa. One of the settlers' major objections to the Swaziland Concession Commission's earlier partition plan was that all Swazis would be in the reserves, leaving them with the all-but-impossible task of coaxing labourers onto the farms. Implicit in the hierarchical partition proposal, and explicit in settler commentary on it, was the argument that farm labour would be secured only by partitioning the land such that some Swazi homesteads were left on the farms. Tenancy regulations could then be promulgated to im-mobilize farm labour *in situ*. The recommendations were warmly received in colonial circles.[108] Recognizing that in Grey's partition, many Swazi homesteads would be left on white farms, Selborne argued that rather than relocating the Swazi immediately to the reserves, the thinking up to that time, they should be allowed a period of grace during which they could move voluntarily. When

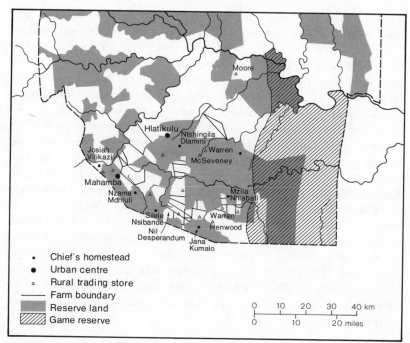

15   Southern Swaziland showing effects of imposition of reserves

this period expired those who remained could be forced to enter into tenancy relations with landowners. Only then could farmers be assured of their labour supply.

Selborne's plan was officially approved in the 1907 Partition Proclamation.[109] Section 6 noted that no Swazi homestead on settler land could be forced to move for five years after the delimiting of reserves and no consideration could be exacted by landowners for such residence. After the five years, Swazi homesteads could continue to occupy white farms if an agreement was drawn up between landlord and tenant, subject to the confirmation of the Resident Commissioner. State control of landlord-tenant relations was consequently ensured from the outset.

Given the colonial desire to foster settler-estate production in Swaziland, the wisdom of allowing the five-year period was questioned at the time.[110] Selborne had rejected suggestions for a shorter period because of his policy of expediency dictated by nervousness: "I want many of the Swazis to stay on the farmers' land and work for them in the same way they do in the Transvaal, and I thought there were more chance of their settling down to these conditions if they had 5 years instead of 3. At the end of 5 years it will rest with the farmer whether he wants any Swazis on his land or not."[111] It is clear that the colonial authorities were worried that the implementation of colonial policy could precipitate considerable trouble from below (see chapter 8). As Lagden pointed out to Selborne in 1906, a policy of forced resettlement would disturb long-established rights and cause ill-feeling and probably unrest.[112] Milner's Swaziland Concessions Commission wanted to minimize Swazi resettlement in constructing reserve boundaries, and Selborne had agreed with this. By including as many homesteads as possible within the reserves, and by allowing a lengthy period prior to the possible resettlement of those who were not, Selborne finally arrived at what he hoped might be a satisfactory resolution of the farm-labour problem. The settlers were optimistic that at least a third of the Swazi would remain as tenants, because they were convinced that many Swazi homesteads wanted to cut themselves loose from the chiefs' control and could be induced to remain on farms as labourers.[113] Colonial officials also anticipated that sufficient Swazi homesteads would enter into relationships with landlords which, under state regulation, would be amenable to both parties.[114] In this they badly miscalculated (see chapter 9).

CHAPTER EIGHT

Policy, Partition, and Protest

We are against class legislation because it must necessarily interfere with our natural progress and makes the European the sole judge to determine which course the evolution of our natural history and ideals should take.
Queen Regent Labotsibeni, 1914

In the early years of British rule in Swaziland, the administration began a careful search for local collaborators. They compiled a detailed register of the chiefs and asked the opinions of white settlers of long standing.[1] Not that it mattered. Between 1904 and 1909, the politics of divide-and-rule largely failed, and the chiefs became united as they rarely had been in Swazi history. Under the common threat, all chiefs – central and regional, Dlamini and non-Dlamini – came together to guard their interests within Swazi society. White settlers and colonial officials were convinced that there were potential collaborators among the chiefs, but they consistently underestimated the powerful binding forces of their own policies.[2] Allister Miller's retrospective observation that "the Swazis were never more united since 1897 than they were under the Queen Regent in 1906" is borne out by the surviving evidence.[3]

At the outset of British rule in 1902, the prospect for an alliance between the central and regional chiefs was not promising. The unity established in the Kruger years of the late 1890s faded during the Anglo-Boer War when the Swazi inner council failed to appoint an immediate successor to Bunu who had died soon after Republican control was lifted in 1899. During a brief but intense succession dispute, one of Bunu's infant sons was designated as heir and the Swazi resigned themselves to a long period of regency. Conscious of the problems this would pose for continued aristocratic domination, the Queen Regent Labotsibeni proposed that another of her sons, Prince Malunge, be appointed. Her pleas were rejected by some of the more powerful members of the council as involving too great a break with tradition.[4] Once British rule was imposed, however, the aristocracy was faced with a more difficult task in securing national consensus over its policies. Although Prince Malunge emerged as a

major force in Swazi politics and played an important role in artic-
ulating Swazi opposition to colonial rule until his death in 1915,
neither he nor his mother could ever aspire to the fullness of regal
power without the actual title. In concert with a coterie of educated
black and white advisers, they nevertheless exercised considerable
authority during the first two decades of British rule.

One indication of growing regional autonomy was that increasing
numbers of *imbutfo* soldiers left for the districts after Bunu's death.
When Johannes Smuts visited Labotsibeni in April 1901 she had
only 400 men with her. Smuts recalled the thousands of soldiers
who attended the *Incwala* in the 1890s and told her that "she must
have become a very small *inkosi* and have very much less power than
previously."[5] General meetings of the council of chiefs were rarely
convened during and after the war, and when the Queen Regent
called a meeting of the council in 1904 to discuss colonial taxation
policy she was forced to levy fines on many local chiefs so that they
would attend.[6] Drought in 1903 and 1905 led many in the drier
reaches of the country to doubt her ability to make rain. As David
Forbes remarked, Swaziland was in the process of becoming "two
countries" in the early twentieth century, as the cleavages inherent
in Swazi social organization deepened.[7] In June 1905, the Resident
Commissioner in Swaziland noted that "as matters now stand a number of chiefs dissent from the Queen's policy and actions and do not
support her [and] as long as this division lasts her power of mischief
need not be feared."[8]

As the nature and implications of British colonial land policy became evident a new alliance was quickly forged. The Swazi delegation
to Selborne in July 1905 included a number of the country's more
powerful chiefs, including some hitherto hostile to the Queen Regent.[9] From then until late 1908, the chiefs buried traditional ani-
mosities in a common quest to reverse the tide of British land policy.
This development was viewed with considerable alarm by the administration. They reacted by downplaying the voluntary nature of the
alliance and attributing it to the "great personal terror" with which
the Regent was regarded.[10] The Swazi chieftainship – fronted by the
Regent, Malunge, and their black and white advisers (the so-called
Zombode Party) – initially adopted the passive strategy of petition
and delegation to progressively higher levels of the colonial hier-
archy. In 1907, in order to finance these activities, all the chiefs
agreed to a national levy and forced their followers to seek work.
When the 1908 Swazi delegation to the Colonial Office returned
empty-handed, the Swazi chiefs began to see the futility of this method
of protest. They then seriously debated the possibility of armed

157   Policy, Partition, and Protest

resistance but finally rejected it. In late 1908 individual chiefs began a scramble to look after their own regional interests and the unity began to crumble.

In early 1908, when the Special Commissioner George Grey was trying to accumulate information from local chiefs for land-partition recommendations, he was confronted by a wall of silence. By the time he reached the Mankiana district in late 1908, he found a more co-operative attitude and a willingness to supply information. In 1909, the Queen Regent refused to appeal the particulars of the partition on the grounds that "the Government knows plainly that [we] have all along disapproved of the division of the land."[11] Despite her explicit instructions, many regional chiefs broke with the Queen Regent's policy and lodged appeals (largely unsuccessfully) to have extra land, favourite grazing grounds, timber stands, and traditional burial-grounds included within the reserves.[12] By mid-1909, the Regent was again having difficulty getting chiefs to attend council meetings, and there was antagonism and hostility concerning her attempts to exercise central control over the flow of Swazi migrant labour (see chapter 4).

Within the country districts local tensions flared, particularly after 1914. Land disputes were not new to Swazi society, but the sudden constriction of the size of many chiefdoms as a result of the land partition led to serious disagreements over chiefdom boundaries and in many cases to "faction fights" between the followers of chiefs. Colonial courts usually came down heavily on these "disturbers of the public peace," but colonial policing and legislation was largely ineffectual in controlling what were often exceedingly bloody fracas. In the early 1920s the Hlatikulu gaol was often "filled to overflowing with faction fighters."[13]

Although the Swazi chiefs did no more than discuss the possibilities of armed revolt, the colonial administration were worried about it.[14] For Selborne in particular, the neighbouring Bambatha Rebellion provided an uncomfortable warning, particularly as the Swazi were more united than the fragmented rebels in Natal.[15] While the Swazi had been peaceably disarmed in 1903, they could potentially form an army of several thousand men. In 1906, after Selborne visited Swaziland, ordinary Swazi began to sport assegais and shields in an ostentatious manner designed to engender alarm. As Coryndon noted, "It is the shield as much as the spear which has so strong an effect in fostering the warlike spirit of the Swazis."[16] Colonial officials were further disquieted by the realization that a revolt under a united chieftainship would take the form of a "mass" uprising. Collaborating chiefs, the ruin of many an anti-colonial revolt, would be hard to locate in such an environment. It was fears such as these, rather than the force of argument in petition and delegation, that gave the Swazi chiefs some influence on colonial state policy and won for them some important concessions, particularly over the size and location of the reserves (see chapter 7).

As the Queen Regent and her closest advisers continued to oppose colonial land policy, the administration debated various proposals to depose the Regent.[17] One of the more startling was Robert Coryndon's plan, formulated in secret meetings with white settlers in 1907, to take advantage of what he perceived to be popular disaffection with the Queen Regent. Totally ignorant of Swazi succession procedures he proposed that Labotsibeni immediately be deposed and replaced by her grandson, Sobhuza, at that time a youth of only eight. As he noted to Selborne, "Till she is safely away I shall never feel happy."[18] He thought the action would divert attention away from the despised 1907 Partition Proclamation, remove from the public stage an intransigent ruler and her "semi-alien" advisers, and "stamp this Administration as a strong Administration."[19] Selborne reserved judgment on the headstrong plan, and in a cautious administrative climate, radical proposals such as this received short shrift.

A closer look at the Swazi chiefs' protests reveals the issues around which a disparate social class could rally. The Swazi's fundamental challenge was that Britain did not have the right to rule the country. Clauses guaranteeing Swazi independence included in Boer-British Conventions of the 1880s were frequently cited to criticize the Swaziland Order-in-Council of 1903 (by which Britain assumed control of Swaziland) and to attack all subsequent legislation passed by the colonial state.[20]

A second major concern of the Swazi rulers was British appropriation of their juridical authority, through the establishment of a colonial legal code and the wide powers of colonial courts. In 1905 Malunge summed up their sentiments in this way: "[The chiefs] are losing their power in the country, because they had not now the power to decide in civil matters between natives. If a native were dissatisfied with the decision of a chief, he went to the Magistrate's court, and got the matter settled there. Their subjects now treated them with contempt, because they know that their chiefs had no power over them."[21]

The Zombode Party was particularly critical that the Swazi were being forced to pay for an administration to which they had fundamental objections. The Queen Regent repeatedly attacked Milner's decision to cancel the Private Revenue Concession which should have garnered her an annual income of £12,000. No payments were made after 1899 and in 1904 Labotsibeni claimed £60,000 as back-payment and demanded that payments be resumed. Milner denied the existence of the debt, cancelled the concession, and expropriated all concession revenues on the grounds that the mass of Swazi would benefit. In fact, his real motives lay in the direction of colonial economy and his desire not to provide the Regent with a large source of revenue with which to contest colonial policy.[22]

Colonial land (and labour) policy provoked the most bitter and impassioned response from the chiefs. Flights of imagery such as "being killed," "living in darkness," "being pushed into the mud," and "being stripped naked" were common in their articulation of the effects of land alienation. The chiefs appealed to the dubious history of concession granting and to white manipulation of Mbandeni in the concessions era of the late 1880s. They quite properly claimed that under the Swazi tenurial system, land was inalienable and therefore by intention and definition only leased to whites. As Malunge pointed out to Selborne in 1906, he did not "consider for a moment that the white man has got any land in Swaziland ... the land is ours and the white people were only lent rights here, [and] we wish the King to govern us in our land with our land."[23]

Underlying these emotional charges was a fear that the colonial state intended to "destroy our national life and put an end to our separate existence, merging us indiscriminately among the scattered tribes of the Transvaal."[24] Loss of control over land, the basis of the chiefs' power over the commoners, threatened to undermine completely their power. The emasculation of the Swazi chiefs of the eastern Transvaal and the weakening of their hold over their followers located on white farms had been observed with alarm by the chiefs of Swaziland. They feared that this process was also on the colonial agenda for Swaziland:

We wish to remain in our country which we chiefs hold for the Paramount Chief. It displeases us to hear that our country will be cut up into farms and we fear that any natives on those farms will cease to have any respect for the chiefs but will transfer their allegiance to the landlords.[25]

In 1908, when partition had become a painful reality, and the Swazi delegation to Britain had returned unsuccessful, the Queen Regent castigated a colonial prospectus which threatened to shatter chief-commoner relations within Swazi society:

Were the people also sold? What I think is being done is that my people are being taken away too. What about them? You are tearing my skirt. My people are just like the land that is said to have been sold ... Where am I going to live with this people of mine? Have they also been sold?[26]

Another important Dlamini chief, Nogcogco, added that "if the land is cut up the farmers will stop the people coming up to work for him [Sobhuza]. Once the land is divided it is done with."[27]

Coryndon's attempts to assuage the chiefs by arguing that the young king would have "half the country" and "plenty of people to plough for him" were no more than a sop. By this stage, the chiefs had no doubt about the real nature of colonial designs on Swazi labour and land. The resolution of the labour problems of the settler-estate sector and the provision of large areas of land for capitalist enterprise had brought the conflict between a pre-capitalist ruling class and a nascent capitalist agricultural sector in the country to a head. It was thus not simply the loss of land *per se* which roused the Swazi ruling class but the concomitant loss of their followers, political authority, and surplus labour which their control over land had given them.

After the mapping of reserve boundaries by George Grey in 1908, the Zombode Party continued to draft petitions and make formal protests challenging the legitimacy of the land partition to successive High Commissioners.[28] But colonial intransigence forced the chiefs to turn to other modes of achieving their ends, particularly as July 1914 approached. Between 1909 and 1914, the Queen Regent had softened her demands by acknowledging the fact of partition and seeking a better deal within it:

Please do not think that we are trying to upset the whole principle of the division of land ... What we now want is a greater amount of land. Even if we got more it would not be sufficient but it would help to make the position less acute. The white man is given more land in proportion than we are. If all the natives who are on concession land left it and entered Native Reserves you would see that there is not sufficient land for us today.[29]

Part of this request for more land was the desire to acquire control over the extensive crown lands. High Commissioner Gladstone stood firmly by his predecessor's position and refused to transfer crown lands to the reserves. The Queen Regent and her advisers consequently decided to adopt a more aggressive strategy to recapture land lost in the partition and Swazi commoners left stranded on that land. As she later recalled: "I felt I must lose no time. I told the Council all our weapons had failed and now with our own strength we must set out with determination to buy back as much as we can of our dear little Swaziland. They all agreed to assist by voluntary contributions."[30]

The black South African activist, Pixley Seme, was drawn into the Swaziland land issue to advise on the best procedure for land re-purchase.[31] As a co-founder of the African National Congress in 1912, Seme was an active campaigner against the South African Native Lands Act of 1913 and was more than willing to lend his weight to the Swazi case. Seme publicized the situation in Swaziland in a vituperative series of articles in the newspaper *Abantu Batho* in early 1913.[32] He predicted that legislation similar to the Native Lands Act would be passed in Swaziland, and observed that the Act would apply to Swaziland anyway if and when the country was transferred to the Union. His advice to the Queen Regent was to purchase as much land as possible with funds garnered from all possible sources, including the Swazi population itself.[33]

This recommendation to raise funds for land repurchase by taxing homesteads was not a new idea. In 1909, the Queen Regent had levied a tax of £3 on all adult male Swazis and demanded that the chiefs "call all their young men to get money to hand over to the Government to repurchase the white man's land for the Swazis."[34] Colonial officials in Swaziland were alarmed that land scheduled for white settlement might find its way back into the reserves. Under pressure from Coryndon, Selborne drafted legislation prohibiting the purchase by Swazis of land outside the reserves. The Colonial Office refused to endorse the legislation on the grounds that it was inconsistent with the prevailing policy in much of southern Africa.[35] Local colonial fears were unwarranted in any event. The Queen Regent's policy was not supported by the regional chiefs, not enough was raised to make any purchases, and the idea was dropped.

What Seme added to the situation in 1913 was his South African experience and his knowledge of alternative sources of funds. Loans of £130,000 were negotiated with South African banks but these fell through after colonial intervention. In addition to concern about Swazi land purchase, colonial officials were opposed to the Swazi chiefs incurring large debts through the acquisition of land at spec-ulative selling prices.[36] The Queen Regent was more successful in securing a smaller loan of £5,000 from the Native Recruiting Corporation in February 1914 with which to purchase a 6,000 acre farm in the Swaziland lowveld. NRC involvement undoubtedly arose from the company's desire to ingratiate itself with the country's chiefs in the interests of the mine labour supply, but the colonial state was less charitable, criticizing the NRC for its actions.[37]

The Zombode Party eventually incurred liabilities of £48,000 for five farms with a total of 75,000 acres. To dampen the continued hostility of the Swazi chieftainship and to absorb Swazi financial resources which might be put to "more embarrassing uses," Coryndon temporarily reversed Selborne's earlier intransigence on the question of crown lands and approved the purchase of 40,000 acres by the Regent.[38] He later added another 28,000 acres of crown land in the south of the country to the reserves.[39] These two concessions did not signal any major shift in colonial policy on the disposal of crown land to white settlers, since these areas were already heavily settled by Swazi and the transfers were simply made to gain political capital.

The bulk of the Zombode Party's debt was eventually met by exactions from Swazi homesteads.[40] In late 1913, an internal tax of £3 per chief and £1 per male adult was imposed by Labotsibeni. This was raised to £10 and £5 respectively in 1914, when Swazi men were urged to "work to the death to earn the money, in the same manner in which in past times they took up their weapons to die for their chiefs."[41] The land repurchase scheme did not get very far, however. Although the brainchild of Seme and the Queen Regent, the other chiefs initially agreed to take part since all stood to gain by having their landholdings augmented. At a meeting at Zombode the chiefs agreed to persuade their followers to take advances from labour recruiters and pay these into the land repurchase fund. Before long however, the Swazi chieftainship was wracked with internal dissension and acrimonious charges and countercharges over the issue of fund raising. Rumours that funds collected from the Swazi were being embezzled by the Queen Regent added fuel to a more serious charge.[42] It quickly became evident to the southern chiefs, who were experiencing the bite of the partition most intensely, that they would reap little benefit from land repurchase and that all funds would be directed to acquiring land in the Dlamini heartland in the Ezulwini valley and other areas of symbolic importance to the aristocracy. As the Queen Regent admitted to Coryndon, purchase of land at Ezulwini was a priority because the area was "intrinsically more sacred and more valuable than gold because it is the circuit of our historic kraals and birthplace of the Nation."[43] The prospect of the land repurchase scheme being used to buttress the aristocracy's position without providing extra land for local rulers and people rankled with the non-Dlamini chiefs. Their vigorous protests to Zombode eventually forced a vaguely worded concession from the Regent that "as far as is possible land will in future be bought near the different chiefs."[44] Although the chiefs finally agreed to continue to force their followers to pay the tax under these conditions, they were thwarted by internal resistance from Swazi commoners to the demands of the land-repurchase program.

In late 1913 chiefs began to demand funds from their followers and forwarded the money to Zombode.[45] Dissatisfied with the general response, Prince Malunge personally supervised collections later in the year, touring the countryside with several labour recruiters, including George Morris of Marwick & Morris. The Queen Regent also appealed to mineworkers on the Rand and collectors were sent to Johannesburg (appendix H).[46] The response was so poor that Malunge visited the mines himself in October 1914 but he also "failed to get any support from the Swazis employed there."[47] The program had ground to a halt again, this time because of the resistance of commoners. Regional chiefs continued to be "extremely dissatisfied with the supervision of the funds" by the Zombode Party though colonial officials detected more general opposition: "Natives complain that they now have to pay three lots of taxes – the usual Government tax, landowners tax and Chief Regent's taxes. It seems to me that the constant demand of money by the Chief Regent, the purpose of which the natives say they are ignorant, is not conducive to the well-being of the natives generally."[48] The colonial state willingly took charge of collected funds at the request of the chiefs who began another concerted effort to collect land repurchase funds. By April 1915, the chiefs were forced to admit, in chief Nomadakolu's words, that "in the matter of land purchases the people have defeated us. They will not bring money."[49] Tax collection meetings at which Zombode representatives were present were widely boycotted and excuses abounded for the tardy response.[50]

The chiefs' failure led them to enlist the state's power in their struggle with the commoners. A Swazi spokesman put the case as follows:

Although the chiefs urge the people to make their contributions, we are powerless, and she [the Queen Regent] wishes the Government to help in collecting the money. She would like ... the District Officials to collect this money at the same time as the collection of the ordinary tax. The natives said that would be harsh but she replied that she was forced to take this step because they had not made a ready and proper response to her requests for money. She wants the Government to assist because it is powerful.[51]

Even the influential southern chief Bokweni Mamba, who had successfully mobilized his followers for mine work to raise funds in 1907–8, supported the call for state intervention:

About the land purchase, do not be tender with the people. They will not obey and they defy us. Request payment at once. Let the Assistant Commissioners collect it all this year. The people take no notice of us but the Government has power and the Chief Regent wishes to avail herself of that power.[52]

The chiefs requested legislation to force all Swazi men to pay a land tax of £5 but this was turned down. Colonial officials agreed that funds had to be raised to meet the debt without aggravating the growing rift between chiefs and commoners.

In 1915, officials responded by making colonial tax camps collection centres for the land-debt fund. While district officials were supposed to accept "whatever was offered," they were not averse to using "moral pressure" which included requests for 10 shillings from each taxpayer.[53] It still took the colonial state more than four years of persuasion and cajoling to liquidate the debt.[54] When this was achieved in 1919, colonial officials refused to continue collections for future land repurchase, claiming that "the people have been very dissatisfied about this matter and it is now hard to get money."[55]

The commoners' resistance was partially a function of the sheer size of the internal tax, the largest yet demanded, which threatened to cut into the reproductive needs of the homestead. As long as Swazi homesteads could acquire continued short-term access to land either in the reserves or on crown or private land, the Queen Regent's plea that they should remember "that your chief is not buying [land] for himself but for you and your children" lacked much conviction.[56] The general erosion of the chiefs' authority which had begun with colonial rule also meant that increasingly the chiefs could be defied without retribution (see chapter 10). In addition, the earners of the bulk of the Swazi wage – young migrant mineworkers – must have resented further inroads into their earning power, as the lack of success of collections from mineworkers in Johannesburg seems to show.[57] Yet, while there was widespread opposition to the demands of the Swazi ruling class, the poorest response came from a particular section of the commoner population – the farm-tenant homestead.

The failure of the Swazi chiefs to generate the funds necessary to make land repatriation a self-sustaining venture meant that the colonial state could respond relatively freely to the demand of white landowners that the whole program be stopped. The settlers' response to the Zombode Party's scheme was hostile from the start. They ordered their tenants not to pay and the tenant homesteads were of course happy to obey.[58] While the more far-sighted settlers opposed the chiefs, on the basis that land suitable for white settlement would be returned to the reserves, the majority were more concerned about labour cost. The Assistant Commissioner at Mankiana commented that, "where they have advised the natives not to pay, it is only with the object of getting labour cheap as possible."[59] The farmers were aware that the collection of funds from tenants would in all probability lead to demands for increased wages for farm work.

When colonial officials began their collections on behalf of the Swazi chiefs in 1915, they trod cautiously and made no demands from tenant homesteads at all since "it is undesirable that natives should be subjected on any large scale to risk of ejectment for non-payment of rent by reason of contributing to the land fund."[60] Hence, the response of the colonial state to the entreaty of the Swazi chiefs was strictly conditional. Overt state coercion was not available to them, and their requests were also subject to the anterior needs of the settler-estate sector. The support of the colonial state for the chiefs' campaign to exact funds from the commoners certainly did not imply tacit consent for the land repatriation program as a whole. Colonial officials remained concerned about their ability to regulate Swazi land purchase and in January 1915, legislation was passed which vested control of all Swazi land purchases in the High Commissioner. This effectively removed the Swazi chiefs from the open land market, even had they the means to raise sufficient funds.[61]

Colonial legislation sought to control and inhibit, though not necessarily prohibit, land purchase by the Swazi.[62] It was enacted in part to avoid a repetition of the serious financial difficulties which an over-enthusiastic chieftainship had got themselves into in 1913 and 1914. It was also meant to discourage land speculators from buying land cheaply from the crown and reselling it to Swazi chiefs. But it was first and foremost a response to longstanding "unease" on the part of colonial officials and white settlers that land earmarked for white settlement would be lost to the reserves.[63] The legislation was designed to pacify the settlers as well as to control further land purchase in the more fertile areas of the Swaziland middleveld and in the Ezulwini valley. The failure of the chiefs' policy proved to be another victory for the white settler over the Swazi chief. However, the settler triumph was to be rather hollow. While they managed to prevent large additional areas of land falling under the chiefs' sway they remained unable to exercise the necessary degree of control over tenant homesteads. The tenants seized the chance to hide behind their landlords in dealings with their chiefs, but equally refused to defer to the landlords' own demands. Indeed, the intensity of tenant resistance to the domination of white settlers was one of the major reasons that the land partition failed to achieve colonial aims for a flourishing settler-estate sector in Swaziland.

CHAPTER NINE

Landlords, Tenants, and Farm Workers

Mr. Hintze came to the ground and said he had come to plough. Before that we did not know that we were on his land. We thought we were in native area. He told us that if we did not want to be under him we must move. We moved at once. But we moved back later without telling him.

Cabukela Mkonta, 1916

Settler-estate production in Swaziland experienced a slow and halting process of expansion after the land partition. White immigration fell short of the vision that had sustained both colonial official and landowner through the disturbed partition years. By the early 1920s, the number of farms in the country had increased to over 300 and the number of whites involved in agriculture to around 500. The major farming areas were in the south of the country and around Bremersdorp, but large tracts of land remained unoccupied and uncultivated by white landowners. Farming was small-scale, under-capitalized, and labour-intensive, characteristics of settler agriculture not only confined to Swaziland at this time. The constraints on capital accumulation were many. Poor access to external markets, Union embargoes and tariff barriers, and limited credit facilities all provided considerable obstacles to settlers trying to compete with South African capitalist agriculture that received massive infusions of state support.[1]

Maize for the local market continued to be the main crop on white farms. In 1921, despite some diversification in cropping patterns, maize still occupied 70 per cent of the area under cultivation. Repeated efforts to reduce costs, particularly through the wage bill, were nullified by cheaper imported South African maize. In 1910, the Swaziland Farmers Association attempted to secure an exclusive contract to supply all the maize needs of the government and the local mines. The plan was scotched by a poor harvest in 1911.[2] During and after the First World War, cotton, tobacco, and citrus were added to the farm roster. Tobacco farmers joined the Union Co-operative Society and assured themselves of a regular market for their product. Cotton growers were less fortunately placed since "the high cost of machinery and the unorganised state of native labour

[made] the production of this commodity prohibitive from a commercial point of view."[3] The precarious position of most farmers was brought home in 1921 when the National Bank of South Africa called in all Swaziland overdrafts: "The financial outlook is very grave. The majority of farmers are without capital and will be crippled this season if they cannot raise money to tide them over the current very bad period ... in some cases farmers have no money to pay wages and naturally the natives are not prepared to wait for their wages."[4] Capital shortages were a recurrent problem for settler producers. In desperation some of them took to mine recruiting as a sideline in order to raise capital from capitation fees.[5] This practice led to a great deal of acrimony in the settler community as the mines posed one of the major threats to the farm labour supply. While capital shortages were an important constraint on settler-estate production, they were compounded by problems experienced with the farm labour force.

The only reasonably successful form of settler production in the country was cattle ranching. By 1921, there were over 63,000 head of cattle (with a cash value of £250,000) on several ranches in the Swaziland lowveld.[6] A number of individual settlers ran large herds of several thousand head, but the major operators were companies controlled by British and Natal capital.[7] In 1919, the Bar R Ranch of the Swaziland Ranching & Development Company had close to 10,000 head, and an estimated carrying capacity of 35,000 head. The Natalia Ranching Company had 8,500 head (18,000 by 1922) and the Swazi Coal Mines Company a further 5,000. Herds were built up by extensive purchase from Swazi homesteads and stock was imported from South Africa, Australia, and New Zealand for cross-breeding.[8] By 1918, the various companies had invested £130,000 in imported cattle. When the Union Government relaxed its restrictions on cattle importation to South Africa in 1916, the companies were able to export slaughter cattle to Johannesburg and Durban. Exports increased from 389 head in 1917 to over 3,000 head in 1920. In 1921, slaughter cattle to the value of £26,240 and hides worth £2,099 were exported. Capital shortages were not a great problem for the ranching companies, particularly in the early years of production. But they did still require a large labour force. While they were in a better position to secure labour than the other types of farmer, their operations were far from problem-free. The ranchers also tended to see labour tenancy as a means of controlling labour costs, and faced the same general problems which accompanied this form of labour control.[9]

The final element in the mix of white agricultural producers were trek farmers from the eastern Transvaal who used the Swaziland highveld as winter grazing for their sheep. By 1920, close to 300,000 sheep were being brought into the country each year. With grazing land at a premium, these farmers extended their grazing eastwards and even leased highveld land from the chiefs within the reserves. While their labour needs were much less significant than those of the settler-estate producers and the ranching companies, the trek farmers were anxious to retain tenants on their Swaziland properties. Shepherds were needed to look after their flocks, tenant families in Swaziland could be "kaffir farmed" to raise funds for agricultural operations in the Transvaal, and tenants under their control in Swaziland could be used to ease their labour problems across the border.

Prior to July 1914 and the expiry of Selborne's "period of grace" white landowners could take little advantage of the new relations with "squatters" on their land. Some landowners tried to cajole Swazi homesteads into signing agreements but the latter were under no compulsion to accede to these demands. The owner of the aptly titled farm "Nil Desperandum" in southern Swaziland made agreements with the fifteen homesteads on his property to supply labour but the arrangement was simply a verbal one which the tenants broke with impunity.[10] In the main, settlers in search of farm labour were forced to submit to the unsatisfactory "free market" conditions which had prevailed in the pre-partition years. They continued to have serious problems acquiring and controlling farm workers, particularly since many Swazi homesteads refused to acknowledge their new overlords and withheld their labour as one means of protest:

There are a number of natives ... who refuse to work or move off the farm and who in a high handed manner tell us that the ground is theirs and they acknowledge no white man as owner ... They worked on the farm for the owners when they lived there for seven years from 1887 to 1894, but now will agree to nothing. I am willing to allow the natives residing on the farm to remain there if they provide labour or pay rent, but they cannot I think be in a position to defy us today.[11]

The weak position of the settlers was exaggerated by the massive flight of male Swazis to the Rand mines after 1910 (see chapter 5). Farm wages increased steadily between 1909 and 1914, surpassing those for farm work in the Transvaal, although they still compared unfavourably with those on offer at the local mines and on the Rand.[12]

One of Selborne's intentions in allowing a five-year gestation period before the system of labour tenancy came into effect was to give

TABLE 16

Distribution of Swazi Population after Partition

District	Homesteads in Reserves		Homesteads outside Reserves		Total
	Number	%	Number	%	
Mbabane	513	46.8	582	53.2	752
Mankiana	727	55.4	585	44.6	1,095
Hlatikulu	1,755	66.8	874	33.2	2,629
Peak	389	51.7	363	48.3	752
Ubombo	530	53.1	469	46.9	999
Total	3,914	57.7	2,873	42.3	6,787

Source: SA, D09/2, Grey to Selborne, 11 February 1909.

colonial officials time to direct a gradual removal of Swazi homesteads to the reserves. This strategy was supposed to minimize the
need for mass forced eviction and the social unrest likely to follow.
Assistant Commissioners were given explicit instructions "to use their
influence with both landowners and natives, to ensure that the end
of the term of concurrent occupation shall entail as little disturbance
as is possible and to induce natives, who will not desire to come to
arrangements with landowners, to move into native area before the
date arrives."[13] Despite the fact that reserve boundaries were drawn
with the explicit intention of including as many Swazis as possible
within the reserves, more than 40 per cent of Swazi homesteads were
excluded (table 16).[14] Forced resettlement therefore had the potential to be quite extensive. Colonial officials quickly became aware that
this "voluntary" movement was not taking place as anticipated and
that the majority of homesteads were remaining in situ despite considerable efforts to persuade them to move.[15]

It is difficult to ascertain precisely what degree of resettlement
took place between 1909 and 1914; contemporary records simply
note how slight it was. Indeed, it appears that by 1914 the number
of Swazi homesteads on settler land had actually increased by several
hundred (table 17). In the Hlatikulu district, for example, 117 homesteads had moved off white farms by June 1914, yet there were 313
more homesteads on the farms than there had been in 1909. The
Mbabane and Ubombo districts experienced a net decrease of homesteads on white land, probably as a result of a greater degree of
resettlement (and/or a lower rate of homestead formation) in these

TABLE 17
Population Redistribution, 1909–14

District	Number of Homesteads outside Reserves		Difference
	1909	1914	
Mbabane	582	395	− 187
Mankiana	585	704	+ 119
Hlatikulu	874	1,187	+ 313
Peak	363	649	+ 286
Ubombo	469	270	− 199
Total	2,873	3,205	+ 332

Source: Compiled from D09/2 and RCS 405/14.

two districts.[16] There are suggestions in the record that some chiefs encouraged their followers to resettle in the reserves. In April 1914, reports circulated that the Queen Regent had told all Swazi that they should move to reserves rather than submit to tenancy agreements, and colonial officials expressed concern that such an order might lead to a mass exodus of farm labour.[17] In general, however, the various forces encouraging population immobility far outweighed these considerations.

First, a number of commoners undoubtedly saw an opportunity to loosen their ties with the Swazi chiefs by remaining on alienated land and acquiring a productive base independent of the chiefs' control.[18] The primary constraint on this option was the type of tenancy relationship which could be expected from the landlord. Many Swazi had an astute idea of what this was likely to be given their dealings with settlers in the past, but the option would certainly have been attractive to homesteads on the estates of absentee landlords. On the evidence from other parts of the region, one might speculate that homesteads engaging in production for market might have looked for as unfettered a degree of access to land as possible, whether in farms or on the reserves. In practice, with so few Swazi homesteads producing marketable surpluses, this factor probably had little effect.

To a much larger number of homesteads it was not clear why they should voluntarily abandon established homestead sites and cultivated fields. In many areas there were no obvious signs of settler production and some landowners would never even have been seen

by their prospective tenants. After 1914, colonial officials often commented that there were landlords who had taken no steps to avail
themselves of the new tenancy arrangements and that Swazi homesteads on those estates remained undisturbed.[19] Landowners holding
land for speculative purposes deliberately made no attempt either
before or after 1914 to induce tenants to move, arguing that a resident labour pool on the estate would make the land more attractive
to potential settlers.[20] Homesteads on crown land (about 34 per cent
of the total population on alienated land) were allowed to remain
by the colonial state, pending sale to incoming settlers. This proved
to be no more than a temporary respite for tenants as crown-land
sales began to accelerate, especially after the First World War.

A number of other factors also inhibited resettlement in the period
before July 1914. Between 1909 and 1912, the feeling in the rural
districts was that the colonial decision to "cut up the land" might
somehow be reversed or at least postponed until Sobhuza came of
age in 1920. When the Swazi chiefs began to collect funds for land
repurchase in 1912, they tacitly acknowledged the intractability of
the colonial position. A second factor then came into play. In order
to expedite their collections the chiefs held out the hope to all Swazi
tenants that the farms on which they were resident were scheduled
for repurchase and incorporation into the reserves. Many probably
saw little point in moving to the reserves in these circumstances.[21]

In conducting the land partition in 1908, George Grey had stressed:

The principle that no native chief has exclusive control of any area, or
portion of an area, must be adopted and insisted upon. The native areas
are for the use of the Swazi Nation as a whole, every Swazi has the right to
enter native area. It will be the duty of the Assistant Commissioners to see
that no chief is able to exclude any native from the area.[22]

Grey therefore did not try and allocate reserve land proportional in
size to the existing chiefdoms. Some chiefs had virtually all of the
land formerly under their jurisdiction included within the reserves,
others had very little. The proportion of followers who were incorporated also varied considerably from chief to chief. In the Mankiana
district, for example, virtually all of chief Dalada Dlamini's followers
were included, while 60 per cent of those of a neighbouring chief,
Mpapela Mabuza, were not.[23] The more important chiefs tended to
be better accommodated in this respect than their minor counterparts. To have ensured that each chief received an area of reserve
land proportional in size to his former chiefdom or to the number
of his followers would have been virtually impossible given the nature

of the partition procedure adopted by the colonial state. But Grey considered such logistical constraints irrelevant in any case:

The chiefs do not appear to understand that no chiefs have exclusive ownership in any reserves. The result of the partition must be that the present division of Swaziland among the various chiefs come to an end; the native areas must be looked upon as open ... to all Swazis.[24]

In support of this position, Selborne informed the chiefs in 1908 that the reserves were to be regarded as "national property" and that individual chiefs could not lay exclusive claim to reserve land formerly under their control, and therefore prevent Swazi resettlement on that land.[25]

What these colonial social engineers failed to anticipate was the opposition which this would arouse from the chiefs. As early as 1909, some chiefs, particularly in the south of the country, began to express opposition to the colonial attempt to "make the natives treat these areas as national lands, and not as those of any particular tribe or tribes."[26] Confronted with the loss of land and labour to white settlers, they feared that this added constraint would weaken their powers still further. By 1913, this viewpoint was held by most of the ruling stratum and led the Resident Commissioner to issue an official warning that no resettled homestead could be excluded from the reserves.[27] Legislation was enacted in late 1913 to give the Assistant Commissioners power to locate resettled homesteads anywhere in the reserves and to prosecute chiefs who resisted forced resettlement.[28] By February 1914, as the period of concurrent occupation drew to a close, colonial officials conceded that "it is useless to expect that natives will look upon native area as common to the whole tribe."[29] As a result of Swazi opposition and the incapacity of the state to restructure land rights the partition consequently produced no fundamental alteration in the pre-colonial principle of territorial jurisdiction nor in the modes of land control and allocation to commoners, at least within the reserves.

The implications of this development for population mobility must now be spelled out. In many cases, chiefs simply did not have sufficient land within the reserves to allocate to their own followers stranded on white farms. These homesteads were generally unwilling to *khonta* (give allegiance) to other chiefs who did have land for them, and who insisted on this as a condition of occupation. They preferred to remain on crown or private land.[30] While some homestead heads undoubtedly balked at the idea of being treated as new arrivals in a different chiefdom, with all that that implied for loss of status, many chiefs also reacted negatively to the prospect of their followers coming under another chief's control. Some homesteads attempted to move to reserves and to disregard the authority of the local chief. They invariably met with opposition from those already there if they refused to *khonta*.[31] Other homesteads did move and did *khonta*. The result was an upsurge of bad feeling between chiefs which, on occasion, led to eruptions of violence between their followers.

Neighbouring chiefs on good terms compromised by extending a practice which had been carried out on a small scale in the nineteenth century.[32] The followers of a chief with limited land resources were "lent" to a neighbouring chief with ample land, in similar fashion to the traditional practice of *kusisa* (or cattle loaning). The loaned followers were settled on land under the host chief and, in exchange for access to land, provided him with tribute labour, while remaining liable for tribute and tribute labour to their own chief.[33] This eventually led to a far greater degree of inter-mixing amongst the followers of different chiefs. In the short term, however, the option was not particularly attractive to many homesteads, who preferred to remain where they were and take their chances on the settler-estates of the country:

A considerable number of natives have reluctantly entered into agreements [with landowners] because they believe they have no reasonable hope of getting suitable sites in native areas without very considerable trouble ... They have said that will arouse the hostility and obstruction of the chiefs and natives in those areas and that they prefer not to take this course and would rather enter into agreements with landowners.[34]

In the longer term, the impact of population immobility produced a distinctive spatial pattern in which "some areas are thickly populated while other areas in the vicinity, just as suitable, are not looked upon with favour, although there may be lots of room, because it would mean living under another than their own chief."[35] Any analysis of the "underdevelopment" and ecological deterioration of the Swazi reserves after 1914 would certainly have to take this factor into account. It is quite likely, for example, that some areas consequently experienced rapid ecological decline while others remained relatively stable.[36] Hence, the impoverished state of the reserves identified by some observers in the 1930s may have reflected a maldistribution in reserve resources resulting from the persistence of pre-capitalist structures of territoriality as much as any absolute shortage of grazing and agricultural land in the reserves.

Many of the forces encouraging population immobility in Swazi-

TABLE 18
Evictions from Farms in Mbabane District, 1914–18

Year	Notices of Ejectment	Households Affected	Numbers Moved	Written Contracts
1914–15	23	114	65	47
1915–16	8	42	24	6
1916–17	13	35	31	1
1917–18	11	20	14	0
Total	55	211	134	54

Source: SA, RCS 759/15, 141/16, 578/16

land persisted after 1914, although there was an upsurge in resettlement as landlords began to exercise their new powers of eviction. Assistant Commissioners in all districts reported spasmodic population movement in the years after 1914 as a result of tenant resistance to landlord demands and the forced evictions which followed. In the Mbabane district at least, forced evictions fell off steadily after an initial rush in 1914 (table 18). Between 1914 and 1918, a total of 134 homesteads were evicted from settler-estates. In the Hlatikulu district, 170 homesteads had moved or been moved by July 1916. In neither district would these movements necessarily have been to the reserves.[37] In the early 1920s, there was a temporary upsurge in forced evictions with a renewed influx of white settlers into the country under the colonial state's Returned Soldier scheme.[38] The fact that there was never any mass forced expulsion from concessions does not mean that Swazi homesteads simply acquiesced in the new social relations of production imposed by the conditions of tenancy.

The regulations governing conditions of tenancy promulgated in 1907 had been kept deliberately vague by Selborne. No specific guidelines were laid down as to terms of service, the Resident Commissioner simply reserved the right to vet all tenancy agreements. A subsequent colonial decision to permit two alternative forms of tenancy – rental payment or labour service – arose from the conviction that any appearance of forcing Swazi tenants to provide labour might lead to discontent and a mass movement to the reserves. As colonial officials were well aware, this policy provided no more than an illusion of choice since landlords had the power to evict tenants who refused to offer labour service on demand. Despite his desire to avoid the growth of "kaffir farming" in Swaziland, Selborne also decided to exact rent from tenants on estates where labour was not required in order to avoid a massive shift of population to those areas.

Attempts to standardize the terms of service began in 1911 in order to try and avoid tenant discontent from variable landlord demands, to ensure that all landlords would have at least a modicum of labour, and to clamp down on any move towards "farming of natives on a large scale."³⁹ The opinions of white landowners were sought through the Swaziland Farmers Association. Those of the Swazi chiefs and people were not since by and large they still rejected the whole principle of tenancy.⁴⁰ Not surprisingly, the proposals of the Farmers Association were strongly weighted in their own favour. They included demands that the land on which tenants could "squat," and how much land and stock they could have, should be determined by the landlord; that "squatters" should pay a minimum rental of £1 per adult per annum in advance (or supply an equivalent amount of labour service); that tenants could contract to supply continuous labour at current farm wage rates; and that they should no longer have any responsibility to their chiefs or be regarded as constituents of the chiefs for tax-collection purposes.⁴¹

The final request was rejected by the Resident Commissioner since it would have interfered with a tax-collection system which was serving the state reasonably well.⁴² The other terms were accepted with minor modifications. Rental charges were set at a maximum of £3 per adult per annum. In lieu of rent each adult tenant could be forced to provide between two and six months of unpaid labour service on demand. Alternatively, landlords and tenants could contract for the latter to provide up to six months of labour at a minimum wage of 15 shillings per month. The colonial state appropriated powers of eviction of tenants who refused to submit to landlord demands, since colonial officials feared violent conflagration between landlords and tenants if they did not. In 1913, a standard tenancy form was drawn up with the assistance of the Swaziland Farmers Association "to materially assist both farmers and natives" and copies were printed ready for distribution.⁴³

With these basic guidelines established to the satisfaction of the landlords, Coryndon appealed to the Swazi chiefs to assist him in ensuring a peaceful transition:

I have never proposed to induce Swazis to remain on private land if they do not wish to do so ... My object is not to assist the owners of land to get labour but to assist the Swazis. I look forward to your assistance and the assistance of the chiefs to prevent a large number of people being moved at the same time. I believe many of the Swazis desire to enter into agreements and it is better that they do so than that all the people on private land should be required to move into native area at the same time.[44]

Coryndon was well aware of the threat posed by the chiefs, and realized that the whole colonial design to resolve the farm-labour issue might flounder without their co-operation. He reckoned that the chiefs had ample motive for opposing labour tenancy since they were highly averse to any relationships that would tend to weaken or dissipate their hold over their followers. He feared that the chiefs would either precipitate a mass movement to the reserves or, more likely, advise their followers to resist entering into agreements with landlords. The alarmist reaction to the activities of a Mankiana district chief, Sicunusa Dlamini, is an instance.

Sicunusa, a member of the ruling lineage with a large following, found that the land partition had left 39 of his followers' homesteads (containing approximately 470 people) and one of his own scattered across four farms. Sicunusa ordered his followers not to enter into any tenancy arrangement with landlords. Challenged by the Assistant Commissioner, Sicunusa twice fobbed him off, claiming that he would do nothing without the orders of the Queen Regent and refusing to speak to the landowners on behalf of his followers: "Sicunusa refuses to assist or to take any initiative, despite every endeavour to persuade him that the Chief Regent, nor anybody else for that matter, could alter the present state of affairs ... The landlords concerned are anxious to retain the natives on their land on apparently most advantageous terms, but the natives tell me they are afraid to do anything on account of their chief."[45] Sicunusa was also incensed that two of the landlords were trying to evict some of his followers and ordered them to stay, arguing that he had nowhere in the reserves to move them to. He refused to move his own homestead off one of the farms. A frustrated Assistant Commissioner recommended that "if the Chief is reluctant to move in the matter, he be ejected, and his natives be made to make their own arrangements."[46]

Conscious that Sicunusa's actions might be imitated by other chiefs, Coryndon moved quickly to head off the threat by issuing a stiff warning to the Queen Regent that "if your people are prevented from making reasonable arrangements now they will have to move on to native area."[47] The Queen Regent eventually agreed to tell Sicunusa not to prevent his followers from signing agreements if they wished to do so, though she was sceptical that that was what they desired.[48] Coryndon's general belief that "many of the Swazis desire to enter into agreements" was little more than wishful thinking. Most homestead heads on expropriated land had very little option but to submit to tenancy relations. However, the form and content of the relationship became the object of sustained struggle after 1914.

As July 1914 approached, rumours flew in Swaziland's white-settler community and in the eastern Transvaal that a Swazi rising was imminent. Arms and ammunition were distributed to white farmers and traders living along the Swaziland/Transvaal border but the crucial month came and went without incident.[49] Thus encouraged, landlords began the task of reorganizing their labour supply in earnest. With the full backing of the colonial state, the tables had turned in their favour and the long battle to secure a farm labour force seemed all but won. Cattle farmers in the lowveld and some trek-sheep farmers in the highveld immediately began to clear their lands of Swazi homesteads superfluous to their needs.[50] Landlords elsewhere were more circumspect. Absentee landowners from the Transvaal tried either to exact rent from tenants or to use their control over tenants in Swaziland to ease their labour problems on farms in the eastern Transvaal. Swazi homesteads were ordered to send their young men to serve a period of labour service in the Transvaal in lieu of rent for occupation of the Swaziland estate. This practice aroused the opposition of the Swazi chiefs and *umnumzana*, but it appears to have gone on notwithstanding.[51] Colonial officials were not prepared to intervene except in cases where children were being taken without their parents' consent or where there was evidence of large-scale recruiting by landlords not in possession of recruiters' licences.[52]

Settlers within Swaziland adopted a variety of strategies to secure farm labour from their tenants. Initially they reorganized Swazi settlement on their estates to appointed sites (usually grouped in one area) and expelled homesteads whose labour was not needed.[53] In some cases, tenants were ordered to remove their stock from the farm, even though they themselves were allowed to remain. The landlords then tried to reach formal agreements with their tenants. In practice, slight modifications were made to the basic forms of tenancy agreement established by the administration.

In some cases landlords demanded an annual rental of £1 or £2 per male (or per married male) or per hut from tenants. Many absentee landlords and local landlords not engaged in farming operations adopted this form. Such rent tenancy was most common in the highveld and northern middleveld and lowveld, and could amount to a tidy sum each year. A southern trader, Henwood, who had profited largely by cattle trading in the 1890s, had 174 homesteads on his Hlatikulu estate, "Petrus Keus," in 1914. He made an agreement with his tenants for a rental charge of £1 per annum per hut, which gave him an annual income supplement of over £500; an example of the "kaffir farming" that Selborne had been so anxious to avoid.[54] On some farms, particularly in the south of the country, landlords simply demanded unpaid labour service in exchange for rent-free occupation of the estate by tenants. Exactly how long this period of unpaid service should be and how many homestead members should provide it became a matter of considerable disagreement between landlords and tenants. Most landlords demanded at least three to six months of labour per adult; not many got it.

Under a third form of tenancy relation, the landlord agreed to provide all able-bodied labour on the estate with employment at current farm wage rates, on condition that he was always given first call on the tenant's service and that each period of service be for a continuous period of six months. This form was common on the more productive estates in the south and centre of the country, on ranches, and on farms with a small number of tenants where landlords were anxious to retain a labour supply through guaranteed employment. Actually tenant wages were usually fixed well below the current farm wage for migrant workers, since landlords often built an implicit rental payment into the wage. In 1917, for example, the ordinary farm wage for male labour was 15 to 20 shillings per month whereas tenant labourers earned only 10 to 12 shillings. Some landlords attempted to obtain both labour and a rental fee by binding Swazi homesteads to six months of wage labour at current rates and levying a rental charge of £1 per annum (in effect one or two months of unpaid labour).[55]

Within this basic framework, landlords devised their own variations on a theme. On his lowveld estate, for example, David Forbes demanded "6 months of work at 10/– to 15/– per month, and such small jobs as weeding mealies, reaping and branding cattle etc. unpaid in return for ground to plough and graze cattle on."[56] On the northern mining property of the Piggs Peak Development Company, the conditions of tenancy were tied to mine work:

In exchange for the right to live, cultivate and graze on assigned portions by way of rental ... the native undertakes to render service whenever he may be required and at the current rate of wages – either underground or surface work – up to a maximum of 6 months or 180 shifts per annum. Natives shall be given reasonable time to plough, sow and reap. Rations to be supplied while working.[57]

The guarantee of employment at wages well in excess of local farm

rates proved a reasonably attractive proposition for many homesteads, at least until the mine closed in 1917. The Company was
even able to attract extra tenants to add to the 59 homesteads already
on the property in 1914. In this manner it partially resolved its
problems of labour stabilization (see chapter 6). There is no evidence
that landlords were able to enforce share-cropping arrangements
upon their new tenants. Whereas sharecropping was a vital stage in
the capitalization of settler agriculture in parts of the South African
grain belt, the circumstances in Swaziland were much less propi-
tious.[58] As long as there were alternative routes to the means of
subsistence, sharecropping remained singularly unattractive to Swazi
homesteads however desirable it might have appeared to landlords.

Most white farmers tried to force their tenants to provide labour
rather than rent, but there was widespread resistance to this type of
service. Homestead heads withheld homestead labour and assented
only to rental agreements.[59] In some cases, the smaller homesteads
would not perhaps have been in a position to supply such service.
In every case, the struggle of Swazi homesteads to maintain their
independence vis-à-vis the various labour markets of the region, and
to avoid farm work, were undoubtedly major factors. The diversion
of a regular portion of homestead income from wage labour in South
Africa was a small price to pay for avoiding the unattractive conditions of local farm work. Homestead labour was remunerated at
a better rate on the South African mines and homestead heads and
young men reacted strongly to the implied loss in income and
transgression of their freedom to proceed to labour markets of their
choice. One inventive landowner, aware of this situation, allowed his
tenants to live rent-free on his land, on condition that they allowed
him to recruit them for minework on the Rand. This scheme was
more readily agreed to.[60]

The landlords' response took a number of forms. They raised
rents in an attempt to make labour service look more attractive. They
appointed African headmen at relatively high rates of pay to collect
labour from tenant homesteads for the landlord. Many threatened
tenants with eviction if they continued to refuse to offer labour as
a condition of tenancy. David Forbes gave immediate notice to any
tenant who refused to submit to his rigorous terms. He could hardly
have been surprised when there was a mass exodus of tenants from
his estate.[61] On eviction, some landlords unsuccessfully attempted to
claim back rent from their tenants. If conditions improved at a later
stage, it was not unusual to find tenants approaching the landlord
to be allowed to return. More common, particularly where landlords
were not in permanent residence, was a movement back to the estate

to "squat." The description by Cabukela Mkonta at the head of this chapter typified this process. In their search for cheap labour, some farmers took to scouring the reserves for potential tenants. Some homesteads did respond to the offer of land in exchange for free labour but in those cases on record, the sons and daughters flatly refused to work and deserted when pressed.[62]

The threat of eviction rarely extracted any concessions from tenants, since they always had the option of moving to another farm where conditions were more to their liking, to crown land, or to the reserves. It was this relative freedom of movement which gave tenants some bargaining power and severely emasculated the landlord threat. Some tenants threatened with eviction moved over the border into the Transvaal. Swazi homesteads seem to have been well aware of the alternative tenancy conditions in the eastern Transvaal and where these appeared to be better they moved. In 1914, for example, some 700 followers of the Mankiana chief Mtshengu Mdhluli were scattered over seven farms in the district. A program of forced eviction was adopted by some landowners and unacceptable conditions of tenancy were demanded by others. This led to a "great number" of homesteads leaving Swaziland to live in the Transvaal.[63] In 1915, there was a further movement of tenant homesteads from the Mankiana district to squat on farms in the eastern Transvaal. Several Swazi chiefs complained that they were losing their followers and that they could find no trace of many of them after they left for the Transvaal. Farm tenants in the eastern Transvaal were known to make the opposite move if they could find more attractive conditions in Swaziland.[64]

The temporary expedient of stalling over tenancy agreements was adopted by some homesteads. By delaying a decision until the ploughing season, tenants were assured by law of another year's occupation of their sites.[65] Tenants also defaulted on rent payments and ignored the terms of agreements with landlords. On the farm, Nooitgedacht, in the Hlatikulu district the heads of five homesteads agreed to a rental charge of £1 per annum each. When called upon to pay, the tenants immediately claimed hardship. The landlord gave them six months to find the money. When they still did not pay, the landlord issued an eviction notice. The money was immediately forthcoming.[66]

Tenants consistently refused to enter into written contracts with their landlords. As the Assistant Commissioner at Mankiana observed, "Superstitious as the native usually is, they mostly do not like the idea of signing agreements but prefer to remain on the land simply by verbal agreement."[67] The real reasons for avoiding signed contracts had very little to do with irrational superstition. In the Mbabane district, for example, forty seven contracts were signed in 1914–15, seven in 1915–16, and only one in 1916–17. Clearly the binding effects of a written contract soon began to make themselves felt. But there were other factors involved here too. Some homestead heads, not without a hint of irony, observed that it was only through the signing of contracts in the 1880s that they were in their present situation and that they had no desire to be hoodwinked again.[68] The supply of printed agreement forms prepared by the colonial state for the purpose began to gather dust in the administration buildings in Mbabane.

Colonial officials suspected that the whole anti-contract movement was being engineered by the chiefs and the case of chief Sicunusa Dlamini gave credence to this view. Nevertheless, there were certainly ample reason for Swazi resistance without chiefly direction:

The simple fact is that the Swazis are only too well acquainted with the corresponding conditions of occupation on private farms in the Transvaal and Natal. The private owner who wishes so courteously to come to some agreement with the Swazis privately has nothing to recommend him except the gross abuses and bad treatment which the Swazis hear too often about and which in many cases they have witnessed with their own eyes among their own relations and friends who happen to live over the Transvaal border.[69]

Any attempt by landlords to force Swazi homesteads into disagreeable tenancy relations, from which they could not immediately escape if circumstances warranted, was doomed to failure. The rural information network had disseminated a blanket suspicion of all white farmers. Consequently very few tenants were prepared to commit themselves to binding written agreements. Frustrated landlords were forced to accept verbal agreements in order to secure labour. In the well-farmed Hlatikulu district, for example, there was not a single written tenancy contract in existence by 1917.

For the tenant homestead the major advantage of the verbal agreement was that it did not, and could not, have state backing. The homestead could thus leave a landlord's estate at a moment's notice if conditions became too onerous or those elsewhere more attractive. Individual homestead members in farm service were not quite so immune since landlords were quick to harness the authority of the Masters and Servants Act of the Transvaal as a means of worker control. Between 1913 and 1916, 138 Swazis were tried for desertion under the Act, with a conviction rate of 88 per cent. Nevertheless, desertion remained a perennial problem which was hard to control. In some cases farm labourers required only the slightest of excuses to desert. An unpleasant task such as manure preparation, the refusal of a landlord to pay a full day's wages when the labourer arrived for work in mid-morning rather than at 5 a.m., and the threat of a beating from a landlord all provided workers, at one time or another, with sufficient grounds for desertion.[70]

There were much broader forces at work, however, which encouraged permanent or temporary desertion amongst farm workers and which rendered the farm labour supply continuously and inherently unstable. The first of these was a factor of the landlords' own making for the conditions of service on many farms were degrading and brutal. Much farm labour was, of course, unpaid as a condition of tenancy. Where payment was due, wages were often a pittance and the labourer was never guaranteed regular or sufficient payment. On Lionel Cameron's farm at Ntambana, Mtshakela Dlamini was promised the relatively high wage of £20 per annum. After working for five months, all he had received from Cameron was "plenty of food" and a "present of one shilling every Saturday" which he was supposed to share with Mbulisa, another farm worker. When Mtshakela demanded his wages from Cameron's wife, Cameron issued the blunt warning that "if anyone fights with my missus I'll kill him." Mtshakela chose the lesser of two evils and deserted without being paid.[71]

Other farm workers were less fortunate with the response to their demands for payment. Mehlamane Mandhlope worked as a casual labourer for Jan Snyman for a mere 10 shillings a month, but received nothing for his first two months' work. Frustrated at his treatment, he confronted Snyman about his working conditions and the fact that he had not been paid. Mehlamane recalled Snyman's response:

I told him I had only two meals a day and that he was always asking me to work at night too. Early the next morning he caught me, put his foot on my neck and held me down and thrashed me with a short leather strap. He hit me many times. Once I got away he chased me and thrashed me again. When I got away the second time I ran some distance and asked him to pay me. I ran to Mr Middleton's. Mr Middleton intervened and he then left. He chased me because I demanded my wages.[72]

Middleton, a neighbour of Snyman's, confirmed that Snyman had "given the boy a hammering" and testified against Snyman in court since he was undoubtedly aware of the harm such an incident would do on the rural grapevine.[73] With a touching display of colonial magnanimity, Snyman was fined 10 shillings for assault and cautioned about his failure to pay wages. Assaults of this sort were common and for every one that came to the attention of the authorities there were scores that remained within the confines of the farmyard.[74] Female workers on farms were by no means immune. When Solomon Maritz discovered Vangile Nhlabati absconding with a few of his mealies, he beat and kicked her senseless.[75]

The actual conditions of farm work were hard, particularly during periods of ploughing, planting, and harvesting when the farmer was more likely to supervise his labour force directly. Long hours, poor rations, constant verbal and physical abuse, and the fear of serious physical violence were hardly much of an incentive for farm work. In addition, the farm labourer was an isolated worker and had no channels of expression for his grievances. The lack of redress when workers finally did take their landlords to colonial courts must have been particularly embittering. For many, desertion was the logical option. Landlord attempts to force the state to act against deserting tenants, above and beyond application of the ambiguous Masters and Servants legislation, elicited a contradictory response. In 1917, the Hlatikulu Farmers Association called on the administration to legislate against a practice which was rendering the farm labour supply "very unstable."[76] Over the next three years, the issue was debated at length by colonial officials at various levels. Legislation was drafted but was then shelved; it was believed that the Act would inhibit the flow of labour to the mines and would moreover be impossible to implement. As a result, landlords were unable to secure the degree of control which they sought and complaints about labour shortages and inefficiency echoed into the 1920s and 1930s.

Many farm deserters simply took out a mine contract or went to work elsewhere in South Africa to put distance between themselves and the Masters and Servants Act. Recruiters were never prepared to wait on farm deserters, however, and actively attempted to recruit on the farms using African runners. When Kwentula Mkonza, a runner for the NRC labour agent Gert Dekker, recruited three of his relatives for work in Johannesburg, the landowner Adolf Hintze offered to pay back their advances if they would remain on the farm. The men rejected his offer.[77] Incidents such as these invariably led to public outbursts by settlers that their farm labour was being poached by mine recruiters. Farmers desperate and solvent enough to match labour recruiters by advancing wages to farm workers found that this too was no guarantee that they could secure the promised labour.[78] The problem of how to outcompete the mines exercised landlords for some considerable time. One group unsuccessfully suggested the introduction of that old standby, a differential labour tax for farm workers.[79] Landlords eventually tried to cut off the avenues of escape to the mines by enforcing a quasi-contract upon tenant workers. They devised a scheme which won colonial approval whereby the tax receipts of farm tenants were endorsed with the landlord's name at the time of tax collection. Landlords were informed in advance of the time and place of collection so that they could be present to ensure that the receipts were endorsed. Mine recruiters were instructed that the holders of endorsed receipts could not be recruited for mine work since they were in breach of contract with landlords. For its success the plan required the full co-operation of the recruiters, but since they had already shown scant respect for the farm labour supply, this method of controlling farm workers all too rarely proved successful.[80]

In an environment of high rates of desertion, landlords turned to what they believed to be a more trustworthy labour source: that of the women, children, and underage males of tenant homesteads. To some degree this complemented the attempts by homestead heads to achieve some sort of internal division of labour by encouraging adult sons to migrate to the mines while directing their female and child labour towards the fulfilment of the homestead's tenancy obligations.[81] For various reasons, the labour of underage males was increasingly directed towards the mines as well, a trend which mine recruiters were quick to seize on and landlords to rail against:

Members of the Association respectfully suggest ... the natives under tax paying age be not allowed to proceed to work outside of Swaziland that owing to the demand for labour on the mines and the increasing number proceeding to work on the mines, farmers today find great difficulty in obtaining sufficient labour to do their work and that if such a course were adopted ... it would greatly assist the farming community and would protect youths from the bad moral influence they almost invariably come under in the industrial centres to which they go.[82]

Under pressure from local farmers and the Union authorities, efforts were made by the colonial state to control the more excessive instances of recruiting of minors. But without the means to establish the exact age of a potential recruit many teenagers slipped through the net.

White settlers unable to secure or retain sufficient male labour were forced to adopt other methods to keep their farming operations afloat. Some ranchers farmed out their stock to Swazi homesteads in the reserves, in much the same fashion as wealthier homesteads would loan cattle to other needier homesteads. Poorer Swazi homesteads were more than willing to loan cattle from white settlers and avail themselves of the dairy produce. As an added incentive, ranchers sometimes paid the taxes of the herders. This reciprocal arrangement had considerable attractions for both parties and became quite widespread in the country.[83] White agriculturalists were unable to take their product to the labour supply in this way and remained vulnerable to tenant recalcitrance. As a result, after 1914 the settlers turned increasingly to female and child labour. The use of this labour was enthusiastically endorsed by the colonial state, since it resolved one of the perennial colonial dilemmas.[84] The primary advantage of female and child labour for landlords was that it was inherently more stable and therefore afforded greater facility for manipulation and control. It was also not subject to the constant pressure of alternative and more lucrative forms of employment such as the local and Rand mines. But female and child labour was never completely docile and compliant, as landlords quickly discovered.

The wages paid to female and child farm workers were atrocious, even by the low standards of the day. At a time when farm wages for male adults were running at 15 to 20 shillings, women were paid 5 to 10 shillings and children 3 to 5 shillings for a month's work. The common response of these workers was to take in kind what they lost in cash. Crop theft was the almost universal response with which most landlords had to live. Women and children working in the fields would take a few maize cobs home with them every day secreted in their bags. Most daylight theft was on a small scale, as one woman, Dambile Mapalala, explained:

I went to Watts to reap for him. I worked two days and on the day I finished I took these few mealies. They were poor mealies. Those with only a few on the cob and I shelled them for my baby. I left it in the garden and later I fetched it. Watts said I had stolen them.[85]

A slightly larger scale of operation was described by a farmer, J. Robberts, who periodically spied on his workers from his house:

I could see them where they were working from my house. They were working but from time to time one or another would go out into the veld as though to make water. On the third day I became suspicious that mealies were being stolen from the fields.[86]

Robberts' suspicions were confirmed when he apprehended the mealie-laden culprits on their way home from work. Theft of maize and vegetables occurred on a much larger scale at night. The rash of crop thefts reached epidemic proportions in 1918 and the landlords finally moved to crush the practice. They spied on workers, waited with dogs and guns in the fields, and called in constant police patrols. Many women and children were arrested. Consistent with the double standards of colonial justice, and in marked contrast to the leniency shown to landlords who assaulted workers, the full weight of the law descended. Dambile Mapalala was imprisoned for one month's hard labour. Another women, Mzanwayo Nhlengetwa, who had stolen a dish of maize from a farmer, H. Rose, received three months' hard labour. Other women and minors were imprisoned for terms of one to three months.[87] The respite was a temporary one for settler producers. By 1922 white farmers were again threatening to take up arms against crop thieves who "look upon the European farmers' crops as their own property."[88]

The final destabilizing factor in the farm labour market was the continued vitality of relations between chiefs and commoners in the country. The pull on farm homestead labour from central and local chiefs was naturally at its greatest at precisely the periods that labour was most in demand on the settler-estates. Chiefs had very little direct control over their followers away at work in South Africa and the calls on male subjects working on farms probably increased. The labour tenants found themselves constantly pulled in two directions. That they often opted to desert temporarily if farm duties could not be made to mesh with other rural obligations was hardly surprising. Substituting the drudgery and isolation of farm work for the *esprit de corps* of a tribute labour party must have been a constant temptation for the farm labourer. The case of Mantinta Nsibande provides a pertinent case study of the competing pressures to which farm labour was subjected.

As part of his homestead's tenancy obligations, Mantinta worked as a general farm worker on the estate of a maize farmer August Muller in the Hlatikulu district. The exacting arrangement with Muller placed Mantinta on call whenever the farmer required his services. Any labour rendered by Mantinta was unpaid. He first fell foul of Muller in November 1914 when he assaulted a fellow worker, refused to work, and left. He returned the same day when he heard that Muller had gone to Mahamba to start proceedings against him for desertion under the Masters and Servants Act. He worked for another two days and then deserted again. This time he did not return. Muller was hard-pressed for labour and had him arrested, tried, and fined under the Act. At the end of December, Muller demanded that Mantinta undertake some ploughing on the farm. Mantinta again refused to work and left immediately for Zombode, the resident of the Queen Regent, probably to participate in some organized labour activity with his *emabutfo*. Two weeks later he reappeared at the farm with his father and started work, on condition that Muller did not prosecute him again. The following day he was gone again, sending word to Muller that he was ill. In fact, he had gone to the village of his chief, Silele Nsibande, where he spent the next few days working in Silele's fields helping to bring in the early harvest. Mantinta pleaded guilty to desertion at his second trial under the Masters and Servants Act. The Assistant Commissioner, aware of the competing rural demands on Mantinta's labour power, found him not guilty and discharged him.[89]

If one of the reasons for the labour difficulties experienced by white farmers in Swaziland was that they were unable to break farm workers from their traditional obligations to their chiefs, it would be incorrect to imply that Swazi homesteads responded to demands of the chiefs as rapidly or as freely as they had in the nineteenth century. Indeed there is evidence of a considerable dilution in the powers of the chiefs in the period covered by this study. It is to the problem of transformation in relations between chiefs and commoners that we now turn.

CHAPTER TEN

Continuity, Conflict, and Change

When the ruling class is despised, law and order is threatened.
W.A. Challis, 1912

The confrontation between August Muller and Mantinta Nsibande described in the previous chapter had a lesson for their contemporaries. For the white settlers of Swaziland, frustrated by their continuing inability to exploit fully the country's rich natural and labour resources, here was further proof (if any were needed) of the errancy of colonial policy. The verdict itself was irrelevant: the real case had been fought, and lost, ten years earlier when Milner first declared his intention to partition the country between white and black. Selborne's "climbdown of expediency and nervousness" in 1907–8 and his failure to reduce the Swazi ruling class to a mere appendage of the colonial state had guaranteed that the farmer would never be able to exercise complete and exclusive control over his tenant workers.[1] Some colonial officials might have been inclined to agree: those who had not been privy to the agonized deliberations of Selborne and his two Resident Commissioners Moony and Coryndon and those more concerned with questions of economic exploitation than social order. Others could argue that properly handled Mantinta Nsibande's deference to traditional authority was a hopeful sign. His evident frustrations as a wage worker were being constructively channelled away from an unmade future towards a secure past. The case would undoubtedly have given greatest satisfaction to the representatives of local and regional mining interests in the country. Local mine managers could take some solace from the realization that they did not struggle alone to cut the rural ties of the Swazi worker. And labour agents for the Rand mines had the power to turn the whole situation to their own advantage by offering workers like Nsibande a third way. Silele Nsibande, the local chief, would have expected such loyalty from his followers and would probably have been satisfied, though probably somewhat surprised, to see him

exonerated in court. For the chieftainship as a whole, however, isolated actions of loyalty were cold comfort indeed.

In early 1915, when Nsibande went to trial, the Swazi chiefs were
occupied with much weightier matters. Only weeks later Chief No-
madakulu expressed the mounting frustration of the Swazi rulers
when he declared that "the people have defeated us" on the issue
of land repurchase.[2] The inability of the chiefs to marshall support
of the commoners for their program provides a much clearer insight
into the state of chief-commoner relations in the post-partition era
and illustrates the declining power of the chiefs over commoner
homesteads. The chiefs' failure to mobilize the country ideologically
gave rise to the first mass revolt by commoners against the ruling
class in Swazi history. Termination of the revolt required colonial
intervention, and was thus the first occasion on which the chiefs
managed to capture colonial state power for use against the commoners. The effective banning of the Swazi from the private land
market thereafter mitigated against any further conflict in this particular area, leaving colonial chiefs and the aristocracy to contest the
dilution of their powers and position on different terrain.

The commoners' response was in fact symptomatic of a more
general erosion of the chiefs' authority in Swaziland. The Swazi
rulers had been placed in an increasingly vulnerable position during
the first two decades of British colonial rule. Repeated attempts to
roll back the constraints of state power or to capture it for their own
ends met with only limited success. Some chiefs sought to appropriate the symbols and artifacts of colonial and capitalist domination
to forge a new culture of dependency:

In the matter of art the chief is exceedingly catholic in his tastes. His picture
gallery is small but distinctly choice ... side by side with a representation of
the Crucifixion is one of Satan armed with his pitchfork, and above them
are pictures of the King and Queen and of the late President Kruger. On
the dining table stands a rhinoceros-horn snuff box and an earthen-ware
hand basin and jug, whilst overhead are hung portmanteaux, riding breeches,
boots, shirts, hats, coats, shooting jackets, saddles, bridles and guns. Thus
are the tribesmen impressed with the great possessions of their chief.[3]

But the counterweight was very powerful. Divested of many of the
legal and political endorsements of chieftainship by an "effloresence
of legislation," stripped of a large proportion of the land area which
bound their followers to them and by means of which they could
attract new followers, and co-opted into the colonial structures of
coercion, the peeling away of their power left the chiefs weakened

and embittered. The effects of this potent combination of factors were exacerbated by further forces emanating directly, or in part, from the participation of Swazi commoners in wage labour. While the social relations and political alignments of Swazi society had a notable impact on the ways in which Swazi labour was made available to the developing capitalist economy, it is also apparent that as wage labour became entrenched so Swazi society itself was forced to adjust and change.

In the first place, a faster rate of homestead formation, smaller homestead size, and the development of a new division of domestic labour which all accompanied the emergence of mass migrancy would in all likelihood have reduced the ability of the chiefs to extract labour from commoner homesteads (see chapter 4). The existence of alternative methods of acquiring homestead subsistence needs from labour migration and the possibilities for "squatting" on white farms or crown land outside the chiefs' control meant that Swazi homesteads were no longer exclusively dependent on the Swazi chiefs for access to a material base. The struggle by the Swazi chiefs against a colonial policy which threatened to strip them of land and the labour and allegiance of commoner homesteads, led them to turn to those very homesteads for the funds to achieve their ends. However, the chiefs only succeeded in alienating many commoners by their constant and onerous exactions.

The strength of chief-commoner relations also showed considerable dilution in other more tangible ways during the period under examination. The numbers of men in permanent residence at the villages of local chiefs rapidly declined. Contrasting two eras, Kuper noted in the 1930s that formerly the villages of local chiefs "were inhabited by large numbers of men, but today there are rarely more than fifteen in residence for any length of time."[4]

The regimental system was removed from centre stage of Swazi society during the first twenty years of British rule, despite the best efforts of the aristocracy to preserve and adapt it to a new milieu. The massive mobilizations of regimental labour which occurred as late as the 1890s were never to be repeated and the power of the aristocracy to extract *imbutfo* and *emabutfo* labour in various branches of production declined over time. The large hunting parties of the nineteenth century were severely circumscribed by colonial edict and the precipitous decline in game stocks in the country. In 1914, when he organized a royal hunt in the south of the country, Prince Malunge even found himself in conflict with white settlers in court over the traditional practice of grass burning to flush out game.[5] The use of the *emabutfo* for agricultural labour by the aristocracy declined as the twentieth century progressed, although this function was never completely extinguished, and persisted well beyond the period of study, albeit in attenuated form. In 1913, William Penfold, comparing the situation with that prevailing twenty-five years earlier at the end of Mbandeni's reign, lamented the passing of the regimental system "and with it the old soldierly discipline and spirit."[6] By the time of Sobhuza II's assumption to the throne in 1921, the numbers of *imbutfo* soldiers permanently in residence at the royal villages had "drastically declined."[7] In the early 1930s, the three royal villages in the Ezulwini valley had a combined population of less than 500, and the number of *imbutfo* soldiers in residence at the king's village was "rarely over 70."[8] When Hilda Kuper first observed the regimental system, *egoli* ("the city of gold" or Johannesburg) was "better known to a number of Swazis than their own royal villages."[9] The declining significance of the *emabutfo* appears to have been hastened by a number of factors including the long period of regency during Sobhuza's minority. While this did not prevent the aristocracy from exercising traditional Dlamini rights over the labour of commoner homesteads, one of the major mechanisms for this, and for renewing Dlamini dominance, was the *Incwala* ceremony. The *Incwala* was held in abeyance during the whole period when the Swazi were without a king. Hence the annual obligatory gathering of a large proportion of the men of the kingdom at year end was in disuse until the 1920s. Even then it failed to recapture its former glory. By the mid-1930s, fully fifteen years into Sobhuza's rule, only 1,000 men attended the *Incwala*, and only 20 per cent of adult males were "still active members of the military organization."[10]

The attractiveness of life at the royal villages for the young men of the realm had clearly declined. All Swazi men had to acquire some cash income to meet colonial taxation demands, and service in the ranks provided little opportunity for this.[11] The royal villages had ceased to be places where the nucleus of a herd might be started. And the *imbutfo* soldiers in residence increasingly had to make arrangements for their own support while at the royal villages: "Formerly, when cattle were raided from hostile tribes the men were better fed; the present rulers are less able to support financially a large permanent retinue ... Those who stay lead a precarious hand-to-mouth existence, relying largely on the generosity of the women in the neighbourhood for whom they do occasional jobs, in their spare time, and wandering from beer drink to beer drink."[12] There was thus little material incentive to be gained from permanent residence at the royal villages. In the nineteenth century most homestead heads had made sure that at least one member of the homestead joined the *imbutfo* force; under the new dispensation these same individuals represented a potential source of income. Hence, homestead support for the *imbutfo* did not operate to anything like the same degree.

The need of the aristocracy to raise funds to sustain its defence against a far more fundamental challenge to ruling-class integrity also affected the fate of the regimental system. Having failed to harness the *emabutfo* for the purposes of raising funds on the capitalist labour market of the Rand, the aristocracy had to call on individual chiefs to exercise their local powers to induce labour migration and to support internal taxation. In effect, this was a tacit devolution of control over the labour power of commoner homesteads to the local level. Withdrawal of labour from the *imbutfo* was encouraged by local chiefs who saw in such a strategy the means to appropriate a proportion of migrant earnings which might otherwise have been lost to the central authorities.[13] The very fact of widespread and growing participation by Swazi males in wage employment meant that the pool of labour on which the aristocracy could draw at any point in the year would inevitably have been smaller than in the past. As James Stuart observed in 1922, "A counterattraction has been afforded the young men, who in the ordinary course would have formed part of the army personnel."[14] But the labour pool was circumscribed in yet another way. With declining homestead size and a falling age of marriage, the proportion of single males available for the *imbutfo* was reduced. In addition, men drawn more directly into homestead agricultural production tied up labour formerly available to the Dlamini.

Yet despite these mounting social pressures, local productive relations between chiefs and commoners showed considerable resilience. To some extent this was related to the essential flexibility of the relationship, which allowed the chiefs to substitute cash payment for tribute labour and adapt the concept of tribute to a new situation (see chapter 4). But reports of Swazi men and *umemo* parties working in the fields of local chiefs are common right up until 1920. While the land partition undoubtedly exercised a negative effect on chief-commoner relations in general, there was at least one way in which it may inadvertently have strengthened local loyalties since land disputes provided points around which chiefs could rally their followers.

To a large degree, the continuing bind of local chief-commoner relations was a result of the perpetuation of pre-capitalist forms of land control in the Swazi reserves, a victory won by the Swazi rulers in the face of concerted opposition from white settlers and many colonial officials. This ensured that the majority of Swazi homesteads remained dependent on local chiefs for access to land for agricultural production. The structural insecurity of many tenant homesteads may also have ensured that amicable relations were maintained with local Swazi authorities. For most Swazi ultimate sanction for land control and distribution in the reserves remained in the hands of the aristocracy. During the early 1920s, for example, Sobhuza II was several times called on to arbitrate in land disputes between southern chiefs. Such intervention was avidly promoted by a colonial administration seeking to manipulate and co-opt the young and inexperienced king. Without the retention of these actual and symbolic powers over land it is doubtful that Sobhuza would have been as successful in rejuvenating the central role of the aristocracy as he was in later years.

With regard to the new Swazi worker-peasant class, however, neither the king nor the Swazi chiefs expected that traditional ties would continue to bind without their direct intervention. Chapter 4 showed how the aristocracy tried, and failed, to use the *emabutfo* system as a means both of countering regional autonomy and controlling the migrant movement in its own interests. As a result, the first two decades of the twentieth century provided the southern chiefdoms with much greater space within which to pursue their own interests. Both chiefs and aristocracy felt a common need to reach out to workers at the place of work in order to exert greater influence over migrant workers from Swaziland. When the Swazi migrant workforce was scattered around the small towns of the eastern Transvaal this strategy was much less feasible. With the growing concentration of Swazi workers on the Witwatersrand after 1910 the Swazi authorities seized the opportunity.

Perhaps the most striking feature of Swazi employment patterns on the Rand after 1910 was the strong preference displayed for certain mines. Many of these were located near the East Rand mining towns of Boksburg, Benoni, and Germiston (figures 16 and 17). A small number of mines dominated the affections of Swazi labourers (table 19). Of these the East Rand Proprietary Mine (ERPM) was by far the most important, receiving over 50 per cent of Swazi mine recruits between 1912 and 1920. The Van Ryn Mine also proved a consistent employer of Swazi migrants: in 1912–13, 24 per cent of the mine workforce was from Swaziland. Much Swazi independent labour was drawn to Van Ryn as well (table 20). Indeed, the mines most popular with non-recruited Swazi migrants were also those where the bulk of Swazi recruits were working.

A primary determinant of such congregation was the fruitful relationship which developed in Swaziland between the recruiting

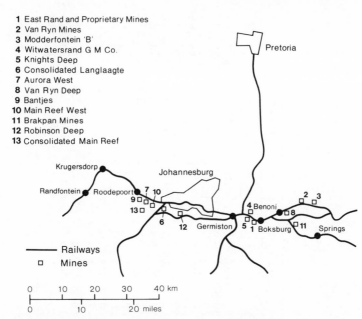

1 East Rand and Proprietary Mines
2 Van Ryn Mines
3 Modderfontein 'B'
4 Witwatersrand G M Co.
5 Knights Deep
6 Consolidated Langlaagte
7 Aurora West
8 Van Ryn Deep
9 Bantjes
10 Main Reef West
11 Brakpan Mines
12 Robinson Deep
13 Consolidated Main Reef

16 Location of Witwatersrand mining towns and selected gold mines

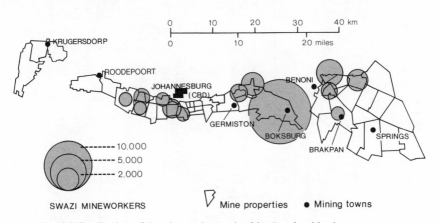

17 Spatial distribution of Swazi recruits received by Rand gold mines

agencies of certain mines and the Swazi worker (see chapter 5). By linking the most productive recruiters in the country (Marwick & Morris, Howe & Murray, Taberer's Labour Organization, and the Neumann Group) with the mines to which the bulk of Swazi recruited labour was sent (ERPM, Van Ryn, Modderfontein "B" and Main Reef West respectively), it is evident that the recruiters were successful insofar as they built upon existing patterns of migration and upon

TABLE 19

Swazi Recruits Received by Witwatersrand Gold Mines, 1912–21

Mine	1912–13		1913–14		1914–15		1915–16		1916–17		1917–18		1918–19		1919–20	
	No	%	No	%	No	%	No	%	No	%	No	%	No	%	No	%
ERPM	2,500	56.7	1,200	39.3	2,100	45.5	2,495	47.4	2,072	56.3	2,082	48.3	1,639	45.8	1,557	41.4
Van Ryn Mines	636	14.4	305	10.0	399	8.7	316	6.0	424	11.5	436	10.1	158	4.4	215	5.7
Modderfontein B	437	9.9	839	27.4	554	12.0	121	2.3	13	0.4	18	0.4	0	0.0	2	0.1
Witwatersrand GMC	54	0.3	139	4.5	324	7.0	194	3.7	266	7.2	328	7.6	250	7.0	308	8.2
Knights Deep	5	0.1	34	1.1	51	1.1	367	7.0	88	2.4	309	7.2	166	4.6	256	6.8
Cons. Langlaagte	3	0.1	155	5.1	219	4.7	78	1.5	11	0.3	248	5.8	314	8.8	227	6.0
Aurora West	0	0.0	0	0.0	149	3.2	259	4.9	194	5.3	120	2.8	121	3.4	138	3.7
Van Ryn Deep	0	0.0	1	0.0	13	0.3	3	0.1	10	0.3	143	3.3	406	11.3	356	9.5
Bantjes	122	2.8	64	2.1	293	6.4	153	2.9	2	0.1	9	0.2	17	0.5	83	2.2
Main Reef West	391	8.9	30	1.0	26	0.6	129	2.5	102	2.8	0	0.0	0	0.0	0	0.0
Brakpan Mines	0	0.0	2	0.1	40	0.9	209	4.0	133	3.6	181	4.2	81	2.3	0	0.0
Robinson Deep	22	0.5	110	3.6	224	4.9	229	4.4	2	0.1	0	0.0	20	0.6	25	0.7
Cons. Main Reef	47	1.1	4	0.1	38	0.8	135	2.6	36	1.0	109	2.5	118	3.3	87	2.3
Ginsberg	3	0.1	33	1.1	23	0.5	126	2.4	152	4.1	114	2.6	49	3.0	0	0.0
Others	229	5.2	141	7.6	158	3.4	446	8.5	177	4.8	213	4.9	240	6.7	509	13.5

Source: NRC Annual Reports, 1913–1920.

TABLE 20
Swazi Independents Engaged at Rand Mines, 1911–14

Mine	1911–12		1912–13		1913–14		Total	
	No	%	No	%	No	%	No	%
Van Ryn Mines	185	55.4	193	33.6	210	49.5	588	44.1
ERPM	4	1.2	127	22.1	12	2.8	143	10.7
Modderfontein B	3	0.9	92	16.0	28	6.6	123	9.2
Knights Deep	10	3.0	15	2.6	11	2.6	36	2.7
New Klienfontein	11	3.3	15	2.6	6	1.4	32	2.4
Van Ryn Deep	2	0.6	1	0.2	24	5.7	27	2.0
Rose Deep	16	4.8	4	0.7	6	1.4	26	2.0
Witwatersrand GMC	2	0.6	2	0.3	21	5.0	25	1.9
Simmer Deep	11	3.3	8	1.4	1	0.2	20	1.5
Others	58	17.4	70	12.2	71	16.7	199	14.9

Source: NRC Annual Reports, 1912–14.

Swazi preferences for particular mines. Taberer's supplied Swazi recruits in any number to only two of Central Mining's seven mines, and Howe & Murray to only one of General Mining's eight mines. Other recruiting operations such as those of Consolidated Goldfields (with as many as eight recruiters in Swaziland in 1911) and the contractor J.E. Palmer for JCI represented mines traditionally avoided by Swazi migrants and were much less successful in their Swaziland recruiting effort.

Congregation may also be viewed as a rational defensive strategy adopted by workers themselves to cope with the oppressive and debilitating environment of minework and compound life. Moroney has argued that "it is important to view the development of ethnic solidarity in an industrial environment as a particular response to that environment, rather than a simple transferral of tribal values."[15] Cultural resources such as friendship, kinship, and language similarities could be more readily marshalled in the context of congregation. A large complement of labour from one area could also mean better representation with mine management. The isolated worker was the unprotected worker, and it is noteworthy that Swazi on mines with small complements from Swaziland had to vent their grievances through other channels.[16] In the case of ERPM, the Swazi recruits of labour contractors Marwick & Morris had a separate compound and their own "police boys" and they could air their complaints through the Marwick & Morris compound manager.[17] Labour contractors

stood between the worker and mine management with a vested interest in ensuring that grievances were attended to since, in the long
run, their own reputation and livelihood were at stake. In 1916,
Marwick & Morris were absorbed by the NRC. The ERPM simultaneously embarked on an economy drive in which "compound meat,
bread, vegetables and nearly everything [was] cut down to the lowest
possible point."[18] The number of Swazi employed on the mine began
to decline almost immediately (table 19).

In his anxiety to downplay the penetration of the countryside into
the compound, Moroney tends to miss another important determinant of congregation on the Rand. Congregation by Swazi workers
was actively encouraged both by the Swazi chiefs and the aristocracy,
who perceived a number of advantages in having their followers
grouped together at a limited number of mines. Congregation tended
to mitigate the dissolution of rural loyalties in the urban-industrial
environment, particularly since Swazi mine "boss boys" were often
the sons of chiefs.[19] It also allowed the chief to know exactly where
his followers were to be found in the mushrooming urban complex
of the Witwatersrand, an important consideration when he wanted
to make some exaction from them. Personal visits to the Rand by
Swazi chiefs became increasingly common. Whenever the Mamba
chief, Bokweni, visited his numerous followers on the Rand he was
"feasted, assured of their fealty and left for his own country laden
with presents."[20] Controlled mine visits were generally encouraged
by the colonial administration in Swaziland, mine management, and
the Native Recruiting Corporation as a mode of fostering worker
control. Swazi chiefs were cordially received by NRC officials and
compound managers so long as they did not encourage worker
protest.[21]

Mine management was well pleased with the Swazi chiefs. Swazi
migrants were discouraged from participation in worker resistance
and strike activity which might jeopardize their security of employment. The disturbances on the Rand in 1913, for example, were
greeted with great concern by the Swazi chiefs and rulers who gave
their verbal support not to striking miners but to the Union Government which was complimented on the "satisfactory manner" in
which the strike was settled.[22] During that strike, all 600 Swazi workers at the Van Ryn mine refused to go underground and other
workers followed suite. The latter group eventually succumbed to
pressure and threat from the compound manager. Yet the Swazi
workers still refused to work, "gave their war-cry and rushed up to
the other natives ... throwing stones and assaulting with sticks." The
action was forcibly quashed by compound police and the Swazi work-

ers were subsequently disciplined.[23] Further evidence of Swazi participation in early industrial action comes from 1920 where, as Bonner points out, the networks of Swazi mobilization were again primarily "ethnic or regional" in character. At a strike at Knights Deep mine in February that year there was a confrontation between striking and non-striking workers during which "the Swazi complement ... switched sides en masse and happily belaboured their colleagues of a few moments before."[24] While news of such actions could only have caused alarm in Swaziland itself, some comfort was undoubtedly drawn from the ethnic solidarity displayed by Swazi workers.

By the second decade of British rule the essential contradiction of Swazi participation in wage labour was consequently making itself felt in the rural districts of Swaziland. W.A. Challis, an uneasy missionary, observed of the Swazi migrant workforce at this time that "a tribe well-governed by its native chiefs and headmen under the British Government is apt to degenerate into a lawless horde, and in the case of those who come down from the mines, a dangerous as well as lawless horde of savages, with a very thin veneer of civilization."[25] Implicit in this "veneer" was the development of new forms of consciousness in the capitalist workplace which filtered back into the Swazi countryside. Chiefly diatribes and missionary reports of the time are replete with complaints about the new attitudes being shed abroad in Swazi society towards figures of traditional authority, homestead heads, and the colonial state.[26]

It is significant therefore that one of Sobhuza's first acts when he came to power in Swaziland was to take firm action to reverse this trend. In 1920, he visited Johannesburg with five other chiefs, the Swaziland Resident Commissioner, and the Commissioner of Police at the expense of the Swaziland administration. Sobhuza was allowed to make his first appointment of mine *ndunas* at the ERPM and other mines. Later, in 1921, Sobhuza bought six stands in the black township of Sophiatown. A house on one of the stands was used by Sobhuza on his periodic visits to the Rand and the "house of the King" became a central meeting point for Swazi workers on the Rand.[27] With his assumption to the Swazi throne, a new phase was consequently inaugurated in the struggle to check degeneration of the Swazi workforce into a "lawless and dangerous horde."

In the 1920s Sobhuza resumed the attempts earlier abandoned by his grandmother to challenge the land partition decision in the courts. In 1926, in a test case brought before the Privy Council, he also found the colonial administration totally intransigent on the issue. With this failure weighing heavy, Sobhuza turned to other more orthodox methods of re-asserting central authority through intermarriage and placing. In the 1930s Sobhuza attempted to regain royal control, lost in the late nineteenth and early twentieth century, over the marriage age of young men but he discovered that his targets had already "taken wives and made girls pregnant." Attempts to levy fines on the offenders were largely unsuccessful.[28] Sobhuza also made serious efforts to resuscitate the *emabutfo* by introducing the system into the schools. Later, three thousand Swazi were mobilized along regimental lines to participate in the British war effort. By the 1950s, John Gamede could refer to the southern chiefdoms as being much less free and independent than in "the old days."[29] In sum, the 1920s appear to mark the onset of a new phase in the assertion of centralized control within Swazi society, albeit within the limits of continued colonial domination. When that particular story is told it must of necessity be related to the course of the struggle for land and labour in earlier decades.

Conclusion

The consequence of all this will be that the Nation will be broken up into locations, its National Life ended, and it will be turned into a congeries of small crowded locations.

Pietermaritzburg Lawyer Parsonson, 1905

Although South Africa's industrial revolution failed to match the scope and scale of Europe's, it was just as destructive of the earlier social and economic order and as devastating in its impact on the lives of its victims.[1] The British and Portuguese colonies of the subcontinent were profoundly influenced by their economic incorporation into the emerging capitalist system of South Africa. Swaziland was no exception. One cannot examine the historical development of Swazi society outside the broader context of this regional political economy. Today, when external influence and determination are so transparent, this is obvious. Yet the literature on Swaziland has traditionally exhibited a profound uncertainty regarding the external influences on historical change in the economic and social organization of Swazi society.

Hilda Kuper's detailed reconstructions beginning in the 1930s have provided the basis for measuring subsequent change.[2] Kuper herself was aware that the Swaziland she saw was very different from that of fifty, twenty, or even ten years before. But neither she nor any subsequent Swaziland scholar has set out to explore systematically the explosive period of social and political transformation which followed the discovery of gold on the Witwatersrand in 1886. Powerful forces from abroad shook the roots of agrarian society and wrought fundamental changes in Swazi modes of living and survival. In the late 1880s, Swazi society was still virtually self-sufficient and few homesteads had recourse to the produce and labour markets of the region. Over the next thirty years the integrity of that society underwent a systematic and relentless challenge. By 1920 the main lines of incorporation had been firmly drawn. The majority of Swazi men were engaged in wage labour on the Rand, in other parts of South Africa, and in Swaziland itself, many homesteads were heavily dependent upon imported foodstuffs for their survival, and some of the most important institutions of nineteenth-century Swazi society (such as the regimental system) had been severely undermined. While the Swazi experienced much of the rural degradation and impoverishment that was a common consequence of integration into an expanding capitalist economy the path taken was still in many ways quite distinct from that of their confrères.

In the late nineteenth century the land and labour of the Swazi became the object of intense desire amongst white settlers, land companies, Boer pastoralists, and mining capitalists. What they confronted in their sometimes complementary, but often conflicting, drive for control was a powerful, centralized society which retained much of its pre-capitalist vitality and integrity. There was little resemblance to the fractured and shattered social remnants to the north and south which had born the brunt of European expansion in the nineteenth century. Even the Zulu, who are sometimes held up as an example of a consolidated and obdurate society, had been greatly fragmented by the time that gold was discovered on the Rand.[3] The strategies of capital and colonial state in the era of the mining revolution, and the outcome of their quest, were conditioned by the character of Swazi society and by the reactions of Swazis to these pressures. Swaziland consequently became the site of some of the most intense, though remarkably peaceful, struggles over land and labour witnessed anywhere in the region during this period.

It would be a mistake, however, simply to set European aggressors against Swazi defenders without paying due attention to the lines of social and political division across the Swazi countryside.[4] These included, first, the historically contentious relationship between the ruling Dlamini aristocracy and subordinate provincial chiefs and chiefdoms of the country districts. The advent of colonialism altered the conditions of the struggle between aristocracy and local chiefs for without the traditional resolution by armed confrontation, economic and cultural conflict became more pronounced. Second, within each chiefdom there were the relations of dominance and dependence between the chiefs and their followers at the local level. Third, and in many ways dependent on the first two, there were the productive relations within the basic unit of society, the Swazi *umuti*. These relations, both within and without the homestead, in which every Swazi was caught and the struggles which surrounded them are of critical importance to an understanding of the ways in which the country was incorporated into new circuits of capitalist production and exchange. These internal social relations placed certain demands and obligations on most Swazi which in practice often worked in opposition to one another. The Dlamini aristocracy, one hundred or more regional chiefs, and the mass of commoners reacted within these constraining social relations not simply in defence of the existing order but in their definition and pursuit of new class goals and interests. The internal relations and their effect on the external forces were complicated because these relations were refashioned by interaction with white settlers, merchant and mining capitalists, and the colonial state.

An approach to rural transformation that focuses only on the changing material needs and domestic relations of the homestead is typical of the usual analysis both of the rise and fall of the southern African peasantry and of societies with a high degree of homestead autonomy.[5] Yet the notion of atomistic, self-contained homesteads interacting individually with the natural environment and commodity markets is inadequate for many parts of the sub-continent, Swaziland included. Kimble, Delius, and Harries have all recently drawn attention to the importance of pre-colonial, extra-homestead relations in commodity production and labour migration from Basutoland, the northern Transvaal, and southern Mozambique.[6] Less attention has been paid to the pre-colonial Swazi, an example where both market production and migration were largely absent.

The comparative lateness of Swaziland's subordination to colonial rule helps to explain the lack of Swazi men on the labour markets of the region for most of the nineteenth century. Swazi indifference was underwritten by the productive independence of the individual homestead. As long as Swazi homesteads had continued access to abundant natural resources, could participate in a number of complementary branches of production, and could cope with an uncertain physical environment this situation could persist. Within the homestead, the emergence and consolidation of a distinctive sexual division of labour led to a far greater degree of geographical mobility for men than women. However, most of the male labour resources of Swazi society were locked into a set of extraneous relations of subordination and tribute with local chiefs (predominantly in the south of the country) and the central Dlamini authorities. These relations, particularly the regimental system, were important determinants of the pre-colonial labour immobility which characterized Swaziland in the nineteenth century. The young Swazi male was no stranger to migration or to spending extended periods away from home. Appropriation of labour from the commoner homestead by king and chief depended upon the spatial transfer of labour power to a designated point of production – whether by military expeditions, hunting parties, or working the fields of the rulers. The problem which confronted capital and colonial state in the late nineteenth century was how to break the binding power of pre-capitalist relations and redirect this movement of labour for capitalist enterprise.

A distinguishing feature of Swaziland's extremely brief period of peasant export production in the late 1880s and early 1890s was that it bore little direct connection to labour migrancy. Studies in other areas have emphasized the existence of such linkages, in both an enabling and inhibiting sense. Bundy and others have stressed that commodity production was often a hedge against and a viable alternative to labour migration, and that a sustained extra-economic assault on the commodity producer was necessary in order to free African labour for capitalist enterprise.[7] As agricultural viability was undermined, so the labour flow blossomed. In Pondoland, by contrast, migrancy and commodity production expanded simultaneously, as the proceeds of labour migration were reinvested in the rural economy.[8] Neither scenario adequately captures the situation in Swaziland. While the early 1890s did witness a brief reorientation of agricultural production towards the market, it did not occur in response to colonial demands for labour nor was it accompanied by any upsurge in Swazi labour migration. Export production was dominated by the larger domestic production units in Swazi society, those of the Swazi ruling class. The terms of participation were thus clearly established by the pre-existing productive relations of Swazi society. With access to the requisite land and labour resources, and strong political sanctions over commoner accumulation, the chiefs were ideally placed to take advantage of new market opportunities. In addition, with their extensive stock reserves, they were able to use the new regional market for beef and *lobola* cattle by reinvesting the proceeds of cattle trading in agricultural innovation. The increased demand for agricultural labour at the homesteads of the chiefs seems to have rendered migrancy even less likely among Swazi commoners and labour migration from Swaziland remained extremely limited until the late 1890s.

In the aftermath of ecological calamity between 1896 and 1899, the constraints on Swazi labour migration were, of necessity, waived by the Swazi chiefs. But such participation, however ephemeral, tended to draw male labour back into the orbit of homestead reproduction. Hence a new dimension was introduced into the developing struggle for Swazi labour, as the heads of homesteads attempted to direct their members to the wage labour markets to acquire the basic means for homestead survival. With Swazi cattle holdings remaining in a depleted state for the first decade of British rule and endemic food shortages plaguing the Swazi countryside this trend was sustained well beyond the 1890s.

Superficially, at least, the situation in the Swazi countryside came increasingly to resemble that described for the southern African periphery by various underdevelopment theorists: declining rural productivity accompanied by and reinforcing an upsurge in male labour migrancy. Yet there is little substance to the argument that land expropriation *per se* was initially responsible for the depressed state of Swazi agriculture, since the Swazi did not lose effective control of two-thirds of the land surface until 1914 and grain purchase had become ubiquitous well before then. The lack of accessible markets, shortages of draft power in the wake of cattle disease, a series of drought years, and the erection of a relatively efficient distribution network for imported grain all conspired against agricultural self-sufficiency. In turn, the availability of imported grain for homestead purchase and the integration of the plough into the domestic agricultural cycle reinforced a new domestic division of labour in which men took on much greater responsibilities for homestead production than before. Declining homestead size, a direct result of incorporation into the migratory labour system, also demanded greater male commitment to agriculture. But availability of purchased grain and a new domestic division of labour also seem to have facilitated (and may even have been hastened by) the withdrawal of labour from the fields by Swazi women. It would be difficult to argue that homestead incorporation into the capitalist economy was unequivocally liberating for rural women but it did allow many to win a greater degree of space and more control over their own time than the onerous agricultural calendar of the nineteenth century had ever permitted.

Before 1907 and to some degree thereafter, Swazi men who looked for work did not do so out of any real sense of duty to the colonial state. In order to acquire money for homestead food purchase and *lobola* payments young Swazi men worked sporadically, and as close to Swaziland as possible. Balancing the higher wages of the Rand against their catastrophic experiences of the late 1890s, the majority chose to avoid the mines. Those who did go to Johannesburg were careful to play the mine labour market to their best advantage. They shunned labour recruiters, would only work on a small number of mines, and quickly deserted when conditions fell below expectations. The poorer or smaller homestead without access to a wage and the migrant who resented colonial appropriation of a large proportion of his earnings, tried either to find other means of meeting colonial demands or to avoid making payment altogether. The former strategy, which demanded a reorganization of homestead labour and productive activity, eventually led to increased indebtedness and hardship. Yet Swazi homesteads reacted far more intricately than is suggested by some of the literature on the rural response to colonial coercion. The road to underdevelopment is littered with innovative, though ultimately unsuccessful, attempts to keep proletarianization at bay.

Tax evasion became much less viable after the colonial state honed its instruments of coercion in 1907–8. Swazi men could ill afford to spend long spells in crowded, unsanitary colonial jails if the loss of potential wage earnings threatened to undermine homestead reproduction. For the chiefs, with a higher profile in the countryside, tax evasion was never a realistic option. They simply intensified their demands upon their followers. The struggle to control the terms and fruits of migrancy consequently intensified dramatically after 1908. Within the domestic unit struggles over homestead income crystallized around the conflict between *lobola* and food purchase. The *umnumzana* needed to maximize the proportion of migrant earnings accruing to the homestead to avoid migrating themselves and to meet homestead consumption needs. How successful they were determined how quickly sons could accumulate sufficient *lobola*. There were, however, other interests also actively contending for the migrant wage. The claims of South African and local employers on Swazi workers and the competing demands of colonial state, chief, and homestead head all exercised an inevitable upward pressure on the scope and timing of Swazi participation in migrancy.

When the British assumed control of Swaziland after the Anglo-Boer War, they were confronted by a kingless society, but one in which pre-capitalist relations were still the dominant mode of social organization for the majority of the country's population. The control of the Swazi aristocracy and chiefs over land, and hence the labour, of Swazi homesteads was preserved intact. It was quickly manifest to white settlers, mining interests, and the colonial administration that they would not be surrendered without a struggle. There were also clear regional differences in the degree of political control exercised by the aristocracy over the country, with the southern districts remaining more loosely tied by the centralizing institutions of Swazi society. The Swazi chiefs in general, and the Dlamini rulers in particular, were provided with ample evidence of the threat posed by mass Swazi participation in wage employment and of the contradictions inherent in any attempt on their part to encourage the migratory flow. Such endorsement, ostensibly to further their own struggle with the colonial state, carried the constant danger of undermining the very foundations upon which chief-commoner relations were built. Hence, the ruling class had to build into the system both the means of appropriating a proportion of the fruits of Swazi wage labour and ways in which to exercise some control over those movements. While local chiefs devised their own means of achieving these ends, building on pre-capitalist notions of dependency and tribute, the aristocracy came up with its own grand design to hold the outskirts in place. This inevitably brought the central authorities into direct conflict with local chiefs and their followers.

The dilution of Dlamini powers during periods of regency was not a new phenomenon; the prospective length of that period certainly was. Queen Regent Labotsibeni and her advisers were forced to devise alternative strategies to control the drift from the royal villages, to hold regional chiefdoms in check, and to manipulate the migratory labour movement in royal interests. They turned, quite logically, to the institution which had given the Dlamini aristocracy actual or nominal control over all young Swazi men in the nineteenth century. The longevity and resilience of the Swazi regimental system set it apart from those of other Nguni societies whose redoubtable regiments had been reduced to a hollow shell by the twin agencies of capital penetration and imperial reconstruction. It was this particular institution, so central to Dlamini dominance in the nineteenth century, which the aristocracy struggled to retain, manipulate, and adapt in the twentieth. Plans to legitimize wage labour in the industrial army of the Transvaal as a suitable regimental activity and to exercise central control over the migrant labour flow, were furthered by the presence in Swaziland of a frustrated band of recruiters who calculated that their path to the labour resources of the country lay in the regiments. An alliance between aristocracy and recruiter was quickly forged. The Dlamini strategy was actively contested by the southern chiefs and by homestead heads, but its ultimate failure must be laid at the door of resistance by migrants to central directives concerning the conditions and location of employment, and to the intervention of a colonial state attempting to defuse the tension in the countryside.

Between 1909 and 1912 the Witwatersrand gold mines emerged as the major (though by no means exclusive) employer of Swazi workers, in sharp contrast to their earlier avoidance of this place of work. Characteristic patterns and processes of labour migration were established which came to typify the country's labour history until the 1940s. The erratic movement of Swazi workseekers during the early years of colonial rule was replaced by one in which a large and relatively consistent number of migrants began to divide their annual calendar into two parts, one half spent in Swaziland and the other away working on the South African mines. The seasonality of labour movement became more, rather than less, marked as new forms of productive organisation and homestead structure developed.

Central to the genesis of the mines' migrant labour system as a whole was the role of merchant capital in forging links between the rural districts and particular labour markets. The complexities and conflicts which pervaded the formative years of the mine recruiting system, disguised until recently by all-embracing concepts like "monopsony," have recently been uncovered by Jeeves' regional analysis of the system at work.[9] His explanation for the massive regional conversion to mine employment after the repatriation of Chinese labour finds a ready echo in Swaziland. A social history of recruiting activity in the Swazi countryside provides added detail to the overall picture.

If the country proved to be barren territory for the recruiter before 1910, recruited mine labour rapidly became the dominant form of migrancy thereafter. Swaziland was overrun by labour recruiters, spearheaded by the labour contractors Marwick & Morris, who were remarkably successful in their quest to secure Swazi recruits. This was in marked contrast to the two decades of ineffectual recruiting which preceded it. A narrowing of the options on the regional labour market, the role of the recruiter as trader, the vital intermediary role of the black runner, and the opportunities for workers to "play" the system (both legally and illicitly) were all important factors. However, the cash advance proved to be the crucial determinant, not only because it allowed the migrant to hold off repressive taxation by the colonial state, but because it afforded the homesteads and chiefs of migrants potentially greater control over the fate of the mine wage. Even after the competitive excesses of the years before 1912 were brought under control by the NRC, the advance continued to exercise its effects.

Swaziland also provides direct evidence of the important intermediary role of the black runner who, though he was in one sense a collaborator, was no passive instrument of the recruiter or, ultimately, of mining capital. The profession was highly sought after as the gains were considerable if the runner plied his trade successfully. The recruiter's anxiety to reduce recruiting costs, colonial legislation, the preferences of migrants for certain mines, and the amount of time spent in non-productive activity, all rendered running an inherently unstable enterprise. But it was a niche in the developing migrant labour system that Swazi men, and the sons of chiefs and aristocrats in particular, were only too anxious to fill.

The integration of Swaziland into the goldmines' migrant labour system did not go uncontested by capitalist interests within Swaziland itself. In contrast to "consolidated" areas such as Basutoland and Pondoland, Swaziland was a mineral-rich area and also offered attractive opportunities for commercial agriculture. As a result, early colonial Swaziland bore many of the hallmarks of a frontier society as white settlers, pastoralists, land companies, and mining concerns scrambled to secure a stake in the mineral and land resources of the country. Although this community was relatively successful in harnessing state support to secure unfettered control over resources, they were much less successful in persuading Swazi workers to expend their labour on the estates and mines of the country. Fierce contests for labour consequently developed on the ground. On the local tin and gold mines, for example, mine management had continuous problems with worker stabilization and discipline.

Migrant labour systems in southern Africa have traditionally depended on a marked spatial separation of home and workplace on the part of an oscillating workforce. Without the incessant intervention of the countryside, the beneficiaries of those systems were able to enforce a greater degree of time-discipline during the production process. The checkered history of the Swaziland mining industry in the early decades of this century provides an important illustration of the peculiar difficulties which confronted capitalist enterprise in a rural setting where traditional social relationships and obligations were still strong. Struggles between capital and labour on the mines were amplified not simply by the proximity of the worker's own homestead but by demands of the Swazi ruling class which did not diminish when the migrant moved to work on adjacent mining properties. Even with the weight of state backing the mines were unable to enforce their concept of time-thrift on local miners, with severe repercussions for production and profitability.

The British colonial state responded favourably to the overtures of local mine managers for formal and informal assistance with their irreverent labour force. But on many occasions the administration's response to the demands of actual and aspirant capitalist was less helpful. In the late 1890s, Republican attitudes and policy towards Swaziland were transparent. The country was a potential source of labour for the mines and farms of the Transvaal; Swazi aversion to wage labour therefore had to be broken. Kruger's Swaziland administration under J.C. Krogh used a mixture of coercion and incentive to try and undermine the independence of the Swazi homestead and shatter the power of chief-commoner relations. Because of the Anglo-Boer War, and the loss of Republican control over Swaziland, the fate of these strategies remains imponderable. After the Anglo-Boer War, the British colonial state was confronted with much the same need to mobilize Swazi labour for the South African market and with many of the same frustrations doing so.

The brooding presence of the South African economy and the Rand goldfields can be detected in virtually all aspects of British policy making in Swaziland. In the eyes of colonial officialdom, the ultimate political fate of Swaziland was for it to be incorporated into the Transvaal. The time for this was, for one reason or another, continuously extended.[10] But the colonial state saw no point in delaying the country's economic integration. Indeed, closer economic union would undoubtedly make the case for transfer more palatable. The British administration avidly pursued a policy consistent with this end. The Swazi were to supply labour to the South African mines. Their land was to be used by productive British settlers. Swaziland's incorporation into the migratory labour system had been achieved within a decade of the imposition of imperial rule when in Kuper's vivid phrase "the mine dump had replaced the peaceful countryside in the foreground of much Swazi life." But the local state could hardly take all of the credit for this achievement, since it had as much to do with conditions internal to Swazi society and the choices offered to Swazi homesteads and migrants by competitive recruiting conditions as it did with the colonial instruments of labour mobilization. Indeed the striking feature of early colonial labour policy in Swaziland was the limited ability of the state to direct a large flow of Swazi labour to the Rand mines. By pressing extremely hard on the Swazi homestead the colonial state was able to squeeze labour into the market but it had little control over where that labour would go and how long it would remain there. When the end had been achieved by other means the administration was forced to oversee a recruiting system ripe for manipulation and abuse by all parties. As for the migrants themselves, their new commitment to the Rand was far from unconditional. Strategies of survival, including ethnic solidarity, helped Swazi miners to cope with the social and physical costs of minework.

Colonial strategy in Swaziland was also complicated by the competing demands of the local mines and a nascent settler-estate sector. Attempts to resolve these various pressures by freeing land and generating labour for capitalist enterprise, while simultaneously attempting to maintain social order, show the real constraints on state power in Swaziland and its sensitivity to local conditions. The Swazi countryside proved anything but "peaceful." Milner and his successors shared the vision of Swaziland as a haven for a class of British rural accumulators. In Milner's case the country dovetailed neatly into his reconstruction plans for the Transvaal. Selborne was concerned to have the country stocked with agrarian capitalists before transfer to avoid it being used as a dumping ground for poor whites. Both did all they could to further settler interests in the country. The anticipated influx of settlers did not take place and large amounts of land freed for the purpose lay idle.

What the colonial state could deliver was far less than white settlers and other concession holders were demanding. Commentators on the land partition, by means of which over 60 per cent of the area of Swaziland passed out of Swazi hands, have tended to stress the ineffectiveness of peaceful Swazi opposition to an intransigent colonial administration bent on securing land for settler enterprise and creating labour reserves totally inadequate for Swazi needs. The argument developed here proposes a more nuanced interpretation. It suggests that colonial policy was in practice governed not simply by the needs of agrarian capital for land but was also constrained by the reactions of the Swazi themselves to various mooted policies. Colonial response to calls for far-reaching land expropriation was governed by "interaction between social engineering and the art of the possible."[11] The administration constantly desired to avoid an armed uprising. The Bambatha revolt in Zululand and the uncharacteristically united front of the Swazi chieftainship in the face of a common threat, underscored the value of caution. Both colonial and, more reluctantly, settler ideology consequently underwent a significant shift away from confrontation towards accommodation of the existing political framework of Swazi society. Not only did the Swazi receive more land, in quantity and quality, than they might otherwise have done, but the delimitation of reserve boundaries kowtowed to the pre-capitalist geography of Swazi society. While the Swazi ruling class lost the war against land alienation, to their undoubted cost, they did win some victories on the way. The upshot was that the Swazi chiefs and aristocracy were eventually able to secure for themselves a much greater stake in the colonial (and later post-colonial) order than might once have seemed likely and than white settlers originally demanded.

In concentrating solely on the provision of land for white settlement in Swaziland, studies of the land partition have tended to lose sight of another piece of colonial social engineering integral to the planning and execution of the partition. There has thus been an unfortunate tendency to drive a wedge between colonial land and labour policy when, in reality, the two were inseparable. Those who have made the connection have drawn, perhaps unsurprisingly, on the work of the labour reserve theorists.[12] There is no real evidence, however, that the creation of Swazi reserves was conceived at the behest of South African mining capital as part of "a policy which would maintain the 'reserves' in order to subsidize the costs of re-producing a migrant labour force."[13] Although segregationist ideas were gelling, as the SANAC Report attests, there was no party line which officials such as Milner and Selborne felt compelled to follow in Swaziland. It is also improbable that the reproductive costs of a group of Africans who shunned mine labour, and who did not have the numbers to form a large share of the mine labour force, should have needed subsidizing. And in the years leading up to the partition, no colonial official in Swaziland ever made the connection.

The partition was intended to be as much a labour as a land partition. It was designed to provide two of the basic preconditions for settler-estate production in the country: private property and a land market. But it also sought to mark off a portion of the Swazi labour force for the exclusive use of a weak agricultural sector. The perennial problem of securing Swazi for farm work in the country, first in evidence in the 1890s, resurfaced in the early years of British rule. While the colonial state remained committed to mobilizing Swazi for the Rand, appeals from local white settlers for aid with their labour difficulties met with a positive response from colonial officials. Drawing strongly on precedent and example from elsewhere in the sub-continent, and motivated by the persistent demands of land-owners, colonial officials concluded that the imposition of a system of labour tenancy was the best way forward.[14] Swazi labour divided off for settler-estate production by the land partition was to be im-mobilized on the farms through binding tenancy contracts. Prior to July 1914, the date chosen for the legalization of tenancy relations, colonial officials were engaged in persuading the Swazi chiefs and people of the finality of partition, directing the resettlement of Swazi homesteads, and establishing the guidelines for a system of farm tenancy. White landlords were given leave to "experiment" with their new tenants. Thereafter, those who refused to submit to a new set of social controls could be summarily evicted.

The colonial solution to the farm labour problem was very tidy in principle. On the ground, however, the conditions of tenancy be-came a perpetual source of conflict between landlords and tenants. This struggle was to have a significant impact on the development of the settler-estate sector in the country, not only in the very early years looked at in this study, but through to the advent of agri-business capital in the country in the 1950s and 1960s. As for the material context of production, land control was secure, but the estate sector remained shackled by capital shortages, Union embargoes, and lack of access to external markets. But on the farms Swazi tenants did not passively submit to the new dispensation. While many homesteads opted or were forced by social conditions within Swazi society to remain on white farms, this did not signal any desire to submit to the terms of farm employment. Attempts by landlords to enforce onerous tenancy conditions met with strong and sustained opposition, as homesteads and workers struggled to maintain a degree of independence in relation to the various labour markets of the region. The insecurity of the landlords was exacerbated by the response of local chiefs to the loss of their followers and by the presence in the countryside of the agents of Rand mining capital. Tenant reactions to these competing demands on their labour proved to be a major reason for the early failure of the system of labour tenancy in Swaziland.

The result was that the 1907 land partition was never the straightforward solution to the farm labour problem that colonial social engineers once hoped it might be. In 1912, Robert Coryndon informed the Swazi chiefs that it was his intention to introduce white settlers and thereby "promote the interests and welfare of the whole country in every way."[15] There proved to be very little community of interest and social harmony in the estate sector during either the period considered here or thereafter. At the behest of the landlords, the colonial state was repeatedly drawn into the messy battles that continued to threaten the farm labour supply; legislating here, buttressing there, and at all times moving with the caution which the contradictory pressures upon it necessitated.

Labour tenancy and the expropriation of land for settler enterprise intensified the conflict between an indigenous ruling class and an emerging agrarian capitalism. Ruling class opposition to colonial policy was aroused both by the loss of land and by the concomitant loss of political authority, prestige, and tribute from commoners on white farms. After rejecting armed resistance as a viable strategy of opposition, the Swazi chieftainship chose to work within the limits set by the new colonial order by purchasing alienated land on the open market. For its effectiveness the land repurchase scheme depended on a united chieftainship and the full co-operation of Swazi commoners who were needed to supply the necessary funds. Neither was forthcoming. Internal rifts between the Queen Regent and the regional chiefs, and between all chiefs and their commoner subjects, seriously compromised the effectiveness of the scheme. Unable to mobilize their followers in the cause, the chiefs managed to capture colonial state power for a limited season in order to extort funds to meet their land debt.

For the colonial state the entry of the Swazi rulers into the land market was contradictory. It certainly signified tacit acceptance of the reality of partition and private property, an important concession which allowed the state to manipulate the terrain of the contest over land policy in the interests of white settlers. By contrast, the possibility that land earmarked for white settlement would return to the Swazi fold was viewed with great concern. With the full backing of the settlers the colonial state effectively forced the Swazis off an open land market and set the seal on colonial land policy until at least the 1940s.

Nonetheless, the concessions extracted from the colonial state in the pre-partition period ensured that the chiefs and aristocracy continued to control a depleted, but relatively significant, portion of the material base of the country; some 37 per cent of the country as a whole, and almost 50 per cent of the more heavily settled middleveld zone. Hence, although Swazi homesteads now had alternative access to land on the newlycreated white farms of the country, the pre-capitalist basis of chief-commoner relations was preserved over at least a third of the country. The majority of Swazi homesteads remained directly dependent on the chiefs in order to acquire access to the means of production. Those who stayed on white farms or crown land had no ultimate security in the event of eviction and may also have wished to cultivate good relations with their local chief. This, in the final analysis, explains why the Swazi chiefs were able to hold on to their dominant position within Swazi society despite considerable political, juridical, and economic erosion of their nineteenth-century powers. It was also the foundation upon which Sobhuza II was to build after his ascension to the throne in his quest to reassert the political and cultural hegemony of the Dlamini aristocracy within Swazi society.

This account draws to a close with the coronation of Sobhuza II, but the next fifty years of British colonial rule witnessed the embellishment and elaboration of many of the processes discussed here. The continuing struggles of the chieftainship to regain land and control the commoner populace; intensified conflict between landlords and tenants with increased white settlement of the country; ever-deepening dependence of Swazi homesteads on wage labour and food purchase; the rejuvenation of Dlamini dominance under Sobhuza; and the renewal of competitive recruiting in the 1940s and 1950s as British and South African capital began a second colonial occupation of Swaziland, all await detailed exploration.[16] Their study should benefit from an understanding of the tumultous years between 1890 and 1920. In turn, light may be shed on the contemporary economic subordination of Swaziland to South Africa and on the resurgence of the traditional in the post-colonial period. As recent events indicate, the "residuum of the past" here remains unusually strong.[17]

Appendixes

APPENDIX A

Swazi 'Emabutfo' in the Nineteenth Century

King	Regiment	Approximate Age (1900)
Mswati	Inyati	56–67
	Mgadhlela	52–57
	Giba	47–56
	Balondolozi	45–52
Mbandeni	Ndhlavela	38–47
	Giba	30–37
	Mgadhlela	24–29
Bunu	Ngulube	18–24
	Halaza	13–17
	Lisaka/Lomkhele	8–12

Sources: SA, RCS 408/33; Webb and Wright, *James Stuart Archive*, vol. 1, 153–4.

APPENDIX B

Contract between Bunu and M.J.J. Grobler, 3 May 1899

Whereas it has appeared that during recent Months, so called labour agents, under which head are included various undesirable and irresponsible persons, have visited and still visit Swaziland with the alleged object of recruiting Swazies as labourers for the mining companies in the S.A.R. and thereby conveying beyond my realm my Swazi subjects without my knowledge and consent. And recognising the desirability and necessity that Swazies should leave (my realm) under better control and proper supervision to labour in the S.A.R. in order that they should be placed in a better position to pay their taxes to the authorities. Now therefore these present witness that I the undersigned Ungwane, alias N'Bili alias N'Bunu declare herewith to empower and irrevocably to appoint Matthias Johannes Jacobus Grobler for the period of 15 consecutive years as my lawful Agent for me, and on my behalf from me personally and by his representatives to deal and have the control over the conveyance and proper supervision of the labourer from time to time to good mines and other companies and persons in the South African Republic (and in Swaziland), upon the following terms and conditions to wit: I undertake and bind myself on every occasion to deliver to the said Matthias Johannes Jacobus Grobler or his representative or his proxy holder on their demand within fourteen days as many sound, healthy Swazies apparently between the ages of 17 and 45 years as possible (in no case however less than 50 upon each demand).

He the said Matthias Johannes Jacobus Grobler shall convey and employ the Swazies to the general labour Agencies, mining companies and such like at his own expense including pass money (and moreover shall pay to me the sum of 10/- per Swazie so delivered by me to him). Any overplus over and above the aforesaid disbursements arising out of the transaction may be appropriated by the said Matthias Johannes Jacobus Grobler to cover his own expenses. I promise and bind myself further to give no other person any privilege whatsoever to convey Swazies as labourers etc. from Swaziland or to employ them on any place.

This done and signed at Zomboti in Swaziland on this 3rd day of May 1899.

As Witnesses: Signed By:
Chris Botha   Bunu
Maaciban   Labotsibeni
H. de Jager   Sebokwane
                       Gudluluku

Note: On May 9 1899 a modified contract was also signed. This gave Grobler the right to prevent other recruiters from working in Swaziland:

Whereas it appears that during the last months so-called labour agents amongst whom certain undesirable and irresponsible persons are found in Swaziland and have and are still visiting Swaziland alleging that they are recruiting labourers for the Mining Companies in the South African Republic and in that manner are taking away my Swazis without my knowledge and consent. Seeing the desirability that the Swazis should leave the country under better regulations and supervision to work in the South African Republic with the object of being placed in a position to enable their taxes to be paid to the Authorities. Now therefore, I, the undersigned Ungwana alias Unhili alias Ubunu hereby declare to empower and irrevocably appoint Matthias Johannes Jacobus Grobler for a period of 15 consecutive years as my lawful agent in my name and on my behalf personally and through his power to act, supervise and direct, the transport of the labourers delivered by me to him from time to time to good Mines and other Companies or other persons in the South African Republic under the following conditions that is to say. I undertake and bind myself to deliver as occasion demands to the said Matthias Johannes Jacobus Grobler, his Substitute or representative and at their request to deliver within fourteen days as many good healthy Swazis as possible from 17 to 45 years of age. These Swazis, he the said Matthias Johannes Jacobus Grobler shall take to the various labour Depots or Mine Companies or otherwise and place them. Further I promise and bind myself to give no one else whomever any permission to take Swazis as labourers or otherwise out of Swaziland to work on any place. *Further the said Matthias Johannes Jacobus Grobler is hereby authorised to prevent all persons whomsoever and if necessary to do so of right from deporting any Swazis from Swaziland* [my italics]. In case it can be proved that the said Matthias Johannes Jacobus Grobler has not faithfully carried out the conditions of this Power of Attorney, then I shall have the right to revoke the same.

This done and signed at Bremersdorp on this 9th day of May 1899.

As Witnesses: Signed By:
C.A. Koevoort   Unhili alias Ubunu
Chris Botha   Labotsibene
H. de Jager   Mgudhlula
A.P. Moritz   Bili
Maacibaan

Sources: SA, S7A; SA, RCS 23/10.

APPENDIX C

Contract between A. Bremer and Robinson Group of Companies, 1907

Robinson Group of Companies
Labour Department,
Mayfair Office.

Albert Bremer, Esq.

Dear Sir,

This is to confirm the arrangement entered into between yourself and this Group for supply of Five Hundred (500) Swazies on the following terms and conditions:

1. One hundred Swazies to be supplied within one month from date of due notice.
2. The balance of 400 to be supplied as required by us.
3. All natives to sign on for at least six months and you will use your utmost endeavour to get them to sign on for twelve months.
4. All natives to be underground boys.
5. The natives to receive pay at the rate of 2/– per shift.

220   Appendixes

6. We to pay you the following premium for boys delivered at the
   Mine:– 6 month boys 50/– (fifty shillings)
            12 month boys £5:10:0 per head
In consideration of the sum of £1,000 – which we advance you, and which sum is to
be deducted from amount which will become due to you as boys are delivered, you
guarantee to do your utmost to supply us with *as many* boys beyond the aforemen-
tioned 500 boys as we may in the future require.

Yours faithfully,
John E.Seccull
For Labour Department

Source: BRA, HE 254/149/942.

APPENDIX D

*Agreement between Swaziland Tin Ltd. and
Prince Malunge, 1906*

Embekelweni
24th September 1906

To Prince Malunge
EMBEKELWENI
Dear Sir,
Referring to our recent discussion on the labour question, I am now prepared to pay
you the sum of 10/– per boy for the first 500 boys sent to the Swaziland Tin Mine,
Mbabane, under the following conditions:–

1st   That the boys be engaged to work for not less than six months.
2nd   Their payments be made for every batch of 50 boys delivered on the Com-
       pany's property.
3rd   That you agree not to divert or supply labour to other Companys or indi-
       viduals without first submitting such labour to the Swaziland Tin Company

Yours faithfully,
S.T. Ryan

Source: SA, RCS 100/15.

APPENDIX E

*Contract Signed between 50 Swazis and
B. Armstrong at Mbabane, September 1908*

We, the undersigned members of the Ngulube, Masotha, Isaka and Magdhlela regiments of the Swazi people, are proceeding to Johannesburg to work underground
as drill boys on the York Mine, Krugersdorp. We are going of our own free will, at
the invitation of the Ndhlovukazi, the Chief Regent of the Swazi people and we have

been dispatched "in the kraal" as an impi. We are instructed by the Chief Regent to learn rock drilling and to do our utmost to prove to the white people at the mines that the Swazi nation is equal to any other nation at drill work, so that we may win for our nation a good reputation amongst the mines and ensure satisfactory employment and fair treatment in the future. We are proud to be sent on a mission by the Ndhlovukazi. We are going as though we were going to war, and we are resolved to carry out our mission. We are proceeding to the York Mine, Krugersdorp, where we will work for a period of six months as drill boys. We clearly understand that we are not promised any definite wage or rate of pay. We shall be paid according to the manner in which we acquit ourselves. If we do not do the regulation minimum amount of work a shift, we understand that we shall not be paid anything. What the ordinary rates of pay shall be we are willing to wait and learn for ourselves when we get there. We are the scouts of the nation to ascertain how the York Mine will treat us. We ask for no promise.

Source: *Rand Daily Mail*, 16 October 1908.

APPENDIX F

Marwick & Morris Mine Contract

"KWA MUHLE."

AGREEMENT.—It is hereby agreed between Messrs. JOHN SYDNEY MARWICK and GEORGE ABBOT MORRIS, hereinafter called the "Employers," and the undermentioned Natives, hereinafter called the "Labourers," as follows:—

The employers agree to hire the labourers, and the labourers contract to give their services as underground hammer boys on the East Rand Proprietary Mines, Limited, or on any other mines or works to be selected by the employer, for a period of six months, that is to say, one hundred and eighty completed shifts, for wages at the rate of two shillings per shift, a shift to be every completed hole of thirty-six inches drilled in the mine. The labourers agree to do the necessary shovelling to clear the face of the rock before commencing to drill, but the time so occupied shall not exceed two hours.

The labourers shall be paid for the first fourteen days worked in the mine at the rate of two shillings per diem, irrespective of the number of inches drilled by them, but thereafter their time shall be computed on the number of completed shifts only. The employers undertake to provide the labourers with rations and quarters free of cost.

The labourers hereby acknowledge their indebtedness to the employers for advances or value received in the amount set opposite to their respective names hereunder, and they agree to the deduction of such amounts from their wages, and do hereby agree that such indebtedness shall be regarded either as a set off against the wages of the Labourers until the indebtedness is satisfied, or that the Labourers have hereby ceded to the Employers all wages coming due to them until such indebtedness is discharged—whichever course the Employers may deem most expedient.

The Labourers agree to enter upon the terms of this Contract at East Rand, Transvaal, on the.................day of.................1914.

Agent's No.	Travelling Pass No.	Passport No.	Name and Clan and Native's Mark	Father.	Chief.	Residence.	ADVANCES. Particulars.	Amount.	Name of Runner.

Attested by me at.................this.................day of.................1914.

.................Signature of Employer or Agent.

NOTE.—*Agents are requested not to put more than one Native name on each Contract Form.*

MARWICK & MORRIS' CONTRACT.—SCHEDULE OF WAGES.

HAMMER BOYS.—36 in. hole 2/- per shift. From 36 ins. to 48 ins. ½d. per inch, with bonus of 2d. for 42 ins., and a further bonus of 4d. for 48 ins., i.e., for 42 ins. 2/5, and for 48 in. 3/- per diem.

TRAMMING AND SHOVELLING.—1/6 per shift.

MACHINE BOYS.—2/- to 3/- per shift (*Ispisane*).

WINZE BOYS.—2/9 for 36 inches, including cleaning up (*E' Wenjini*).

SHAFT BOYS.—3/- for 36 inches, including cleaning up (*'E Dambula*).

APPENDIX G

Agreement between Messrs Marwick & Morris and the Native Recruiting Corporation, 29 January 1913

Recruiters

1. Both parties agree not to engage recruiters, runners, or other employes of either party until such recruiter, runner, or other employe has been out of employment for three months.

2. Both parties agree not to engage an assistant in any store where one of the parties has already a Licensed Recruiter.

3. Both parties agree not to engage any recruiter, runner, or other employe, who has been dismissed by either party without the consent in writing of the party lately employing such recruiter, runner, or other employe.

Advances

1. The advances in both Swaziland and Zululand are to be strictly limited to £5, and such advances shall only be made to natives who engage to come out to work within three months after the receipt of such advance. It is understood that the £5 advance covers everything, including fines, taxes etc. This clause is to come into operation as from the lst March 1913.

2. Subject to facilities being granted by the Government concerned, both parties agree to immediately prosecute any native who refuses to come out at the end of such period of three months or any shorter period as he may engage to remain at home.

3. No native in Swaziland is to be advanced any money who has not in his possession a tax receipt or certificate of liability for tax, and such tax receipt or certificate of liability for tax is to be endorsed either with the name of the Native Recruiting Corporation or Messrs Marwick & Morris when the boy is recruited for either of these parties.

Feeding

1. It is agreed that all natives coming forward from Zululand and Swaziland are to be charged 5/– for feeding, this is to come into force for all natives who are attested on or after the 1st April 1913.

Runners

1. It is agreed that in Zululand and Swaziland only actual recruiting agents are to be allowed to have runners, and only three runners are to be licensed to each recruiter, it being understood that if a recruiter refuses to limit his runners to three both parties shall inform such recruiter that they will not bear the cost of any of his runners.

2. In special cases where it is found necessary to increase the number of runners the party wishing to increase same must notify the other party. This provision is to come into force from the 1st March 1913.

Mealies

1. It is agreed that neither party will in future supply mealies to natives under any conditions whatsoever.

Cattle and Horses

1. It is agreed that advances by way of cattle and horses shall be discontinued, and that neither party will have any dealings with natives as regards cattle and horses. This clause shall become operative as soon as Messrs Marwick & Morris have disposed of their existing stores.

Free Railway Fares

1. Messrs Marwick & Morris agree not to pay free rail fares for natives coming forward from the Harding District if they are able to abandon same under Mr Rethman's contract.

2. Messrs Marwick & Morris undertake, if possible, to abandon giving free railway fares to Basuto natives who sign on for a period of not less than six months.

Source: NRC, File 5.

APPENDIX H

Notice by the Chief Regent of Swaziland

SHE SAYS:

All Swazi are informed by means of this notice that the Chief Regent desires that they shall work this year because the final proclamation of the High Commissioner has been promulgated to the effect that on the 1st day of July 1914, in the coming winter, the Swazis are to go one side and the whites to the other.

Therefore it is necessary that all Swazis should pay money to enable the Chief to endeavour to add to the small areas to which it is said they are to go.

This collection will be called "The Swaziland National Land Fund."

In Swaziland it will first be paid at the time when the Government Tax Collection is made.

From Johannesburg to Witbank inclusive the Chief's Son Lomvanzi of Mbandeni, with C.S. Mabaso as his Secretary and Amos Zwane have been selected to collect the money from those working there. Therefore prepare yourselves at the different places.

The programme of the Chief's Son will be as follows:–

At Robinson Deep at 4 p.m. April 5, 1914

Cason	do.	"	12,	"
Van Ryn	do.	"	19,	"
Main Reef West	do.	"	26,	"
Pretoria	do.	May	3,	"
Witbank	do.	"	10,	"
Ermelo	do.	"	17,	"
Carolina	do.	"	24,	"

Those working from Waterval Boven to Barberton will be informed later of the names of the Collectors for those places.

Each man to pay £5.

Source: CO 417/546.

Notes

INTRODUCTION

1 Wolpe, "Capitalism and Cheap Labour Power"; Legassick, "South Africa"; Levy, *Foundations of the South African Cheap Labour System.*
2 Beinart, *Political Economy of Pondoland*; Harries, "Labour Migration from Mozambique"; Shillington, *Colonisation of the Southern Tswana*; Kimble, "Clinging to the Chiefs."
3 Booth, "Priorities and Opportunities for Research in Swaziland," 2.
4 I have explored the theoretical and historiographical background to this study in a number of articles: see Crush, "Southern African Regional Formation"; "Uneven Labour Migration in Southern Africa"; "Capitalist Homoficence, the Frontier and Uneven Development."
5 Berman, "Structure and Process."
6 Booth, *Swaziland*; Daniel, "Comparative Analysis of Lesotho and Swaziland's Relations"; Vieceli, "Swaziland after Sobhuza."
7 Hyam, *Failure of South African Expansion.*
8 Bonner, *Kings.*

CHAPTER ONE

1 Bonner, *Kings*, 155.
2 Ibid.; Bonner, "Factions and Fissions"; Delius, *The Land Belongs to Us*, 181–250.
3 Garson, *The Swaziland Question*; Mashasha, "Road to Colonialism."
4 Sieborger, "Recruitment and Organisation of African Labour," 180–93. In the 1870s and 1880s several employers in Natal applied to introduce labour from Swaziland but it is not clear whether these were for Swazi or not and there is no evidence that the applications came to fruition; NA, SNA, 1844/79, 878/83, 1219/90.

5 Etherington, "Labour Supplies and the Genesis of South African Confederation."

6 Ballard, "Migrant Labour in Natal"; Harries, "Kinship, Ideology and the Nature of Pre-Colonial Labour Migration"; Kimble, "Labour Migration in Basutoland."

7 Mathews, *Incwadi Yami*, 494–506; CO 879/33/840, Enclosure in No 3, Report on Swazieland, 7–8.

8 Settlers Emigration Society, *Land and Farming Prospects*, 17–25.

9 For readily accessible descriptions of these zones see Fair, Murdoch, and Jones, *Development in Swaziland*, 10–15; Booth, *Swaziland*, 80–90.

10 Bonner, *Kings*, 9–46; Murdoch, *Soils and Land Capability*, 39–42, 263–5.

11 SANAC, 1903–5, vol. 5, Written replies by A. Miller, 249; SA, J40/04, Moony to Secretary for Swaziland Affairs, 4 December 1905.

12 Hughes, *Land Tenure*, 28.

13 "Notes from Bulungu," TOS, 8 April 1899, 6 May 1899.

14 Beemer, "Diet of the Swazi," 203–5.

15 Ibid.

16 Milk yields were greatest in the summer months when grain stocks were at their lowest; Kuper, *African Aristocracy*, 36. See also KCL, Miller papers, MS 565, A. Miller, "The Kafir Races of South-East Africa," 15.

17 SA, Transcripts of Interviews with John Gamede, 1953–5; Beemer, "Diet of the Swazi," 205.

18 The geography of the homestead is described in Marwick, *The Swazi*, 11–37; Hughes, *Land Tenure*, 69–75.

19 KCL, Miller papers, MS 567, Alfred Gould to Zillah Gould, 15 November 1891, 4.

20 KCL, Miller papers, MS 565, A. Miller, "The Kafir Races of South-East Africa," 5; Trevor, *Forty Years in Africa*, 63; Griffithes, *From Bedford Row to Swazieland*, 32.

21 KCL, Miller papers, MS 567, Alfred Gould to Zillah Gould, 15 November 1891, 5–6.

22 Bonner, *Kings*, 13.

23 This may have been counterbalanced by increasing general stockwealth. In the early nineteenth century *lobola* payment for a wife was for a larger productive community since her sisters would also transfer their allegiance to the new homestead. This practice disappeared after about 1840 when each daughter became a potential source of cattle. During the nineteenth century bridewealth payments for the woman of even the humblest origins rose from 1 to 2 head to 10 to 12 head; Webb and Wright, eds., *James Stuart Archive*, vol. 1, evidence of Gama, 137–9; evidence of Giba kaSobhuza, 151; vol. 2, evidence of Mabola, 7; KCL, Stuart papers, KCM 24402, evidence of Zibokwana, 92; TLC, 1903, evidence of David Forbes, para. 2330–1.

24 TAD, SNA 259/642/05, Swaziland Concessions Commission, evidence of Godfrey Lagden, 21; KCL, Miller papers, MS 428a, Swaziland Concessions Commission, evidence of Theophilus Shepstone, 12, 14–15.

25 Jeff Guy sees the role of cattle in the latter context as a "self-reproducing store of labour-power [which] allowed the cattle-owner to increase his number of wives – that is ultimately the size of the lineage, homesteads, production communities and number of producers"; Guy, "Ecological Factors," 114. For analysis of cattle accumulation through marriage practices in Swaziland see Engelbrecht, "Swazi Customs Relating to Marriage"; Derman, "Stock and Aristocracy"; Kuper, "Rank and Preferential Marriage."

26 Kuper, *African Aristocracy*, 142.

27 On *lilima* see ibid., 144–8.

28 Ibid., 142.

29 Kuper, *Swazi*, 33–4; Hughes, *Land Tenure*, 158.

30 Kuper, *African Aristocracy*, 44; SANAC, 1903–5, vol. 5, Written replies by D. Forbes, 215; Written replies by A. Miller, 249.

31 Kuper, *African Aristocracy*, 45.

32 Hilda Kuper notes that in the "final heterogenous nation of over 70 clans 20% were *bomdzabiko* (true Swazi), 14% were *emakhandzambile* (those found ahead) and the remainder were *labatik'emuva* (latecomers)"; Kuper, *African Aristocracy*, 17–8, 233–4.

33 SA, D48/07/2205, Register of Hlatikulu Chiefs, 1907.

34 Kuper, "Development of a Primitive Nation," 341.

35 Bonner, *Kings*, 9–46.

36 The rise of the Swazi state has recently been explored in several important works by Phil Bonner: "Rise, Consolidation and Disintegration of Dlamini Power"; "Early State Formation Among the Nguni"; "Mswati II"; "Classes, the Mode of Production and the State"; *Kings*. See also Nyeko, "Rule of the Dlamini"; Jones, "Pre-Colonial Swazi Population."

37 This process was interrupted by major Zulu incursions in 1847 and 1852; Bonner, *Kings*, 57–62; Beemer, "Military Organization," 57. It is noteworthy that no Dlamini chiefs were placed in the drier reaches of the country; ACR, 1907–8, AC Ubombo; RCS 414/11, AC Ubombo, MR, February 1911. For a discussion of the structure and spacing of royal villages see Rosen-Prinz, "Urbanization and Political Change," 61–71.

38 Bonner, *Kings*, 88; KCL, Stuart papers, KCM 23513, File 30 (iii), Suggestions for consideration in connection with the Private Revenue Concession (PRC), 30 December 1922, 6; Forbes, *Life in South Africa*, 97.

39 On the restrictive marriage practices which funneled cattle into the hands of the aristocracy see Bonner, "Classes, the Mode of Production and the State." Figures for the nineteenth century show the wide discrepancies

in bridewealth demanded, ranging from over 200 cattle for a daughter of the king to less than 10 for a commoner woman; KCL, Miller papers, MS 565, A. Miller, "The Kafir Races of South-East Africa," 11; MS 567, Alfred Gould to Zillah Gould, 15 November 1891, 5

40 *The Net*, 1 September 1887, 132; Wilson, *Behind the Scenes*, 80. Another estimate put the total cattle wealth of the country at 35–40,000 in the late 1880s; CO 879/33/480, Enclosure in No 3, Report on Swazieland. Four royal cattle posts were established by Mswati in the 1850s and two by Mbandeni in the 1870s; Kuper, *African Aristocracy*, 171; KCL, Miller papers, MS 602, Incidents in the History of Swaziland.

41 For colourful contemporary descriptions of the *Incwala* see KCL, Miller papers, MS 1479a, "The Incwala" by Allister Miller; Mathews, *Incwadi Yami*, 501–3; Halle, *Mayfair to Maritzburg*, 180–90. Over the years the proper interpretation of the *Incwala* has been debated at length by anthropologists; Cook, "Incwala Ceremony of the Swazi"; Marwick, *The Swazi*, 182–95; Kuper, "Ritual of Kingship Among the Swazi"; "Costume and Cosmology"; and *African Aristocracy*, 197–225; Beidelman, "Swazi Royal Ritual."

42 KCL, Miller papers, MS 1479a, "The Incwala" by Allister Miller, 4.

43 Parallel female age-regiments were also established but their role was never more than nominal; Kuper, "African Aristocracy," 129–33.

44 Descriptions of the age-regiment system are from KCL, Miller papers, MS 565, A. Miller, "The Kafir Races of South-East Africa"; MS 567, Alfred Gould to Zillah Gould, 15 November 1891; SA, RCS 115/14, de Symons Honey, "A History of Swaziland," 30–1; Beemer, "Military Organization," 67–74. Both the Inyati regiment in the 1850s and the Ndhlavela regiment in the 1870s were given permission to marry before proceeding to battle. Thereafter, they remained in the *imbutfo* force for a time; Webb and Wright, eds., *James Stuart Archive*, vol. 2, statement by Mabola.

45 SANAC, 1903–5, vol. 5, Written replies by A. Miller, 253; Beemer, "Military Organization," 49, 64.

46 Bonner, *Kings*, 89.

47 KCL, Miller papers, MS 567, Alfred Gould to Zillah Gould, 15 November 1891.

48 SANAC, 1903–5, vol. 5, Written replies by A. Miller, 253; Davis, *Umbandine*, 104–15; Mathers, *Goldfields Revisited*, 220–1.

49 Beemer, "Military Organization," 178.

50 KCL, Miller papers, MS 567, Alfred Gould to Zillah Gould, 15 November 1891. On the increasing size of royal villages in the 1880s see Jones, "Pre-Colonial Swazi Population," 344.

51 Kidd, *Essential Kafir*, 303.

52 SANAC, 1903–5, vol. 5, Written replies by A. Miller, 253.

53 See, for example, the case of Ndangu Tshongwe in SA, D801/09, Grey's Notes on Partition Appeals.

54 For details of slaving in the nineteenth-century Transvaal see Harries, "Slavery, Social Incorporation and Surplus Extraction," 309–30; Bonner, *Kings*, 80–92.

55 KCL, Miller papers, MS 565, A. Miller, "The Kafir Races of South-East Africa," 9.

56 "Journal of Spencer Walton, 21 November 1891," *South African Pioneer*, 28 (1915): 122–4.

57 Bonner, *Kings*, 89.

58 Etherington, "Labour Supplies and the Genesis of South African Confederation."

59 Mathews, *Incwadi Yami*, 502; UW, William Cullen Library, Nicholson papers, A 82, W. Penfold, "The Romance of Swaziland: Some Hitherto Unwritten Chapters of Its History," 1922.

60 KCL, Miller papers, MS 565, A. Miller, "The Kafir Races of South-East Africa," 19; Halle, *Mayfair to Maritzburg*, 180; Trevor, *Forty Years in Africa*, 66; Mathews, *Incwadi Yami*, 502–3.

61 KCL, Miller papers, MS 542b, Miller Diary, 2–3 August 1890.

62 I have recently begun work on a comparative study of the divergent experience of the two Swazi peoples in the nineteenth and twentieth centuries. For an analysis of the political ramifications of boundary demarcation see Macmillan, "Nation Divided?"

63 Matsebula, *History of Swaziland*, 87–114.

64 Trapido, "Landlord and Tenant," 26–58.

65 Macmillan, "Nation Divided?" 2–7; Eastern Transvaal Natives Land Committee, 1918, evidence of G. Wheelwright, 134–6, and J. Sutherland, 404; Myburgh, *Tribes of Barberton District*.

66 SA, S14D, Smuts to Milner, 3 May 1898; DO 119/236, Smuts to Robinson, 26 June 1896; and *South African Pioneer*, 8 (1895): 14; 10 (1897): 116; 11 (1898): 300.

67 Bonner, *Kings*, 48, 103–6, 128.

68 I am grateful to Mr Huw Jones (personal communication) for this colourful expression. See Jones, "Pre-Colonial Swazi Population," 344–5.

69 Bonner, *Kings*, 29; KCL, Stuart papers, KCM 24402, Statement by Tikuba, 27 November 1898, 89; "Bullets that Stray" *Sunday Times*, 8 March 1912; SA, Transcripts of Interviews with John Gamede, 1953–5, 70; Hughes, *Land Tenure*, 69–75; and Interview with Logwaya and Uhlangamiso Mamba, 15 July 1970, Ka-Mamba, Swaziland (conducted by P. Bonner).

70 Bonner, *Kings*, 128.

71 DO 119/218, Enclosure in No 19, Report of Journey through Eastern Swaziland by James Stuart, 24 January 1895.

72 Swaziland Concessions Commission, *Report of Detailed Decisions.*

73 P. Bonner (personal communication).

74 TAD, SSA 93/348/95, Shepstone to Martin, 22 January 1895.

75 SA, RCS 119/14, Dawson to AC Hlatikulu, 11 December 1916.

76 SA, D48/07/2205, Register of Hlatikulu Chiefs, 1907.

77 DO 119/218, Enclosure in No 19, Report of Journey through Eastern Swaziland by James Stuart, 24 January 1895.

78 Hughes, *Land Tenure*, 206. Interview with Simelane Simelane and Jozi Simelane, 6 May 1970 (conducted by P. Bonner).

79 SA, D48/07/2205, Register of Hlatikulu Chiefs, 1907.

80 DO 119/218, Enclosure in No 19, Report of Journey through Eastern Swaziland by James Stuart, 24 January 1895.

81 SA, RCS 119/14, Dawson to AC Hlatikulu, 11 December 1916.

82 *South African Pioneer*, 8 (1895): 14; TAD, SSA 293/3618/95, Special Commissioner to Secretary of State, 17 October 1895.

83 DO 119/223, Smuts to Robinson, 12 October 1895, 16 October 1895; DO 119/225, Smuts to Robinson, 18 October 1895; TAD, SSA 293/3461/95, Special Commissioner to Secretary of State, 7 October 1895; SSA 293/3526/95, Special Commissioner to Secretary of State, 12 October 1895; SA, Transcripts of Interviews with John Gamede, 1953–5.

84 DO 119/225, Smuts to Robinson, 18 October 1895.

85 TAD, SSA 293/3684/95, Public Prosecutor Bremersdorp to Special Commissioner, 17 October 1895.

86 TAD, SSA 293/3547/95, Special Commissioner to Secretary of State, 14 October 1895. On the death of Thabiti see TAD, SSA 293/104/95, JP Zombode to Special Commissioner, 16 October 1895.

CHAPTER TWO

1 UW, William Cullen Library, A55, R. James, The Diary of Trader James, 1936, 2; KCL, Miller papers, MS 1478, A. Miller, "A Short History of Swaziland," 28; Swaziland Chamber, *Swaziland: The California of South Africa*, 17.

2 *The Net*, 2 March 1891, 36; Bonner, *Kings*, 160.

3 USPG, E45, Report of Rev C. Johnson, 31 March 1890.

4 TAD, GOV 1021/65/22, Mulder to Selborne, 12 February 1906; CO 879/81/729, Enclosure in No 20, statement by Silele Nsibande, 4 July 1905.

5 The Swaziland concessions era is considered at length in Bonner, *Kings*, 160–207.

6 Crush, "Genesis of Colonial Land Policy," 76; "Colonial Division of Space," 72–4.

7 Bonner, *Kings*, 189.

8 Garson, *The Swaziland Question*; Mashasha, "Road to Colonialism."

9 For details of mining in Swaziland in this period see McCarthy, *Further Incidents*, chapters 8 and 9; TAD, Forbes papers, A602, vol. 37, Annual Reports of Henderson and Forbes Gold Mining Co, Southern Forbes Reef Co, Forbes Gold Mining Co; Swaziland Concessions Commission, *Report of Commission*, appendix B; KCL, Miller papers, MS 547a, Report on Mineral Prospects and Concessions in Swaziland, 1910; BRA, HE 277.

10 This account of trading in Swaziland is based on the following sources: CO 879/33/840, Enclosure in No 3, Report on Swazieland, 23–5; DO 119/225, No 32, Smuts to Robinson, 14 November 1895; TAD, SSA 601/1791/97, Foreign Office Diplomatic and Consular Reports on Trade and Finance, No 1996, Swaziland, 1897; "Swaziland Concessions Commission" *TOS*, 15 April 1905 and 22 April 1905; Swaziland Concessions Commission, *Report of the Commission*, 11–70.

11 On Schwab's earlier career see Watson, "History of the Little Free State," 42–7.

12 Swaziland Concessions Commission, *Report of Commission*, 67–8; "Swaziland Concessions Commission," *TOS*, 11 March 1905.

13 Swaziland Concessions Commission, *Report of Commission*.

14 "Editorial," *TOS*, 10 July 1897.

15 For cattle smuggling see TAD, SSA 287/95, Report of Complaints: John A. Major, 199–204.

16 DO 119/231, No 50, Smuts to Milner, 16 August 1897; "A Truculent Swazie," *TOS*, 24 December 1904.

17 TAD, SSA 247/157/95, Krogh to State Secretary, 5 October 1895.

18 "Why Depend on Others?" *TOS*, 26 February 1942; "The Swazi and the Soil," *TOS*, 14 May 1942. Since Miller's statements came in the midst of a polemic against the seeming impotence of Swazi agriculture in the 1940s, they must be carefully evaluated against the contemporary evidence.

19 Wesleyan Methodist Archives, Box 328, No 46, Underwood to Kilner, 30 July 1886; Box 328, No 4, Underwood to Kilner 19 January 1886. See also CO 879/33/840, Enclosure in No 3, Report on Swazieland, 7.

20 "Why Depend on Others?" *TOS*, 26 February 1942.

21 Ibid.; SA, S56, Dawson to Smuts, 23 February 1897.

22 TAD, SNA 259/642/05, Swaziland Concessions Commission, evidence of G.Lagden, 18–19.

23 On the drought of 1889 see DO 119/20/422, de Winton to Knutsford, 7 December 1889. The drier reaches of the country remained sparsely inhabited and low-yielding during the 1890s; DO 119/35/315, Report of JP Lebombo, 1 April 1892; DO 119/149/814, Swaziland Annual Report, 1892.

24 SA, S18, Acting Government Secretary Bremersdorp to Government Secretary, 2 July 1892; DO 119/35, JP Forbes Reef, 3 March 1893. The first plough was introduced in 1890 by the Swazi chief Tekuba Dlamini.

25 *South African Pioneer* 5 (1892): 6. On the growing use of ploughs see DO
    119/225, No 32, Smuts to Robinson, 14 November 1895.

26 SA, DO9/126, J. Dove, Report on Land Settlement in Swaziland, 1909, 13;
    "Why Depend On Others?" TOS, 26 February 1942. For descriptions of
    agricultural activity in the 1890s see *South African Pioneer*, 6 (1893): 8; 10
    (1897): 72, 107 and 115; 12 (1899): 55; DO 119/75, Report of Landrost
    Bremersdorp, 1 April 1893; DO 119/217, Stuart to Martin, 29 December
    1894.

27 For the traders, 1896 was business as usual. Grain to the value of £3500
    was imported by the administration and Bunu also brought in some 300
    bags for sale to the chiefs; DO 119/227, No 49, British Consul to High
    Commissioner, 14 August 1896.

28 "The Tin Mines," TOS, 23 April 1898; SA, S18, Report by Sidney Ryan,
    21 March 1892; KCL, KCM 6943, Forbes Reef Letter Book, 20 June 1893,
    14 August 1893, November 1893, December 1893, January 1894;
    McCarthy, *Further Incidents*, 65. The migrants were constantly pillaged
    by touts from the Rand and by brigands living on the Lubombo Mts;
    Bozzoli, *Political Nature*, 41. As protection, and to avoid paying for passes,
    some migrants employed Swazi guides; DO 119/75, JP Lebombo, 2 Sep-
    tember 1892.

29 "Swaziland Notes," *Goldfields News*, 28 February 1890; "Swaziland Re-
    view," *Goldfields News*, 7 July 1896; "Pressing the Swazies," *Goldfields News*,
    5 August 1898; BRA, HE 277, Penfold to Phillips, 29 January 1893; TAD,
    HC 10/65, Enclosure in No 226, Annual Report of Swaziland Government
    Committee, 6 June 1894.

30 "Native Labour Supply," *Goldfields News*, 23 October 1896.

31 "Pass Laws," *Goldfields News*, 14 July 1896.

32 TOS, 23 April 1898.

33 KCL, Miller papers, Letter Book No 171, Doring to Martin, 17 August
    1889, 309–10; SANAC, 1903–5, vol. 5, Written replies by A. Miller, 254;
    and the comments of Richard Martin in A. Miller, "Swaziland." The
    major trader in the south of Swaziland, J.C. Henwood, employed over
    100 men in the mid-1890s; Swaziland Concessions Commission, *Report of
    the Commission*.

34 SA, Transcript of Interviews with John Gamede, 1953–5.

35 The tendency to work within Swaziland at first and then to leave the
    country in search of higher wages was not untypical; SANAC, 1903–5, vol.
    5, Written replies by A. Miller, 254.

36 "The Weather," TOS, 22 January 1898.

37 DO 119/221, Smuts to Robinson, 30 May 1895; *The Net*, July 1896, March
    1897, January 1899; TAD, HC 11/69, Smuts to Robinson, 14 August 1896;
    SSA, 601/1791/97, Foreign Office Diplomatic and Consular Reports on
    Trade and Finance, No 1996, Swaziland, 1897; "Report from Peak Dis-

trict," *TOS*, 22 October 1898; USPG, E 1898, Report on Swaziland by W. Swinnerton, 31 December 1898; *South African Pioneer* 11 (1898): 193 and 12 (1899): 69.

38 "Swaziland," *Goldfields News*, 7 July 1896; SA, S18, Memorandum of General Trade by Grosvenor Darke, 31 December 1896; "Notes from Bulungu," *TOS*, 6 May 1899, 5 August 1899.

39 On labour migration from Swaziland in 1896, see DO 119/227, No 49, Smuts to Robinson, 14 July 1896; *South African Pioneer* 10 (1897): 194; TAD, SSA 601/1791/97, Foreign Office Diplomatic and Consular Reports on Trade and Finance, No 1996, Swaziland, 1897. On rinderpest see Van Onselen, "Reactions to Rinderpest."

40 *TOS*, 11 September 1897, 29 January 1898.

41 *TOS*, 8 January 1898.

42 Nilsen, *Malla Moe*, 76.

43 SA, Transcripts of Interviews with John Gamede, 1953–5.

44 TLC, 1904, evidence of D. Forbes, para. 2239.

45 Figures are from BRA, HE 250/140/119.

46 KCL, Miller papers, KCM 3497, Swaziland and the Swaziland Corporation, 8; "De Kaap Mine Managers Association Annual Meeting," *Goldfields News*, 14 February 1899; TLC, 1904, evidence of N. Breytenbach, para. 8036–7.

47 *TOS*, 14 January 1899, 11 March 1899, 12 November 1899.

48 *South African Pioneer* 15 (1902): 103; 16 (1903): 106.

49 Under the terms of the 1894 Convention with Britain, the South African Republic agreed not to impose taxes on the Swazi until 1898 as a condition of assumption of control over Swaziland. The role of the SAR in mobilizing labour for the mines is examined in Jeeves, "Control of Migratory Labour," 10–13.

50 TAD, HC 98/100, Confidential Memorandum on the Administration of Swaziland by the SAR; SSA 657, Report on the Swaziland Police by H. Schroder, 1 June 1897.

51 "Sauce for the Goose," *TOS*, 4 June 1898; "The King Orders Up All His Men," *Goldfields News*, 21 June 1898; DO 119/238, Smuts to Milner, 24 June 1898; TAD, SS 7267/7641/98, Tax Collector to Inspector General, Pretoria, 17 June 1898.

52 O'Neil, *Adventures in Swaziland*; Cook, "History and Izibongo"; Private papers of Captain George Wallis.

53 DO 119/241, Milner to Fraser, 3 September 1898.

54 The reasons for Mbabha's death and Bunu's role in the murder were never made clear even at the latter's trial in Bremesdorp. For an account of the "Mbabha Affair" see Mashasha, "Road to Colonialism," 265–85.

55 DO 119/236, Memorandum on Memezi, 10 July 1896.

56 DO 119/236, Smuts to Milner, 9 June 1898; DO 119/236, Memorandum

on Memezi, 10 July 1896; Webb and Wright, eds., *James Stuart Archive*, vol. 1, evidence of John Gama, 135.

57 Milner papers, MSS 9, vol. 7, para. 3, Fraser to Milner, 2 September 1898 (quoted in Mashasha, "Road to Colonialism," 283).

58 Protocol of 5 October 1898 to the 1894 Convention made all Swazi, including the king (now the "Paramount Chief"), liable for criminal prosecution for a wide variety of offences including murder, assault, kidnapping, perjury, arson, malicious damage to property, robbery, and witchcraft.

59 DO 119/244, No 23, Smuts to Milner, 31 August 1899; DO 119/238, Smuts to Milner, 5 August 1898.

60 DO 119/238, No 56, Fraser to Milner, 28 July 1898.

61 DO 119/234, Smuts to Milner, 12 February 1898. For further details of the chiefs' protest against a tax "which is like death" see HC 13/72, Enclosure 1 in No 106, Notes of Special Commissioner's Meeting with Queen Mother, 8 August 1898; Enclosure 1 in No 40, Interview of British Consul with Queen, 24 October 1898. The chiefs did not protest against taxation per se but the heavy amount being levied. Clearly there were benefits to be gained through encouraging migration provided that the state did not appropriate too great a proportion of migrant earnings.

62 TAD, BA 35, Smuts to High Commissioner, 20 December 1897; SA, S14D, Smuts to Milner, 5 August 1898.

63 DO 119/234, No 28, Smuts to Milner, 21 March 1898; Enclosure in No 28 and No 29, Notes of Meeting between Special Commissioner and Paramount Chief, 25 March 1898; *Standard and Diggers News*, 2 May 1898.

64 "Hut Tax," TOS, 20 August 1898, 14 January 1899.

65 Between October 1895 and March 1898, £26,000 passed hands; DO 119/235, Enclosure in No 70. See TAD, GOV 200/955/06, Report of Meeting between Selborne and Swazi Chiefs, 14 September 1906, for details of the fate of this revenue.

66 SA, S14 FIV, General Report on the Effect Produced on Swazi People by the Protocol by James Stuart, 20 March 1899; TAD, SSA 807/1665/99, P. Cronje to State Secretary, 10 April 1899.

67 Jeeves, "Control of Migratory Labour," 11–12.

68 SA, S57, S. Erskine to Stuart, 22 November 1898.

69 SA, S14 FIV, General Report on the Effect Produced on Swazi People by the Protocol by James Stuart, 20 March 1899.

70 Thuys (Mathias) Grobler was a close confidant of Bunu and was also employed by Kruger to ferry the monthly concession revenue to Bunu. According to O'Neil, *Adventures in Swaziland*, much of it ended up in Grobler's own pocket. Johannes Smuts objected to the contract on the

grounds that it was "a monopoly which may hamper British subjects carrying on the business of labour agents" and that it would hinder the acquisition of labour by local mining companies; SA S14D, Smuts to Milner, 26 May 1899.

71 SA, S14D, Smuts to Milner, 28 June 1899.

72 TAD, HC 13/72, Enclosure in No 6, statement by Mkonjwa.

73 "The Native Tax," TOS, 29 October 1898.

74 Miller, "Swaziland," 1900, 274–94.

75 "Native Labour," TOS, 15 July 1898.

76 "Native Labour," TOS, 24 December 1898.

77 KCL, Marwick papers, KCM 2576b, E. Clark, "A Story of Early Natal."

78 CO 291/29, No 2, Smuts to Stephenson, 29 April 1901; TAD, C14, Box 3, TLC Papers, Gillespie to TLC, 22 August 1903; SNA 739/183/03, Lagden to Moony, 6 January 1904.

79 Warwick, *Black People*, 108.

80 CO 879/81/729, Enclosure in No 3, The Case for the Incorporation of Swaziland into the Transvaal by A. Miller, 7 March 1903; NA, PM 18/1900/1322, Resident Magistrate Ndwandwe to Chief Magistrate Eshowe, 14 July 1900; TAD, CS 14/1576, Visit of Johannes Smuts to Swaziland, April 1901; GOV 780/A22, Milner to Secretary of State, nd; SA, J2/01, J. Smuts, Proposals for the Government of Swaziland, 1901; J50/04, Report on Swaziland, 1903; Forbes, *Life in South Africa*, 163, 174. For details of various incidents at chief Bokweni Mamba's in the south see TAD, SNA 21/48/02; "Bullets that Stray," *Sunday Times*, 8 March 1912.

81 Jeeves, "Control of Migratory Labour."

CHAPTER THREE

1 SA, D48/07/2205, Register of Hlatikulu Chiefs, 20 April 1907.

2 The seriousness of this case is illustrated by a massive 90 pages of handwritten evidence taken down during the trial; SA, HCR No 45/11, Rex v Chief Nzama and others, 6 March 1911; HCR 47/11, Rex v Nzama Mdhluli, 7 March 1911.

3 After 1910, an additional amount of approximately £3,000 per annum was raised through a special tax – the Swazi National Fund – which was used for combating stock disease and for educating children of the royal household. Extraordinary revenue included income from sales of crown land.

4 Crush, "Settler-Estate Production."

5 ACR, 1912–13: 6. When colonial revenue began to fall in 1911, this was seen as an opportune moment to "turn to the natives" for further revenue. A dog tax of 5 shillings per dog generated a further £5,000 per

annum. In 1916, ordinary tax was raised by 10 shillings per person; SA, D10/3, Coryndon to Selborne, 7 January 1910; RCS 491/15, Meeting of Chiefs and Acting Resident Commissioner, 26 August 1915.

6 SA, J82/03, Report on Swaziland by Commissioner for Native Affairs, 1902.

7 SA, J2/01, J. Smuts, Proposals for the Government of Swaziland, 1901.

8 SA, J138/05, Statement by Lord Milner to Swazi Queen Regent and Council, 13 July 1904.

9 Ibid; J1/03, Notes of a Meeting with Swazi Queen Regent and Council, Statement by Special Commissioner, 16 March 1903; TAD, SNA 739/183/03, Report on Swaziland, 1903.

10 SA, J64/03, Report on Swaziland, 1902; J134/03, Moony to Lagden, 15 May 1903.

11 TLC, 1904, evidence of David Forbes, Godfrey Lagden, Nicolaas Breytenbach, S. Hulley, William Grant, J.W. Watts, and General Ben Viljoen.

12 TLC, 1904, evidence of Godfrey Lagden, para. 1776.

13 This concept is developed in Guy, "Destruction and Reconstruction of Zulu Society," 175.

14 SA, J175/03, Lagden to Moony, nd.

15 SA, J82/03, Report on Swaziland by Commissioner for Native Affairs, 1902.

16 SA, J1/03, Notes of a Meeting with Swazi Queen Regent and Council, 16 March 1903; J134/03, Moony to Lagden, 15 May 1903.

17 TAD, SNA 739/183/03, Report on Swaziland, 1904. See also TLC, 1904, evidence of D. Forbes, para. 2242, who predicted that payment would be bad due to food shortages in the country. In fact, payment was good in spite of these shortages. Rumours in South African newspapers that a Swazi revolt was imminent were quickly squashed by Swaziland officials; Rand Daily Mail, 5 February 1903; SA, J47/03, Moony to Secretary for Swaziland Affairs, 11 February 1903.

18 SANAC, 1903–5, vol. 3, evidence of A. Miller, para. 41514.

19 SA, RMS 143/05; South African Pioneer 17 (1904): 22.

20 The figures are uncertain here. One source notes that in the 12 months to October 1903, 50,000 head succumbed to ECF. Another notes that between 1902 and 1905 the number of cattle in the country fell from 20,000 to 10,000; "ECF: The Great Scare," TOS, 16 October 1903; TAD, SNA 258/642/05, A. Miller to Swaziland Concessions Commission, 17 February 1905.

21 ACR, 1907–8, AC Peak, 42; SANAC, 1903–5, vol. 5, Written replies by A. Miller, 264; KCL, Miller papers, MS 925, Swaziland: The California of South Africa, 30. This practice was not confined to Swaziland; JPL, Native Grievances Commission, Minutes of Evidence, evidence of H. Taberer, 6 February 1914; Marks, Reluctant Rebellion, 129.

22 SA, D739/183/03, Report on Swaziland 1904; TAD, SNA 259/642/05, Swaziland Concessions Commission, 1905, evidence of G. Lagden, 19.

23 KCL, Miller papers, MS 633b, Swaziland Chamber to Secretary for Swaziland Affairs, 29 June 1906, 6; SANAC, 1903–5, vol. 5, Written replies by A. Miller, 253, 264–5; "Nkoman's Little Game," TOS, 6 May 1905; SA, DO9/125, AC Ubombo, MR, May 1908.

24 "Pictures from Swaziland," *The Mission Field*, May 1906, 135–6; *South African Pioneer* 15 (1905): 181; 20 (1907): 3; SA, RCS 647/09, Coryndon to Secretary of Liquor Commission, 30 September 1909; Beemer, "Development of The Military Organization," 182. Beer production for sale actually began in the late 1890s and continued right throughout the period under study in all areas of the country; SA, HCR 329/19, Rex v Mahlebele Dlamini; "The Question of Kafir Beer," TOS, 12 November 1898.

25 DO 119/244, Enclosure in No 23, Forbes to Smuts, 11 August 1899, 18 August 1899.

26 SA, J146/06, Notes of Meeting between Moony and Queen Regent and Council, 27 June 1906; TOS, 2 December 1905.

27 SA, J138/06, Moony to Secretary for Swaziland Affairs, 27 June 1906. See also CO 879/81/729, No 41, Aborigines Protection Society to Colonial Office, 6 April 1906; No 56, Elgin to Selborne, 2 July 1906, Selborne to Elgin, 21 July 1906.

28 Kuper, *African Aristocracy*, 93.

29 Swaziland Administration Proclamation No 3 of 1904. In addition to its taxation provisions this Proclamation documented the manner in which Swaziland was to be administered under the Governor of the Transvaal.

30 SA, J18/06, Selborne to Honey, 17 January 1906. Details of the first two years' prosecution of tax offenders are contained in SA, Criminal Record Book, 19 August 1906.

31 TAD, GOV 752/337/04, Sub-Native Commissioner Piet Retief to Sub-Native Commissioner Wakkerstroom, 30 June 1904, and Telegram from Special Commissioner for Swaziland, 6 June 1904; GOV 752/96/04, Moony to Secretary for Swaziland Affairs, 25 June 1904, and Nicholson to Moony, 2 June 1904; GOV 752/50/04, Layman to Tyrrell, 1 July 1904. Moony did speculate that the rumours were being fuelled by the Queen Regent to direct attention away from internal political intrigues. However, he advanced no evidence in support of his contention and appears to have been confusing two separate issues. Similar discontent was observed in the Natal countryside; Marks, *Reluctant Rebellion*.

32 SANAC, 1903–5, vol. 4, evidence of A. Miller, para. 41514; SA, J18/06, Moony to Secretary for Swaziland Affairs, 25 January 1906.

33 Engelbrecht, "Swazi Customs Relating to Marriage."

34 SA, J18/06, Moony to Secretary for Swaziland Affairs, 25 January 1906, and Selborne to Honey, 17 January 1906.

35 SANAC, 1903–5, vol. 4, evidence of A. Miller, para. 41449; and "Interview with Mamisa," TOS, 16 October 1903.

36 SA, J138/05, Notes of Meeting between Lord Milner and Queen Regent and Council, 13 July 1904.

37 SA, J138/05, Complaints of Queen Regent to Special Commissioner and Replies, February 1905; J138/06, Parsonson to Elgin, 14 April 1906; J146/06, Notes of Meeting between Moony and Queen Regent and Council, 25 June 1906; TAD, GOV 200/955/06, Report of Interview with Swazi Queen Regent and People, Mbabane, 14 September 1906.

38 SA, J138/05, Complaints of Queen Regent to Special Commissioner and Replies, February 1905.

39 TAD, GOV 200/955/06, Selborne to Elgin, 24 September 1906.

40 TOS, 10 August 1905.

41 TOS, 27 January 1906.

42 Challis, "Swaziland from Within," 307–21. The high turnover of Zulu recruits made this somewhat problematical; SA, J70/03, Moony to Lagden, 4 March 1903.

43 "Nkoman's Little Game," TOS, 6 May 1906.

44 "Hut Tax Defaulters," TOS, 28 October 1905, 11 November 1905, 2 December 1905.

45 Married men also complained about the colonial practice of removing their traditional headrings and shaving their heads while in prison; SA, J18/06, Moony to Secretary for Swaziland Affairs, January 1906.

46 "Swaziland Chamber Annual Meeting," TOS, 1 September 1906; SANAC, 1903–5, vol. 4, evidence of A. Miller and D. Forbes.

47 CO 879/81/729, No 57, Selborne to Elgin, 9 July 1906; TAD, GOV 200/955/06, Selborne to Elgin, 24 September 1906 and Report of Interview with Swazi Queen Regent and People, 14 September 1906.

48 SA, D19/07/1141, AC Mbabane, MR, August 1907.

49 ACR, 1907–8: 17; SA, D45/07/1417, Conference of Assistant Commissioners. For details of Coryndon's career see Youé, "African Career of Robert Thorne Coryndon."

50 SA, D19/07/1141, AC Mbabane, MR, July 1907.

51 SA, D19/07/ʀ141, AC Hlatikulu, MR, August 1907.

52 SA, D19/07/1141, AC Ubombo, MR, October 1907.

53 SA, D19/07/1141, AC Mbabane, MR, October 1907.

54 SA, D19/07/1141, AC Ubombo, MR, February 1908.

55 SA, J294/06, Moony to Secretary for Swaziland Affairs. 24 October 1905, 11 January 1906; J130/06, Report from Hlatikulu District, 13 March 1906, 7 April 1906; RMS 134/06, Moony to Secretary for Swaziland Affairs, 14 June 1906.

56 SA, D09/125, AC Ubombo, MR, April 1908.

57 ACR, 1907–8, AC Hlatikulu, 30; AC Peak, 38; SA, D19/07/1141, AC Hlatikulu, MR, June to October 1907; AC Peak, MR, October 1907.

58 Few chiefs took their collaborative duties as seriously as one southern
chief, Songqagana Dlamini, a member of the ruling Dlamini aristocracy
who was employed in the Swaziland police force; SA, D48/07/2205, Register of Hlatikulu Chiefs, 20 April 1907.

59 ACR, 1907–8, Report of AC Police. In 1909–10 almost 8,000 patrols were
dispatched covering a distance of 447,766 miles; SA, D10/57, Draft ACR,
1909–10, AC Police.

60 SA, D19/07/1141, AC Mbabane, MR, September 1907. In the Hlatikulu
district alone, 28 *ndunas* were prosecuted in July 1908 for obstruction
of colonial justice; SA, D09/125, AC Hlatikulu, MR, July 1908.

61 SA, D19/07/1141, AC Ubombo, MR, October 1907.

62 SA, D09/125, AC Hlatikulu, MR, January 1909; D10/57, AC Mbabane, MR,
April 1909.

63 SA, D19/07/1141, AC Hlatikulu, MR, May 1907.

64 SA, HCR, No 85/11, Rex v N. Nsibandi & M. Matebula; No 188/19, Rex
v Zihlele Gwebu.

65 Cooper, "Africa and the World Economy," 33–4; Jeeves, *Migrant Labour
in South Africa's Mining Economy*, 255.

66 Marks, *Reluctant Rebellion*. On taxation and social protest in colonial
southern Africa see Crush, "Colonial Coercion," 179–81.

CHAPTER FOUR

1 NA, SNA 2905/01, Application of Mr John Major; SA, J18/02, W. Barry
& Co to Secretary for Swaziland Affairs, 19 March 1902; SNA Natal to
Lagden, 21 February 1902; Smuts to Forbes, 28 December 1901. Swaziland was officially thrown open to recruiting in June 1902; TAD, SNA
26/830/02, Telegram, 4 June 1902.

2 TAD, CS 192/16253/02, Grobler and de Jager to Colonial Secretary, 21
November 1902; Assistant Colonial Secretary to de Jager, 2 December
1902; Assistant Secretary for Swaziland Affairs to Assistant Colonial
Secretary, 18 December 1902; de Jager to Colonial Secretary, 6 January
1904.

3 *TOS* 30 September 1905 and 7 October 1905.

4 SA, J50/04, Report of Special Commissioner for Swaziland, 18 September
1903; TLC, 1904, evidence of D. Forbes, para. 2240. The 1904 Census
gave a *de facto* adult male population of 17,583 and the 1911 Census a
population of 22,395 adult males. In 1908, there were 23,204 adult males
over 18 on the colonial tax register; SA, D09/2, Grey to Selborne, 7
December 1908, 31. It is likely that Moony was estimating the numbers

of single men in the country and Forbes the number of able-bodied men available for wage labour.

5 SA, J50/04, Report of Special Commissioner for Swaziland, 18 September 1903; TLC, 1904, evidence of D. Forbes, para. 2239. The discrepancy may be more apparent than real. Moony's figure was based on the issue of passes and would therefore be likely to include migrants who went more than once to South Africa during this period. The Forbes figure is probably a more accurate indicator of the actual number of individual Swazis who migrated. This would mean that about one in five potential migrants actually migrated for wage labour between 1901 and 1904.

6 For details of the post-war labour market see Van Onselen, *Studies in the Social and Economic History of the Witwatersrand*; Denoon, *Grand Illusion*; "Transvaal Labour Crisis."

7 WNLA Annual Report, 1904, 15. Between 1905 and 1915, over 1,400 miles of new track were laid in the Transvaal; Best, *Swaziland Railway*, 64–5.

8 For details of Swazi employment outside the Rand see TLC, 1904, evidence of Godfrey Lagden, N. Breytenbach, D. Forbes; TAD, SNA 259/642/055, Swaziland Concessions Commission, 1905, evidence of G. Lagden, 15 March 1905; SNA 739/183/03, Report on Swaziland; KCL, Miller papers, MS 428a, Swaziland Concessions Commission, evidence of A. Miller; WNLA Annual Report, 1904, Report of General Manager; Jones, "Pre-Colonial Swazi Population," 363. In June 1903 there were 12 labour agents in the country; TAD LTG 125/110/45, Report by Commissioner for Native Affairs, 30 June 1903.

9 TLC, 1904, evidence of Godfrey Lagden, para. 1776; evidence of William Grant, para. 8137; evidence of J. Watts, para. 11666.

10 TLC, 1904, evidence of D. Forbes, para. 2239, 2247–8, 2274–81; evidence of S. Hulley, para. 6920–2; TAD, C14 Box 15, TLC papers, Hulley to TLC, 5 August 1903.

11 TAD, SNA 26/860/02, WNLA Meetings, 10 April 1902.

12 TLC, 1904, evidence of G. Lagden, para. 1776; evidence of W. Grant, para. 8137; evidence of J. Watts, para. 8141.

13 Packard, "White Plague: Black Labour." In 1903, 5,022 workers out of an average mine workforce of 62,000 died from disease or accident. Disease accounted for 63 per cent of mine fatalities in 1903, with pneumonia being the biggest killer. For further details see Richardson, *Chinese Mine Labour*, 8–46; Jeeves, *Migrant Labour in South Africa's Mining Economy*, 17–19, 28–47; Katz, "Silicosis on the South African Gold Mines."

14 Migrants with fewer alternative economic opportunities were drawn considerable distances to the higher wages of the Rand; Van Onselen, *Chibaro*.

15 TLC, 1904, evidence of D. Forbes.

16 WNLA Annual Report, 1908.

17 SA, DO9/125, Draft ACR, 1908–9, AC Hlatikulu.

18 Van Onselen, "Black Workers in Central African Industry," 228–46.

19 SANAC, 1903–5, vol. 4, evidence of A. Miller, para. 41464–77, 41587; evidence of D. Forbes. Cash *lobola* was first introduced in the aftermath of rinderpest in the 1890s; Webb and Wright, eds., *James Stuart Archive*, vol. 2, evidence of Mabola, 8; vol. 3, evidence of Ngoqo, 115. The existence of marriage on credit is in sharp contrast to Harries' findings in southern Mozambique where homestead heads continued to control bridewealth by raising the cash value of daughters out of easy reach; Harries, "Kinship, Ideology and the Nature of Pre-Colonial Labour Migration." In the 1930s Brian Marwick came across women married earlier in the century whose *lobola* was still not fully paid; Marwick, *The Swazi*, 15.

20 Kuper, *African Aristocracy*, 97–8; Marwick, *The Swazi*, 124–6.

21 SANAC, 1903–5, Written reply by David Forbes, 218; TAD, SNA 258/642/05, A. Miller to Swaziland Concessions Commission, 15 February 1905.

22 SA, RCS 647/09, Coryndon to Secretary, Liquor Commission, 30 September 1909; DO 119/608, Grey to Selborne, 29 February 1908.

23 Kuper, *Uniform of Colour*, 149.

24 SA, RMS 143/05.

25 For further details see Reilly and Reilly, "State of Nature Conservation in Swaziland," 6.

26 High Commissioner's Proclamation No 44 of 1907 and No 1 of 1910. For cases of prosecution involving hunts organized by chiefs and the Prince Regent Malunge, see SA, HCR 181/12, 197/14, Rex v Prince Regent, 1914.

27 Jones, *Study of Swazi Nutrition*, 66.

28 SANAC, 1903–5, vol. 5, Written replies by Allister Miller, 265; SA, D19/07/1141, AC Hlatikulu, MR, October 1907.

29 Six chiefs included in the survey had herds ranging from 20 to 150 head. At the royal cattle post on the Lebombo there were over 400 head; CO 879/81/729, Enclosure in No 47, Report of the Swaziland Concessions Commission on work in Swaziland in 1905.

30 Crush, "Landlords, Tenants and Colonial Social Engineers," 239.

31 CO 608/1–4, Swaziland Statistics, 1906/7 to 1909/10.

32 ACR, 1907–8, AC Hlatikulu, 31; *South African Pioneer* 29 (1916): 1; RCS 578/16, Draft ACR, 1916–17, AC Mbabane; RCS 70/23, Minutes of Meeting of Chiefs, Hlatikulu, 17 November 1922; RCS 220/24, Meeting of Native Chiefs with AC Mankiana, 31 January 1924.

33 SA, RCS 578/16, Draft ACR, 1915–16, JP Bremersdorp; RCS 795/15, AC Mankiana, AC Ubombo, MR, September 1915; RCS 141/16, AC Mbabane, AC Mankiana, MR, November 1914; ACR, 1910–11: 8; ACR 1916–17: 6; ACR, 1917–18: 4. By the early 1930s, 50 per cent of the cultivated area

of the country was under the plough; Marwick, *The Swazi*, 293; UW, William Cullen Library, SAIRR Papers, A410/A3(2), W. Hodgson and W. Ballinger, "Swaziland," 1931, 14; NRC, File SWAZ.28, Swaziland Brochures Providing Historical, Ethnographical, and Statistical Information.

34 *South African Pioneer* 30 (1917): 4.

35 Marwick, *The Swazi*, 60–3, 73. By 1921, 2,500 homestead heads were away at work.

36 In Pondoland, Beinart finds a similar pattern emerging with a growing seasonality to migration. He locates the reasons for agricultural innovation in the drive for expanded commodity production, an inadequate explanation in the Swaziland case; Beinart, "Labour Migrancy and Rural Production."

37 SA, J138/05, Notes of Meeting between Lord Milner and Queen Regent and Swazi Council, 13 July 1904.

38 Interview with D. Fitzpatrick, Mbabane, 30 March 1982.

39 SA, D19/07/1141, AC Hlatikulu, MR, June to August 1907.

40 The data available for table 7 are unfortunately incomplete.

41 SA, D09/125, Draft ACR, 1908–9, AC Hlatikulu.

42 Jeeves, *Migrant Labour in South Africa's Mining Economy*, 52–8.

43 TAD, SNA 26/860/02; GNLB 206 1705/14/D110, WNLA Memorandum, 10 April 1902; CM, 14th Annual Report, 1903, 56–7; TLC, 1904, evidence of F. Perry, para. 814–17.

44 TLC, 1904, evidence of D. Forbes, para. 2264–73.

45 The Bechuanaland figure for the same period was only £3; WNLA Annual Report, 1904, Report of General Manager.

46 BRA, HE 251/138/458, Memorandum by General Manager of WNLA, Annexure, 25 February 1904.

47 A year later the contract period was raised to 8 months in the Transvaal and Swaziland, perhaps on the false assumption that the length of contract was unimportant to migrants; CM, 15th Annual Report, 1904: 22; 16th Annual Report, 1905: 258; SANAC, 1903–5, vol. 4, evidence of A. Miller, para. 41604–5.

48 TLC, 1904, evidence of D. Forbes, para. 2309, 2239, 2295.

49 TLC, 1904, evidence of D. Forbes, para. 2310–13. This point is ignored by Isobel Winter and Donald Kowet who see in the agreement evidence that the Swazi chiefs could mobilize Swazi labour at will; Winter, "The Post Colonial State," 28–9; Kowet, *Land, Labour Migration and Politics*, 90.

50 SA, J13/07, Governor's Office to Moony, 19 January 1907; Secretary for Swaziland Affairs to Moony, 19 January 1907.

51 CO 879/106/874, No 190, Selborne to Elgin, 13 March 1907. A year earlier, Bremer's arrival in Swaziland as an unofficial emissary of Selborne was warmly welcomed by Moony. Bremer's subsequent disen-

chantment with the colonial position led to a rapid change of heart on the part of local officials. In June 1906, Bremer was appointed as an agent and adviser by the Queen Regent because of Selborne's persistent refusal to acknowledge the authority of another adviser, the Pietermaritzburg lawyer Parsonson; RHL, Anti-Slavery papers, MSS.BRIT.EMP. S22, G186, Bremer to Fox-Bourne, 19 March 1906; 16 April 1906; Vilikazi to Aborigines Protection Society, 1 July 1906; CO 291/107, Encl. No 3 in No 482, Bremer to Parsonson, 28 April 1906.

52 The Bremer-Vilikazi plan was designed to raise money to pay the legal costs of appealing Milner's cancellation of the Private Revenue Concession. For details of the activities of the Robinson Group see Jeeves, *Migrant Labour in South Africa's Mining Economy*, 199–211.

53 CO 879/106/874, No 197, Elgin to Selborne, 16 March 1907.

54 BRA, HE 254/149/942, J. Secull to A. Bremer, 25 July 1907. It is of interest to note that a copy of the Robinson-Bremer contract found its way into the rival H.Eckstein & Co's files.

55 BRA, HE 277/215S/33, S. Jennings to Chairman, Swaziland Tin Ltd, 18 December 1906; HE 277/215S/26, Ryan to Secretary, Swaziland Tin Ltd, 2 September 1906; SA, RCS 100/15, Ryan to Secretary, Swaziland Tin Ltd, 2 September 1906; Kelly to Boyd, 26 January 1915.

56 The question of whether Malunge had a hand in the resolution of the company's labour shortages in 1907 was later a matter of dispute between the company and Sidney Ryan; SA, RCS 100/15, Various correspondence

57 "Labour Supply," *TOS*, 24 October 1908. In the 1890s Armstrong had been a Native Commissioner in south-west Rhodesia and was involved in the supposed shooting of the Mlimo, a major figure in the Ndebele revolt of 1896. The incident led to his expulsion from the colonial service; Ranger, *Revolt in Southern Rhodesia*, 183–8; Keppel-Jones, *Rhodes and Rhodesia*, 458–9

58 Van Onselen, *Studies in the Social and Economic History of the Witwatersrand*, 188.

59 "Swazi Rising," *Rand Daily Mail*, 16 October 1908. This incident is reconstructed from the following sources; SA, DO9/125, AC Mbabane, MR, September 1908 to January 1909; *TOS*, 16 October 1908, 24 October 1908 and 12 December 1908; *Rand Daily Mail*, 14 and 16 October 1908.

60 "The Swazis and Labour," *TOS*, 12 December 1908.

61 CO 417/487, Coryndon to Hely-Hutchinson, 8 July 1909.

62 "The Swazis and Labour," *TOS*, 12 December 1908. Armstrong resigned from his own company in mid-1909 and worked for a time as a labour supervisor for Swaziland Tin Ltd. In 1911 he tried to sue the company for infringing mining safety regulations and charged certain colonial officials with colluding in a coverup. The case never came to court and Armstrong committed suicide soon thereafter; CO 417/502, Contra-

vention of Mining Law by Swaziland Tin Ltd; Armstrong to Gladstone, 14 June 1910.

63 SA, RCS 23/10, Tatham to Coryndon, 14 January 1910.

64 CO 417/487, Kropwitz to Coryndon, 28 June 1909; Marwick to Acting Government Secretary, 1 July 1909.

65 See correspondence and legal advice in SA, RCS 23/10.

66 High Commissioner's Gazette, Notice No 66 of 1910, 3 September 1910. This clause was also incorporated into the Native Labour Regulation (Swaziland) Proclamation of 1913.

67 CO 417/487, Nicholson to Marwick, 9 July 1909; Enclosure in Marwick to Acting Government Secretary, 1 July 1909, sworn statement by Nduluvula.

68 "Swazis for the Mines," *Rand Daily Mail*, 14 October 1908.

69 SA, J138/05, Notes of Meeting between Lord Milner and Queen Regent and Council, 13 July 1904.

70 "Swazi Rising," *Rand Daily Mail*, 16 October 1908.

71 Ibid.

CHAPTER FIVE

1 ACR, 1910–11, 12.

2 Crush, "Swazi Migrant Workers." The possibility of a movement of female migrants to and from South Africa cannot be discounted but the available evidence suggests that it was slight and consisted mainly of wives accompanying their husbands to work. In 1921, 8,953 men and 183 women were recorded as out of the country working.

3 The proportion of the total mine labour force emanating from Swaziland rose from 0.9 per cent in 1909, to 1.5 per cent in 1910 and 2.07 per cent in 1911; Van der Horst, *Native Labour in South Africa*, 216–7. The mine strikes of July 1913 and January 1914 on the Rand "were to a slight extent reflected in Swaziland, principally owing to the curtailment of the recruiting of native labour"; ACR, 1913–4, 4, 14; NRC Annual Report, 1913, 11; SA, RCS 842/13, Draft ACR, 1913–4, AC Hlatikulu. For details of the strikes themselves see Yudelman, *Emergence of Modern South Africa*. For the effects of the "bumper" harvest of 1920, see SA, RCS 167/21, Draft ACR, 1920–1, AC Police.

4 TAD, GNLB 20 1101/11, GNLB Annual Report 1910–11; Chamber of Mines, 21st Annual Report, 1910, xliv, 327; SA, RCS 414/11, AC Mbabane, MR, August 1910; AC Mankiana, MR, August 1910.

5 Jeeves, *Migrant Labour in South Africa's Mining Economy*.

6 Jeeves and Yudelman, "Mobilization of a Sub-Continent," 7.

7 Jeeves, *Migrant Labour in South Africa's Mining Economy*, 253–64.

8 TAD, SNA 739/183/03, Report on Swaziland, 1904; SA, SCS 90, Monthly Report of Special Commissioner, May 1904.

9 In 1908–9, for example, 1,000 head of cattle were exchanged for grain by lowveld dwellers experiencing "great privations"; SA, D09/125, Draft ACR, 1908–9, AC Ubombo; AC Ubombo, MR, October 1908; Eastern Transvaal Natives Land Committee, 1918, evidence of D. Forbes, 55.

10 Challis, "Three Years in Swaziland."

11 TLC, 1904, evidence of G. Lagden, para. 1852.

12 TLC, 1904, evidence of D. Forbes, para. 2284, 2340; SANAC, 1903–5, evidence of A. Miller, para. 41456–7; SA, RCS 414/11, Draft ACR, AC Mbabane.

13 ACR, 1906–7, 8; ACR, 1907–8, AC Peak, 39; SA, RCS Draft ACR, 1908–9, AC Mbabane.

14 ACR, 1907–8, 23.

15 ACR, 1907–8, AC Mbabane, 44.

16 TOS, 20 November 1903; SA, L. Von Wissell, "Dad's Story," 24.

17 "Land and the Man," TOS, 7 September 1907; ACR, 1907–8, 23–4, 28; AC AC Hlatikulu, 35; ACR, 1909–10, 8; SA, D09/125, J. Dove, Report on Land Settlement in Swaziland, 1909, appendix E.

18 BRA, HE 277/215S/33, S. Jennings to Swaziland Tin Ltd, 18 December 1906.

19 ACR, 1908–9, AC Hlatikulu.

20 Union of South Africa, Report of the Select Committee on the Native Labour Regulation Bill, March 1911, evidence of S. Pritchard, 25–9, 38.

21 J.S. Marwick was a member of a well-known white settler family in Natal. He worked in both the Natal and Transvaal Native Affairs Departments at different times and, in later years, became a Member of Parliament. He was a frequent visitor to Swaziland and also owned land in the Hlatikulu district; KCL, Marwick papers, KCM 2551b, Handwritten Notes on J.S. Marwick.

22 NRC File 78, Groups Committee on Native Labour, Minutes of Meetings, 16 July 1913; NRC Annual Report, 1914; CAD, CA vol. I, Native Grievances Inquiry, evidence of J.S. Marwick, 13 March 1914.

23 SA, D19/07/1141, AC Mbabane, MR, October 1907.

24 SA, D09/125, AC Hlatikulu, MR, January 1909.

25 SA, D10/57, AC Hlatikulu, MR, November 1909.

26 NRC File 5, Marwick to Villiers, 15 January 1913.

27 NRC File 5, Honey to Taberer, 2 May 1913; NRC File 113, Taberer to Villiers, 23 December 1912.

28 SA, RCS 414/11, Draft ACR, 1910–11, AC Mbabane; AC Mbabane, MR, August 1910.

29 SA, RCS 414/11, Draft ACR, 1910–11, AC Hlatikulu.

30 CAD, CA vol. I, Native Grievances Inquiry, evidence of J.S. Marwick, 13
    March 1914; TAD, GNLB 197 1453/14/97. Courtesy of Marwick & Morris,
    ERPM was somewhat inappropriately designated as "the home of the
    Swazi"; TAD, GNLB 97 220/13/218.

31 TAD, SNA 425/344/09, Acting Assistant Director (GNLB) to SNA, 5 April
    1909, 8 April 1909; SNA to Acting Assistant Director (GNLB), 6 April
    1909.

32 SA, RCS 414/11, AC Hlatikulu, MR, August 1910; NRC File 5, Honey to
    Taberer, 2 May 1913.

33 BRA, HE 254/137/1256, H. Eckstein & Co to Wernher, Beit & Co, 2 May
    1910.

34 Challis, "In Swaziland," 8–10.

35 CAD, CA vol. 1, Native Grievances Inquiry, evidence of J.S. Marwick, 13
    March 1914.

36 SA, RCS 440/23, Honey to Connaught, 15 June 1923; RCS 70/23, Minutes
    of Meeting of Chiefs, Mbabane District, 12 March 1923; RCS 124/24,
    Minutes of Meeting of AC Peak and Chiefs, 1924.

37 TAD, GNLB 5 3855/09, Report on Remittance and Deposit Agency; SA,
    DO9/125, AC Hlatikulu, MR, May 1908; AC Mankiana, MR, August 1908.

38 Challis, "In Swaziland."

39 TAD, GNLB 195 1407/14, Director of Native Labour to Marwick & Morris,
    18 August 1914. Colonial concern that wages were being "recklessly
    squandered" on the Rand later led to official endorsement of the NRC's
    Deferred Pay Scheme in 1918; SA, RCS 70/23, Minutes of Meeting of
    Chiefs, Hlatikulu District, 17 November 1922, 8.

40 SA, HCR, No 74/12, Rex v Dinati Langwenya.

41 TAD, GNLB 43 941/12/3020, Letter from G. Godfrey, 22 November 1911;
    GNLB 88 7/13, Report of Director of Native Labour, 1912; CAD, NA 2
    6911/12/F2, Advances to Natives Recruited in Swaziland, Basutoland and
    Bechuanaland.

42 CAD, NA 2 6911/12/F2, Coryndon to Gladstone, 8 March 1912; High
    Commissioner's Gazette, Notice No 20 of 1912 and Proclamation No 19
    of 1913; TAD, GNLB 47 1159/12/187, Marwick & Morris to Director of
    Native Labour, 18 July 1912.

43 TAD, GNLB 43 941/12/D38, Government Secretary to Director of Native
    Labour, 4 April 1914; SA, HCR, No 177/16, Rex v Mgudwa Gamede; No
    301/19, Rex v Charles Warren.

44 SA, HCR, No 254/11, Rex v Madhlohlo Magagula; No 159/13, Rex v
    Mangebeza Ngobe.

45 CAD, NA 2 6911/12/F2, Coryndon to Gladstone, 8 March 1912. The cattle
    advance system found in Pondoland does not appear to have been used
    to anything like the same extent in Swaziland. While this system would

probably have had intrinsic appeal to the Swazi household, the need for cash and grain was more pressing, and it is unlikely that the traders in Swaziland would have had access to the cattle stocks necessary to make the scheme a success. Beinart's explanation for why the system did not appear outside Pondoland was the "smaller size of homesteads and more commodified relationships" elsewhere. This explanation does seem inadequate in the Swaziland context where relationships were far less "commodified" than in Pondoland; Beinart, *Political Economy of Pondoland* 67.

46 High Commissioner's Gazette, Notice No 53 of 1913, Section 12.

47 Union of South Africa, NGI, 1913–14, para. 545–567, 645. In the 1930s, Hilda Kuper observed that Swazi families avoided excessive credit "because of fear and suspicion of being involved with traders." In turn, traders avoided advancing goods on credit since little security could be offered by homesteads. The situation in the 1930s may have resulted from the earlier experiences of both parties; Kuper, *African Aristocracy*, 136.

48 New trader-recruiters in the country usually experienced an initial barren period; SA, RCS 414/11, AC Mankiana, MR, August 1910. One of the more successful trader-recruiters George Bennett "had grown up as a Swazi, knew the Swazis, their ways, and how they thought, was persona grata with the Royal Kraal and was living with a daughter of the Queen Mother"; Private papers of Captain George Wallis, "The Bennetts, The Stewarts and Jimmy Howe."

49 Kuper, *Uniform of Colour*, 41.

50 SA, D10/57, AC Hlatikulu, MR, July 1909.

51 The following discussion of recruiting tactics and Swazi responses is synthesized from descriptions of recruiting activities by witnesses in over one hundred cases from the Hlatikulu Court Records in the Swaziland Archives. Precise documentation is provided only when illustrative material is used.

52 TAD, GNLB 51 1239/12/5447, Recruitment of Under-Age Natives in Swaziland; Marwick & Morris to All Agents, 19 December 1912; Acting Director of Native Labour to SNA, 25 November 1912; KCL, Marwick papers, KCM 3097, Marwick to Director of Native Labour, 17 December 1914.

53 NRC File 113, Taberer to Villiers, 23 December 1912, 13.

54 SA, RCS 859/23, Carter to Nicholson, 28 January 1923.

55 NRC File 113, Taberer to Villers, 23 December 1912, 8; CAD, NTS 2051/77/280, SNA to Government Secretary, Mbabane, 10 February 1923.

56 SA, RCS 146/13, Draft ACR, 1912–13, AC Police; CAD, NTS 2051/7/280, Nicholson to SNA, 1 March 1923.

57 TAD, GNLB 43 941/12/38, Pass Officer (Boksburg) to Director of Native labour, 21 December 1916; NRC to Director of Native Labour, 15 December 1916.

58 SA, HCR, No 195/19, Rex v Kukumba Shongwe.

59 High Commissioner's Gazette, Proclamation No 19 of 1913, Section 9(7).

60 NRC File 5, Notes on Mr Villiers' interview with Marwick & Morris, 29 January 1913; Marwick to Villiers, 19 February 1913; Honey to Taberer, 2 May 1913.

61 TAD, GNLB 130 2443/13, Colenbrander to Chief Native Commissioner, 6 November 1913. Colenbrander's description applied specifically to Marwick & Morris activities just south of the Swaziland border but accurately captures the position within Swaziland itself.

62 SA, HCR, No 73/14, Rex v Percival Howe.

63 High Commissioner's Gazette, Notice No 19 of 1913, Section 9(8). It is possible that this practice was encouraged by the recruiters but there is no evidence for this.

64 NRC File 5, Marwick to Villiers, 1 April 1913.

65 It was the latter offence that Frederick Buckle construed as "depraving the moral standards of the native"; Union of South Africa, NGI, 1913–14, 561. It has recently been argued that there was a considerable community of interest between trader-recruiters and recruits in defrauding the mining companies. There is little evidence of this kind of "joint enterprise" in Swaziland; Jeeves, *Migrant Labour in South Africa's Mining Economy.*

66 NRC File 5, Marwick to Villiers, 20 January 1913; NRC to Marwick & Morris, 12 August 1914; TAD, GNLB 43 941/12/D38, Government Secretary to Director of Native Labour, 21 February 1914.

67 SA, HCR, No 66/15, Rex v Mbilini Lunga.

68 SA, HCR, No 177/16, Rex v Mgudwa Gamede; No 332/17, Rex v Mbambeni Magagule.

69 TAD, GNLB 227 468/15, Statement by Basi Mnisi at Boksburg, 20 May 1915; Marwick & Morris to Native Affairs Department, 21 May 1915.

70 SA, HCR, No 113/13, Rex v Mayiyane Twala.

71 NRC File 5, Honey to Taberer, 2 May 1913; CAD, CA vol. 1, Native Grievances Inquiry, evidence of J.S. Marwick, 13 March 1914.

72 In 1917, legislation was passed making pass fees and the cost of food en route to the mines (four to eight shillings), which had hitherto been met by the recruiter, recoverable as an advance; CO 417/594, Honey to Buxton, 2 June 1917; Buxton to Honey, 15 June 1917.

73 TAD, GNLB 252 357/16, Labour Shortages in Natal.

74 TAD, GNLB 82 3154/12/77; SA, HCR, No 54/18, statement by A. Crocker, 113.

75 CAD, NA 233/1810/F551, Report by SNA on His Visit to Some Natal Col-

lieries, 2 February 1910; Shortage of Native Labour Committee, evidence of J. Horsfall and Dr White; TAD, GNLB 102 729/13/87, Report of Inspection of Certain Coal Mines: Hlobane, Vryheid, November 1917; CAD, NTS 2045/61/280, Chief Native Commissioner Natal to Director of Native Labour, 13 December 1917.

76 NA, CNC 64/13.

77 SA, HCR, No 54/18, statement by A. Crocker, 113.

78 CAD, NTS 2045/61/280, Medical Officer Hlobane to Inspector Dundee, 17 August 1917.

79 SA, HCR, No 54/18, Rex v 59 Natives; CAD, NA 233/1810/F551, Shortage of Native Labour Committee, evidence of Makutshwa.

80 SA, HCR, No 54/18, Rex v 59 Natives, statement by Kufa Nsibande.

81 NA, CNC 2109/1917, Strike at Hlobane Colliery; CAD, NA 213/958/F473, Report of Inspector of Native Labour, Dundee, 6 March 1917; JUS 260, 4/301/17, Strike of Xosas: Hlobane Colliery.

82 SA, HCR, No 407/17, Rex v Mjange Ngwenya.

83 Overall desertion rates on the Natal coalfields were as high as 15 per cent in 1918 and the mines were an estimated 5,000 workers short of their required complement of 13,700; CAD, NA 233/1810/F551, Report and Recommendations of Departmental Committee on Shortage of Labour in Natal, 1918, 12.

84 SA, HCR, No 54/18, Rex v 59 Natives, Judgement of the Court, 124–35. In July 1918, warrants were issued for the arrest of a further 183 Swazi deserters but many could not be located, having already left for the Rand, and charges appear to have been dropped; SA, HCR, HS 6/19/18.

85 NAD, NA 909/18/F473, Hlobane Colliery to Minister of Native Affairs, 24 June 1918.

86 SA, HCR, No 254/11, Rex v Madholhlo Magagule.

87 SA, HCR, No 159/13, Rex v Mangebeza Ngobe.

88 SA, HCR, No 420/18, Rex v Ndhladla Bhembe.

89 SA, HCR, No 372/17, Rex v Zondiwe Hlope.

90 SA, HCR, No 228/14, Rex v Mashingiliza Nhlengetwa, statement by Dhlodhlo Dlamini.

91 See, for example, the incremental changes made to the Transvaal Labour Agents and Compound Overseers Proclamation of 1901, in 1903, 1906, and 1907.

92 TAD, UNAD 186.F473 v9, Notes for Henry Burton's Speech on Native Labour Regulation Act of 1911; Union of South Africa, Report of the Select Committee on the Native Labour Regulation Bill, March 1911.

93 Compare High Commissioner's Gazette, Notice No 66 of 1910 with TAD, SNA 95/82/1910, Government Notice No 1063 of 1907.

94 High Commissioner's Gazette, Notice No 54 of 1911; Notice No 11 of 1912. The inadequacy of existing legislation was revealed in a test case

when the state failed to convict Nganetole Mazibuko for desertion from a recruiter's roll under the Masters and Servants Law of the Transvaal; SA, Swaziland Law Reports, 1907–32, Rex v Nganetole Mazibuko.
95 High Commissioner's Gazette, Proclamation No 19 of 1913; Notice No 53 of 1913.

CHAPTER SIX

1 Hall, "Notes on the Tin Deposits"; Miller, "Gold Production and the Mineral Resources of Swaziland," 375–7.
2 Crush, "Settler-estate Production"; "Tin Mining in the Valley of Heaven."
3 Freund, *Capital and Labour*, 30, 111.
4 "Our Tin Mining Prospects," *South African Mines, Commerce and Industry*, 13 October 1906; "Swaziland Tin Company," *South African Mines, Commerce and Industry*, 11 February 1905.
5 Fawns, *Tin Deposits of the World*, 144; Scott, "Mineral Development in Swaziland."
6 BRA, HE 9, Swaziland Tin Concessions File, S. Ryan to Managing Director (Eckstein & Co), August 1902; Swaziland Chamber, *Swaziland: The California of South Africa*, 44. Another problem faced by the tin mines was inexperienced and incompetent management, a feature which the profit-hungry Randlord found inexcusable; BRA, HE 277/36/202, Oats to Wernher, 23 November 1906; HE 277/202/41, Oats to Phillips, 17 January 1907.
7 Other major shareholders in Swazi Coal Mines included Sir Percy FitzPatrick and Sir Julius Wernher. For details of the stalled operation see KCL, Miller papers, MS 547a, Report on Mineral Prospects and Concessions in Swaziland, 1910; BRA, HE 277/202/98, Evans to Wernher, 13 July 1908.
8 Suggestions to do away with white overseers and concentrate larger labour gangs do not appear to have been carried through; BRA, HE 277/215s/16, Wallers to Swaziland Tin Ltd, 14 August 1906. Earlier proposals to use Swazi families for tribute mining were not followed up either; HE 9, Swaziland Tin Concessions File, Ryan to Managing Director (Eckstein & Co), August 1902.
9 On production methods for tin mining see KCL, Miller papers, MS 547a, Report on Mineral Concessions and Prospects in Swaziland, 1910, 14–18; HE 277/215s/33, Jennings to Swaziland Tin Ltd, 18 December 1906; HE 277/202/42, Rouillard to Jennings, 19 February 1907; "Swaziland Tin Mines," *South African Mines, Commerce and Industry*, 9 May 1908.
10 BRA, HE 277/215s/B3, Jennings to Directors, Swaziland Tin Ltd, 18 December 1906.

11 *South African Pioneer* 21 (1908): 66.

12 SA, DO9/12, Draft ACR, 1908–9, AC Ubombo; Draft ACR, 1909–10, AC Ubombo.

13 SA, J152/06, Handwritten Notes on Meeting between Selborne and various Whites, September 1906, statement by Hollow.

14 "Swaziland Chamber: President's Address," TOS, 1 September 1906.

15 TAD, GOV 200/955/06, Report of Interview with Swazi Queen Regent and People, 14 September 1906, statement by Selborne.

16 BRA, HE 277/215s/26, Heard to Secretary, Swaziland Tin Ltd, 2 September 1906.

17 SA, RCS 100/15, Heard to Swaziland Tin Ltd, 24 June 1914.

18 "Swaziland Chamber: President's Address," TOS, 10 August 1907; "Alluvial Gold," TOS, 19 January 1907.

19 SA, RCS 100/15, Kelly to Business Manager (Swaziland Tin Ltd), 26 January 1915; Boyd to Ryan, 29 January 1915.

20 These figures are from ACR, 1907–8, 25; 1908–9, 8; 1909–10, 7; SA, RCS 44/12, Draft ACR, 1911–12.

21 SA, RCS 144/18, Draft ACR, 1917–18, AC Peak; Erleigh, "Swaziland as Sheep Country," 2–4.

22 KCL, Miller papers, MS 191a, Swaziland Corporation Annual Report, 1911.

23 CO 417/487, Coryndon to Selborne, 12 January 1910; Selborne to Coryndon, 7 July 1910; High Commissioner's Gazette, Notice No 66 of 1910.

24 The absolute number of individual workers hired was probably somewhat less since some undoubtedly signed on more than once for short periods of employment during the course of the year.

25 *South African Pioneer* 29 (1916): 7.

26 DO 119/867, Coryndon to Rodwell, 8 November 1910; SA, D10/57, AC Peak, MR, October 1909; ACR, 1910–11, 9; ACR, 1911–12, 8.

27 DO 119/867, Coryndon to Rodwell, 3 December 1910.

28 DO 119/867, Honey to Gladstone, 26 July 1910; Gladstone to Rodwell, 29 September 1910; Memorandum by A. Balfour, 14 September, 1910; Gladstone to Coryndon, 28 June 1911.

29 Later the mine managers did request a system of *optional* registration of contracts. This was agreed to and enshrined in the Native Labour Regulation Proclamation of 1913; CO 417/529, Coryndon to Gladstone, 19 February 1913.

30 BRA, HE 277/202/98, Evans to Wernher, 13 July 1908.

31 BRA, HE 254/137, H. Eckstein to Wernher, Beit & Co, 26 May 1910.

32 Van Onselen, *Chibaro*.

33 *South African Pioneer* 21 (1908): 4, 66.

34 SA, DO9/41, Honey to Selborne, 3 December 1909. In May 1908, police

raided three Mbabane homesteads and confiscated a "very large quantity
of beer prepared for sale"; DO9/41, AC Mbabane, MR, May 1908; *South
African Pioneer* 25, (1912): 28.

35 SA, J152/06, Handwritten Notes on Meeting between Selborne and Various Chiefs, September 1906; DO9/41, Honey to Selborne, 3 December
1909; RCS 647/09, Coryndon to Secretary, Liquor Commission, 30 September 1909; RCS 761/13, Coryndon to Gladstone, 21 November 1913.
36 TAD, GOV 200/955/06, Speech by Lord Selborne, 17 September 1906.
37 SA, DO9/41, Honey to Selborne, 3 December 1909.
38 SA, DO9/125, AC Mbabane, MR, July 1908.
39 SA, D19/07/1141, AC Mbabane, MR, September 1907.
40 SA, RCS 295/17.
41 *South African Pioneer* 29 (1916): 5.
42 High Commissioner's Gazette, Proclamation No 19 of 1913.

CHAPTER SEVEN

1 "A Native's Vengeance: Narrow Escape from an Awful Death," *TOS*,
13 July 1905.
2 Mashasha, "Swazi and Land Partition"; Fransman, "Colonial State and
the Land Question"; Crush, "Genesis of Colonial Land Policy"; Booth,
"Development of the Swazi Labour Market."
3 Crush, "Landlords, Tenants and Colonial Social Engineers."
4 SA, Swaziland Census Report, 1921.
5 TAD, SNA 739/183/03, Report on Swaziland, 1904.
6 ACR, 1907–8, AC Hlatikulu, 31; ACR, 1908–9, AC Hlatikulu, 13; CO 417/
487, Coryndon to Gladstone, 28 October 1910.
7 KCL, Miller papers, KCM 3497, *Swaziland and the Swaziland Corporation*,
1903. In 1908 Coryndon estimated stock loss at around 800 sheep per
annum which he naively attributed to "the ancient predatory instinct
which has not been checked and the craving for meat food" arising
from excessive beer consumption; ACR, 1907–8, 17.
8 Swaziland Concessions Commission, *Report of Commission*.
9 RHL, Lagden papers, Mss. Afr. s210 2/4, Memorandum on Swaziland
by Godfrey Lagden, 8 September 1906. See SA, J195/03, A. Van Staden
et al to Moony, 28 July 1903; J40/04, Moony to Secretary for Swaziland
Affairs, 4 December 1905 for details of the post-war claims of land
ownership by concession holders.
10 Swaziland Chamber, *Swaziland: the California of South Africa*, 41–2.
11 "Swaziland Crisis," *TOS*, 21 October 1905; "Unanimous Meeting in
Southern Swaziland," *TOS*, 28 October 1905; KCL, Miller papers, MS 298f,
Miller to Breytenbach, 16 September 1906. After the promulgation of
the 1907 Partition Proclamation Transvaal concession holders

reneged on their deal with Swaziland settlers and pushed for a "South African solution" of one or two large reserves. Selborne explained the rationale for the partition in considerable detail and they were quickly mollified; CO 417/456, Enclosure in No 1, Selborne to Elgin, 27 January 1908.

12 Crush, "Settler-estate Production."

13 Ibid.

14 Trapido, "Landlord and Tenant in a Colonial Economy," 26–58. Land settlement policy under Milner is reviewed in Katzenellenbogen, "Reconstruction in the Transvaal," 341–56.

15 For an analysis of the failure of Milner's policy see Denoon, *Grand Illusion*.

16 Mashasha, "Swazi and Land Partition."

17 SA, J190/05, Memorandum Compiled by Lord Milner after Discussions with A. Miller of the Swaziland Corporation Ltd, 28 December 1904. Miller later requested that the land for settlers be sold in 200 acre blocks interspersed with 200 acre blocks of Corporation land to thwart speculation by potential purchasers; see CO 417/456, Enclosure in No 3, Miller to Milner, 30 March 1905.

18 Crush, "Settler-estate Production."

19 The term "landowner" is used retrospectively throughout this chapter to denote holders of land concessions whose rights were converted to freehold by the colonial state in 1907.

20 The Swaziland Corporation's local manager, Allister Miller, was also President of the Chamber at this time.

21 "D'Essai," *TOS*, 18 May 1907. For extended discussion of Swaziland's potential for agrarian capital see the following sources: Miller, "Swaziland," 1900, 274–94; KCL, Miller papers, KCM 3497, *Swaziland and the Swaziland Corporation*, 1903; and MS 191a, Swaziland Corporation Annual Reports, 1903–7; Miller, "Swaziland," 1905; Miller, "Swazieland: Its Agricultural and Pastoral Future"; Settlers Emigration Society, *Land and Farming Prospects*. The advantages of Swaziland as a haven for white settlers were also trumpeted abroad in the British journal *South Africa* whose editor, E.P. Mathers, was a major shareholder in the Swaziland Corporation Ltd. See, for example, "The Swaziland Corporation: A Few Words about the Agricultural Resources and the Great Land Areas of the Corporation," *South Africa*, 4 April 1903, 24–5.

22 Swaziland Chamber, *Swaziland: The California of South Africa*, 38–9; BRA, HE 273/114/113, Memorandum on Concession No 19 by Cohen, Yates and Marais.

23 KCL, Miller papers, MS 191a, Swaziland Corporation Annual Report, 1903.

24 Swaziland Chamber, *Swaziland: The California of South Africa*. The

Chamber planned to offer easy terms of purchase with land to be held rent free for the first three years following which payment was to be made over a twenty year period.

25 SA, J2/01, J. Smuts, Proposals for the Government of Swaziland, 1901, 3–4.

26 SA, DO9/85, Speech by Lord Selborne in Mbabane, 14 May 1909. The 1907 Partition Proclamation reserved the right of the colonial state to fine landowners who failed "beneficially to occupy the land ... to the satisfaction of the High Commissioner"; High Commissioner's Gazette, Proclamation No 28 of 1907, Section 8(c). This clause was never enforced.

27 CO 417/456, Enclosure, Selborne Memorandum. See also TAD, GOV 203/1075/06, Selborne to Elgin, 29 October 1906, where Selborne repeated his desire not to see "one of the evils of South Africa reproduced in Swaziland – absenteeism combined with kaffir farming." For the Natal case see Slater, "Land, Labour and Capital in Natal," 257–83.

28 CO 417/456, Enclosure No 2, Swaziland Concessions Commission to Selborne, 7 July 1905.

29 SA, DO9/2, Grey to Selborne, 11 February 1908, 33. For investigative reports see SA, DO9/125, J. Dove, Report on Land Settlement in Swaziland, 1909; RCS 423/17, Union Department of Agriculture, Report on the Suitability of Swaziland for Tobacco and Cotton Cultivation, 1917. For further details of how the land partition was "arranged" spatially to suit settler interests see Crush, "Colonial Division of Space."

30 Bodleian Library, Selborne papers, Ms Selborne Box 163 f. 157, Statement by Lord Elgin to Swazi Deputation, December 1907; SA, RCS 506/20, Memorandum of Meeting to Explain Land Settlement to Swazi Chiefs, 11 October 1907; D45/07/640, Minutes of Meeting at Mbabane on 6 March 1908, statement by R. Coryndon; ACR, 1907–8, 13.

31 SA, RCS 506/20, Selborne to Coryndon, 23 November 1907; UW, William Cullen Library, SAIRR Papers, AD 843, B.18.1, Secretary of Anti-Slavery & Aborigines Protection Society to Undersecretary of State for the Dominions, 7 December 1942.

32 SA, RCS 178/12, Swazi Petition, 4 May 1911, and Draft Reply of R. Coryndon. DO9/85, Letter from Swaziland Mining, Commercial and Industrial Chamber, 1909, stressed the "extreme necessity of throwing open to suitable European settlers on reasonable terms all lands the property of the crown."

33 BL, Viscount Gladstone papers, 46003, Selborne to Gladstone, 18 May 1910; CO 417/502, Gladstone to Secretary of State, 24 November 1911. In 1910 Gladstone assumed that transfer would probably occur in 1914. By the end of 1912, his revised estimate was five to ten years.

34 CO 417/502, Botha to Gladstone, 21 April 1911; Gladstone to Botha, 24 April 1911; BL, Viscount Gladstone papers, 46006, Gladstone to

Botha, 5 December 1912, 6 December 1912; 46074, Coryndon to Gladstone, 21 December 1912.

35 Lists of incoming and resident settlers to whom land was sold on soft
terms are located in CAD, PM 1/1/301, No 187/2/1913, Coryndon to
Gladstone, 11 July 1913; CO 608, Swaziland Statistics, 1912/13–1918/
19.

36 ACR, 1909–10 to 1924–5. A further 37,000 acres were purchased from
land companies for the Mushroom scheme. In 1912, the Swaziland
Ranching & Development Company, with considerable capital backing
from Natal, bought 84,000 acres of crown land and 87,000 acres of
land from the Anglo-Swazi Corporation. An additional 100,000 acres
were bought in 1917; KCL, Miller papers, KCM 2295 and MS 639; Private
Papers of Captain George Wallis, "Allister Macintosh Miller," 1. On
the rationale for selling land to bywoners see CO 417/487, Coryndon
to Gladstone, 28 October 1910.

37 The sale of crown lands to Lovat caused a rumpus in the South African
Parliament and after representations from Botha, Gladstone agreed to
discuss all future sales in advance; CAD, PM 1/1/301, No 187/2/1913,
Gladstone to Smuts, 20 August 1913; BL, Viscount Gladstone papers,
46074, Gladstone to Coryndon, 14 January 1913.

38 Selborne, "The South African Protectorates"; Youé, "Imperial Land
Policy."

39 CO 879/81/729, Enclosure 2 in No 57, Milner to Moony, 30 January
1905; No 47, Selborne to Elgin, 14 May 1906.

40 Crush, "Genesis of Colonial Land Policy."

41 SA, DO9/2, Selborne to Smuts, 6 January 1908.

42 "Lord Selborne in Swaziland," The Star, 4 September 1906; TAD, GOV
200/965/06, Report of Interview with Swazi Queen Regent at Mbabane,
14 September 1906; GOV 200/1075/06, Selborne to Elgin, 29 October
1906.

43 KCL, Miller papers, MS 298e, Miller to Swaziland Corporation, 10 September 1906.

44 This policy was savaged to no avail by the settlers. In his letter to his
directors Miller railed against Selborne's "climbdown of expediency
and nervousness," the "Basutoland prejudices" of the Resident Commissioner Enraght Moony, the "experienced bluffing" of the Swazi
chiefs and the negrophilistic sentiments of the British Government,
concluding that failure to effect a satisfactory partition would lead to
difficulty in getting "the class of European we wish to see here"; see
ibid.; and MS 298d, Memorandum of Meeting between Selborne and
Miller, 15 September 1906. More considered settler arguments about
the threat to white settlement are to be found in TAD, GOV 203/1075/
06, Enclosure No 2, D. Forbes to Selborne, 20 September 1906; Swa-

ziland Chamber to Secretary for Swaziland Affairs, 29 September 1906. The nature of this protest and of colonial dexterity are discussed in Crush, "Genesis of Colonial Land Policy" and Mashasha, "The Swazi and Land Partition."

45 TLC, 1904, evidence of David Forbes, para. 2294; "Something about the Future," TOS, 10 October 1903; "Swaziland Chamber: President's Address," TOS, 1 September 1906.

46 SA, DO9/85, Memorandum from G. Somers to Lord Selborne on behalf of Hlatikulu Residents.

47 SANAC, 1903–5, vol. 5, Written replies by A. Miller, 250; SA, DO9/126, E. Fraser to J. Dove, 25 November 1909.

48 TLC, 1904, evidence of N. Breytenbach, para. 8020.

49 KCL, Miller papers, KCM 3497, Swaziland and the Swaziland Corporation, 1903, 10.

50 "Land and the Man," TOS, 7 September 1907.

51 SANAC, 1903–5, vol. 5, Written replies by A. Miller, 250.

52 TAD, GOV 1022/65/45/06, Pott to Selborne, 29 September 1906.

53 SA, DO9/126, J. Dove, Report on Land Settlement in Swaziland, appendix D, H. Silburn to W. Pott, 15 August 1908.

54 Swaziland Chamber, Swaziland: The California of South Africa; BRA, HE 273/114/113, Memorandum on Concession No 19 by Cohen, Yates and Marais.

55 Swaziland Chamber, Swaziland: The California of South Africa, 38.

56 SANAC, 1903–5, vol. 4, evidence of A. Miller, para. 41496.

57 KCL, Miller papers, KCM 3497, Swaziland and the Swaziland Corporation, 1903, 10; SANAC, 1903–5, vol. 4, evidence of A. Miller, para. 41652.

58 "Swaziland Mining, Commercial and Industrial Chamber: President's Address," TOS, 22 July 1905.

59 SANAC, 1903–5, vol. 4, evidence of A. Miller. For a discussion of the South African farm labour problem see Lacey, Working for Boroko, 120–60; Keegan, "The Sharecropping Economy."

60 TAD, GOV 1022/65/45/06 and GOV 1057/17/24/07. In a subsequent report on the company concession in 1908, H. Silburn proposed the following alternative sources of labour and wage rates: (a) Mozambican labour at 30 shillings per month, (b) Indian labour from Natal at 30 shillings per month plus rations for men and 15 shillings per month plus rations for women, and (c) indentured labour from India for five year periods, the first year at 10 shillings per month (5 shillings for women) with an annual increase of one shilling per month (6d for women); SA, DO9/125, J. Dove, Report on Land Settlement in Swaziland, appendix D, H. Silburn to W. Pott, 15 August 1908.

61 Swaziland Chamber, Swaziland: The California of South Africa, 39.

62 TAD, GOV 203/1075/06, Enclosure No 3, Swaziland Chamber to Secretary for Swaziland Affairs, 29 September 1906, 5.

63 Ibid.; SA, J53/03, Memorandum of Swaziland Chamber, 31 December 1903; Bodleian Library, Selborne papers, Ms Selborne Box 170, Selborne to Maydon, 3 April 1906.

64 TLC, 1904, evidence of N. Breytenbach.

65 David Forbes divided his time between the family property in McCorkindale's New Scotland settlement and his various interests in Swaziland. He also sat on the Transvaal Labour Commission; Forbes, *My Life in South Africa*.

66 TAD, A 602, Forbes papers, vol. 37, Native Taxation by David Forbes; SANAC, 1903–5, vol. 5, Additional Memoranda: Taxes by D. Forbes. The possibility of a differential labour tax favouring "those by whom a certain amount of agricultural work has been done" was rejected by Selborne as conducive to social discontent; CO 879/81/729, No 49, Selborne to Elgin, 14 June 1906.

67 SANAC, 1903–5, vol. 4, evidence of A. Miller, 577–601; vol. 5, Written replies by A. Miller. These freehold plots were to cover an area of 150,000 acres, with a further 150,000 acres set aside for future purchase by "enlightened" Swazis.

68 SANAC, 1903–5, vol. 4, evidence of A. Miller, para. 41615.

69 SANAC, 1903–5, vol. 4, evidence of A. Miller, para. 41607; KCL, Miller papers, MS 428a, SCC, 1905, evidence of A. Miller.

70 For applications of the target worker argument see SANAC, 1903–5, vol. 5, Written replies by A. Miller, 250; TLC, 1904, evidence of D. Forbes, para. 2360–1.

71 SA, J53/03, Swaziland Chamber to Chamberlain, 31 December 1902.

72 SANAC, 1903–5, vol. 4, evidence of D. Forbes, para. 44617.

73 "The Native Problem," TOS, 30 September 1904.

74 KCL, Miller papers, MS 637b, Swaziland Chamber to NAD, 1903; MS 428a, SCC, evidence of A. Miller and T. Shepstone; TAD, SNA 258/642/05, Miller to SCC, 17 February 1905; SANAC, 1903–5, vol. 5, Written replies by A. Miller, 255. Within the Transvaal, the representatives of agrarian capital saw the solution to the colony's labour shortages as the break up of the "locations" of Basutoland, Zululand, and Swaziland; Marks, "Natal, the Zulu Royal Family and the Ideology of Segregation," 176.

75 KCL, Miller papers, MS 428a, SCC, 1905, evidence of A. Miller, 2.

76 SA, J306/05, Moony to Secretary for Swaziland Affairs, 4 December 1905.

77 SA, J2/01, J. Smuts, Proposals for the Government of Swaziland, 1901, 3–4; Rubie, *The Swaziland Concessions*.

78 SA, J40/04, Milner to Miller, 15 January 1904.

258 Notes to pages 145–8

79 SA, J306/05, Moony to Secretary for Swaziland Affairs, 4 December
   1905; TAD, SNA 258/642/05, SCC, 1905, evidence of E. Moony, 28 January 1905; CO 291/107, Swaziland Concessions Commission Report,
   Meetings of Commission, 7 December 1905.

80 TAD, SNA 258/642/05, SCC, 1905, evidence of G. Lagden.

81 "The Settlement," TOS, 7 October 1905.

82 High Commissioner's Gazette, Proclamation No 3 of 1904. See CO 879/
   81/729, No 10, Milner to Lyttleton, 6 February 1904; No 15, Milner
   to Lyttleton, 17 October 1904.

83 SA, J138/05, Minutes of Interview between Resident Commissioner and
   Swazi Queen Regent & Council, 13 February 1905. See CO 879/81/729,
   Enclosure in No 20, Report of Swazi Deputation to Selborne, 4 July
   1905, for further details of Swazi objections.

84 SA, J18/05, Milner to Moony, 30 January 1905; J138/05, Complaints of
   Queen Regent to Moony and Replies, February 1905.

85 CO 879/81/729, No 17, Lyttleton to Milner, 29 March 1905.

86 Selborne calculated that this would leave about one third of the area
   of the country in Swazi hands, hardly a generous allowance in absolute
   terms but a considerable advance on settler demands; CO 879/81/729,
   No 19a, Selborne to Lyttleton, 26 June 1905; Swaziland Concessions
   Commission, *Report of Commission*, para. 9.

87 SA, J138/05, Moony to Lieutenant Governor of Transvaal, 2 June 1905.

88 CO 879/81/729, Enclosure in No 47, Report of Swaziland Concessions
   Commission on work done in Swaziland during 1905, 11.

89 Crush, "Genesis of Colonial Land Policy"; CO 291/107, Proceedings of
   Meeting of Swaziland Concessions Commission with Concession Holders, 13 December 1905.

90 RHL, Anti-Slavery papers, MSS.BRIT.EMP.522.G186, Parsonson to Fox-
   Bourne, 23 October 1905.

91 "Editorial Comment," TOS, 21 October 1905; KCL, Miller Papers, MS
   632, Memorandum for the Secretary of Swaziland Affairs, 8 March
   1906; MS 633b, Swaziland Chamber to Secretary of Swaziland Affairs,
   29 September 1906. In the latter memorandum the settlers tried again
   to get the area of reserves reduced to 25 per cent.

92 TAD, GOV 203/1075/06, Forbes to Selborne, 20 September 1906. David
   Forbes here sought an assurance from Selborne that at least 50 per
   cent of the land would remain in white hands.

93 TAD, GOV 203/1075/06, Selborne to Elgin, 29 October 1906; KCL, Miller
   papers, MS 248e, Miller to Swaziland Corporation, 16 September 1906.

94 RHL, Lagden papers, Mss. Afr. s210 2/4, Memorandum on Swaziland,
   8 September 1906; DO 119/821, Selborne to Coryndon, 13 March 1908.

95 For an extended discussion of Grey's partition activities see Crush,
   "Colonial Division of Space." For reasons of political expediency Grey,

with the connivance of Selborne, included some tracts of land in the reserves which were of use to neither Swazi nor settler, in an attempt to soften the starkness of the absolute ratio; DO 119/608, Grey to Selborne, 5 October 1908; Selborne to Grey, 10 October 1908.

96 KCL, Miller papers, MS 428a, SCC, 1905, evidence of A. Miller, 5.

97 RHL, Lagden papers, Mss. Afr. s210 2/4, Memorandum on Swaziland, 8 September 1906.

98 The other potential galvanizing force for consolidated reserves and the mass relocation of the Swazi population – that of mining capital – appears to have had little influence. As Lagden commented in 1905, "I do not know that there is much to be gained by collecting the natives into reserves, except that it would be a labour supply to the industrial centres"; TAD, SNA 259/642/05, Swaziland Concessions Commission, 1905, evidence of G. Lagden, 26. One suggestion made at this time was to reserve a large area of Swaziland as a labour reserve for the Rand mines on which non-Swazis could be settled; Bleloch, *The New South Africa*, appendix F, "Swazi Native Reserves" by W. Fraser. Such a system was actually experimented with in various parts of the Transvaal.

99 SANAC, 1903–5, vol. 4, evidence of A. Miller and D. Forbes.

100 SA, J245/02, Miller to Moony, 19 November 1902.

101 "The Swazi: Mr Miller's Opinions," *Transvaal Leader*, 25 November 1904. The missionary community in Swaziland which was having its own problems in advancing its cause continued to hanker after a "bloodless rebellion" which would give the colonial state an excuse to shatter the power of the Swazi chiefs and "scatter the Swazis among European farmers and mines"; Challis, "Three Years in Swaziland."

102 SA, J2/01, J. Smuts, Proposals for the Government of Swaziland, 1901.

103 SA, J245/02, Moony to Lagden, 29 November 1902; J70/03, Moony to Lagden, 4 March 1903.

104 CO 879/81/729, Enclosure in No 57, Swazi Petition to Lord Milner.

105 RHL, Lagden papers, Mss. Afr. s210 2/4, Memorandum on Swaziland, 8 September 1906, para. 5.

106 KCL, Miller papers, MS 429, Miller to Malcolm, 21 December 1906, 5.

107 Colonial officials bent over backwards to accommodate the odd minor collaborating chief they could find. As Grey commented, "[Gucuka] is one of the most loyal and useful men in the district, and it is the strong wish of the Administration that he should be put in undisputed possession of his lands." In contrast, Josiah Vilikazi, an adviser to the Queen Regent who held a concession near Mahamba lost the greater part of his land on the advice of the District Commissioner; SA, D09/2, Grey's Partition Notes; DO 119/608, Grey to Selborne, 4 July 1908.

108 CO 291/107, Swaziland Concessions Commission, Minutes of Meeting on 7 December 1905, statement by A. Miller, 378; CO 879/81/729, No

47, Selborne to Elgin, 2 June 1906. This particular letter has additional significance for in it Selborne requested full and absolute discretionary powers to resolve the land question in Swaziland. That he was granted them, almost without question, is perhaps somewhat surprising given his shaky relationship with the Colonial Office in other areas. It was clearly related to the strong case he made that the "period of unrest" in Swaziland would otherwise be indefinitely prolonged and that it was necessary to "enhance that authority which it is so necessary for me to have in dealing with the natives." See CO 291/107, Swaziland Settlement Memoranda and CO 879/106/87, No 799, Elgin to Selborne, 1 September 1906, for Elgin's affirmative response. For a lone dissenting voice see CO 291/107, Minute by H. Just.

109 High Commissioner's Official Gazette, Proclamation No 28 of 1907, 25 October 1907.

110 CO 879/96/890, Enclosure in No 37, Petition of N. Breytenbach and others; Enclosure in No 38, Ferreira and Olmesdahl to Selborne, 4 January 1908; DO 119/608, Grey to Rodwell, 4 November 1908; SA, DO9/125, J. Dove, Report on Land Settlement in Swaziland, 1909, 11–12.

111 CO 879/96/890, Enclosure in No 37, Statement by Lord Selborne, 19 December 1907; and "Selborne's Speech at Wakkerstroom," *Rand Daily Mail*, 22 November 1909.

112 RHL, Lagden papers, Mss. Afr. s210 2/4, Memorandum on Swaziland, 8 September 1906. See also CO 879/96/890, Enclosure in No 3, Coryndon to Selborne, 6 June 1907.

113 SA, RCS 506/20, Memorandum of Meeting to Explain Land Settlement to Swazis, 11 October 1907; TAD, GOV 203/1075/06, Forbes to Selborne, 20 September 1906; and KCL, Miller papers, MS 429, Miller to Malcolm, 21 December 1906.

114 SA, DO9/2, Grey to Selborne, 11 February 1908, 32.

CHAPTER EIGHT

1 SA, D48/07/2205, Register of Swaziland Chiefs, 1907.

2 TAD, GOV 203/1075/06, Selborne to Elgin, 29 October 1906; CO 879/96/890, Enclosure in No 3, Coryndon to Selborne, 6 June 1907.

3 KCL, Miller papers, MS 542, Miller to Clifford, 19 April 1926.

4 For details of Bunu's untimely death and the succession dispute see SNA, RCS 115/14, de Symons Honey, "A History of Swaziland," 1916, 126(a); DO 119/572, Governor of Natal to Milner, 13 February 1900; Mordaunt to Smuts, 9 February 1900; *South African Pioneer* 16 (1903): 90; SA, J50/03, Moony to Secretary for Swaziland Affairs, 1 August 1904; TAD, GOV

780/65/04, Moony to Walrond, 30 May 1904; Kuper, *Sobhuza II*, 30–3. There were also disputes over whether Malunge should be appointed Prince Regent; TAD, GOV 752/50/04, Report by Two Special Messengers of Chief Usibebu.

5 TAD, CS 14/1576, Visit of J. Smuts to Swaziland, April 1901.

6 SA, J50/04, Report on Swaziland, 1904.

7 TAD, GOV 203/1075/06, Forbes to Selborne, 20 September 1906.

8 SA, J138/05, Moony to Lieutenant Governor of the Transvaal, 2 June 1905.

9 SA, J138/05, Report of Deputation to Selborne, 4 July 1905; Nyeko, "The Extension of British Colonial Administration into Swaziland," 139; RHL, Lagden papers, Mss. Afr. s210 2/4, Memorandum on Swaziland, 8 September 1906.

10 TAD, GOV 203/1075/06, Selborne to Elgin, 29 October 1907, para. 7.

11 CO 417/469, Notes of Meeting at Mbabane, 17 November 1908; SA, D09/2, Grey to Selborne, 7 December 1908; SA, D08/3, Queen Regent to Resident Commissioner, 13 May 1909.

12 CO 879/100/927, Enclosure 1 and 2 in No 101, Report of Interview with Queen Regent and Chiefs, 14 & 15 May 1909.

13 SA, RCS 70/23, Minutes of Meeting of Chiefs, Hlatikulu District, 17 January 1922. See also SA, RCS 414/11, AC Mankiana, MR, January 1911; RCS 146/13, Draft ACR, 1912–13, AC Hlatikulu; RCS 724/13–31/14, AC Hlatikulu, MR, November 1913; HCR, AC Hlatikulu, MR, September 1918; HCR 271/18, 504/18, 202/19, 237/19, 329/19, 383/19.

14 Throughout these years, rumours that a Swazi rising was imminent continued to surface in reports by "loyal natives"; SA, J8/1907, Moony to Secretary for Swaziland Affairs, 22 October 1906; Acting Assistant Resident Magistrate to Secretary for Swaziland Affairs, 11 January 1907.

15 The ruthless crushing of the Bambatha rebels undoubtedly proved an equally uncomfortable precedent for a Swazi council debating an anticolonial revolt.

16 CO 417/456, Coryndon to Selborne, 12 December 1907.

17 TAD, GOV 203/1075/06, Taberer to Selborne, 24 September 1906; CO 879/96/890, No 43, Selborne to Elgin, 30 March 1908; No 48, Elgin to Selborne, 6 May 1908.

18 DO 119/814, Coryndon to Selborne, 21 December 1907.

19 DO 119/795, Coryndon to Selborne, 20 June 1907; Selborne to Coryndon, 29 June 1907; Forbes to Coryndon, 20 June 1907; SA, D45/07/1418, Coryndon to Selborne, 22 August 1907; Selborne to Coryndon, 2 September 1907.

20 For a detailed diplomatic history of these various Conventions and their impact on Swaziland see Garson, "The Swaziland Question."

21 CO 879/81/729, Enclosure in No 20, Statement by Malunge, 4 July 1905; TAD, GOV 200/955/06, Report of Meeting between Selborne and Queen Regent and Council, 14 September 1906.

22 Fransman, "Colonial State and the Land Question," 39–48, discusses colonial policy on the Private Revenue Concession.

23 TAD, GOV 200/955/06, Report of Meeting between Selborne and Queen Regent and Council, 14 September 1906, statement by Malunge.

24 SA, J138/05, Swazi Petition to Lord Milner, 30 December 1904.

25 SA, J138/05, Interview between Resident Commissioner and Queen and Council, 13 February 1905, statement by Jokovu.

26 CO 879/96/890, Enclosure 1 in No 42, Minutes of Meeting at Mbabane, 3 June 1908, statement by Queen Regent.

27 CO 879/96/890, Enclosure 1 in No 42, statement by Nogcogco.

28 SA, RCS 178/12, Swazi Petition to Lord Gladstone, 4 May 1911.

29 SA, RCS 478/13, Minutes of Meeting between Resident Commissioner and Chief Regent and Council, 26 August 1913, statement by Malunge.

30 SA, RCS 375/14, Queen Regent to RC, 16 June 1914; RCS 732/13, Report of Meeting between Gladstone and Swazi Chiefs at Barberton, August 1913.

31 Walshe, *Rise of African Nationalism*, 30–42; Kuper, *Sobhuza II*, 47; SA, RCS 141/16, Draft ACR, 1914–15, AC Police.

32 *Abantu Batho* was launched with the aid of a grant of £3,000 from Labotsibeni. Seme's association with the Swazi royal house was long and fruitful for both parties. He later took one of Mbandeni's daughters as his third wife and in 1922 he was one of two lawyers sent with a Swazi deputation to England. In the 1940s he was still closely involved in the Swazi land case; SA, RCS 360/21, Memorandum, 30 October 1930; UW, William Cullen Library, SAIRR Papers, AD 843.B.18.1, Seme to Rheinalt Jones, 14 March 1942, 8 April 1942, 21 July 1942; Matsebula, *History of Swaziland*, 168.

33 KCL, Miller papers, MS 725b, Memorandum Relating to Purchase of Land by Natives, 1914. In February 1914, Malunge attended the Kimberley Conference of the SANNC called to protest the 1913 Native Lands Act in South Africa; CO 417/546, Coryndon to Gladstone, 14 March 1914; Kuper, *Sobhuza II*, 48.

34 SA, DO9/88, JP Mankiana to AC Mbabane, 25 June 1909; Coryndon to Imperial Secretary, 3 July 1909.

35 CO 417/470, Coryndon to Selborne, 2 June 1909; Selborne to Secretary of State, 3 July 1909; Secretary of State to Selborne, 13 August 1909; CO 417/502, Coryndon to Selborne, 29 September 1909.

36 SA, RCS 375/14, Queen Regent to RC, 16 June 1914.

37 CO 417/546, Coryndon to Gladstone, 14 March 1914; Gladstone to Cor-

yndon, 3 April 1914; SA, RCS 158/14, Rodwell to Honey, 19 November 1914.

38 CO 417/546, Coryndon to Gladstone, 14 March 1914; CO 417/581, Honey to Buxton, 7 October 1916.

39 CO 417/546, Honey to Gladstone, 20 June 1914; CO 417/581, Honey to Buxton, 16 September 1916.

40 SA, RCS 45/13, Correspondence in Connection with Purchase of Land by Swazi Nation from H. Kelly.

41 *Abantu Batho*, 20 March 1914; SA, RCS 146/13, Draft ACR, 1912–13, AC Mbabane; RCS 842/13, Draft ACR, 1913–14, AC Mbabane.

42 CO 417/546, Honey to Gladstone, 6 June 1914; SA, RCS 718/14, Meeting of Swazi Chiefs and RC, 19 October 1914; RCS 801/14, RC's Report on Meeting. At the request of the local chiefs and with the assent of an angry Queen Regent, the colonial state took over responsibility for managing land repurchase funds.

43 SA, RCS 375/14, Queen Regent to Honey, 16 June 1914; CO 417/546, Honey to Gladstone, 6 June 1914.

44 SA, RCS 126/15, Meeting of Swazi Chiefs and Resident Commissioner, 6 April 1915.

45 SA, RCS 371/14, AC Hlatikulu, MR, April 1914.

46 SA, RCS 506/14, Grudden to ACS, 3 July 1914; RCS 511/14; RCS 141/16, AC Hlatikulu, MR, August 1914; AC Mankiana, MR, July 1914.

47 NRC, File 5, Marwick & Morris to Horseman, 30 October 1914; Labotsibeni to Marwick & Morris, 7 October 1914.

48 SA, RCS 471/14, AC Mankiana, MR, May 1914.

49 SA, RCS 126/15, Meeting of Resident Commissioner and Swazi Chiefs, 6 April 1915, statement by Nomadakolu.

50 SA, RCS 141/16, Draft ACR, 1915–16, AC Hlatikulu.

51 SA, RCS 126/15, Meeting of Resident Commissioner and Swazi Chiefs, 6 April 1915, statement by Nogcogco Dlamini.

52 Ibid., statement by Bokweni Mamba.

53 SA, RCS 186/15, Resident Commissioner's Report on Meeting with Chiefs, April 1915.

54 SA, RCS 369/18, Honey to Queen Regent, 8 September 1918.

55 SA, RCS 518/17, AC Police to RC, 17 September 1917; RCS 369/18, Government Secretary to ACS, 1 October 1918.

56 *Abantu Batho*, 20 March 1914.

57 SA, RCS 141/16, AC Ubombo, MR, March 1915.

58 SA, RCS 471/14, AC Mankiana, MR, May 1914; RCS 126/15, Meeting of Resident Commissioner and Swazi Chiefs, 6 April 1915, statement by Silele Nsibande; RCS 491/15, Meeting of Resident Commissioner and Chiefs, 26 August 1915.

59 SA, RCS 281/18, AC Mankiana to Honey, 15 May 1918.

60 SA, RCS 273/15, Acting RC to AC's, 17 December 1915.

61 High Commissioner's Gazette, Proclamation No 2 of 1915; CAD, PM 1/ 1/301, 155/33A/1914, Memorandum: Swaziland. Purchase of Land by Natives, 22 September 1914.

62 CO 417/566, Honey to Buxton, 17 October 1914.

63 SA, RCS 375/14, Miller to Coryndon, 30 April 1914; CO 417/546, Coryndon to Gladstone, 27 June 1914; KCL, Miller papers, MS 725b, Memorandum Relating to Purchase of Land by Natives, 1914.

CHAPTER NINE

1 Keegan, "Restructuring of Agrarian Class Relations in a Colonial Economy"; "Sharecropping Economy on the South African Highveld."

2 SA, RCS 414/11, Draft ACR, 1910–11, AC Mbabane.

3 SA, RCS 578/16, Draft ACR, 1915–16, JP Bremersdorp.

4 SA, RCS 167/21, Draft ACR, 1920–21, AC Hlatikulu.

5 SA, HCR, No 27/13, NRC v H. Muller.

6 ACR, 1917–18, 6.

7 The largest of these, the Swaziland Ranching & Development Company Limited had an issued share capital of £220,000 in 1919. The industry as a whole was beset with problems in the early 1920s, and in 1926 this company was forced into liquidation. The Natalia Company was liquidated in 1922. For details of the fluctuating fortunes of cattle ranching in Swaziland see KCL, Miller papers, KCM 2310, 2312, 2392, 2420–2, 2432–8, MS 639–46, 681.

8 KCL, Miller papers, KCM 2295, Evans to Miller, 24 August 1917.

9 Crush, "Landlords, Tenants and Colonial Social Engineers," 235–6.

10 SA, RCS 371/14, AC Hlatikulu, MR, April 1914.

11 SA, DO8/80, J. Flemming to Swaziland Administrator, 3 January 1909.

12 SA, RCS 450/11, Miller to Government Secretary, 31 July 1914.

13 SA, RCS 506/14, RC to AC's; CAD, GG 923/19/237, Gladstone's Report to Secretary of State, 11 July 1914.

14 Crush, "Colonial Division of Space."

15 SA, RCS 842/13, Draft ACR, 1913–14, AC Mankiana, AC Ubombo, MR, August 1913.

16 Any resettlement in the Mbabane district would probably have taken place in 1913 and early 1914 since at the end of 1912, the Assistant Commissioner commented on how few homesteads had moved; SA, RCS 21/12, AC Mbabane to Government Secretary, 4 December 1912. The lowveld crop of 1912 was a complete failure and a population shift out of the area or within the lowveld itself may have been responsible for the net decrease in the Ubombo district.

17 SA, RCS 371/14, AC Hlatikulu, MR, April 1914.
18 SA, RCS 842/13, Draft ACR, 1913–14, AC Mbabane.
19 SA, RCS 759/15, Draft ACR, 1915–16, AC Mbabane; RCS 337/14, Honey to Gladstone, 20 June 1914; RCS 424/24, AC Mankiana to Government Secretary, 27 August 1924.
20 KCL, Miller papers, MS MIL 1.08.1, Swaziland Corporation Report, 18.
21 SA, RCS, 21/12, AC Mbabane to Government Secretary, 4 December 1912; RCS 842/13, Draft ACR, 1913–14, AC Mbabane; CO 417/546, Coryndon to Gladstone, 18 May 1914.
22 SA, D807/09, Grey's Notes on Partition Appeals, 1909.
23 SA, RCS 405/14; RCS 528/l5.
24 SA, D807/09, Grey's Notes on Partition Appeals, 1909.
25 SA, RCS 504/18, Marwick to Honey, 1 October 1918; D08/3, Meeting of Acting RC and Swazi Chiefs, 17 December 1908.
26 ACR, 1908–9, AC Hlatikulu; ACR, 1909–10, AC Hlatikulu.
27 SA, RCS 478/14, Minutes of Meeting between Resident Commissioner and Queen Regent and Council, 26 August 1913.
28 High Commissioner's Gazette, Proclamation No 24 of 1913, Sections 7 and 8. For the background to this legislation see CO 417/529, Coryndon to Gladstone, 5 September 1913.
29 SA, RCS 215/14, AC Hlatikulu, MR, February 1914. I have argued elsewhere that the colonial state deliberately preserved the powers of land distribution of the chiefs. The new evidence presented here suggests that it would be more accurate to say that the state reluctantly acquiesced in the situation; Crush, "Southern African Regional Formation." See SA, RCS 141/16, Draft ACR, 1915–16, AC Mbabane, for a discussion of this question between two colonial officials, Marwick and Honey. Marwick attempted to salvage the situation through presentation of a case for "territorial jurisdiction" as a useful means of colonial administration.
30 SA, RCS 842/13, Draft ACR, 1913–14, AC Mbabane; RCS 215/14, AC Hlatikulu, MR, February 1914; Kuper, African Aristocracy, 67.
31 SA, RCS 371/14, AC Hlatikulu, MR, April 1914.
32 SANAC, 1903–5, vol. 5, Written replies by D. Forbes, 215.
33 Kuper, Uniform of Colour, 6–9.
34 SA, RCS 141/16, Draft ACR, 1915–16, AC Mbabane.
35 SA, RCS 115/14, de Symons Honey, "A History of Swaziland," 1916, 152.
36 This would allow sense to be made of conflicting reports on the condition of the Swazi reserves in the early 1930s; Pim, Financial and Economic Situation of Swaziland; UW, William Cullen Library, SAIRR Papers, A410/A3(2), V. Hodgson and M. Ballinger, "Swaziland," 1931.
37 Confusion over how many Swazi homesteads actually moved continued for many years. In 1932, for example, Pim talked of "extensive removals" and "displacement of a considerable number of natives" yet concluded

that "the numbers actually displaced are not known and were probably not very large." In 1932, an estimated 20,000 Swazi (approximately 15 per cent of the population) were still resident outside the reserves; Pim, *Financial and Economic Situation of Swaziland*, 12, 19, 22.

38 Private Papers of Captain George Wallis.

39 SA, RCS 21/12, Government Secretary to AC's, 28 November 1911.

40 SA, RCS 732/13, Report of Meeting between High Commissioner and Swazi Chiefs at Barberton.

41 SA, RCS 450/11, A. Mordaunt to Government Secretary, 29 September 1911.

42 SA, RCS 21/12, Government Secretary to Swaziland Farmers Association, 2 April 1912.

43 CO 417/529, Coryndon to Gladstone, 5 September 1913.

44 SA, RCS 270/14, Coryndon to Queen Regent, 28 March 1914. Landowners were asked "to ensure that the date for removal should come and go with as little dislocation as possible to the interests of every section of the community"; SA, RCS 115/14, de Symons Honey, "A History of Swaziland," 1916, 152.

45 SA, RCS 187/14, AC Mankiana to Government Secretary, 21 February 1914; RCS 478/13, Meeting between RC and Chief Regent and Council, 26 August 1913, statement by Sicunusa Dlamini.

46 RCS 130/14, AC Mankiana, MR, January 1914; RCS 371/14, AC Mankiana, MR, April 1914.

47 SA, RCS 198/14, Coryndon to Queen Regent, 3 March 1914.

48 SA, RCS 270/14, Queen Regent to Coryndon, 17 March 1914.

49 CAD, GG 1426/50/376, Coryndon to Gladstone, 23 December 1913, 10 January 1914; CAD, JUS 178 3/1423/13, Coryndon to Gladstone, 9 February 1914; "The Swazi Scare," *Cape Times*, 5 January 1914.

50 SA, RCS 371/14, AC Hlatikulu, MR, April 1914; RCS 81/15, AC Hlatikulu, MR, January 1915; RCS 646/15, AC Hlatikulu, MR, October 1915; RCS 759/15, Draft ACR, 1915–16, AC Peak.

51 SA, RCS 130/14, AC Mankiana, MR, January 1914.

52 SA, RCS 295/16, Government Secretary to AC Police, 8 June 1916.

53 SA, RCS 552/14, AC Hlatikulu, MR, June 1914.

54 SA, RCS 371/14, AC Hlatikulu, MR, April 1914.

55 SA, RCS 215/14, AC Hlatikulu, MR, February 1914; AC Mbabane, MR, March 1914; RCS 613/14, AC Hlatikulu, MR, July 1914; RCS 493/17, AC Hlatikulu to Government Secretary, 11 September 1917.

56 SA, RCS 471/14, AC Ubombo, MR, May 1914.

57 SA, RCS 854/14; KCL, Miller papers, Piggs Peak Development Company Ltd Report, 3. For a description of the settlement that sprang up around the mine see Schmelzenbach, *Missionary Prospector*, 49.

58 Keegan, "Sharecropping Economy on the South African Highveld."

59 SA, RCS 215/14, AC Hlatikulu, MR, February 1914; AC Mankiana, MR, March 1914; RCS 471/14, AC Ubombo, MR, May 1914.

60 SA, RCS 471/14, AC Peak, MR, May 1914.

61 SA, RCS 854/14; RCS 509/16, AC Ubombo, MR, September, 1916.

62 SA, RCS 371/14, AC Hlatikulu, MR, April 1914; RCS 569/15, AC Mankiana, MR, September 1915; RCS 708/15, AC Ubombo, MR, November 1915; RCS 424/24, AC Hlatikulu to Government Secretary, 5 September 1924.

63 SA, RCS 528/15, AC Mankiana to Government Secretary, January 1922.

64 SA, RCS 759/15, AC Mankiana, MR, May 1915; RCS 220/24, Meeting of AC Mankiana and Chiefs, statement by Somtseu.

65 SA, RCS 639/14, AC Mbabane, MR, August 1914.

66 SA, RCS 81/15, AC Hlatikulu, MR, January 1915; RCS 418/15, AC Hlatikulu, MR, July 1915.

67 SA, RCS 842/13, Draft ACR, 1913–14, AC Mankiana.

68 SA, RCS 337/14, Honey to Murray, nd; RCS 471/14, AC Hlatikulu, MR, May 1914; RCS 474/24, AC Mankiana to Government Secretary, 27 August 1924.

69 SA, RCS 270/14, Queen Regent to Coryndon, 17 March 1914.

70 SA, HCR 270/14, Rex v Mantinta Nsibande; HCR 126/15, Rex v Mjakela Twala; HCR 232/16, Rex v Mvulane Msibi; HCR 402/18, Rex v Sikonyane Dlamini.

71 SA, HCR 286/16, Rex v Mtshakela Dlamini.

72 SA, HCR 224/16, Rex v Jan Snyman, statement by Mehlamane Mandhlope.

73 SA, HCR 224/16, statement by H. Middleton.

74 SA, HCR 224/16; HCR 286/14, Rex v Theunis Dekker; HCR 216/20, Rex v Mkehli Dlamini, Five, Parrafin and Sixpence; HCR 217/20, Rex v Mkehli Dlamini.

75 SA, HCR 8/3/18, Rex v Solomon Maritz.

76 SA, RCS 493/17, Petition of Hlatikulu Farmers Association; RCS 654/18, Resolutions passed by Hlatikulu Farmers Association.

77 SA, HCR 279/18, Rex v Kwentula Mkonza.

78 SA, RCS 859/23, Carter to Nicholson, 28 January 1923.

79 SA, RCS 293/16, AC Mankiana, MR, May 1916; RCS 489/17, Meeting of European Residents and High Commissioner; RCS 493/17, Petition of Hlatikulu Farmers Association.

80 See SA, RCS 529/15 for further details.

81 SA, HCR 279/18, Rex v Kwentula Mkonza; Wood, "Cotton in Swaziland," 13–19.

82 SA, RCS 592/19, Resolution of Hlatikulu Farmers Association.

83 Private papers of Captain George Wallis, "A Journey to Ingwavuma," 4.

84 SA, RCS 423/17, Honey to Buxton, 14 March 1918.

85 SA, HCR 119/18, Rex v Dambile Mapalala.

86 SA, HCR 346/18, Rex v Balambile Mkonta and 5 others, statement by J. Robberts.
87 SA, HCR 62/18, Rex v Natalonye Gininda and 6 others; HCR 282/18, Rex v Ntondo Mkalela and 2 others; HCR 323/18, Rex v Lomazulu Dlamini and 6 others; HCR 333/19, Rex v Mzanwayo Nhlengetwa.
88 SA, RCS 371/22, Government Secretary to ACS, 20 June 1922; RCS 70/23, Minutes of Meeting of Chiefs and AC Hlatikulu, 15 February 1923.
89 SA, HCR 270/14 and 30/15, Rex v Mantinta Nsibande.

CHAPTER 10

1 Crush, "Landlords, Tenants and Colonial Social Engineers."
2 SA, RCS 126/15, Meeting of RC and Swazi Chiefs, 6 April 1915, statement by Nomadakolu.
3 "Bullets That Stray," *Sunday Times*, 8 March 1912.
4 Beemer, "Military Organization," 64.
5 SA, HCR, Rex v Malunge Dlamini, August 1914.
6 "Letter from W. Penfold," *Transvaal Leader*, 24 December 1913.
7 KCL, James Stuart Papers, KCM 23513, File 30 (iii); Kuper, "Monarchy and the Military in Swaziland," 226.
8 Beemer, "Military Organization," 64.
9 Kuper, *African Aristocracy*, 22, 150.
10 Beemer, "Military Organization," 188; Diaries of H. Raney, 1899–1915, 27 March 1908.
11 Ibid., 191–2.
12 Kuper, *The Swazi*, 55.
13 On growing regional autonomy in the twentieth century see the comments of Beemer, "Primitive Nation," 36.
14 KCL, James Stuart Papers, KCM 23513, File 30 (iii).
15 Moroney, "Mine Worker Protest," 40.
16 TAD, GNLB 275 294/17, Inspector of Native Labour (Roodeport) to Director of Native Labour, 4 August 1917.
17 CAD, CA vol. 1, Native Grievances Enquiry, Minutes of Evidence, evidence of J.S. Marwick.
18 KCL, Marwick papers, KCM 3096, Day to Marwick, 3 November 1916.
19 JPL, Native Grievances Committee, Minutes of Evidence, 1914, evidence of C. Villiers, 3 March 1914.
20 According to one report, in 1912 over 1,000 Swazi mineworkers (approximately 20 per cent of the Swazi mine workforce) were followers of Bokweni Mamba; "Bullets That Stray," *Sunday Times*, 8 March 1912.
21 TAD, GNLB 97 220/13/218; 150 136/14/37; 200 1562/14; 275 294/17, Memorandum by AC Mankiana, 8 June 1917.
22 CO 417/529, Queen Regent to Coryndon, 19 August 1913.

23 NRC File 75, Statement by the General Superintendent of the NRC Ltd, 29 July 1913.

24 Bonner, "The 1920 Black Mineworkers' Strike," 284.

25 Challis, "In Swaziland," 8–10; "Revolt of Youth," in Kuper, *Uniform of Colour*, 148–50; Beemer, "Military Organization," 184.

26 A systematic analysis of Swazi mine culture and consciousness, and its intersection with the demands of the countryside, would necessitate moving well beyond the period under study and is therefore reserved for another occasion.

27 TAD, GNLB 150 136/14/37; Kuper, *Uniform of Colour*, 21.

28 Kuper, *African Aristocracy*, 121; Kuper, *The Swazi*, 52–3; Matsebula, *The King's Eye*, 15–32.

29 SA, Interviews with John Gamede, 1953–5.

CONCLUSION

1 Marks and Rathbone, *Industrialisation and Social Change in South Africa*, 1.

2 Particularly Kuper, *African Aristocracy*.

3 Guy, "Destruction and Reconstruction of Zulu Society," 167–94.

4 Isaacman and Isaacman, "Resistance and Collaboration," 33.

5 Bundy, *Rise and Fall*; Beinart, *Political Economy of Pondoland*.

6 Kimble, "Labour Migration in Basutoland"; Delius, "Migrant Labour and the Pedi"; Harries, "Kinship, Ideology and the Nature of Pre-Colonial Labour Migration."

7 Bundy, *Rise and Fall*; Palmer and Parsons, *Roots of Rural Poverty*.

8 Beinart, "Labour Migrancy and Rural Production."

9 Jeeves, *Migrant Labour in South Africa's Mining Economy*.

10 Hyam, "African Interests"; *Failure of South African Expansion*.

11 Marks and Trapido, "Lord Milner and the South African State," 71.

12 Crush, "Uneven Labour Migration," 121–3.

13 Marks and Trapido, "Lord Milner and the South African State."

14 Crush, "Landlords, Tenants and Colonial Social Engineers," 255–7.

15 SA, RCS 178/12, Reply of Coryndon to Swazi Petition, 1912.

16 For a beginning see Macmillan, "A Nation Divided?"; Packard, "Maize, Cattle and Mosquitoes"; Booth, "Capitalism and the Competition for Swazi Labour."

17 Kuper, *The Swazi*, 84.

Bibliography

I. PRIMARY SOURCES: UNPUBLISHED

A. Official

Central Archives Depot, Pretoria (CAD)
  GG   Governor General (1910–1920)
  JUS   Secretary of Justice (1900–1920)
  NA   Native Affairs Department (1910–1920)

NGI   Native Grievances Inquiry, Minutes of Evidence (1914)
PM   Prime Minister (1910–1920)
Natal Archives, Pietermaritzburg (NA)
SNA   Secretary of Native Affairs
Public Record Office, London (PRO)
Colonial Office Original Correspondence:
    CO   291 Transvaal
    CO   417 South Africa
    CO   608 Swaziland Statistics
    DO   119 High Commission Papers
Swaziland Archives, Lobamba (SA)
    D   British Colonial Correspondence (1907–9)
    J   British Colonial Correspondence (1901–6)
    HCR   Hlatikulu Court Records (1909–1920)
    RCS   British Colonial Correspondence (1909–30)
    S   Joint Governing Committee Records (1890–1894)
    S   South African Republic Colonial Records (1895–1899)
Transvaal Archives Depot, Pretoria (TAD)
    BA   British Agent (1896–1899)
    CA   Commission Archives
    CS   Colonial Secretary (1900–1916)
    CT   Colonial Treasurer (1900–1910)
    GNLB   Government Native Labour Bureau (1908–1920)
    GOV   Governor of the Transvaal Colony (1901–1910)
    HC   High Commissioner (1890–1910)
    LTG   Lieutenant Governor (1902–1907)
    SNA   Secretary of Native Affairs (1900–1910)
    SS   Staatsekretaris (1890–1899)
    SSA   Staatsekretaris (Buiteland) (1894–1899)

B. Non-official

Africa Evangelical Fellowship Records, London
    Misc. Correspondence
    South African Pioneer
Barlow Rand Archives, Johannesburg (BRA)
    HE   Archives of H. Eckstein & Co. (1890–1910)
Bodleian Library, Oxford
    Selborne Papers
British Library (BL)
    Viscount Gladstone papers
Johannesburg Public Library (JPL)
    Native Grievances Inquiry, Transcripts of Evidence (1914)

Killie Campbell Africana Library, Durban (KCL)
  Marwick papers
  Miller papers
  Stuart papers
Natal Archives, Pietermaritzburg (NA)
  Offy Shepstone papers
  Sir Theophilus Shepstone papers
Native Recruiting Corporation Records, Johannesburg (NRC)
  Files 1–113
Rhodes House Library, Oxford (RHL)
  Anti-Slavery Papers
  Coryndon Papers
  Lagden Papers
Transvaal Archives Depot, Pretoria (TAD)
  Forbes Papers
United Society for Propagation of the Gospel, London (USPG)
  Letter Books, E Series
Wesleyan Methodist Archives, University of London
  Boxes 46, 328
William Cullen Library, University of Witwatersrand (UW)
  Nicholson Papers
  South African Institute of Race Relations Papers

C. Other

Interviews
  D. Fitzpatrick, Mbabane, 30 March 1982
  John Gamede, Transcripts of Interviews, 1953–55 (copies in Swaziland Archives)
  C. Gilson, Johannesburg, 11 June 1982
  Logwaya Mamba, Uhlangamiso Mamba, 15 July 1970 (conducted by P. Bonner)
  T. Marwick, Johannesburg, 10 June 1982
  Simelane Simelane & Jozi Simelane, 6 May 1970 (conducted by P. Bonner)
  F. Whittle, Johannesburg, 7 June 1982
Private Collections
  Diaries of H. Raney, 1899–1925 (in private hands)
  Private papers of Captain George Wallis (held by Mrs J. Oliver)
Unpublished Typescripts
  Hodgson, W. and Ballinger, W. "Swaziland." University of Witwatersrand, 1931.
  Honey, de Symons. "A History of Swaziland." Swaziland Archives, 1916.
  Miller, A. "The *Incwala*." Killie Campbell Africana Library, nd.

- "The Kafir Races of South-East Africa." Killie Campbell Africana Library, nd.
- "Swaziland." Paper read at Public Lecture, Government Library, Pretoria, 1905.
Penfold, W. "The Romance of Swaziland: Some Hitherto Unwritten Chapters in Its History." University of Witwatersrand, c.1920.
Von Wissell, L. "Dad's Story." Swaziland Archives, nd.

II. PRIMARY SOURCES: PUBLISHED

A. Official

Public Record Office, London
  CO 879 Colonial Office Confidential Print
Swaziland Archives, Lobamba
  Annual Colonial Reports (1907/8 – 1920/21)
  High Commissioner's Gazettes (1906–1920)
Official Reports
  Pim, A. *Report on the Financial and Economic Situation of Swaziland*, London, 1932.
  Rubie, J. *The Swaziland Concessions*, Pretoria, 1903.
  South African Native Affairs Commission, Report and Minutes of Evidence, 5 Volumes, 1903–5.
  Swaziland Concessions Commission, *Report of Commission Appointed Under Swaziland Administration Proclamation 1904 as to the Expropriation of Rights in Swaziland*, Pretoria, 1905.
  Swaziland Concessions Commission, *Report of Detailed Decisions Relative to Boundaries etc. in Respect of Land, Grazing and Mineral Concessions*, Pretoria, 1908.
  Transvaal Labour Commission, Report and Minutes of Evidence, London, 1904.
  Union of South Africa, Eastern Transvaal Natives Land Committee, Minutes of Evidence, 1918. Pretoria UG 32, 1918.
  Union of South Africa, Report of Native Grievances Inquiry, 1913–14. Pretoria UG 37, 1914.
  Union of South Africa, Report of Select Committee into Native Labour Regulation Bill, 1910.

B. Non-official

Chamber of Mines Library, Johannesburg
  Chamber of Mines Annual Reports, 1890–1920
  Witwatersrand Native Labour Association Reports, 1903–1920

Native Recruiting Corporation Records
Native Recruiting Corporation Annual Reports, 1912–1920

C. Newspapers and Periodicals

Abantu Batho
Cape Times
The East and the West
Goldfields News
Johannesburg Star
The Mission Field
The Net
Rand Daily Mail
South Africa
South African Mines, Commerce and Industry
South African Mining Journal
South African Pioneer
Standard and Diggers News
Sunday Times
Times of Swaziland
Transvaal Leader

D. Contemporary Books

Bleloch, W. *The New South Africa: Its Value and Development,* New York: Doubleday, Page and Company 1901.

Davis, A. *Umbandine: A Romance of Swaziland.* London 1898.

Fawns, S. *Tin Deposits of the World.* London: Mining Journal 1905.

Forbes, D. *My Life in South Africa,* London: Witherby 1938.

Fraser, M., and A. Jeeves, eds. *All That Glittered.* Cape Town: Oxford University Press 1977.

Griffithes, T. *From Bedford Row to Swazieland.* London: Bradley 1898.

Halle, G. *Mayfair to Maritzburg: Reminiscences of 80 Years.* London: John Murray 1933.

Headlam, C., ed. *The Milner Papers: South Africa, 1899–1905, Volume 2.* London: Cassell 1933.

Kidd, D. *The Essential Kafir.* London: Adam and Charles Black 1904.

Mathers, E. *The Goldfields Revisited.* Durban: Davis and Sons 1887.

Mathews, J. *Incwadi Yami.* New York: Rogers and Sherwood 1897.

McCarthy, E. *Further Incidents in the Life of a Mining Engineer.* London: George Routledge and Sons 1920.

Nilsen, M. *Malla Moe.* Chicago: Moody Press 1960.

O'Neil, O. *Adventures in Swaziland.* New York: Century 1921.

Ronan, B. *Forty South African Years*. London: Heath Cranston 1919.
Schmelzenbach, L. *The Missionary Prospector*. Kansas City: Nazarene Publishing House 1937.
Settlers Emigration Society. *Land and Farming Prospects in the Transvaal and Swaziland*. London: R. Clay and Sons 1910.
Swaziland Chamber. *Swaziland: The California of South Africa*. Mbabane 1907.
Trevor, T. *Forty Years in Africa*. London: Blackett 1932.
Webb, C., and J. Wright, eds. *The James Stuart Archive, Volumes 1 to 3*. Pietermaritzburg: University of Natal Press 1976–83.
Wilson, D. *Behind the Scenes in the Transvaal*. London: Cassell and Company 1901.

E. Contemporary Articles

Anon. "Cotton Growing in Swaziland." *Bulletin of the Imperial Institute* 20 (1922): 468–74.
Challis, W. "In Swaziland. *The Net* September 1912, 8–10.
– "Swaziland from Within." *The East and the West* 6 (1908): 307–321.
– "Three Years in Swaziland." *The Mission Field* March 1908.
Coryndon, R. "Swaziland." *Journal of African Society* 14 (1914): 250–65.
Erleigh, N. "Swaziland as a Sheep Country." *Sun and Agricultural Journal of South Africa* March 1928, 262–4.
Hall, A. "Notes on the Tin Deposits of Embabaan and Forbes Reef in Swaziland." *Transactions of the Geological Society of South Africa* 16 (1913).
Miller, A. "Swaziland." *Proceedings of the Royal Colonial Institute* 31 (1900): 274–94.
– "Swazieland: Its Agricultural and Pastoral Future." *Transvaal Agricultural Journal* (1906): 1–11.
– "Gold Production and Mineral Resources of Swaziland, South East Africa." In *Gold Resources of the World, Proceedings of XV International Geological Congress*. South Africa 1929.
Selborne. "The South African Protectorates." *Journal of African Society* 14 (1914): 353–64.
Wood, C. "Cotton in Swaziland." *Empire Cotton Growing Review* 4 (1927): 13–19.

III. SECONDARY SOURCES

A. Books

Beinart, W. *The Political Economy of Pondoland, 1860 to 1930*. Cambridge: Cambridge University Press 1982.

Best, A. *The Swaziland Railway: A Study in Politico-Economic Geography.* East Lansing: Michigan State University 1966.

Bonner, P. *Kings Commoners and Concessionaires: The Evolution and Dissolution of the Ninteenth Century Swazi State.* Cambridge: Cambridge University Press 1983.

Booth, A. *Swaziland: Tradition and Change in a Southern African Kingdom.* Boulder: Westview Press 1983.

Bozzoli, B. *The Political Nature of a Ruling Class: Capital and Ideology in South Africa, 1890–1933.* London: Routledge and Kegan Paul 1981.

Bundy, C. *The Rise and Fall of the South African Peasantry.* London: Heinemann 1979.

Delius, P. *The Land Belongs to Us: The Pedi Polity, the Boers and the British in the Nineteenth Century Transvaal.* Johannesburg: Ravan Press 1983.

Denoon, D. *A Grand Illusion: The Failure of Imperial Policy in the Transvaal Colony During the Period of Reconstruction, 1900–1905.* London: Longman 1973.

Doveton, D. *The Human Geography of Swaziland.* London: Institute of British Geographers 1937.

Fair, D., G. Murdoch, and H. Jones. *Development in Swaziland.* Johannesburg: University of Witwatersrand Press 1969.

Freund, W. *Capital and Labour in the Nigerian Tin Mines.* London: Longman 1981.

Garson, N. "The Swaziland Question and a Road to the Sea, 1887–1895." *Archives Yearbook for South African History.* Cape Town 1957.

Hughes, A. *Land Tenure, Land Rights and Land Communities on Swazi Nation Land in Swaziland.* Durban: Institute for Social Research 1972.

Hyam, R. *The Failure of South African Expansion, 1908–48.* London 1972.

Jeeves, A. *Migrant Labour in South Africa's Mining Economy: The Struggle for the Gold Mines' Labour Supply 1890–1920.* Montreal: McGill-Queen's University Press 1985.

Jones, S. *Study of Swazi Nutrition* Durban: University of Natal 1963.

Kepple-Jones, A. *Rhodes and Rhodesia.* Montreal: McGill-Queen's University Press 1983.

Kowet, D. *Land, Labour Migration and Politics in Southern Africa.* Uppsala: Scandinavian Institute of African Studies 1978.

Kuper, H. *An African Aristocracy.* London: International African Institute 1947.

— *The Uniform of Colour.* Johannesburg: University of Witwatersrand Press 1947.

— *The Swazi: A South African Kingdom.* New York: Holt, Rinehart and Winston 1963.

— *Sobhuza II: Ngwenyama and King of Swaziland.* London: Duckworth 1978.

Lacey, M. *Working for Boroko: The Origins of a Coercive Labour System in South Africa.* Johannesburg: Ravan Press 1981.

Levy, N. *The Foundations of the South African Cheap Labour System.* London: Routledge and Kegan Paul 1982.

Marks, S. *Reluctant Rebellion: The 1906–8 Disturbances in Natal.* Oxford: Clarendon Press 1970.

Marks, S. and A. Atmore, eds. *Economy and Society in Pre-Industrial South Africa.* London: Longman 1980.

Marks, S. and R. Rathbone, eds. *Industrialisation and Social Change in South Africa.* London: Longman 1982.

Marwick, B. *The Swazi.* Cambridge: Cambridge University Press 1940.

Matsebula, J. *A History of Swaziland.* Cape Town: Longman 1976.

– *The King's Eye.* Cape Town: Longman 1983.

Murdoch, G. *Soils and Land Capability in Swaziland.* Mbabane: Ministry of Agriculture 1968.

Myburgh, A. *The Tribes of the Barberton District.* Pretoria: Government Printer 1949.

Palmer, R., and N. Parsons, eds. *The Roots of Rural Poverty in Central and Southern Africa.* London: Heinemann 1977.

Ranger, T. *Revolt in Southern Rhodesia, 1896–7.* Evanston: Northwestern University Press 1967.

Richardson, P. *Chinese Mine Labour in the Transvaal.* London: Macmillan 1983.

Shillington, K. *The Colonisation of the Southern Tswana, 1870–1900.* Johannesburg: Ravan Press 1985.

Van der Horst, S. *Native Labour in South Africa.* Oxford: Oxford University Press 1942.

Van Onselen, C. *Chibaro.* London: Pluto Press 1976.

– *Studies in the Social and Economic History of the Witwatersrand, 1886–1914.* London: Longman 1982.

Walshe, P. *The Rise of African Nationalism in South Africa.* London: Hunt and Co 1970.

Warwick, P. *Black People and the South African War, 1899–1902.* Cambridge: Cambridge University Press 1983.

Yudelman, D. *The Emergence of Modern South Africa.* Westport: Greenwood Press 1983.

B. Articles (includes essays in edited collections)

Ballard, C. "Migrant Labour in Natal, 1860–1879: With Special Reference to Zululand and the Delagoa Bay Hinterland." *Journal of Natal and Zulu History* 1 (1978): 25–42.

Beemer, H. "The Development of the Military Organization of Swaziland."
   Africa 10 (1937): 55–74.
– "Notes on the Diet of the Swazi of the Protectorate." *African Studies* 13
   (1939): 199–236.
– "The Swazi Rainmaking Ceremony: Comments on Schoeman." *Bantu
   Studies* 9 (1935): 273–80.
Beidelman, T. "Swazi Royal Ritual." *Africa* 36 (1966): 373–405.
Beinart, W. *"Joyini Inkomo*: Cattle Advances and the Origins of Migrancy
   from Pondoland." *Journal of Southern African Studies* 5 (1979): 199–219.
– "Labour Migrancy and Rural Production: Pondoland, c.1900–1950." In
   Black Villagers in an Industrial Society, edited by P. Mayer. Cape Town:
   Oxford University Press 1980.
Berman, B. "Structure and Process in the Bureaucratic States of Colonial
   Africa." *Development and Change* 15 (1984): 161–202.
Bonner, P. "Classes, the Mode of Production and the State in Pre-Colonial
   Swaziland." In *Economy and Society in Pre-Industrial South Africa*, edited by
   S. Marks and A. Atmore. London: Longman 1980.
– "Factions and Fissions: Transvaal-Swazi Politics in the Mid-Nineteenth
   Century." *Journal of African History* 19 (1979): 219–38.
– "Mswati II." In *Black Leaders in Southern African History*, edited by C. Saun-
   ders. London: Heinemann 1979.
– "The 1920 Black Mine Workers Strike: A Preliminary Account." In *Labour,
   Townships and Protest*, edited by B. Bozzoli. Johannesburg: Ravan Press
   1979.
Booth, A. "The Development of the Swazi Labour Market, 1900–1968."
   South African Labour Bulletin 7 (1982): 34–57.
Cook, P. "History and Izibongo of the Swazi Chiefs." *Bantu Studies* 5 (1931).
– "The *Incwala* Ceremony of the Swazi." *Bantu Studies* 4 (1930): 205–210.
Cooper, F. "Africa and the World Economy." *African Studies Review* 24 (1981):
   1–86.
– "Peasants, Capitalists and Historians: A Review Article." *Journal of South-
   ern African Studies* 7 (1981): 283–314.
Crush, J. "Capitalist Homoficence, the Frontier and Uneven Development
   in Southern Africa," *Geojournal* 12 (1986): 129–36.
– "Colonial Coercion and the Swazi Tax Revolt of 1903–7." *Political Geog-
   raphy Quarterly* 4 (1985): 179–90.
– "The Colonial Division of Space: The Significance of the Swaziland Land
   Partition." *International Journal of African Historical Studies* 13 (1980): 71–
   86.
– "The Genesis of Colonial Land Policy in Swaziland." *South African Geo-
   graphical Journal* 62 (1980): 73–88.
– "Landlords, Tenants and Colonial Social Engineers: The Farm Labour

Question in Early Colonial Swaziland." *Journal of Southern African Studies* 11 (1985): 235–57.

– "Settler-Estate Production, Monopoly Control and the Imperial Response: The Case of the Swaziland Corporation Ltd." *African Economic History* 8 (1979): 183–197.

– "The Southern African Regional Formation: A Geographical Perspective." *Tijdschrift voor Economische en Sociale Geografie* 73 (1982): 200–212.

– "Swazi Migrant Workers and the Witwatersrand Gold Mines, 1886–1920." *Journal of Historical Geography* 12 (1986): 27–40.

– "Uneven Labour Migration in Southern Africa: Conceptions and Misconceptions." *South African Geographical Journal* 67 (1984): 115–32.

Daniel, J. "A Comparative Analysis of Lesotho and Swaziland's Relations with South Africa." In *South African Review Two*, edited by SARS. Johannesburg: Ravan Press 1984.

Delius, P. "Migrant Labour and the Pedi, 1840–80." In *Economy and Society in Pre-Industrial South Africa*, edited by S. Marks and A. Atmore. London: Longman 1980.

Denoon, D. "The Transvaal Labour Crisis, 1901–1906." *Journal of African History* 7 (1967): 481–94.

Derman, P. "Stock and Aristocracy: The Political Implications of Swazi Marriage." *African Studies* 36 (1977): 119–39.

Doveton, D. "The Economic Geography of Swaziland." *Geographical Journal* 88 (1936): 322–31.

Engelbrecht, J. "Swazi Customs Relating to Marriage." *Annals of the University of Stellenbosch* 8 (1930): 1–27.

Etherington, N. "Labour Supplies and the Genesis of South African Confederation in the 1870's." *Journal of African History* 20 (1978): 235–54.

Guy, J. "The Destruction and Reconstruction of Zulu Society." In *Industrialisation and Social Change in South Africa*, edited by S. Marks and R. Rathbone. London: Longman 1982.

– "Ecological Factors in the Rise of Shaka and the Zulu Kingdom." In *Economy and Society in Pre-Industrial South Africa*, edited by S. Marks and A. Atmore. London: Longman 1980.

Harries, P. "Kinship, Ideology and the Nature of Pre-Colonial Labour Migration: Labour Migration from the Delagoa Bay Hinterland to South Africa, up to 1895." In *Industrialisation and Social Change in South Africa*, edited by S. Marks and R. Rathbone. London: Longman 1982.

– "Slavery, Social Incorporation and Surplus Extraction: The Nature of Free and Unfree Labour in South East Africa." *Journal of African History* 22 (1981): 309–30.

Hoernle, A., and I. Schapera. "Advisability and Possibility of Introducing the *Imbuto* System of the Swazi People into the Educational System." In B. Marwick, *The Swazi*. Cambridge: Cambridge University Press 1940.

Hyam, R. "African Interests and the South Africa Act, 1908–10." *Historical Journal* 13 (1970): 85–105.

Isaacman, A., and B. Isaacman. "Resistance and Collaboration in Southern and Central Africa, c.1850–1920." *International Journal of African Historical Studies* 10 (1977): 31–62.

Jeeves, A. "The Control of Migratory Labour on the South African Gold Mines in the Era of Kruger and Milner." *Journal of Southern African Studies* 2 (1975): 3–29.

Jones, H. "The Pre-Colonial Distribution of the Swazi Population." In *African Historical Demography, Volume 2*, Centre for African Studies, University of Edinburgh, 1981.

Katz, E. "Silicosis on the South African Goldmines." In *Hunger, Work and Health*, edited by F. Wilson and G. Westcott. Johannesburg: Ravan Press 1980.

Katzenellenbogen, S. "Reconstruction in the Transvaal." In *The South African War*, edited by P. Warwick. London: Longman 1981.

Keegan, T. "The Restructuring of Agrarian Class Relations in a Colonial Economy: The Orange River Colony, 1902–1910." *Journal of Southern African Studies* 5 (1979): 234–54.

– "The Sharecropping Economy, African Class Formation and the Native Lands Act of 1913 in the Highveld Maize Belt." In *Industrialisation and Social Change in South Africa*, edited by S. Marks and R. Rathbone. London: Longman 1982.

– "The Sharecropping Economy on the South African Highveld in the Early Twentieth Century." *Journal of Peasant Studies* 10 (1983): 201–26.

Kimble, J. "Clinging to the Chiefs: Some Contradictions of Colonial Rule in Basutoland, c1890–1930." In *Contradictions of Accumulation in Africa*, edited by H. Bernstein and B. Campbell. Beverly Hills: Sage 1985.

– "Labour Migration in Basutoland, c.1870–1885." In *Industrialisation and Social Change in South Africa*, edited by S. Marks and R. Rathbone. London: Longman 1982.

Kuper, A. "Rank and Preferential Marriage in Southern Africa: The Swazi." *Man* 13 (1978): 567–79.

Kuper, H. "Colour, Categories and Colonialism: The Swazi Case." In *Colonialism in Africa, 1870–1960*, Volume 3, edited by V. Turner. Cambridge: Cambridge University Press 1971.

– "Costume and Cosmology: The Animal Symbolism of the *Incwala*." *Man* 8 (1973): 348–67.

– "The Development of a Primitive Nation." *African Studies* 15 (1941): 339–68.

– "Kinship Among the Swazi." In *African Systems of Kinship and Marriage*, edited by A.Radcliffe-Brown and D. Forde. Oxford: Oxford University Press 1970.

- "The Monarchy and the Military in Swaziland." In *Social System and Tradition in Southern Africa*, edited by J. Argyle and E. Preston-Whyte. Cape Town: Oxford University Press 1978.
- "A Ritual of Kingship Among the Swazi." *Africa* 14 (1944): 230–56.

Legassick, M. "South Africa: Capital Accumulation and Violence." *Economy and Society* 3 (1974): 253–91.

Marks, S. "Natal, the Zulu Royal Family and the Ideology of Segregation." *Journal of Southern African Studies* 4 (1978): 172–94.

Marks, S., and S. Trapido. "Lord Milner and the South African State." *History Workshop Journal* 8 (1979): 50–81.

Moroney, S. "Mine Worker Protest on the Witwatersrand, 1901–1912." In *Essays in Southern African Labour History*, edited by E. Webster. Johannesburg: Ravan Press 1978.

Nyeko, B. "The Extension of British Colonial Administration into Swaziland, 1902–1906." *Makerere Historical Journal* 2 (1976): 133–44.
- "Pre-nationalist Resistance to Colonial Rule: Swaziland on the Eve of the Imposition of British Administration, 1890–1902." *Trans African Journal of History* 5 (1975): 61–84.
- "The Rule of the Dlamini in Nineteenth Century Swaziland." *Tarikh* 4 (1972): 42–83.

Packard, R. "Maize, Cattle and Mosquitoes: The Political Economy of Malaria Epidemics in Colonial Swaziland." *Journal of African History* 25 (1984): 189–212.

Scott, P. "Mineral Development in Swaziland." *Economic Geography* 26 (1950): 196–213.

Slater, H. "Land, Labour and Capital in Natal: The Natal Land and Colonization Company, 1860–1948." *Journal of African History* 8 (1975): 257–83.

Trapido, S. "Landlord and Tenant in a Colonial Economy: The Transvaal, 1880–1910." *Journal of Southern African Studies* 5 (1978): 26–58.
- "Reflections on Land, Office and Wealth in the South African Republic, 1850–1900." In *Economy and Society in Pre-Industrial South Africa*, edited by S. Marks and A. Atmore. London: Longman 1980.

Van Onselen, C. "Black Workers in Central African Industry: A Critical Essay on the Historiography and Sociology of Rhodesia." *Journal of Southern African Studies* 1 (1975): 228–46.
- "Reactions to Rinderpest in Southern Africa, 1896–7." *Journal of African History* 13 (1972): 473–88.
- "Worker Consciousness in Black Miners: Southern Rhodesia, 1900–1920." *Journal of African History* 14 (1973): 237–55.

Vieceli, J. "Swaziland after Sobhuza: Stability or Crisis?" *Issue* 12 (1982): 56–63.

Winter, I. "The Post-Colonial State and the Forces and Relations of Production: Swaziland." *Review of African Political Economy* 9 (1978): 27–43.

Wolpe, H. "Capitalism and Cheap Labour Power in South Africa: From Segregation to Apartheid." *Economy and Society* 1 (1972): 425–56.

Youé, C. "Imperial Land Policy and the Swazi Response." *Journal of Imperial and Commonwealth History* 7 (1978): 56–70.

C. Unpublished Material

Bonner, P. "Early State Formation Among the Nguni: The Relevance of the Swazi Case." African History Seminar Paper, University of London, 1978.

– "The Rise, Consolidation and Disintegration of Dlamini Power in Swaziland, 1820–1889." PHD thesis, University of London, 1977.

Booth, A. "Priorities and Opportunities for Research in Swaziland." Paper presented at Workshop on Research Priorities in Southern Africa, Roma, Lesotho, 1981.

– "Capitalism and the Competition for Swazi Labour, 1945–1960." Paper presented at African Studies Association Meetings, New Orleans, 1985.

Crush, J. "Tin Mining in the Valley of Heaven." Paper presented at African Studies Association Meetings, New Orleans, 1985.

Fransman, M. "The Colonial State and the Land Question in Swaziland, 1902–7." In *The Societies of Southern Africa in the 19th and 20th Centuries, Volume 9*. London: Institute of Commonwealth Studies 1978.

Harries, P. "Labour Migration from Mozambique to South Africa." PHD thesis, University of London, 1983.

Jeeves, A., and D. Yudelman. "The Mobilization of a Sub-Continent: Migrant Labour for the South African Gold Mines, 1920–1983." Paper presented at History Workshop, University of Witwatersrand, Johannesburg, 1984.

Macmillan, H. "A Nation Divided? The Swazi in Swaziland and the Transvaal, 1865–1982." Paper presented at International Conference on the History of Ethnic Awareness in Southern Africa, Charlottesville, 1983.

Mashasha, F. "The Swazi and Land Partition, 1902–10." In *The Societies of Southern Africa in the 19th and 20th Centuries*, Volume 4, London: Institute of Commonwealth Studies 1972.

– "The Road to Colonialism: Concessions and the Collapse of Swazi Independence." DPhil thesis, University of Oxford 1977.

Packard, R. "White Plague: Black Labour: Industrialisation and Tuberculosis in Southern Africa, 1850–1960." Paper presented at African Studies Association Meetings, Boston, 1983.

Reilly, T., and E. Reilly. "The State of Nature Conservation in Swaziland: Past and Present." Unpublished paper, 1976.

Rosen-Prinz, B. "Urbanization and Political Change: A Study of Urban Local Government in Swaziland." PHD thesis, University of California, Los Angeles, 1976.

Sieborger, R. "The Recruitment and Organisation of African Labour for the Kimberley Diamond Mines, 1871–1888." MA thesis, Rhodes University, Grahamstown 1975.

Watson, E. "The History of the Little Free State and Swaziland Affairs Relating Thereto." MA thesis, University of Witwatersrand, Johannesburg, 1941.

Youé, C. "The African Career of Robert Thorne Coryndon." PHD thesis, Dalhousie University, 1978.

Index

Ngwane, 21
Nhlabati, Mzila, chief, 61
Nsibande, Mantinta,
187–91
Nsibande, Silele, chief,
29, 61, 188
Nsibande chiefdom, 29
Ntshongise, Sitambe,
chief, 30

Orange Free State, 134,
138

partition, *see* land
partition
passes, 40, 51–2, 40, 64,
90
Peak district, 59
peasantry, 37–9, 203–4
Pedi, 13, 25–6, 31
Piet Retief district, 26, 30,
44
Piggs Peak Development
Company Ltd, 116–8,
122, 179
Pilgrim's Rest, 67
placing, of new chief-
doms, 20–1, 31, 200; *see
also* aristocracy; chiefs
ploughs, *see* agricultural
innovations
police, black, 51–2,
59–64, 114, 187
Pondoland, 204, 209,
242n. 36, 246n. 45
poor whites, *see* bywoners
population, Swazi: distribution, 16, 30, 78,
231n. 23; numbers, 16,
239n. 4; redistribution,
41–2, 170–5, 178, 181
Private Revenue Conces-
sion, 158–9, 243n. 52
protest, anti-colonial, *see*
colonial policy; delega-
tions; land partition;
strikes

Queen Regent, *see*
Labotsibeni

raiding, *see* captives; cattle

ranches, white, 138, 168,
179, 186, 264n. 7; *see
also* Swaziland Ranching
& Development Co Ltd
Rand, *see* Witwatersrand
Rand Native Labour
Association, 46; *see also*
WNLA
recruits, *see* migrant
workers; recruiters
recruiters: and chiefs, 47,
102, 104; competition
between, 46, 86–8, 93–4,
104, 110–15, 121–3;
contracts with aristoc-
racy, 46–8, 66, 78, 83–9,
207; defrauding of, by
recruits, 108–11, 114–
15; methods, 46–7, 78–
89, 99–115, 121–2, 180,
184; Swazi attitudes to-
wards, 47, 68–70, 78–81,
98–9, 101; *see also* colonial policy, on recruiting;
runners; trader-recrui-
ters; wages
refugees, 29–30
regency, periods of, 25,
78, 155, 192, 207
"regiment of the hills", 85
regiments: decline of,
191–3; demobilization
of, 25, 27, 78, 156; and
labour migration, 26–7,
43, 53, 78, 85–9, 191–3,
203–4, 207; Mamba, 29;
and military campaigns,
13, 25–6; size, 13, 22,
26–7, 78; socializing
role, 25, 88–9, 192;
tasks, 24–7, 37–8; under
Bunu, 31, 43; under
Sobhuza II, 199–200
repurchase of land, *see*
Land Repurchase
Program
reserves, Swazi: accom-
modation of chiefs, 136,
146–52, 157, 172–3;
forced resettlement in,
152–4, 159–60, 169–79,
212, 259n. 98; and

labour-reserve theory,
211–12, 259n. 98; qual-
ity and size, 144–8, 162;
underdevelopment, 174;
see also land partition
Resident Commissioners,
see Coryndon, Robert;
Moony, Enraght
ritual: agricultural, 22; of
non-Dlamini chiefdoms,
22, 29–30; *umbengo*
ceremony, 31; *see also*
Incwala
rinderpest epidemic, of
1897–8, 37, 41–2, 48,
54–5, 73
Robinson Group, 83–4
royal cattle posts: establishment, 20–2,
228n. 40; included in
reserves, 151; loan from,
73; size of herds at, 22,
41, 48, 228n. 40,
241n. 29; theft from, 37,
83
royal graves, 29, 51, 151
royal villages: Embekel-
weni, 24; Nkanini, 24,
35; old Zombode, 29;
political disputes at, 25,
44; size of, 24, 192; in
the Transvaal, 26;
upkeep of, 24–7, 38, 45,
127, 192–3; Zombode,
27, 44, 46, 63, 85,
162–3, 188
runners: duties, 104–9,
111, 184–5, 208–9;
numbers, 96, 106;
payment of, 99, 106;
prosecution, 106–7; *see
also* recruiters; trader-
recruiters

Schwab, Gustav, 35–6
Selborne, William Walde-
grave Palmer, second
Earl of: on alcohol, 127;
and colonial land policy,
60, 134–40, 146–8, 161–
2, 173, 211, 259n. 95,
260n. 108; on plans to